Francis of Assisi

FRANCIS OF ASSISI

The Life and Afterlife of a Medieval Saint

André Vauchez

Translated by Michael F. Cusato

Yale

UNIVERSITY

PRESS

New Haven & London

Yale University Press books may be purchased in quantity for educational, business, or
promotional use. For information, please e-mail sales.press@yale.edu (U.S. office) or
sales@yaleup.co.uk (U.K. office).

Set in Electra and Trajan types by Westchester Book Group.
Printed in the United States of America.

Library of Congress Cataloging-in-Publication Data

Vauchez, André.
  [François d'Assise. English]
  Francis of Assisi : the life and afterlife of a medieval saint / André Vauchez ; translated
by Michael F. Cusato.—1st English ed.
      p.   cm.
  Includes bibliographical references and index.
  ISBN 978-0-300-17894-4 (cloth : alk. paper)   1. Francis, of Assisi, Saint, 1182–1226.
2. Christian saints—Italy—Assisi—Biography.   I. Cusato, Michael F.   II. Title.
  BX4700.F6V34313 2012
  271′.302—dc23
  [B]

2012012742

A catalogue record for this book is available from the British Library.

This paper meets the requirements of ANSI/NISO Z39.48-1992 (Permanence of Paper).

10 9 8 7 6 5 4 3 2 1

To Denise,
without whose support this book would never have been completed;
To Étienne, Anne, and Antoine, who have heard me talk about it
for such a long time;
And to those friends who have patiently waited for it.

No matter how hard we try, we always rebuild monuments in our own fashion. But to build with only genuine stones requires a lot of work.
—Marguerite Yourcenar, *Mémoires d'Hadrien*

CONTENTS

PREFACE

You might be saying to yourself upon opening this book, "Not another life of Francis of Assisi!" There are already so many! Besides, he seems so well known, so familiar to us. Who has not heard of this saint who loved poverty, preached to the birds, and was the first to bear the stigmata? Writing a biography is a legitimate undertaking when it corrects the oblivion into which someone has fallen after playing such an important role while alive; or to rehabilitate the reputation of a man or woman who has been misunderstood or poorly treated by earlier authors. Francis belongs to neither of these categories. For a long time, he has been famous and universally recognized as one of the great spiritual figures of the human race, as was shown yet again when representatives of the principal world religions gathered in Assisi in 1986, at the call of Pope John Paul II, in order to pray for peace and to reflect on how to help bring it about in our world.

But in spite of the renown of Francis and his native town of Assisi, it is not at all certain that many of our contemporaries—outside of Italy, where he is still a popular figure—know who he really was. Numerous authors who have been interested in him both in the past and in our own time have sought above all to edify their readers by presenting him as a model to follow; or to invite us to share the emotion, even the enthusiasm, that some aspect of his fascinating personality has inspired in them. Others have even devoted brilliant essays to him, sometimes based upon an enlightened intuition, like *Le Très Bas* (The lowliest) of Christian Bobin, or sometimes anchored in the study of his social and cultural context, like Jacques Le Goff's *Saint Francis of Assisi*, but without trying to present a complete view of his life or his message.[1] We can also mention as illustration the numerous films, more or less romanticized, that have been devoted to the Poor Man of Assisi in an attempt to reconstruct his life through its principal episodes.

With only a few rare exceptions—like the splendid *Francesco, giullare di Dio* (known in English as *The Flowers of Saint Francis*) by the Italian filmmaker Roberto Rossellini (1950)—such reconstructions are but figments of the imagination or fanciful creations. These presentations are inevitably artificial because the search for a consistency—after-the-fact—leads one to paper over the gaps in the documentation, thereby transforming into a singular and straightforward destiny a life which, like that of every human being, is marked by uncertainty and discontinuities.

These deficient presentations first of all result from the fact that, very often, those who are interested in Francis of Assisi have not gone back to the sources, which are numerous and varied, or have not used them properly. Indeed, the lack of knowledge about the specific character of hagiographical texts and the refusal to approach them in a comparative perspective have too often led biographers of Francis of Assisi to stitch together a kind of patchwork, lining up bits of information drawn from texts written for different purposes and in different periods. The image, in large measure artificial, that derives from these more or less arbitrary combinations reflects more accurately the subjectivity of their authors than it does the climate of the period in which the Poor Man of Assisi lived.

One of the major problems posed by the biography of Francis is that everyone thinks he or she knows Francis well enough to interpret him however one wishes; his personality is so rich that it can indeed give rise to different "readings." For centuries, we have celebrated him as the ascetic and the stigmatic, the founder of a great religious order and the paragon of Catholic orthodoxy. Then, at the end of the nineteenth century, he was considered a romantic hero, upholding an evangelical and mystical Christianity which had been destroyed by the ecclesiastical institution. In our own day, we have placed more emphasis on the image of the defender of the poor, the promoter of peace between individuals and religions, the man in love with nature, the protector and patron of ecology, or even the ecumenical saint whom Protestants, Orthodox Catholics, and even non-Christians can relate to. To each his or her own Francis, one is tempted to say, just as Paul Valéry spoke of "[his] Faust," thus claiming the right to interpret for himself this great literary myth. Such a situation, which attests to the importance of the person and the fascination which Francis has never ceased to exercise on people, is probably inevitable. It corresponds to the multifaceted character of the personality of the saint of Assisi that is mirrored in the variety of sources through which we know him. But the historian, faced with such multiple aspects, immediately feels uneasy and willingly leaves to popular writers the task of producing synthetic works (unsatisfactory from a scientific point of view), which, except for a few details, are scarcely remembered in a later era. Because this popular literature exists, moreover, the historian is more inclined to take refuge in erudition and "pure" research. Indeed, contemporary historiography has often been marked by the assumption, given the current state of our knowledge, that an authentic biographical reconstruction of the person of Francis may not even be possible.

However, Francis is neither a myth nor a legendary person, even if many *legendae* were written about him during the Middle Ages. And there is no reason that he should remain more out of reach than his contemporaries like Saint Louis or Frederick II, both of whom have been the subject of remarkable biographies and whose historicity no one has ever questioned. Surely, since Henri-Irénée Marrou, we know that absolute objectivity does not exist in this domain and that any claim to know things "as they really happened" is illusory. But a biographer who wants to produce a work of history must not renounce his or her objectivity simply because biography, like history, is written in the present and reflects the hopes of its time. The author of this book is well aware that it is the work of an individual belonging to a time, place, and culture that will by necessity determine his way of framing the questions. He is interested in Francis, for example, because he had for a long time lived and worked in Italy and has regularly visited Assisi and Umbria. He has been able to measure the profound impact of Franciscanism in that country, where he met numerous people for whom the saint of Assisi remains a living point of reference. As a medievalist, he has dedicated his research to the history of holiness and to the study of hagiographical texts—legends and miracle collections—which constitute the core of the documentation that we have at our disposal for knowing the figure of the "Poverello"—the Little Poor One.

But acknowledging the factors which might have influenced him is not in contradiction with the search for a certain methodological rigor. The historian, even and especially when he avoids this subjectivity, is necessarily engaged in his subject in some manner. That does not prevent him from doing his work honestly, or rather exercising his "craft as an historian"—to use the apt expression of Marc Bloch—while taking his distance vis-à-vis all legends, golden or black, and while approaching the study of the broadest possible documentation with the maximum of objectivity. When the historian proceeds thus, he shows that "we do not have anything better than the testimony and the criticism of the testimony to validate the historical representation of the past."[2] He or she must also have the humility not to claim to be saying everything or to know everything about the life and personality of one's subject, of whom it is necessary to recognize that certain aspects—and not just a few—escape our grasp or remain opaque to us. Indeed, as the documentation relative to Francis betrays, as we shall see, certain *lacunae*, the great temptation is to fill in the gaps by recourse to conjecture and to confer on his existence a unity and logic which it obviously did not have. Thus the historian must be careful to stress the evolution of his subject without covering over the subject's hesitations and contradictions: a task especially difficult in this case, where the hagiographical texts that speak of the Poor Man of Assisi have a tendency to "make an abstraction" of his lived reality and present his life as an exemplary account in which the person counts less than the personality. Jacques Le Goff, however, has shown in his *Saint Louis* to what extent the medieval sources contemporary to his subject, in spite of their partial and biased character, are fundamental to understanding how the image of the sovereign was created.[3] In the case of Francis as well, it is important to analyze with precision the first steps of the tormented genesis of the historical recollections about him, as well as the interpretations, sometimes contradictory, of which his person and project were the object throughout the centuries that followed his death and even beyond. If the documentation that we have at our disposal only rarely permits us to get at the "real" Francis, it does highlight the considerable impact that he had on his contemporaries and upon generations afterward.

Thus this work does not present itself as a biography in the classic sense, moving from the birth to the death of its subject. It devotes considerable space, after a description of the principal steps of his earthly life, to the study of his posthumous destiny and of the impact of his message through the centuries: in short, to all that is meant by the German term *Nachleben* (afterlife). For the beginning does not determine everything; and truth cannot be separated from its transmission. The story of the Poor Man of Assisi did not stop the day of his death. We can even say that, in a certain sense, he knew a second life in this world after he had left it. Thus the "historical" Francis—the only one we can grasp—results from what he managed to reveal of himself in his writings and, at the same time, from the different perceptions of his person and life by his contemporaries and those interested in him through the ages.

The critical approach that I will endeavor to use in this book is not meant to throw suspicion—as is fashionable today—on a universally admired person; even less is it meant, through any sort of iconoclastic spirit, to cast doubt on the greatness of the man. Rather, I strive to rediscover Francis especially in those things which make him different from us. Not a Francis who is the forerunner of our modern times or the poetic hero of harmonious concord between human beings and nature; but a person who lived in the Italy of the communes between the end of the twelfth and beginning of the thirteenth centuries whose life

I shall try to retrace in all its uniqueness. The worst pitfall for a historian is anachronism. By seeking at all cost to adapt the Poor Man of Assisi to our present day under the pretext of making him acceptable and interesting for our contemporaries, we risk distorting him and losing sight of his original characteristics, as well as the concrete issues of his life. As Peter Brown has said, "We must never read Augustine as if he is our contemporary." Making Francis "relevant," as is often attempted, is only a surreptitious way of speaking about ourselves while making it seem we are speaking about someone else.[4] Let us thus seek, first of all, to place Francis within his own time, without nourishing the illusion that we are rediscovering the Francis of Assisi who traveled the pathways of Umbria with a few rag-tag companions and whose lived reality will always escape our grasp. The main difficulty consists in reconstructing for today's reader a world which has become foreign to us and to render it understandable, in spite of the insurmountable discontinuity that exists between its categories of thought, its forms of sensibility, and our own. But only when one has made this attempt of distancing does it become legitimate to ask ourselves what it is in the life and witness of the Poor Man of Assisi that still interests us.

For Francis, like Jesus or Socrates, is one of those spiritual masters whom each generation must remake as its own by rediscovering them through reflection, study, and a comparison between the teachings that come from such figures and from that generation's own experience. Like these masters, the Poor Man of Assisi escapes all appropriation, to the extent that he is like all other human beings, beyond their respective beliefs, in their search for a model of humanity and wisdom. Moreover, his story continues to fascinate and to touch each one of us to the extent that it incarnates in an exemplary manner the conflict between a creative experience (which is, at root, distinguishable from every prescriptive observance) and the requirements of an institutionalization that assures the survival of a founding charism (but which simultaneously alters certain essential characteristics of the original project). Here we discover a dialectical tension that is fundamental in the history of Christianity and the Church, but which goes beyond the sphere of religious experience and concerns all movements and ideologies that, to use the words of Charles Péguy, begin in "the realm of the mystical" only to end up in "the realm of the political." Nor should we forget the famous phrase attributed to the same author: "They have clean hands because they do not use their hands." This allows us to measure, in this area, the futility of overly simplistic dichotomies in historical reconstructions.

If the fact of writing a new biography of Francis finds in this approach sufficient justification, is it not necessary to still say something new about him so that the enterprise might actually be worth the effort? Such is the case today, thanks to the profound renewal which has marked Franciscan studies for forty years or so, particularly in Italy, thanks to the works of numerous philologists and historians whose research has helped advance the understanding that we can have of the life of the Poor Man of Assisi. This statement will perhaps appear somewhat surprising since the majority of sources on which we work today have been known for a long time; and, in the absence of any sensational new discovery in this area, one can wonder where anything new might come from.

But if the body of texts upon which our knowledge of Francis rests has not been enriched in the course of the past half-century, new editions and especially the progress of critical reflection have allowed us to better date and situate certain sources in relationship to others. For the historian's work does not consist, as we have already said, in merely juxtaposing the information coming from various documents, placing them all on the same level, stripped of context; it is rather to establish among the sources a hierarchy founded on their proximity to the events which they report on, the particular contexts of their authors, and the intentions underlying their composition. Scholars have long dreamed of discovering, hidden in a hitherto unknown manuscript, the "real" *Life of Francis* that one of his companions would have been able to write, perhaps Brother Leo, who was his secretary. We know today that we will probably never find this text—if such a text ever existed in this form (which is doubtful). So rather than wandering off on this hopeless quest, researchers concern themselves with establishing the relative value of each of the known sources that tell us about the Poor Man of Assisi, and with drawing from these their historical significance.

These works remain for the most part inaccessible to nonspecialists, few of whom even suspect that such sources exist. Thus it seemed to me that, as we come to the end of this rich season of historiography, the time for harvesting has come: it is time to bring to the awareness of a larger reading public the results of these recent studies which now allow us to speak about Francis in new ways—and even oblige us to do so. Their authors are too numerous to mention all of them here; one will find their names in the notes and in the bibliography which appear at the end of this volume. I want, however, to recognize a particular debt that I owe to two of them who have now passed away: Raoul Manselli, who introduced me *verbo et opere*, by word and deed, to the history of Franciscanism during my sojourns in Rome, and Father Théophile Desbonnets, O.F.M.: the latter, in particular, continued and enriched the tradition of Franciscan studies in France at a time when this area was scarcely a matter of interest. And at the heart of the Italian historiography to which I owe so much, allow me to give a special place of honor to Giovanni Miccoli and Grado Giovanni

Merlo, who, among living authors, are the ones whose studies probably have contributed the most to renewing the historical approach to Francis and to medieval Franciscanism.[5]

I would like to especially thank Nicole Bériou, Jacques Dalarun, and Chiara Mercuri, who have kindly read through my manuscript and shared with me observations that helped me to avoid various errors or imprecisions. Those that remain are attributable to me alone.

Part I

A Biographical Sketch
1182–1226

FRANCESCO DI BERNARDONE

A CITY, A MAN: ASSISI AND FRANCIS

Few historical figures have been as associated with a place and, more precisely, with a city than Francis of Assisi. Saint Thomas is "Aquinas" only by virtue of his birth. Saint Bernard, although in principle constrained by monastic stability, was often absent from the abbey of Clairvaux to which his name remains associated. In contrast, Francis is tied to Assisi with every fiber of his being. This is where he was born at the end of 1181 or the beginning of 1182; where he died during the night of the third and the fourth of October 1226; and where he was buried, before his body was transferred—in 1230—to the basilica built in his honor on the western edge of the city. He spent his whole childhood in his native city. And if he often left it after the birth of his fraternity, he was not away from it for very long, except when he went to Egypt and Palestine in 1219–1220. The rest of the time, at the conclusion of his preaching campaigns in central and northern Italy, he always faithfully returned there or, in any case, to the church of the Portiuncula, located about a little more than a mile outside its walls: the cradle of his order, which always remained for him a primary point of reference. Franciscanism is really the only Christian religious movement that might be able to speak of having a capital (Assisi) and a center (Umbria). The imprint which the Poverello has left is nowhere stronger than in those places where he lived and sojourned for a long time.

When Francis came into the world at the end of the twelfth century, what was this city like where his human and religious experience would take root? In his *Divine Comedy*, Dante admirably evoked its natural surroundings:

> Between Topino's stream and that which flows down
> from the hill chosen by the blessed Ubaldo,

> from a high peak there hangs a fertile slope;
> from there Perugia feels both heat and cold
> at Porta Sole; while behind it grieve
> Nocera and Gualdo under their heavy yoke.[1]

Assisi was at this time a settlement of moderate importance, less extensive than it is today. For we have to imagine the absence of the basilica of San Francesco and the immense convent to the west of it (which reminds one a little of the Potala of Lhassa in Tibet!), both constructed in the thirteenth century. The city is located in the heart of Umbria, between the Apennine Mountains and the vast plain that extends from Spoleto up to Perugia—an area which, during the Middle Ages, was called the Spoleto Valley. The medieval town was the successor of the Roman municipality upon whose ruins it was built, as is evidenced even today by the temple of Minerva (transformed into a church) on the Piazza del Comune, as well as by a part of its ancient walls and numerous private and public structures, like the ruins of the amphitheater in the upper part of the town. We know very little with precision about the history of Assisi during the Early Middle Ages, though it seems that the city might have begun its rebirth and expansion around the tenth century under the influence—here as elsewhere—of the resident bishop, the canons of the cathedral chapter, and a few Benedictine monasteries in the town, like those of Saint Peter (which had been reformed by Cluny and rebuilt between the end of the twelfth and the middle of the thirteenth century) and of Saint Benedict. On the slopes of Mount Subasio, at the foot of this high mountain, often covered with snow during the winter, hovering above Assisi from a height of more than four thousand feet, are to be found numerous grottoes, like the Carceri, where hermits lived. At the time of Francis, there were eleven monastic establishments for men and seven for women within the city and its immediate environs, in addition to the great neighboring landowning abbeys of Sassovivo and Vallegloria out in the *contado*, the countryside under the control of the town. In the twelfth century, the two principal religious poles of Assisi were the abbey of Saint Peter, symbol of monastic power, and the cathedral, which had been transferred from Saint Mary Major (the church whose foundation is attributed to Saint Savino in the fourth century) to the church of San Rufino. At San Rufino, in the upper part of the city, the relics of this bishop and local martyr, who died, according to tradition, in 238, had been transferred and placed in an ancient sarcophagus. The structure was completely rebuilt and embellished between 1140 and 1220; its main altar was consecrated by Gregory IX in 1228. It is there, according to tradition, that Francesco di Bernardone—such is the real name of the one we call Francis of Assisi—was baptized in October 1181 or 1182, while the cathedral was under construction, during the episcopacy of Rufino of Assisi, prelate between 1179 and 1185 and author of the important treatise "On the Good of Peace." These construction projects illustrate the growing strength of the power of the bishop, who possessed sizable landed properties—of which a portion was granted as a fief to lay vassals—and who exercised a considerable influence over the city and its contado.

The town was surrounded by a fortified wall, definitely much smaller than it is today: it extended seventy-five hundred feet around the city by the end of the thirteenth century, already much larger than the Roman wall of five thousand feet celebrated by the poet Propertius at the time of Augustus. Yesterday as today, its houses of pink and white stone of one or two stories clung to the edges of terraces, separated by small walls, and connected to each other by narrow alleyways and winding staircases. On the marketplace and especially in the aristocratic quarter of Murorupto, rose tall house-towers, similar to those that one can still see at San Gimignano or Bologna, where the members of the principal aristocratic clans or families (*consorterie*) who dominated city life at that time resided. A few main streets rose into the city, on steep inclines, in diagonals from the gates of the city up to a few flat areas made into piazzas, of which the principal ones were the Piazza del Comune, with the façade of the temple of Minerva immortalized by Giotto, and the one that extended out in front of the cathedral of San Rufino. On the summit, outside the city walls, the town was dominated by a fortress perched upon a peak, the "Rocca," which, in its present state, dates only to the fourteenth century but gives a good idea of what this fearsome bastion could have looked like at the end of the twelfth. Overshadowing the town and the road that led from Perugia to Spoleto, by way of Foligno and the springs of Clitunno, the Rocca occupied a strategic position of the first magnitude.

We do not know the exact size of the population of Assisi at this time. It probably counted scarcely more than three thousand to four thousand inhabitants, since the total population of the diocese, including the countryside, has been estimated at about fifteen thousand by the end of the thirteenth century. Located between the ancient Via Flaminia, which rose toward the Adriatic Coast and down through the Tiber Valley, the city of Francis in the thirteenth century was one step on the road to Rome and to the Holy Land. Indeed, numerous pilgrims went to embark for the East at Ancona in the neighboring Marches, as attested to by the itineraries followed by the monk and chronicler Matthew Paris (1253) and by the archbishop of Rouen, Eudes Rigaud (1254). Several hospices, like the one known as de Fontanellis run by the Crosiers, were there to welcome them.

Like the majority of cities within Italy, Assisi drew most of its revenues from the surrounding countryside. In the period of accelerated demographic and economic expansion that marked the second half of the twelfth century, the relationship between the Umbrian city and the contado, which had been placed under its authority in 1160 by the emperor Frederick I Barbarossa (r. 1152–1190), was evolving considerably. The units of production which for centuries had established the great landowning nobility, lay as well as ecclesiastical, were now beginning to fragment through the sale—more or less obligatory—by feudal lords unable to adapt to developments in the monetary economy and to the hike in prices that this entailed. In the mountainous zones that extended north of the city, the clearing of the land was undertaken by a few wealthy Benedictine abbeys, like Saint Benedict of Subasio or Saint Mary of Valfabbrica (which was a dependent of Nonantola in Emilia Romagna). But it was done especially by those elements of urban society that had capital at their disposal and who sought to make it earn more in the most cost-effective way possible. This is the period when the rural countryside surrounding the town— which one could still admire at the beginning of the 1960s—was really establishing itself. Here, fields sown with cereals and rows of fruit trees predominated which, together, constituted the base of agricultural exploitation that is called in Italian *coltura promiscua*. To the west and to the east, on the watered terraces and the low-lying foothills of the mountains, terraces were created and systems of waterways developed to irrigate the rocky soils on which the new planting of vines and especially olives was going to produce its fruits. To the south of Assisi, between Spello and Perugia, stretched a low and poorly drained plain where the waters of two modest waterways, the Chiascio and the Topino, stagnated. Here peasants pastured their cattle as the raising of livestock expanded at the time, but only a few people actually lived there. Yet it was in this unhealthy zone—where swamp-sickness and malaria were rampant—that Francis and his first companions established themselves at the beginning of their experience of community life: first at Rivo Torto, in a hut from which they were expelled because the owner wanted his mule to stay there, and then next to a little church in terrible shape, Saint Mary of "the Portiuncula," which the people called Saint Mary of the Angels, built on the ruins of a Roman villa.

The wealth of Assisi and its inhabitants was also due to economic activities proper to the city itself; and there were probably a few textile workshops there already by the year 1200. One must not, however, exaggerate their importance. Before the fourteenth century, Francis' native town produced barely enough articles for local consumption. And squeezed as it was between the two great commercial cities of Perugia to the west and Foligno to the east, it was never anything other than a second-rate economic center. Nonetheless, side by side with an aristocracy that remained politically and ideologically dominant, there developed an urban middle class that knew how to take advantage of the growth in demand created by a general rise in the standard of living. Not content to just sell the agricultural produce and the products of local artisans, this social group on the rise gave itself over to loans with interest, in spite of condemnations of usury by the Church which were hardly respected but which left in people's minds a vague feeling of guilt.

The society in which Francis grew up was in many ways more feudal than mercantile. His father, Pietro di Bernardone, was hardly a capitalist, and it would be wrong to imagine him to have been a great businessman, in the manner of a Francesco Datini, the famous merchant of Prato of the fourteenth century. In fact, it does not seem that he was a maker of cloth at all; rather, his activity was that of a seller who, in his shop as well as at markets and fairs, offered clients cloth which he had sought out in places where it was produced or exchanged. His wealth—which one can estimate with a certain amount of precision—consisted partly in cash, deposited or loaned with interest, and partly in revenues from lands out in the contado, but especially from real estate which he had acquired inside of Assisi. Indeed, if local scholars still debate about which house Francis was born in, it is because his father sat atop a comfortable landed patrimony that must have had a good return in this period of demographic growth and rapid increase of the urban population. Thus, son of a rich man and probably of a nouveau riche, very early on Francis acquired a concrete experience of money, whose importance and power in social relationships he could measure.

MERCHANT OR KNIGHT?
THE ADOLESCENCE OF A RICH MAN'S SON

It is into this urban environment, then in the process of change, that Francis was born and spent his youth. We are rather well informed about these years by a text drawn up in Assisi during the years 1244–1246 and known as the *Legend of the Three Companions*. Its author, whose identity escapes us, in spite of the title that it traditionally bears, was born in the same town, whose institutions he knew well. His principal aim was to correct certain details about the life led by the saint before his conversion as it had been described—in terms too general and moralistic—in the first *Life of Saint Francis*, composed in 1228–1229 by the friar Thomas of Celano.[2] According to this source, Francis was first named John by his mother. But when Pietro di Bernardone, whose trade as a cloth

merchant had taken him away from Assisi at the moment of the birth, returned home, he demanded that his son be called Francesco—Francis, the
"Frenchman"—perhaps because he himself had recently gone to France on
business. The anecdote is suspect, inasmuch as certain hagiographers commented on the change of name in order to present Francis as a new John the
Baptist, the Precursor come into the world to prepare the way of the Lord. In
any case, the choice of the name by which he is known to us was purposeful.
Though not absolutely unique, the name was essentially unknown at that time
in Italy. And if his father did give it to him, it was probably due to a trend of
prizing everything that came from over the mountains. For were not Italian
merchants going at that time in search of the heavy, richly colored cloth made
in Flanders and Artois—like the famous scarlet cloth so sought after in upper-
class circles—at the fairs of Champagne (Provins, Lagny, Troyes, Bar-sur-Aube)?

Indeed, the cultural influence of the France of Philippe Augustus was starting to have a profound effect upon the urban elites of Italy. Like the majority of
regions in the West between the end of the twelfth and the beginning of the
thirteenth century, Umbria welcomed and enthusiastically adopted the literary
expressions and ideals of the knightly epic and courtly poetry. Romances of
adventure, _chansons de geste et d'amour_, were known by all; and their heroes—
Charlemagne, Roland, Merlin, Lancelot—were likewise depicted on the en-
trances and pavements of cathedrals in northern and southern Italy, as one can
still see in Modena and Otranto. There is no need to imagine—as many have
without any proof whatsoever—that Francis' mother was French in order to explain the fact, at first surprising, that the young man who became Francis often
sang poems in French. In so doing, perhaps he expressed his most intimate
feelings or thoughts in the language of those regions north of the Loire where
he dreamed about going but where he was never able to go. He certainly had
not studied French in his parish school of San Giorgio, where he had received
during his childhood a level of instruction that one would today call elementary education. But French was at that time in Italy what English is today: the
language in which lyrical and musical culture was expressed, especially appreciated by the young who discovered it through songs and poetry.

We must resign ourselves to not knowing a lot about Francis' youth. He never
mentioned it in his writings, except to say in his _Testament_ that he had lived "in
sin" (_cum essem in peccatis_). His medieval biographers, in line with hagiographical traditions, devoted little attention to these formative years, eager as they
were to address the more significant part of his life: his conversion and commitment to the evangelical life.[3] We know that he had blood brothers—one of

them, Angelo, harshly mocked him after he had abandoned the family home—
and that his mother especially cherished him. In the *Lives* that were consecrated to her son, Pietro di Bernardone is not presented in a flattering light: a
"carnal" man, attached to money and his goods, he eventually entered into
open conflict with Francis and publicly renounced him for giving away some of
those same goods. Numerous painters, of whom Giotto is only the most famous, have immortalized the scene where the newly converted, in the first
months of 1206, renounces his father's goods—and even his clothes—in order to
place himself naked under the protection of the bishop of Assisi. We can wonder whether this complete reversal might not have been exaggerated later by
hagiographers in order to better highlight the contrast between an undoubtedly
greedy father—who, after all, was acting in accord with the norms governing
family relationships in his society—and a son whose rebellion was about to give
birth to a religious movement of great import. Nor should we forget that the
vocation of Francis was not at all obvious in the beginning, since he refused to
enter into the institutional structures provided by the Church for those who
were aspiring to lead a life of perfection outside the world and because he did
not envision himself becoming a monk. The *Legend of the Three Companions*
allows us a glimpse of the suffering that Francis experienced when he broke
with his family. For the young convert, the family belonged to the world of
carnal attachments; but for almost twenty-five years, he had led a life there that
was as enjoyable as it was sheltered. To enter into adulthood, even as a religious,
bearing a paternal curse, was not an easy undertaking, especially at a time
when the individual existed only in relation to his extended family and by virtue of belonging to it. We know from the same source that, in order to erase the
cataclysmic consequences of his disownment, "he chose for himself, as a father,
a very poor and despised man whom he asked to accompany him, in return for
an alms, in order to bless him, by making the sign of the cross over his head,
every time that his father, meeting him in the streets of Assisi, repeated his
curse."[4] The same legend tells us that, in order to force his son to give him back
his money and renounce his portion of the inheritance, Pietro di Bernardone
first went to speak to the consuls of the city. However, having learned that Francis was moving toward the religious life, the consuls sent him on to the bishop
of Assisi, Guido I (r. 1197–1212), who had jurisdiction over the clerics of his diocese and over those who were aspiring to lead a life consecrated to God.

   This detail invites a brief mention of the political and institutional situation
of the city in this period. From Lombardy to Latium, throughout the twelfth century, Italy had been marked by the appearance and expansion of the communal

regime. Thanks to the struggle that for decades opposed popes to German emperors, numerous Italian cities had acquired a broad administrative autonomy which made them—exceptional in Europe at the time, other than for a few towns in Flanders and in Languedoc—independent centers of power. Detaching themselves from their feudal ties to bishop or count, these urban republics gradually created their own political and judicial institutions. These were in the hands of a ruling group consisting of various vassals of the local prelates, men of law well versed in the knowledge of the law and customs, in addition to a few merchants who had become wealthy in business and through the practice of moneylending. The communes, as they were now known, were ruled by councils comprising elected consuls who controlled power within the city and were its representatives to the outside world.

At the beginning of the thirteenth century, there was little harmony in the Italian communes. In most of them, the struggles between the aristocratic clans and families were so intense that they preferred to entrust executive power to an outside authority—that is, one from another Italian town—the *podestà*, chosen to serve for one year. Given that he did not belong to any of the rival factions, he was able to arbitrate these internal conflicts more easily. But the party struggles, bitter as they were, did not impede the citizens from uniting among themselves to defend the common interest of their town against its adversaries and to help its expansion. In fact, it was at this very moment that the Umbrian cities were extending their control over the surrounding countryside—the contado—and seeking to reduce the influence of feudal lords who were often obliged to come and reside in the towns in order to be integrated into the political game. The aspirations of Italian towns for autonomy were countered by the emperors. But in spite of more than thirty years of strenuous effort to bring the towns to obedience, Frederick Barbarossa never succeeded in wiping out the movement; and, in the Peace of Constance of 1183, he had to resign himself to recognizing their right to administer their own affairs.

This process of urban emancipation had not, however, developed everywhere at the same pace. While it occurred quite early on in the great maritime cities like Genoa and Pisa and in the economic and political metropolises like Milan and Bologna, it manifested itself much later in central Italy, where the influence of the papacy—just as hostile to communal freedoms as was the Holy Roman Germanic Empire—was making itself felt. This was the case in Umbria: a region where the Holy See and the Hohenstaufen continuously confronted each other, directly or indirectly, up to the middle of the thirteenth century. If Perugia fell within the pontifical sphere of influence while still enjoying a wide measure of autonomy, Assisi, barely twelve miles away, was part of the Duchy of Spoleto and was, at least since 1176, subject to German lords who, with their troops, occupied the Rocca, the imposing fortress that even today looms over the town.

Francis, in his teens, was probably a witness to the event that changed the history of his little native town and the status of its inhabitants. In 1197 the emperor Henry VI suddenly died, just as he had come to firmly reestablish his authority over southern Italy and Sicily and was getting ready to do the same throughout the rest of the country. Shortly afterward, the population of Assisi rose up and expelled the garrison which the duke of Spoleto, the German Conrad of Urslingen, had stationed there. To avoid falling under the domination of yet another outsider, the rebels destroyed the Rocca, to the great regret of Pope Innocent III, who had hoped to take possession of it within the context of his policy of restoring and expanding the Papal States. With the stones that the insurgents recovered, they reinforced the walls of the town. They also took over the houses and especially the fortified towers which the principal aristocratic families were living in—those whom the charters of the period called the *boni homines*, the people of property—since they were considered to be allies of the former political and social regime.

In this turbulent context the commune of Assisi was born, formed by the sworn association of the free men of the city. We do not know whether Francis took an active part in these revolutionary activities, but it is hardly possible that he remained indifferent to them, given his age at the time—sixteen or seventeen years old—and his social class. By virtue of his family origins, he belonged to this rising class, which, in the Italy of the 1200s, was called the *popolo*. Strictly speaking, this was not "the people" as we use the term today, but rather a bourgeoisie which, in spite of its wealth and abilities, had remained excluded from the circles of power monopolized by the boni homines. These last—about twenty families in Assisi at the time—actually constituted an aristocracy of feudal origin that drew its revenues and strength from its possessions in the contado and from the legal authority that it exercised over them. In contrast, the popolo, of which Pietro di Bernardone was a typical representative, had made its wealth in commerce or manufacturing and drew important profits from landed and propertied investments as well as from moneylending. The popolo are the ones who, in 1198, created the commune of Assisi and who strove over the next years to expand their prerogatives at the expense of the nobles.

Out of this conflict between antagonistic social groups was born a civil war that ultimately provoked open conflict with Perugia, the powerful neighboring city. Indeed, chased out of Assisi, a number of noble families found refuge in this town, among them the family of Favarone di Offreduccio, the father of the future Saint Clare. Eager to eliminate a rival whose growth and unruliness had become worrisome, Perugia took up the cause of the fleeing aristocrats: its troops invaded the territory of Assisi in November 1202. According to the *Legend of the Three Companions*, Francis participated in the battle of Collestrada, near the San Giovanni Bridge, where the military forces of the city were defeated by those from Perugia, reinforced by the exiled nobles of Assisi.[5] This was not a major event having echoes throughout Christianity or even in Italy; but at the regional and local levels, the consequences of this battle were significant. Defeated militarily, the commune of Assisi had to accept in 1203 the conditions of the victors, beginning with the reintegration of the aristocratic families expelled a few years earlier. An accord between the leaders of the popolo and the boni homines was concluded, stipulating that the homes of the latter would be rebuilt within the city and that they would be compensated for the losses they had suffered. The town also had to look outside itself for support in order to safeguard its independence. In 1204 the commune swore fidelity to a papal legate and sought the support of the emperor, Philip of Swabia, who issued an official letter on its behalf in 1205.

For Francis, about twenty years old at the time, the defeat at Collestrada also had serious repercussions. Made a prisoner after having fought as a knight on horseback, he remained in Perugia for almost a year in an insalubrious prison from which he was freed only after his father paid a ransom—as was then the custom for nobles and people of means. Moreover, it seems that during his time in prison he contracted various illnesses that seriously weakened his health, which thereafter always remained fragile.

Peace did not last long between these two social groups, as the exiles, who had returned almost like foreigners, were viewed with suspicion by their fellow citizens. On the other hand, certain lords of the contado had judged the treaty of 1203 insufficiently favorable to their own interests and continued, with the help of Perugia, to stir up trouble against the commune of Assisi. Not until 1210 was a definitive treaty reached between those whom the compromise text calls the *maiores* (that is, the members of the noble families)—some of whom had up to now remained in exile in Perugia—and the rest of the citizens, the *minores*. This document is particularly important for the history of Assisi in that it put an end to a period of troubles that had begun in 1198 but also because it explicitly mentioned the enfranchisement of all the inhabitants of the town who had still been subject to obligations to a master or lord by virtue of their servile condition. Indeed, the commune, having come of age and sure of itself, could not accept that some citizens might not be fully free at a time when it was being said that "the air of the city makes one free." But we would be wrong to imagine the commune of Assisi as a fully democratic regime, for the poorest citizens had no chance to play an active role in civic life.

The aspiration to freedom was one of the fundamental givens of the time and place in which Francis lived. And this climate had to have an effect upon his personal life. What the treaty of 1210 guaranteed to all inhabitants of the city, including former serfs, was actually quite different from our modern notions of human rights or constitutional guarantees. In the Middle Ages, freedom was defined not by the prerogatives of the individual but rather by one's incorporation into a protective collective order. Hereditary subjection to a lord was being replaced by a voluntary submission to the commune, which was now considered to be the only power validly exercising authority over the inhabitants of the city, except for clerics, who were subject to the authority of the Church and, concretely, of the local bishop.

The signs of this renewed unity among the classes were apparent during the following years. Between 1212 and 1215, the communal palace of Assisi was built on the piazza that dominates the city, close to the temple of Minerva (later a church dedicated to Saint Mary). Construction of the new cathedral of San Rufino, interrupted by years of internal struggles, began once again by common accord, and in 1217 for the first time the existence of communal statutes is mentioned (they probably existed a few years before). In other words, there is now a veritable body of civil law, valid for all inhabitants of the town and imposed upon all. Thus civic patriotism had won out over social tensions—at least for the moment—and a community of citizens now united into a commune, apart from which only the bishop still retained a certain measure of power.

Francis grew up in this context of emancipation and expansion of freedoms; and it probably helped inspire his fundamental optimism and the certitude always firing him that it was possible to change the human person and to move society forward. But it would be going too far to make of him, even during this period of his life about which we know so little, a young militant revolutionary against the feudal order. Francis was never taken in by any mythology of progress. Even if he would have been aware of the positive dimension of the political and social transformations that were at work in his day, he probably would also have perceived their limits and ambiguities.

Barely established, the commune of Assisi threw itself into a campaign of annexations. In 1206 its consuls had gone to Valfabbrica to place this abbey and its territories under the protection of the city. A little later, it annexed the little towns of Postignano (1217) and Bettona (1222). Thus, before the very eyes of Francis, the ascendency of the communal regime in his city ended up depriving the inhabitants of smaller urban centers of their freedom and contributed to exacerbating conflicts with neighboring villages, who were then led to enter into war against Assisi in order to oppose its territorial expansion.

Moreover, the freedom which its inhabitants came to attain was a privilege reserved to citizens alone. In the countryside, serfs remained under the domination of lay and ecclesiastical lords who controlled a good part of the contado. The new masters of the land, the bourgeoisie of Assisi, which had begun to make a place for itself side by side with the aristocracy, were no less greedy and demanding of their dependents or renters than had been the nobles. As elsewhere throughout Italy in this period, we see a gap growing between the inhabitants of the towns—protected by the communal regime which could enrich itself here much more easily and quickly than in the countryside—and the *villani:* the mass of country folk, deprived of any real rights, strangers to the refinements of urban culture and despised by the citizens, who mocked their country ways. Moreover, even after Francis had acquired a great reputation for holiness, it seems, according to some testimonies, that he may have been regarded with some suspicion by the peasants whom he encountered, perhaps because he was a typical representative of this bourgeoisie and an urban culture that signified for them economic exploitation and disdain.

Thanks to his social origins and lifestyle, Francis was clearly located on the side of the privileged. Son of a wealthy merchant, he had, as we have seen, fought on horseback at the battle of Collestrada. In a different climate, such a situation would have been difficult to imagine; for it is precisely in this period that the bond between nobility and knighthood had become tightly connected north of the Alps. Was not the ideal of the lord to go to war mounted on horseback while the "little people of the world" fought on foot? The very term "foot soldier" served to designate those fighters of modest rank. The Italian communal society did not know these same divisions, and, as had been noted with scandalized shock by the German bishop and chronicler, Otto of Freising, after the middle of the twelfth century: "Over there, one does not hesitate to give the knight's belt and the status of this dignity to young men of inferior condition and to artisans of the manufacturing class whom all other countries bar like the plague from such honorable and professional careers."[6] Thus is explained how Francis, son of a commoner but endowed with considerable wealth, had been able to go into battle in the manner of nobles without actually belonging to an aristocratic family. And it is not without consequence for his later destiny that the son of Pietro di Bernardone found himself, by virtue of his family context and personal aspirations, at the meeting point of these two social groups. Of a rather modest social origin, Francis had indeed aspired from his youth to raise himself above his condition and to live like a lord. The wealth and lavish generosity that helped others forget his modest roots allowed him to mingle with nobles of his own age and, having reached his majority (fourteen years old), he seems to have been part of a band of revelers that brought together the most rowdy elements of the golden youths of Assisi. Perhaps it was the Society of Dancers of Assisi, which certain documents of the thirteenth century mention, or the Society of the Staff, attested to at a later date, who noisily came out on the occasion of religious feasts, especially during that of Saint Vittorino—former bishop and one of the patron saints of the town—on June 13, or during the feast of San Rufino on August 11, or San Nicolò, or other more secular feasts, like the Calends of May, which marked the return of summer, or even the feast of wine, after the harvests. These confraternities of youths, called *brigate* in central Italy, also participated in farcical parades, for example, during the feast of the Holy Innocents or in danced parodies, like those of Herodias and Salome on the occasion of the feast of John the Baptist, which consisted of demonstrations marked by ritualized perversions.

Francis seems to have taken a particular pleasure in these masquerades, occasionally, in his search for frivolity, sewing together into a single garment expensive fabric and cloth of shabby quality. In this young man's exaggerated taste for patchwork—presented in the hagiography as a characteristic of juvenile immaturity—it is not too far off the mark to see also a show of snobbery by this son of a merchant full of ambition and of knightly dreams. Throughout his life, he was to evince a marked taste for disguise and even dressing up, which, by blurring established boundaries, laid bare the reality of his thoughts and impulsive actions. In any case, abolition of the distinctions between social classes by challenging the ways in which one was supposed to appear and the symbolic clothing associated with it was the sign of a subtly provocative spirit in a young man who dreamed—initially only to amuse himself—of an upside-down world where gaiety and beauty would be the only criteria of success. In this sense, Francis was, according to the apt phrase of Carlo Ginzburg, "a carnival-like personality," if by that one means that he considered hierarchical distinctions nothing more than flexible standards which should not be treated like barriers—without, of course, ever claiming to abolish them or to deny their reality.[7]

The confraternities of youth, like the one that the son of Pietro di Bernardone hung around with, consisted of structures of social connection whereby members of the same age group and of a certain social milieu met to eat, drink, and sing. The importance of these confraternities in the life of the city is attested by the fact that they possessed their own statutes and that the communes, in many cases, recognized their existence, if only to try to redirect their excesses.

In Assisi the leader of such a confraternity was elected by its members and carried a staff as the sign of his authority. He thus had the power to condemn one of the revelers to pay all expenses of the group's partying. Francis, affable and charming, soon rose to this position. He was elected "king" because of his energy and extravagance, since he spent all that he could obtain or earn on merrymaking. In fact, he did not disappoint his drinking companions for, far from making others pay in his place, he always showed himself disposed to pay with his own money for the nights of drinking and fine meals that this festive group periodically threw for itself. The author of the *Legend of the Three Companions*, who reports this habit of Francis', sees there the precursor of a generosity and charity that would later extend to all of humanity and especially to the most disadvantaged. But this interpretation *a posteriori* probably idealizes a more prosaic reality: son of a merchant and nouveau riche, friendly with young aristocrats, Francis had to get them to forget his unremarkable origins and the source of this money that he was so generous with. Moreover, the activities of these bands of youths had nothing edifying about them; and there is no reason to think that Francis might have behaved differently from his companions. Bon vivant, ready for every good or bad turn, he probably did not limit himself to the "stupidities, farces, and clownishness" which the hagiographical texts report about him relative to this period of his life. Sexual games, muggings, and rapes were part of the normal activities of these bands of well-to-do bachelors. And these confraternities of youths will even be accused—two centuries later, it is true—of being gathering places for homosexuals. It would be pointless to try to say more, given the silence of contemporary sources on this subject. But why not read literally the short passage of the *Testament* in which Francis says, regarding the life he had led before his conversion: "When I was in sin . . . ?" Surely, the saints have a tendency to blacken their own portraits and to consider as serious faults what might appear to us as simple peccadilloes. But this seductive young man had no reason to behave other than as the customs of his time and age group dictated.

If we place Francis in this perspective, it becomes easier to understand the extreme reserve that he manifested in his later relationships with women—including and especially those whom he was closest to and who were dearest to him—and the strict limitations that he imposed on the Friars Minor in this domain. Such actions are surprising from a man whose behavior cast doubt on the majority of taboos and fundamental divisions existing in medieval society. Such pessimism, a marked mistrust with respect to the body and its spontaneous reactions, cannot but find its origin in a personal experience of sexuality and perhaps even of sexual dysfunction.

Among the qualities that had brought Francis to the attention of his companions when they had made him the "Prince of the Youth" of Assisi, we have already mentioned his generosity. The *Legend of the Three Companions*—our best guide for this period of his life—even says specifically that "he lacked measure in his manner of dressing" and that to see him "one would have thought him to be the son of a prince, not the son of merchants."[8] Even when he was an adolescent, his reactions were not those that characterized the world of buying and selling, even if such were the activities that he was involved in at that time. Rejecting the dominant values of his social class—eagerness for gain, a spirit of thrift, and concern for profit making—Francis, on the contrary, refused to hoard the money his father had given him, spending it instead without counting the cost. In fact, this "inheritor," born into the business-minded middle class, aspired to live like a knight (*miles*, in medieval Latin) and to lead the life of a nobleman. His ideal was that which the chansons de geste and courtly romances extolled at the time—this French material that had invaded Italy at the end of the twelfth century and whose most representative works he must have known. Ideal warrior, certainly: for this literature exalted the military exploits of courage—Charlemagne, Roland, Olivier, and so many others; but even more so, ethical and romantic ones, like Parsifal, Lancelot, and the knights of the Round Table.

Moved by these models, the young man endeavored to imitate them and to distinguish himself by the practice of their virtues—magnanimity, generosity, and especially courtliness—which was not simple affability but a particular manner of behaving in society. For fundamentally, the courtly attitude consisted of standing back from (or at least some distance from) the rawness of desire and the aggressive assertion of one's own power. Refined behavior, appropriate for an elite, which had value only among people of the same cultural world who alone were capable of understanding the significance of this aristocratic code that excluded and rejected those whose crudeness of manners and language placed them in the sphere of the unrefined or the parsimonious: peasants, avaricious bourgeois, lawyers, and the like. It is not difficult to understand that the young merchant of Assisi might have been seduced by this courtly ideology, which stood in sharp contrast to the pedestrian realism of his family's social milieu. Under these influences—we do not know how or where he encountered them—his ambition was ignited. Not content just to dream of adventures and to aspire vaguely to social promotion, Francis wanted to achieve glory through noteworthy actions and deeds of arms that would make him famous. He was deeply convinced—all the sources agree on this point—that a great destiny awaited him, this romantic hero who sought at all cost to draw attention to himself and purposely cultivated excess: had he not declared to his companions, when he was held prisoner in Perugia: "Know that one day I will be venerated throughout the whole world"?[9] It is this young knight, full of ambition, who was going to throw himself enthusiastically into the knightly adventure.

After his release from the prisons of Perugia and a long illness that immobilized him for the greater part of 1204, Francis decided to follow a man of arms from the region who was going to join Walter of Brienne and a few knights in Apulia. This French *condottiere* who claimed the title of king of Sicily was recruiting troops at the request of Pope Innocent III to fight the partisans of the emperor, who was seeking to maintain control over southern Italy—something that the papacy judged to be injurious to its own temporal interests. The hagiographical texts concerning Saint Francis have mentioned in this regard two visions he received, which, in the eyes of their authors, marked a first step in a process of conversion that was destined to last for almost two years. According to the *Legend of the Three Companions*, the young squire dreamed, before his departure on this expedition, that he found himself in a palace whose walls were decorated with lances, shining shields, and all the things that constituted the military hardware of a knight. Convinced that he was soon to become famous by exploits in battle, the sleeper asked: "For whom are such treasures intended?" and a mysterious voice answered: "These weapons are for you and your companions," which he interpreted as a favorable omen for the expedition that he was going to undertake.[10] For was he not going to accomplish noteworthy deeds there that would allow him to obtain the title of knight, to make him master of a castle, where he might lead the life of a lord that he had dreamed of? Thomas of Celano even adds that there was present in this dream "a beautiful fiancée," promise of a union that would allow him to enter into the nobility.[11] But the second vision is already marked by a less happy tone, if only because it is situated within a context of failure and disappointment. Scarcely having left with this little group of knights, Francis fell ill in Spoleto, about twenty miles east of Assisi, and his companions continued on their journey without him. He was hoping to join up with them after his recovery when he heard, while drowsing, a voice that said to him:

"Who can do more good, the master or the servant?" The master, he answered. "Then why are you looking for the servant, rather than the master?" Ah! Lord, what would you have me do? "Return home; and there you will learn what is right for you to do. The vision that you had had in a dream, you must interpret in a completely new way."[12]

The recourse to premonitory dreams and visions is common in medieval literature and especially in hagiographical texts. They constitute pedagogical means—the Bible furnishes numerous examples of this—for getting the substance of an important message into the soul of a person (then into the listener or reader of the text), by conferring on it a supernatural guarantee of authenticity. We would be wrong to take these famous episodes literally and to lose time wondering whether these conversations actually happened. For their universal meaning is very clear: on the occasion of his failed departure for Apulia, Francis perceived the limits of the knightly ideal which up to then had been animating him. And now he has been led to question it: all people, including Walter of Brienne and Pope Innocent III, are they not but servants, too? There is only one master who deserves to be followed. But who is this Lord and how can one know him? His mind filled with these questions, Francis returned to Assisi in the summer of 1205 and resumed his previous life, combining work at his father's side with the pleasures of life in the company of his joyful band of friends. He did not have to wait long before taking another path.

THE TURNAROUND

In the biographies of Francis, ancient or modern, the term "conversion" is often used to describe the period between his return from Spoleto in the summer of 1205 and the final revelation at the beginning of 1208 of the kind of life that was to become his and his first companions'. It is a convenient term but one which historians are not happy with because it encompasses a whole series of very different episodes among which it is not easy to find a connecting thread, especially since the hagiographers do not recount the progression of events in the same order. Even more: the first among them, Thomas of Celano, has contributed to the confusion by presenting two very different versions of the conditions and steps of Francis' evolution, first in his *Life of Saint Francis*, composed in 1228–1229 (1Cel 1–7), and then in his *Memorial of the Acts and Virtues of Saint Francis* or *Second Life* (2Cel 1–8).[13] In the first *Life*, the conversion of the Poor Man of Assisi is presented as the consequence of a sudden eruption of grace in the soul of a profoundly corrupted sinner. The author sees in Francis a few natural virtues, like magnanimity and generosity, but, according to him, these gifts had been virtually wiped out by a willful descent into sin. Influenced by the *Confessions* of Saint Augustine and by the spiritual journey of Saint Paul converted by God on the road to Damascus, Thomas of Celano describes Francis' return to God as a snatching back that was to free him both from a sinful nature and from a perverted society which was Christian in name only. This grace was not at all merited, but God chose to make Francis an instrument of his providential design for the world. The author of the first *Life* is imprecise about the exact moment when his subject was truly transformed, underlining Francis' long resistance to the divine will. But once Francis acquiesced in this account, the change was total and definitive. And it quickly made of him a man of exceptional holiness, the cause of salvation for many and of the renewal of the Church.

Less than twenty years later, the same author describes the process of the sanctification of Francis in his *Memorial* of 1246–1247 in very different terms.[14] The severe criticisms that Thomas of Celano had previously levied against Francis' family and his conduct now pass into the background, and the accent is put instead on his natural qualities and the merits of his parents. The author is intent on stripping his subject of every perversity and even of all singularity: his conversion appears simply as a return to his true nature and the fruit of his personal efforts, divine grace merely completing and crowning the action of a man who gladly renounced the delights of the flesh and acquired the freedom of the spirit. His conversion is presented as an imperceptible transition whose culmination was the embrace of the leper, on which occasion Francis comported himself as the perfect imitator of Christ and the saints who had preceded him. His whole life, in this account, was a continuous and constantly renewed conversion; so numerous and difficult to overcome were the temptations that assailed him that he seemed no more advanced at the end than at the beginning.

This contrast between the two lives of Francis by Thomas of Celano ought not shock us, even if it is somewhat surprising to a modern reader. The hagiographer of the Middle Ages had to conform to predetermined rules: he was not claiming to write a historical biography of his subject in the sense that we understand it. Rather, he sought to present his subject as conforming to certain particularly prestigious models of holiness, like those whom one could find in existing authoritative texts: the *Life of Saint Martin* by Sulpicius Severus, the *Life of Saint Antony* by Athanasius of Alexandria, or even the *Life of Saint Bernard*. Depending on whether the author was influenced by this model or that, important nuances or even divergences could emerge from one text to another.

Add to this that the life of the founder of the order of Friars Minor had quickly become an essential issue for hagiographers. There could be no neutral biography; each of the lives written in the century that followed the death of Francis reflects an interpretation, a partisan "reading," of the Franciscan phenomenon, inspired more by the burning issues that the order knew at each step of its evolution than by a concern for historical objectivity. Thus in the *Life of*

Saint Francis written shortly after his death, Thomas of Celano is inspired by the desire to account for the rapid development and prodigious success that the Friars Minor were experiencing at the time. This led him to attribute to the person of Francis a trait characteristic of the beginning of the order by presenting his conversion as the sudden and overwhelming eruption of grace in a merchant of hard heart. In the *Memorial*, by contrast, composed at a time when the Franciscan order was especially endeavoring to insert itself into the structures of the Church and to have its providential role there recognized, the same author sought in some way to "normalize" the holiness of Francis, at the risk of stripping it of its uniqueness and making it banal. Thus does he present Francis' conversion in a more classic and nuanced way on the psychological level. More satisfying than its predecessor for the modern reader, this interpretation is not necessarily "truer," even if one assumes that the firsthand information which Thomas of Celano received from the early companions of Francis between 1244 and 1246 allowed him to better assess the complexity of the person.

The existence of such differences in the two *Lives* fairly close in time to the life of the subject they celebrated is inherently discouraging. For if everything is a matter of conventions and appropriateness in the hagiographical texts, we can be tempted to think that it is useless to rely on them in trying to understand what might have been the spiritual experience of Francis. However, the turnaround that occurred in him during these three years had such importance to his later destiny that one cannot just give up trying to analyze its unfolding and to understand its significance. As none of the interpretations proposed by Thomas of Celano about him is fully satisfying, I stand by the events on which the sources are in agreement, while preferring to follow, when they do differ, the *Legend of the Three Companions*, more precise and better informed than the others on the early years of Francis.

After his return from Spoleto, Francis reconnected with his past, taking up his work again, as well as the habits of a joyful bon vivant. However, even to his pleasure-seeking companions it soon became obvious that he was no longer the same. Lost in meditation, he often seemed distracted and said strange things about his upcoming marriage with a most noble fiancée, richer and more beautiful than all the other women he had ever known. Furthermore, secretly, he was giving alms generously to the poor and devoting more and more time to prayer and meditation. Going to Rome on pilgrimage, he was shocked by the small number of offerings that visitors were placing at the tomb of Saint Peter. He thus flung the whole content of his purse through the grill surrounding the altar. Then, as he left the church, he exchanged his clothes for the rags of a beggar who was standing outside and, taking his place, began to ask for alms in

French—which was the best way for him to be neither understood nor recognized. The episode has perhaps been made up by the author of the *Legend of the Three Companions* to highlight the piety and orthodoxy of his subject, as well as to foreshadow his attachment to poverty and the process that was going to lead him from generosity to charity. But it illustrates well what might have been the state of mind of this failed knight who was going to find his voice only in long and painful fits and starts. Rather than the word "conversion," which in our vocabulary evokes a brutal rupture with previous beliefs and practices, the term "turnaround" is probably more appropriate to describe this period of searching, marked by the progressive passage from knightly values to a program of life founded on the Gospel.

This interior transformation occurred in a climate of torpor and melancholy, interspersed now and then with new feelings and revelations, ever more specific, about what meaning to give to his life, even as he maintained his previous aspirations. Francis seems to have thus traversed a difficult period during which interludes of physical weakness and confusion alternated with moments of intense exhilaration. He often withdrew at a distance to pray, especially into a grotto, but he never found any real serenity there. One day he had a vision of a horrible hunchback who was living at the time in Assisi. According to his first biographer, "the devil made him think about this woman and threatened to inflict him with this same deformity if he did not give up his plan." This clearly meant that Francis was hesitating to make a decision for fear of becoming an object of derision for his friends.[15] Little by little, however, the crisis in which he found himself immersed began to fade. Modern psychologists have shed light on the link that exists, in certain cases, between illness, conversion, and creativity, which the medieval hagiographers evoked via the conventions of their genre. After a period of depression marked by an intellectual or profoundly prayerful effort, the saint-to-be becomes obsessed with an overriding idea which never leaves but never fully satisfies the subject's desires. Finally, a release from the suffering occurs, tied to an energizing inspiration, which leads to a transformation of personality. One recognizes in the case of Francis this process of creative illness, at the end of which he finds the courage necessary to act and do certain irreversible things in order to break with his past.

According to Francis' own words in his *Testament*, the event that determined his turnabout was the encounter with lepers. "The Lord led me to begin to do penance in this way: when I was in sin, it seemed very bitter for me to see lepers. And the Lord led me among them and I did mercy to them . . . and after that, I did not wait long before I left the world."[16] If we pause for a moment on this fundamental text, we will notice first that it includes no mention whatsoever of an "embrace of the leper," which can only be a "mystification"—in the double sense of sublimation and deceptive invention—on the part of the hagiographers. In fact, the sight of lepers seems to have acted on Francis like a mirror of his own condition of sin. In not turning away from these repulsive people who, in the medieval mind, incarnated not only a horrible malady but also the suspicion of a hereditary defect or some abnormal sexual behavior which would have caused it, Francis overcame the obstacle and humbly recognized that he, too, shared an analogous condition.

In the Middle Ages, lepers were considered the dregs of society. A leper had to shake a rattle when he moved about in order to alert healthy people against sudden encounters—so much did they dread the contagion that was attributed to the leper's breath, which supposedly corrupted the air around him. Thus political authorities strove to shut lepers away in hospices, where they were fed and cared for by a few dedicated laity with whom, being dead to the world, they formed a religious community under the direction of a cleric. But for most people seeing lepers, the normal reaction was flight and rejection. In approaching them as he did, Francis not only made a charitable gesture but demonstrated heroic courage, which became, contrary to every expectation, a rewarding deed: "And in going among them, what had seemed to me bitter was changed for me into sweetness of soul and of body."[17] Instead of the feeling of horror experienced by Isolde in the *Tristan* of Béroul when her husband, King Mark, handed her over to lepers in order to avenge himself for her infidelity, Francis felt a kind of happiness. For him, the disadvantaged were no longer lepers but brothers, since he had experienced in himself a radical change.[18]

This fateful association with the most despised part of humanity was going to enable Francis to find God in the person of Christ, who had identified himself with the misery of the world by becoming united with the inhuman suffering of these marginalized persons. Francis' reaction is captured in the little phrase in the *Testament* where he mentions this decisive encounter: "And I did mercy to them."[19] Whatever might have been the specific "mercy," it reflects an essential element of the lay spirituality of the period. Mercy consists of an attitude toward the other that we are inclined to think has always been part of the range of human reactions to misfortune or sin. But in fact, there is nothing automatic or obvious here. We can even date the appearance of such mercy—or at least its diffusion within Christianity—to the time in which Francis of Assisi lived. Mercy—as a feeling as well as an institution—finds its origin in the Gospels, but especially in the interpretation that was given to them beginning in the last decades of the twelfth century. It is during this period, following the exhortation of

Christ in his Beatitudes ("Blessed are the merciful," Matt 5:7), that this notion began to be applied not only to sinners but also to the poor, to pilgrims, to the sick and prisoners, and that the aid that one might bring to these unfortunates—the works of mercy—could be a privileged means for entering the Kingdom of Heaven (Matt 25:34–37). The most remarkable form of this evolution that became part of the mindset of the time was the creation of associations and institutions under different names (*maison-Dieu*, hospice, hospital) bringing together willing believers under the sign of fraternity and solidarity with the disadvantaged. A considerable number of men and women at the time committed themselves to trying to remedy the persistent evils afflicting their society. Charitable assistance, organized into hospices and leprosaria founded by individuals or municipal authorities, constitutes one such remedy, while at the same time offering to the faithful the opportunity for spiritual perfection.

Thus Francis did not invent the notion of mercy; it was something that he inherited from the lay religious movements of his day. He was deeply influenced by this new sensibility to the suffering and misfortunes of others, which enabled him to recognize in lepers the palpable form and presence of Christ in human beings. Penance, peace, and mercy were to become the watchwords of Franciscan preaching and to inspire concrete actions through which people could make amends for their faults. Francis did not found any leprosaria; he did not commit himself in any permanent way to the service of these lowly ones, even if he sought their company everywhere he went. Indeed, he even was led in 1220 to prohibit his brothers from totally devoting themselves to them. But in "doing mercy" to the lepers, he made their reintegration into human society possible, thus helping to extend the idea of justice to human and social relationships without giving it the appearance of an aggressive demand, which would have rendered it unacceptable to the Church and society of his time.

By emphasizing in his *Testament* that his encounter with lepers had been at the origin of his process of conversion, Francis clearly indicates that it was neither his praying nor his earlier dreams that changed his life, but rather this particular event. His generous attitude toward the disadvantaged had not been the fruit of his religious evolution; on the contrary, it had preceded his discovery of the Gospel and was the cause of that discovery. Such a sequence did not conform to the canons of hagiography, which were obliged to showcase spiritual evolution and its manifestation as a charitable deed toward one's neighbor. This is what Thomas of Celano does in his *First Life*: he places the embrace of the leper at the end of a process of conversion and presents it as an illustration of the disdain for the self at which the saint had eventually arrived, and as a victory won by Francis over himself. The majority of the later biographers of Francis either do not even mention the incident or, if they write about it, prefer—as does the author of the *Legend of the Three Companions*—to put the emphasis on the wondrous experience of the crucifix in the church of San Damiano, which, as we shall see, spoke to Francis. Similarly, the iconography of the Poor Man of Assisi—however abundant—devoted little space in the thirteenth and fourteenth centuries to the encounter with the lepers—with the notable exception of the Bardi Retable of Santa Croce in Florence. Nor do we find any trace of it in the great cycles which Giotto consecrated to his life, neither in Assisi nor in Florence. In fact, the testimony which Francis left us in his *Testament* ("the Lord led me among the lepers and I did mercy to them") helps us to understand that it is precisely because he had encountered the lepers and because he had been overwhelmed by this event that he was, consequently, moved by the depicted representation of the God-man, poor and suffering, which he was contemplating at San Damiano. In other words, Francis' conscience needed the mediation of his neighbor in order to encounter God.[20]

Indeed, Francis' vocation was affirmed and concretized over the weeks that followed this fundamental encounter. At the end of 1205, while he was praying in the little church of San Damiano below the ramparts of Assisi, kneeling before the large wooden crucifix, he heard a voice that said to him: "Francis, do you not see that my house is falling into ruin? Go, therefore, and repair the house out of love for me."[21] Here again, it is appropriate to step back from the miraculous versions of this episode which rapidly gained acceptance. Moreover, we should note that the author of the *Legend of the Three Companions*, where this episode appears for the first time, does not tell us that it was the crucifix that spoke to Francis, as Thomas of Celano later did in his *Memorial* (2Cel 10), but simply that he heard an "inner voice"—the same that had spoken to him previously on different occasions. Thus, to bring this experience back to its primary meaning, we can say that, probably for the first time in the history of Christianity, a person had been so overwhelmed at the sight of an image of Christ on the cross that a new type of relationship was being established between God and Francis—and that his life was changed as a result. Taking the words that he had heard literally, Francis immediately began to work on the restoration of this ruined structure. To procure the necessary money, he did not hesitate to go to Foligno to sell a few pieces of cloth which his father had given to him, as well as a horse—which illustrates how thoroughly he was still involved in the business of his father. When the priest who serviced the little church refused the sum of money that was offered to him for fear of angering Pietro di Bernardone, Francis threw the purse on the window sill and went to hide in a nearby grotto in order to escape his father's condemnation. After a few days, however, he came out and went back to Assisi, pale and haggard from the mortifications which he had imposed on himself during his withdrawal. Those who had known him when he was in his glory now threw mud and stones at him, treating him like some crazy person.

Pietro, shocked by the behavior of his son, had tolerated Francis' extravagances as long as he could hope that they would give him access to a higher class. But they were no longer bearable now that his son's generosity had nothing to do with any plan of social promotion. Pietro thus intended to drag Francis before the municipal authorities in order to disown him and have him expelled from the territory of the commune. But the consuls declared that Francis no longer fell within their jurisdiction. Pietro thus brought his case before the bishop, Guido I. Guido, who was aware of Francis' spiritual evolution and had counseled him throughout this crisis, asked him to make restitution of the money that his father was claiming, if only because at least some of it seemed likely to have derived from usury. The Church was not allowed to accept such money, even on behalf of the poor or for places of worship. This is that famous scene illustrated by so many painters, especially by Giotto in the upper basilica of Assisi: in front of the bishop's palace on the piazza of Saint Mary Major, the young man, not content simply to give the money back to his father, strips himself of his clothing and places himself under the protection of the prelate, who wraps his mantle around Francis' shoulders—to hide his nakedness, it is often said. In fact, this gesture of the bishop has a totally different meaning: in placing Francis under his jurisdiction, Guido was recognizing him as "a religious" in the juridical sense of the term: that is, as a person who no longer fell under the power of his father or of the lay authorities, but of the Church. Francis was not an outlaw nor would he ever be. He was simply detaching himself from institutions which had become oppressive—the family and the commune—and was going to find a status within the institutional Church as a penitent, thus guaranteeing his spiritual freedom.

But to leave "the world," as Francis tells us in his *Testament* when alluding to this episode, was not so easy. Even before this, his exaggerated feasting and his purposely provocative behavior appeared to some of his compatriots as signs of real instability. The extraordinary events which followed could only confirm this impression and make of Francis a stranger in his own town. This was a rejection difficult to stomach for a person as urbane—in every sense of the term—and as sensitive to the opinion of others as was the son of Pietro di Bernardone. To leave the world was, in effect, to break with all the protections and structures of normal life: family, first of all, from which he had been excluded by virtue of the paternal curse, reinforced by the insults of his brother when he encountered him in the streets of Assisi, and even alienation from the affection of his mother, who had supported him for a long time, but who could no longer do anything for him. This rejection of the family and by the family, far from being a simple hagiographical theme, is found in numerous biographies of the first half of the thirteenth century. Think of the account by the Franciscan chronicler Salimbene of Parma of his own vocation, opposed by his family; or of so many lives of holy Beguines of Flanders and Brabant, contemporaries of Francis. Relatives having recently settled in town and having become newly prosperous through commerce and usury, often tolerant regarding sin and sometimes even heresy, now found themselves at odds with rebellious sons and daughters, gripped by an ideal and aspiring to enter into a group of "brothers" or "sisters." These children of the wealthy, looking for greater prestige through the service of God, developed a mindset that led them to put into perspective the values which their families held in high esteem—the search for profit and the desire to hoard—and to reject a world whose vulgarity and materialism they now despised. Jacques de Vitry has described particularly well this reaction, which helped inspire the vocation of numerous young women of northern France and present-day Belgium who, "Despising the wealth of their relatives, and refusing noble and powerful husbands that were offered to them, . . . preferred instead to live in poverty and to possess nothing other than what they could acquire by sewing and working with their own hands, content with rough clothing and modest food."[22] Thus, in all the well-urbanized regions of Christianity at the beginning of the thirteenth century, the aspiration for new forms of piety created a gap between the generations, while the *Sturm und Drang* of conversion, expressed in the language of visions and dreams and through rejuvenating illnesses, eventually resulted in a radical reevaluation of the individual's relationship to his or her normal environment. This is probably what Francis was trying to express when, in front of the bishop of Assisi, he declared that henceforth he would say only, "Our Father who art in heaven": the only father he wanted to know. For this father was not a tyrant; he was simply asking to be served as a lord would be by his vassal, in all loyalty and sincerity.

By placing himself under the protection of Bishop Guido, Francis had also broken with the commune of Assisi, to which he no longer owed allegiance. And this was not less risky. For as we have seen, at the beginning of the thirteenth century the inhabitants of the towns had a privileged status in comparison with those of the countryside in Umbria. Not only were they free, but the commune, the collective authority having autonomous power, guaranteed their rights against encroachments or attacks against their persons or their goods. This is the security that the young man willingly gave up. And it is significant that, from then on, he usually resided outside of the commune's walls, near the little churches he was repairing in the contado, and even in the forests of the mountainous areas that extended toward Gubbio, where he was one day accosted by brigands and left for dead in the snow. By placing himself outside the protection of the institutions of the city, he became a wild man, a kind of savage closer to nature than to civilization, which was at that time equated with urban and cultured life.

"To leave the world," at this time, was to lead a life consecrated to God. Early on, as we have seen, Francis had rejected the bourgeois values of his father and made the knightly ideal his own. After the failure of Spoleto, he felt himself called, according to Thomas of Celano, to leave the knighthood of this world (*militia saeculi*) in order to become a "knight of Christ." There was nothing original in this: since the eleventh century, the choice of a religious vocation was presented in these terms for numerous laity belonging to the ruling classes of the society. To become a monk at Cluny or Cîteaux: was it not the path for a well-born man to pursue, in the shelter of the cloister, the battles previously fought out in the world? Only the weapons were changed: prayer and asceticism substituting for the sword and shield. And the adversary, henceforth identified as Satan, from whom it was important to snatch the bodies of the living and the souls of the dead. With the Crusades, new avenues were opened to Christian warriors. Assured of their salvation, they placed their weapons at the service of God and the Church in the Holy Land. Such was the program that Saint Bernard, in his *In Praise of the New Knighthood,* had assigned, since the 1120s, to the emergent Knights Templar.

But this was not the ideal that Francis had known and which he had become excited about in his youth. To become a knight of Christ, in Italy of the 1200s, was no longer to enter a monastery. The age of fervor had passed and most abbeys had become unattractive to a person intent on perfection. Moreover, when, after having broken with his family, he sought refuge among the Benedictines of the abbey of San Verecundo to the north of Assisi, working there as a servant in order to stave off hunger and cold, he was so roughly treated that he left after a little while. He then visited a friend in Gubbio, where he got himself hired at the leprosarium of San Lazarus. On the other hand, leaving for the East in order to avenge the honor of God—as preachers were urging people to do—hardly had much meaning anymore, either. For after so many failures, and the scandalous rerouting of the Fourth Crusade, which had ended with the seizure and pillage of Constantinople by the French barons and Venetians in 1204, what spiritual good could one hope to obtain from any of this? It remained for Francis to find his way forward by himself—or, rather, to place himself into the hands of God for that.

BETWEEN EREMITISM AND RELIGIOUS
WANDERING (1206–1208)

According to Thomas of Celano, the habit which Francis wore at that time resembled that of a hermit, with leather belt, staff, and shoes.[23] Eremitism, which goes back to the first centuries of Christianity, was a way of life that was recognized by the Church and enjoyed a great prestige among the peoples of central Italy, where wooded forests, grottoes with limestone reliefs, and craggy hills offered numerous favorable sites. It is not surprising that Francis might have chosen it, at least at the beginning, because it was a state that could be embraced by laity as well as by clerics or monks. Since the eleventh century, hermitages had been proliferating on the ridge of the Apennines which served as a border between Umbria and the Marches and which extended westward into Tuscany. Some such cells orbited a monastic establishment like Camaldoli or Fonte Avellana; others were simple hideaways for isolated individuals living in grottoes or little huts, like at Monteluco—the Thebes of Umbria—near Spoleto. Some anchorites enjoyed a great reputation of holiness. While Francis was alive and in the years that followed his death, there was a hermit famous in the region, Lawrence Loricatus († 1243), who led a life of withdrawal at the bottom of a grotto, on the lands of the abbey of Subiaco. Having come from Apulia, where Byzantine-influenced traditions of extreme ascetic rigor prevailed, he inflicted on himself the most horrible mortifications, always wearing against his skin a kind of metal breastplate furnished on the inside with nails, which tore at his flesh when, exhausted by mortifications and privations, he allowed himself to sleep. But in the Middle Ages, the term "hermit" also designated, in the broadest sense, any person who led, alone or within a little informal community, an austere religious life at a distance from towns and settlements.

Fed at first by the priest at San Damiano, Francis soon refused his help and began to beg his food in the streets of Assisi by urging—in French, the language of inner feeling and lyrical enthusiasm—neighbors and passersby to join him on the roads. But the imperative for him was to work with his hands, and it seems that he may have devoted most of his time in 1207 and at the beginning of 1208 to the restoration of a few churches. Such work was not lacking; for the clergy of Assisi, preoccupied with the reconstruction of the cathedral of San Rufino, seems to have neglected the little structures in the neighboring countryside:

San Damiano, where Francis had perhaps been received as a lay brother (*conversus*) or oblate, but also a chapel dedicated to Saint Peter, as well as the church of Saint Mary of the Angels, called the Portiuncula, which belonged to the abbey of Saint Benedict of Subiaco. To restore or construct a church was certainly a meritorious work, often recompensed with the granting of indulgences. But that is not why Francis devoted himself with such ardor to this pursuit. For him, the church as an edifice was first of all a place of prayer and encounter with God. When he mentions in his *Testament* the beginnings of his religious experience, he uses a phrase which remains somewhat strange for us: "The Lord gave me such a faith in churches that I was praying simply in this way and said: "'We adore you, Lord Jesus, and we bless you because by your holy cross you have redeemed the world.'"[24]

One would understand if he had written that he had great faith in the Church. But the use of the plural precludes this interpretation. We must recognize that he wanted to signify by this that churches as buildings had played an essential role in his conversion, for it was there, while meditating and praying in front of the crucifix and the altar, that he had encountered God and understood the meaning of the mysteries of salvation, especially the Incarnation and Passion of Christ. A passage in the *Legend of the Three Companions* confirms this; one day during this period,

> He was walking in the vicinity of the church of Saint Mary of the Portiuncula, weeping and groaning out loud. A pious man heard him and, thinking that Francis was suffering from an illness or sorrow, was moved with pity and asked him the reason for his tears. The man of God answered: "I am weeping over the Passion of my Lord Jesus Christ. Out of love for him, I ought not be embarrassed to go through the world groaning in this way and crying."[25]

In spite of everything, this very physical engagement in manual work was for him only a temporary situation; he was looking for something else. It is then that an inspiration occurred, in the course of which his real vocation was revealed. According to Thomas of Celano, after having heard in the church of the Portiuncula the passage of the Gospel about the sending of disciples on mission for Christ, Francis cried out: "This is what I want, this is what I seek, this is what I long to do with all my heart!"[26] From that time on, he wore only a poor and course habit, girding his waist with a cord and going out to preach penance and peace. The hagiographers' accounts about this moment of fundamental intuition are not, however, in agreement. Thomas of Celano refers not to any specific passage from the Gospel but rather to a collection of texts indiscriminately borrowed from the three synoptic Gospels (Matt 10:9–10; Mark 6:9;

Luke 9:3 and 10:4), about Jesus' prohibition to his disciples against carrying gold, silver, money, moneybag, bread, staff, shoes, or two tunics on the road, and about his order that they go preach the kingdom of God and penance. According to other legendae, Francis' revelation took place after a few men from Assisi had joined him and become his companions. In any case, at the conclusion of a profound and intimate conversation with God in prayer, Francis finally understood what was expected of him. From then on, neither his profound humility nor his obedience to the Church and its hierarchy would ever interfere with his certitude of having been called to do great things, as he had predicted and announced from a very early age, in becoming "the herald of the Great King" in this world.[27]

The account of the "conversion" of Francis as presented in his medieval and modern biographies invests the story with a kind of obviousness, giving a deceptive coherence to a succession of episodes that were, in fact, rather disparate. Our reliance upon this handy notion, moreover, absolves us from asking what, in the surprising behavior of the young man, was consistent with his previous aspirations and what now separated him from them. By "doing mercy" to lepers and seeking to be poor among the poor, Francis was not giving up his juvenile ideal of generosity; he was instead broadening it and elevating it. If one can believe an episode of the *Fioretti* which has a ring of authenticity to it and which many similar anecdotes in earlier sources confirm, Francis, having been welcomed kindly and with great generosity by a knight some years later, declared to his companions that such a courteous man could not fail one day to place himself at the service of God. And this is what effectively happened a little bit later.[28] Far from being an obstacle, the knightly ideal, if taken seriously, could constitute the point of departure for an authentic religious experience, on the condition that it go beyond the sociological limits within which it was usually practiced.

In the last analysis, it was a question of giving up the logic of exclusion which predominates in this world in order to live according to "mercy," which, on the contrary, puts the excluded and the poor at the center of the feast. For Francis, this fundamental reversal was translated into an overturning of the logic of his reactions: "And going away from them [the lepers], all that had seemed bitter to me was changed for me into sweetness of soul and body," as he writes in his *Testament.*[29] A similar reversal also occurs with respect to food: this rich young man, who was used to choice and refined cuisine and had never touched food that was not to his liking, took a bowl and went begging from door to door. But the mélange of wretched foods in his bowl threatened to make him nauseous. However, overcoming his repugnance, he began to eat, and "it seemed to him that he had never tasted foods of such deliciousness."[30] These remarks on taste are not hagiographical or literary clichés. There is in Francis a knowledge of people and things according to taste, smell, and flavor which places him miles apart from any purely intellectual knowledge of the divine mystery.

At the end of this evolution, Francis is thus both the same person and yet another person. To the end of his life, he was to maintain (using the vocabulary of *courtoisie*), the lyrical sense of happiness and the taste for conquering hero-ism. But the encounter with the lepers changed his perspective by leading him to reestablish a communion with the most wretched of human beings via the free gift of love, and to "leave the world" in order to devote himself to this task. We would be on the wrong track, however, if we gave to this expression the meaning that it often had in monastic spirituality: of a flight from or a despising of earthly realities. Francis does not flee the world. On the contrary, he rushes to plunge himself into it in order, like his Lord, to conquer it and to reintegrate back into society the poor and all those whom power and money have excluded from it.

2

BROTHER FRANCIS:
A LAYMAN IN THE CHRISTIANITY OF THE EARLY THIRTEENTH CENTURY

Up to now, we have been trying to understand the behavior of Francis by limiting ourselves to an analysis of his psychological motivations and his social and cultural environment. But before 1208, Francis was just an isolated individual whose actions had hardly attracted anyone's attention. On this period of his life, his biographers have shown extreme discretion and have not sought to embellish it. For example, whereas the *Life of Saint Martin* recounts that, while crossing the Alps, the saint succeeded in cajoling, even converting a group of brigands whom he had encountered along the way, those whom Francis met during the first period of his wandering were hardly even listening to his words and simply threw him into a snow-filled ditch after beating him up. Likewise, if the theme of his encounter with the leper does indeed appear in all of his *Lives*, none of them tells us that Francis ever healed him. And it is obvious from his *Testament* that Francis is the one who emerged from this encounter transformed.[1] Had he died at that moment, who would ever have remembered this eccentric young man who had thought it right to break with his circle of friends and social milieu in order to live as a hermit and to work at restoring a few small churches in the environs of Assisi?

But before going any further and tackling what we might call the years of the "public life" of Francis (echoing those of Christ, his model), it is appropriate to define as clearly as possible the religious context that helped shape his own experience. Indeed, too often the biographers have presented the Poor Man of Assisi as an exceptional character who invented everything and received nothing. This tendency to make of him a kind of spiritual meteorite is particularly prominent in the first *Life* that Thomas of Celano dedicated to him, in 1228, in which he emphasized the radical newness of the Franciscan message and its capacity to reform the Church. But the historian has to react against this exaggerated supernaturalism devoid of all nuance. As impressive as the figure of the saint might have been, the form of life that he was going to propose would not have been nearly as successful if it had not been connected by a straight line to previous religious experiences, whether to pick up from them some of their most worthwhile elements or to avoid the excesses and failures they had sometimes led to.

Indeed, since the eleventh century, a general aspiration for reform of the Church had appeared in Western Christianity, an impulse translated into a desire to go back to the "apostolic life," such as the first Christian community of Jerusalem had lived it, according to the description in the Acts of the Apostles (Acts 4:32–35). Limited at first to monastic circles and to the clergy, this claim had gained ground and had extended itself to certain elements of the laity. Such individuals aspired to lead a life that was both in conformity with the Gospel and adapted to the needs of their state, characterized by manual work, marriage, and family life. Numerous members of the faithful thus devoted themselves to works of mercy toward the poor and travelers—for example, Saint Allucio († 1134) in Tuscany, who built a hospice by the side of the road, as well as a bridge over the Arno at a place where pilgrims on their way to Rome were being extorted by a local lord, who made them pay dearly for transport across the river. Others went farther, like Waldo (Valdesius), a layman from Lyons who, around 1170, having heard in church the passage from the Beatitudes where the poor are exalted, devoted himself thereafter to announcing the Gospel. He was soon joined by companions, men and women, whose claim to have the right to preach everywhere quickly put them in conflict with Church authorities. During the Third Lateran Council in Rome in 1179, however, Waldo and a delegation of Waldensians—the name given to his disciples—were received by Pope Alexander III, who authorized them to persevere in their apostolic activity on the condition that they not preach in public without the permission of the local clergy. In fact, the clergy were at first reserved, then openly hostile toward these laymen and -women, who were having the Scriptures translated for them into the vernacular and were sometimes claiming to be teaching their pastors. Ignoring these warrants, the Waldensians persisted in their itinerant preaching and life of evangelical poverty, citing the word of Saint Peter as reported in the Acts of the Apostles that it was better "to obey God rather than men" (5:29). This refusal to obey earned them a condemnation as heretics by Pope Lucius III in 1184, along with a group of similar religious movements which had sprung up in northern Italy: the Arnoldists, for example—disciples of Arnold of Brescia († 1155), who had advocated the renunciation of temporal power and wealth by papacy and clergy—and the Humiliati of Lombardy. But the Waldensians survived these condemnations by going into hiding, even if their movement was weakened by the split that occurred between 1205 and 1218, between the "Poor of Lombardy" who had created worker-communities and the rest of the movement, strongly entrenched in southern France, which emphasized itinerant preaching and begging.

Thus a contentiousness developed among the laity that took progressively more radical forms, depending on the region. But the same themes were found almost everywhere: all these movements were in agreement about taking the clergy as a group to task for its wealth, lavishness, and thirst for power, as well as for its overinvolvement in political issues, often leading it to neglect its pastoral duties and to lead lives contrary to the precepts of the Gospel. Certain groups, like the Italian Patarini, even went so far as to deny the validity of the sacraments conferred by morally unworthy priests—indeed, to deny the very reality of the sacraments, like the "*bons hommes*," whom learned clergy were beginning to call Cathars. The lay reformist movements did not go as far. In their view, conformity to the witness of the apostles was to be identified no longer with a separation from the world and withdrawal into a monastery, or even in living by a religious rule, but in the witness of an authentically Christian life attested to by poverty and expressing itself through a public proclamation of the Gospel message.

At the end of the twelfth century, the papacy put an end to these movements and attacks by the clergy multiplied against these presumptuous laity, who had intended to transmit the Word of God but were incapable of understanding it and interpreting it correctly. As Innocent III wrote in 1199, borrowing the words of the bishop of Metz, who had denounced to the pope the activities of various groups of laity of his city: "Certain ones among them had only disdain for the stupidity of their priests; and when the latter do present the word of salvation to them, they murmur in secret that they find better instruction in books and are able to present it better than they."[2] After this, the Roman pontiff reminded lay reformers that even if the priests were not up to their task, the faithful did not have the right to judge them or to hold secret meetings which could destroy the unity of the Church. Thus, around 1200, laity desiring to commit themselves to a religious life while remaining in their state found themselves confronted with a dilemma: either give up living in conformity with the Gospel, or ignore the ecclesiastical interdicts and be accused of rebellion, indeed heresy, by the hierarchy.

This situation was not without danger for the Church, which was in the process of cutting itself off, if not from the masses, at least from the most dynamic

levels of the urban society of the day. By exalting the role of the clerics and endeavoring constantly to extend the prerogatives of its spiritual authority, the
Church was becoming a sluggish structure whose theocratic claims were increasingly unpersuasive to the laity. The risk of conflict was particularly high in
Italy, where the ascendant classes (referred to as *popolo:* merchants, master artisans, lawyers) were claiming the right to play a leading or at least more important role in the political life of the cities. These classes thus often came in
conflict with their bishop, whose authority was not solely spiritual. This hostility between clerics and laity also had religious motives, for the clergy had been
unable to give satisfactory answers to the questions that their flocks posed to
them about, for example, the use of money and lending with interest, which
the Church condemned as contrary to Christian charity. But their fundamental questions were above all of a spiritual nature. It was, at the end of the day,
a matter of knowing whether "the world" that Jesus had rejected with such
force according to certain passages of the Gospels—especially those in John—
referred to the whole of creation, contaminated by the intervention of Satan, as
the bons hommes or Cathars were saying; or the totality of worldly realities,
as the Cistercians and the majority of clerics of the period were teaching; or
whether the curse spoken by Christ was aimed only at the wrongful use of these
things, contravening the demands of the Gospel. The doctrinal debate concerned only a small number of educated persons who had access to the biblical
texts, but they felt its importance deeply: did the Sacred Scriptures constitute "a
forest of symbols" (to use the expression of Baudelaire in another context), so
dense that only learned clerics were able to elucidate their abstruse matters by
means of a spiritual exegesis, or a living and accessible word, capable of inspiring
the behavior of all Christians? Was the Gospel made to be venerated in ritual actions and commented on by learned clerics, or to be received and lived by everyone? And did it not have a meaning, purely spiritual, which the Church kept
hidden from the greatest number, as the bons hommes were claiming?

There was another problem roiling many people at the turn of the twelfth
and thirteenth centuries: in a Church generally rich and powerful, as it had
become with the success of the Gregorian Reform, what was the place of the
poor? Clerics exalted the virtue of poverty, and the best among them founded
and undertook with their own resources truly meritorious works of mercy and
assistance. But this was not the case with the most. And many religious—in
particular, the monks whom the Church placed at the top of the hierarchy of
the states of perfection—never found a satisfactory balance between the necessities of a religious life in common and the demands of the Gospel. Even a
relatively recent order like that of Cîteaux, which had grown spectacularly

throughout the West between 1120 and 1170, underwent an economic expansion so rapid that it ended up destroying the quality of its spiritual life. In numerous regions, these "white monks," as they were called, which Bernard had wanted to make models of asceticism and austerity, had become enriched by the sale of wool and meat and had at their disposal large financial reserves at a time when famines were still prevalent. Sometimes even the search of the most favorable conditions for the expansion of religious life went against the demands of charity or even of simple humanity. Had not Cistercians or Carthusians more than once been seen chasing peasants from their lands and houses in order to create around their abbeys "deserts" indispensable for guaranteeing the monks solitude and peace? Finally, even when certain elements of the ecclesiastical hierarchy seemed to understand and sometimes even support the most legitimate aspirations of the disadvantaged in terms of justice and peace, it always ended up condemning their protest movements the moment when these were translated into collective action; the pretext for such repression was that the poor were challenging a social order which the Church had made sacred by presenting it as willed by God and thus necessarily unchangeable.

This was seen, for example, in France in 1182—the probable year of the birth of Francis—when the peace processions of the Capuciati of Le Puy, led by a pious carpenter and claiming their inspiration from Christ and Mary, were condemned and then brutally dispersed by royal authority and the nobles of the region, with the blessing of the clergy. The movement was suppressed for having challenged the feudal structures by criticizing bellicose lords or those who had been treating their subjects unjustly. By accusing of heresy those who were contesting its power and wealth, the hierarchy only radicalized the antiestablishment elements, like the Patarines in Italy, who, rejecting the mediating role of hierarchy and clergy, longed for a purely spiritual Church and saw in poverty the necessary condition for attaining Christian perfection. At the beginning of the 1200s, the gap only widened between the poor and a Church that was rich and in league with the powerful—in spite of the efforts of a few clerics, more clear-eyed and generous than others, like Raoul l'Ardent, Peter the Chanter, or Fulk of Neuilly in France. How could bishops and abbots, almost all born into the world of the nobility, whose ideas and interests they shared, do other than counsel the wealthy to show themselves generous, and the indigent to suffer their hardship patiently?

It would be too easy to heap sarcasm upon the clerics at the beginning of the thirteenth century and to reproach them, through vague moralizing, for their indifference toward the disadvantaged. For if they scarcely perceived the social reality of the poverty around them, this resulted less—in many cases—from the hardness of their hearts than from the rapid evolution of the world in which they were living and their inability to adapt to the new realities. Indeed, in "the century of great progress" (to borrow the apt expression used by Georges Duby to describe the years 1080–1230), those to be counted among the poor included not only men and women living in indigence, as always has been true, but also those left behind in the expansion: those who were not able to maintain their social rank, like the poor knight whom Francis met one day on the streets of Assisi and to whom he gave his own garments, so much had the spectacle of the man's decline moved him. There were those numerous "shameful poor" in the towns, whose aristocratic origins or bourgeois respectability impeded them from going out to beg and to whom it was necessary to go and discreetly help in their homes so that they would not face humiliation.[3] Confronted with this mass of poor who were too disparate to have a class consciousness or to express any coherent claims, certain individuals within the society of the well-off began to feel a sense of guilt. Thus did voluntary poverty come to have an essential place in the ideology of the majority of dissident or simply reform-minded religious movements of the time. A society in which power and wealth were once considered signs of divine favor—like that of the Early Middle Ages and the first feudal age—now gave way to a more broad-minded world, from the second half of the twelfth century forward, in which the criteria of success— nobility, victory, fortune—were no longer the same as the criteria of perfection, now become more spiritual. Paradoxically, the economic expansion, by increasing inequities and by rendering the fate of the excluded more tragic, restored to the Beatitudes a timeliness that they had lost for centuries. From this time on, the conditions were ripe so that we witness, according to the famous phrase of Marie-Dominique Chenu, "an evangelical awakening due to the changing of the world."[4] Yet that awakening required perceptive individuals who were aware of the changes occurring before their eyes, and to draw all the necessary conclusions.

THE FIRST COMPANIONS AND THE FRATERNITY OF THE PENITENTS OF ASSISI (1208–1209)

The kind of life led by Francis—and his perseverance—ended up conquering the hostility or indifference that had been surrounding him ever since he had left his worldly life. Indeed, beginning in spring 1208, some of his fellow citizens began to join him, one by one, and came to share his way of life. Tradition has it that there were eleven in the beginning—which, with Francis himself, constituted a group of twelve people, like Jesus' apostles. Fourteenth-century sources were to separate Francis from the lot and add the name of a twelfth friar, at the same time detailing that one of them, John Capella, abandoned the Christian faith and, like Judas, hanged himself.[5] The parallel is too perfect to be true. Moreover, the names of the first companions are not always cited in the same order, nor are they identical in the different biographies of Francis. All sources agree, however, that the first followers were all from Assisi.

In his *Testament*, Francis recalled the origin of the fraternity in these terms: "And after the Lord had given me brothers, no one showed me what I had to do, but the Most High Himself revealed to me that I was to live according to the form of the Holy Gospel."[6] These few words have a decisive importance, first to the extent that they depict the arrival of Francis' first companions as a grace given to him by God. Francis did not proselytize; he did not seek to found a religious congregation. But he did rejoice that "brothers" were joining him and that his personal experience was unexpectedly leading to the formation of a little community.

Moreover, we should note that Francis himself locates his discovery of the evangelical life after the brothers' arrival. This emphasis contradicts the assertion of Thomas of Celano, who emphasizes that Francis had had the revelation of his future form of life while he was still alone. Because Thomas wrote in 1228, when the majority of the first companions were still living, it is difficult to imagine that he could have distorted or misinterpreted an event of this importance without raising some heated protests among his confrères. It thus seems more probable that Francis' awareness of the fundamental intuition, which was at the origin of the form of life and, later, of the rule of the Friars Minor, occurred in two moments: the personal vocation to the Gospel life that we have already examined, followed, a few months later, by the discovery with his first brothers of its concrete demands, notably with respect to poverty. Indeed, according to the *Anonymous of Perugia* and the *Legend of the Three Companions*, Francis, accompanied by Bernard and Peter, entered the church of Saint Nicholas in Assisi and, after praying, opened the book of the Gospels three times. Each time, he opened to a passage dealing with the demands of self-sacrifice required by Jesus for the one who would follow him: "If you would be perfect, go, sell all that you possess, give it to the poor and you will have treasure in heaven" (Matt 19:21); then, "Take nothing for your journey" (Luke 9:3); and finally: "The one who wishes to follow me must renounce one's very self" (Matt 16:24 and Luke 9:23).[7] By this triple opening of the Bible or missal, though one could be tempted to see a magical usage of the text or a kind of martingale and which Saint Augustine had already labeled *sortes biblicae* (a random opening of the Bible), Francis is implicitly reacting against a tradition that had obscured the radicalism of the evangelical message. He rediscovers the simple, original, and unique truth of the Scriptures, thus restoring a direct relationship, interrupted for centuries, with the sacred text. On this occasion, he discovered that the Gospel was not a collection of stories or counsels but rather a way of life and the only one that securely leads to salvation.

Francis then abandoned the state and habit of a hermit for the simple clothing that was to become the uniform of the newborn fraternity: a single tunic—in conformity with the Gospel counsel "Do not have two tunics!" (Luke 9:3)—fastened by a cord, like peasants wore, as a kind of belt; no walking stick or sandals, but undergarments or breeches, unlike monks, who did without them since their vocation did not include moving about; a humble habit of coarse cloth in the form of a cross or Tau, a symbol of penance, with a capuche, or hood, like that of rural workers. At the most, the friars could wear a mantle in cold weather or when sick. But numerous episodes, reported by the medieval biographers of Francis, show him stripping himself even of this piece of clothing for the sake of a beggar or a poor shivering woman whom he encountered along the way. These details about clothing, which can seem secondary to us, were in fact very important. Indeed, in the Middle Ages, attire was—much more than it is in our day—a social indicator. The habit made the monk, or rather the friar, in the most concrete sense of the term, since, in the first years of the fraternity, simply putting on this attire meant being admitted, and it was taken away from those who rendered themselves unworthy by their behavior, before they were expelled from the community. In choosing a modest habit, Francis demonstrated his refusal to be slotted into a set social or religious category and clearly indicated that his little group wished to blend into the mass of those who had no social standing.[8] Finally, for him, "to live according to the holy Gospel" meant to lead an itinerant and poor life with his brothers, dedicated to a call to conversion addressed to all people. The *Legend of the Three Companions* summarized this in terms whose specific formulation was probably constructed after the fact but whose substance seems authentic: "Beloved brothers, God in his mercy has chosen us not only for our own salvation but also to save many souls. Let us go throughout the world and, by our example more than by our words, let us exhort people to do penance for their sins and to remember the divine commandments."[9] When they were four in number, Francis and Giles left to preach in the Marches of Ancona. And when they arrived in the villages and castles and were asked who they were, they simply responded: "penitents from Assisi" (*viri poenitentiales de Assisio oriundi*).

It is important to pause for a moment on this word "penance," which holds such a place of importance in the personal experience and message of the Poor

Man of Assisi. At the beginning of his *Testament*, does not Francis say: "This is how the Lord gave me, brother Francis, to begin to do penance"? According to the *Legend of the Three Companions*, this was a new idea in the Christianity of the day: "Love and fear of God were, in a manner of speaking, extinguished everywhere and people were profoundly ignorant of the ways of penance. Such a thing even passed for foolishness."[10] There is a certain dramatization of the situation on the part of the hagiographer, who aims to enhance the glory of his subject by attributing to him the merit of a real innovation. But the reality is more complex. Since at least the years 1170–1180, communities of male and female penitents existed in northern Italy, especially in rural areas. Initially, these were mostly peasants who, wanting to lead a religious life without renouncing their state, gathered to work and pray together. They followed ascetic observances and liturgical particulars, just like the conversi of Cistercian monasteries. But unlike the conversi, they had never felt the need to place themselves under the tutelage of a monastic order or religious house and were subject only to the bishop of the diocese.[11] The movement expanded afterward to the towns of Lombardy, especially among the Humiliati, who formed communities of laymen and laywomen, associating work and prayer. These last merit special mention, for certain characteristics of their movement prefigure the Franciscan experience. According to the words of a chronicler from the beginning of the thirteenth century, these were "citizens who, leaving all for Christ, lived by the work of their hands, often preached the word of God and listened to it with right intention, perfect and solid in the faith, effective in works."[12] Putting their goods in common, some lived in community in an urban environment, where they endeavored to associate work with prayer and to confer an evangelical value on their work. They did not flout orthodoxy, but other aspects of their life appeared shocking to churchmen, especially the mixed genders of their communities, where men and women coexisted on the level of strict equality, and their refusal to swear oaths before the courts, based on the word of Christ: "Let your yes mean yes and your no mean no."

In the regions near Umbria, like the Romagna, there were from the year 1215 communities of urban penitents who were living according to a rule of life (*propositum*) whose abridged version—in which they are described as "brothers and sisters of Penance who remain in their homes"—was approved by Honorius III in 1221.[13] These were pious confraternities bringing together laity of both sexes, who had readily accepted a one-piece habit of gray or beige cloth as visible sign of their profession. In addition, the men grew beards while the women cut their hair. The penitents especially distinguished themselves from other laity by their style of life: while remaining in the world, they rejected a worldly life,

abstaining from banquets and spectacles and from exercising public functions
in order to avoid committing an injustice. To remain faithful to the evangelical
commands, they refused to bear arms and to swear oaths. Those who adopted
the penitential state while they were yet single were bound to observe chastity.
Nor were married people excluded from this constraint, required as they were
to observe periodic continence during vigils and certain religious feasts and the
high moments of the liturgical season, like Lent. This is why they were often
called "continents" (*continentes* in Latin, *pinzocheri* or *pinzochere* in Italian).
And finally, every day the penitent had to say one hundred *Pater nosters*; this
was considered the equivalent of the Psalter for the unlettered.

Since Late Antiquity, the Church had imposed this form of life on public
sinners who, having made honest atonement, were reconciled to God before
being reintegrated into the Christian community by the bishop. What is new,
in the Italy of the 1200s as in Flanders and the Brabant of the same period, is
that men and women began to adopt this way of life voluntarily in large numbers, and to conform to its demands, sometimes while living as recluses in their
own homes, sometimes in the context of small communities. In this regard, the
loca (living spaces) of the first Franciscan fraternity were very similar to the *domus* (houses or béguinages) that were multiplying in the north of France and
what is today's Belgium, since in both cases the separation from the exterior
world was not concretized by an impregnable enclosure.

However, the form of life of the penitents of Assisi was distinguishable from
that of these other fraternities on one essential point: the itinerant preaching
which, from the beginning, was part of the program of Francis and his companions. This practice went beyond the penitential life or, more precisely,
added to it an apostolic dimension which it did not usually have. What were the
influences that caused this? The hagiographical sources are content, as we have
seen, to mention the repeated consultation of a missal which miraculously
opened each time to the very pages of the Gospel that concerned the sending
on mission, two by two, of the apostles. It is reasonable to ask, however,
whether Francis might have been inspired by certain popular religious—or
even dissident—movements, like the Waldensians, with whom Francis' companions were sometimes initially confused by certain ecclesiastical chroniclers,
or again with hermit-preachers who sometimes sprang up unexpectedly in the
public places to harangue the crowds and urge them to change their lives.

To speak of preaching with respect to Francis and his companions, especially
in this first phase of their community life, however, risks leading us into error,
for at the beginning of their apostolate, they were not preaching sermons. They
were content simply to exhort their listeners, in a language familiar to them, to

"do penance." This way of speaking proved their legitimacy by recalling the model of Saint John the Baptist, whose penitential preaching was really quite different from the "kerygmatic" proclamation of the word of God announced afterward by Saint Paul. But penance—in the sense that Francis understood it—was not a sacrament and was not identical with confession, even if it could ultimately lead to it. This change of attitude was to be translated into behavior toward God and others. The penitent had first to recognize him- or herself as a sinner: "When I was in sin . . . ," writes Francis at the beginning of his *Testament*. "Sin" is not a matter of a moral judgment, but a real-life condition in which the individual attributes to himself the merit of the good things that God has given him and then directs his action toward the exaltation of the self. This makes a person lapse into indifference, if not hostility, toward his neighbor. When Francis had "begun to do penance," he had become aware of the vanity of his life. But this emptiness had soon been filled by the certitude that God loves the world and the creatures to whom he has given life, and that he wants to save them. Once this fundamental relationship, obscured by sin, has been reestablished, the penitent has to live in conformity with this conviction by turning toward others, especially toward those most in distress: living images of the poor and humbled Christ. This was the experience which Francis had had when, having encountered the lepers, he had "done mercy" to them, thereby rediscovering the very mindset of God, who shows himself merciful toward men and women.

One cannot understand the success of the proclamation of this message by the penitents of Assisi, however, without situating it within the spiritual climate of the time, strongly marked by a certain eschatological expectation—that is, by a collective anxiety about the coming of a new era. Not that belief in the imminence of the end of the world was any more prevalent than at other times, but the idea that the time was ripe for a better understanding of the Gospel message "in spirit and in truth" was gaining currency beyond the narrow circle of educated clerics and monks familiar with the works of Joachim of Fiore († 1202), who had announced the imminent coming of an "age of the Spirit." The text of the Gospel to which Francis and his companions never ceased referring in their preaching included this dimension: "Do penance! The kingdom of heaven is at hand!" (or "is coming," according to the other version of Matthew 4:17 then in circulation). But the conversion to which they were inviting their listeners was not presented as a simple preparation or preliminary step that was necessary to pass through in order to attain perfection. It already included entry into this "kingdom of heaven," which it was helping to create here and now (*hinc et nunc*). Far from any millenarian speculation or complex divisions of the history of salvation which certain ecclesiastical authors had given themselves over to, Francis was calling for the realization of a new world that each person must make happen in his or her own life.

In 1209 these perspectives were not yet obvious. The penitents of Assisi comprised only one small group among others who, in the same period, were claiming to live, voluntarily poor, an experience of a return to the Gospel. Since almost nothing distinguished them from the real poor, they were often treated like rogues, prostitutes, or wild men, like those coal miners living on the edges of villages and stirring up reactions of fear when they left their forests.[14] Women locked themselves in their houses with their children when penitents arrived in a village or neighborhood. And clerics regarded these visionaries with a certain distrust since, on many points, they looked much like heretics to them. But "following the exhortations of Saint Francis, they supported everything with courage and resignation, without cursing those who did them harm."[15] Some people, impressed by their patience, showed them sympathy, like the anonymous woman and a bourgeois named Guido who, in Florence, gave lodging in their homes to Bernard of Quintavalle and his traveling companion—probably Giles—during their first expedition outside of Umbria.[16] And since each of the brothers had received from Francis the authority to accept into the community those who desired to enter, new recruits soon began arriving, some of whom were from outside Assisi, like Masseo of Marignano, a knight of Perugia, and Riccerio, a noble from the Marches of Ancona.

Who were these men who came to join Francis after his conversion? Many uncertainties remain. Thomas of Celano, who wrote his *Life* in 1228 while almost all the early companions were still alive, gives only a few names and very few details about them, both to honor their modesty and to avoid dividing the attention of his readers among several figures, for his intention was to exalt Francis. But the hagiographical sources of the thirteenth century say little more, so imposing does the personality of the founder seem to have been in comparison with his entourage, which for the most part remains in the shadows. Thus one still wonders about the personality of that "inhabitant of Assisi, of simple and pious bearing," mentioned but never named in the *Vita prima*; he was the first to follow Francis, but we hear nothing about him afterward.[17] Still, all the sources agree that Bernard of Quintavalle was Francis' first real disciple. Bernard was a well-known person—called "*dominus*" (lord) in the sources—who possessed great lands and who undoubtedly belonged to a higher social class than Francis. It was he who was chosen to lead the little group of early friars when they went to Rome to meet the pope; afterward he became one of the closest associates of the Poverello.

Then came Peter Cattani—a name which goes back not, as has sometimes been thought, to the town of Catania in Sicily but to a family line known in Assisi, where his brother Tebaldus appears as a knight in the acts of the commune between 1228 and 1233. Peter succeeded Francis at the head of the order of Friars Minors in 1220, but died a few months later. After these, we find Giles, who had accompanied Francis into the Marches at the time of his first expedition outside of Umbria and who later took the road toward Saint James of Compostela with Bernard, while Francis and Peter went to evangelize the Rieti Valley; then Sylvester—a priest from Assisi who had sold stones to Francis (at too high a price) when he was repairing San Damiano, and who afterward repented of his bad deed; Sabbatino, John of the Hat (de capella), Morico the Short, Philip Longo (the Tall), John of San Costanzo, Barbaro, Bernard of Vigilante, and Angelo Tancredo, a knight from Rieti. The hagiographical sources give other names as well, like Rufino and Leonard of Assisi or Masseo of Marignano, without our being able to date with any precision the men's entry into the fraternity.

Of all those who came to join him, Francis demanded that they sell what they possessed and distribute the money to the poor. In a society where the rights of the individual counted less than those of the family, it was not easy for an owner to get rid of his goods, for he had to obtain the agreement of all those having rights and to compensate them before proceeding to their alienation. Thus in almost every case, the entrance into the fraternity of the disciples of Francis created a kind of social upheaval and sparked within public opinion reactions ranging from misgivings to outright hostility toward this little handful of crazies who were disrupting the typical manner of parceling out goods among successors and the strategies of the family clan. According to the *Anonymous of Perugia*, which was again quite close to these events, "Their very relatives and close friends went after them; and their fellow citizens, small and great, men and women, showed them their disdain and greeted them with derision."[18] For Francis, this renunciation constituted an indispensable precondition to the renunciation of the world. As tough as it was for those brothers who possessed lands and properties, this requirement was not unprecedented: it pertained as well to monks, who, at the time of their profession of faith, had to abandon everything that belonged to them. The difference was that, upon entering a monastery, one became a member of a community that itself possessed buildings, lands, and revenues and materially took into its care those who were joining them. By contrast, Francis and his companions, without any possessions or resources, had to work with their hands and beg bread and turnips in order to assure their subsistence; and they lived in a hovel which did not belong to them, at Rivo Torto, on the marshy plain that extended from the base of Assisi.

Unfortunately, the early Franciscan sources are not very helpful for determining the social origins of these personages, and they have a tendency, for understandable reasons, to highlight those who belonged to the elite. In those days, before the little group that gathered around Francis had a well-defined status and enjoyed any notice in Assisi, the entrance of an aristocrat would draw more attention than that of a simple peasant or manual worker. Indeed, to join the fraternity was to make a religious choice with a strong social connotation, since his form of life was marked by three characteristic traits of the humblest classes: manual work, submission, and lack of learning. That some rich men were consenting to submit themselves to such a rude discipline was, for the public, a subject of astonishment. There were probably also poor among them, in the economic sense of the term: men like John the Simple, whom Francis had exceptionally allowed to leave to his family the cow that he owned, for without it, the family would have been plunged into indigence. But it seems that the majority belonged to the upper-middle class—the milieu of notables and the well-off of Assisi—who gave up a relatively privileged situation in order to live in voluntary poverty.

On the social and cultural level, then, at the beginning, those who came from comfortable surroundings had nothing in common with the others. For the well-off to renounce all their goods and live among the lowly and rough-edged people—with whom they would never have had contact had they remained in the world—constituted a profound and painful rupture. For those who were poor and uninstructed, in contrast, the entry into the fraternity simply represented a sacralization of their previous form of life, transposed into the framework of a religious community. This duality at the level of recruitment already existed in monasticism. But the Cistercians, imitated on this point by the majority of other orders, were content to juxtapose within the same monastery two rather distinct communities: that of the choir monks—who had for the most part been born in the upper classes, who knew how to read and write, and who consecrated themselves to the life of prayer and the liturgy—and that of the lay brothers, of peasant stock and mostly unlettered, who attended to the material tasks of the monastery and were subject to the first group, as the body is to the soul.

At this level, the novelty introduced by the Franciscan fraternity was considerable, for those who had been poor in the world found themselves on the same equal footing as former landowners and clerics who had passed through the schools, all now united by the common desire to "follow the humility and poverty of Our Lord Jesus Christ."[19] Within such a group, tensions and strains were surely not lacking. We notice them in the grumpy reactions of certain friars, born of the nobility, toward Francis, who had been, after all, only a bourgeois wanna-be. Only the mutual affection which the members showed one another, often in a very demonstrative fashion, could assure cohesion and peace within a group of people who had no common temporal interest but only a shared program of evangelical life. As Jacques Paul has noted, if they had recruited only among the poor or the little people, the brothers would have been suspected of pursuing social or political objectives under cover of a religious institution. And if the fraternity had counted among its own only the formerly rich, joining it could have seemed a show of snobbery or a somewhat derisory idealism.[20] By devoting themselves to poverty, the knights and patricians who took the Franciscan habit conferred dignity and respectability on the way of life of the poor. Chosen by such men, begging ceased to be degrading. But in exchange, the presence of the poor within the community brought to this unusual experience a dose of realism and illustrated the ability of the followers of thoroughgoing evangelicalism to transcend these social struggles, without ever denying the existence of the factors and situations which had given birth to them.

It is difficult to imagine exactly what form of life of Francis and his companions might have followed during the period before the foundation of the order of Friars Minor, for the hagiographical texts readily present it as a kind of golden age. Nothing is more normal than this process of embellishment: every group that gives itself a history and rereads its own past in that perspective tends to attribute a more or less mythical perfection to its origins. By holding ourselves to the most certain givens, especially those provided by Francis' *Testament*, we can, nevertheless, reconstruct the earlier period without falsifying it through overidealization.

The life of the friars is presented, first, as a wandering in the manner of Christ, whose footprints they desired to follow: "to follow naked the naked Christ," in conformity with the adage frequently cited in the monastic literature of the twelfth century and taken literally by the evangelical movements that were developing in the West around 1200. They moved around constantly, not wanting to set down roots in any one place or to allow themselves a residence other than the huts near Assisi to which they returned periodically to reconnect with one another. This instability had inherent witness value, demonstrating as it did, in a visible and concrete manner, the friars' intention to live in this world "as pilgrims and strangers." In the spirit of the men and women of the Middle Ages, the pilgrim was a sacred personage, a figure of Christ who himself had never ceased to go about Galilee and Judaea with his apostles and who had walked with the pilgrims of Emmaus after his resurrection. The people, if not the Church, happily worshiped those pilgrims who died on the road from illness or were killed by robbers, venerating them as the equal of martyrs.[21] Thus were the brothers, who went from village to village and did not have any fixed home, welcomed by villagers assured of their honesty and orthodoxy. But for Francis, the refusal of every permanent place went hand in hand with the radical rejection of every possession. Wandering had meaning only if it was accompanied by complete disappropriation and a break with all family and social relationships. Thus his early companions asked him not to send them on mission into those places where they had lived for fear that the ties of solidarity that they often had taken such pains to sever might form once again. It is on this condition alone that mobility could become an element of this "following of Christ" (*sequela Christi*), which was at the heart of their vocation and toward which they wanted to invite their listeners by their example. The pastoral concern—to urge the faithful to penance and to help simple priests in their ministry—was secondary. In the eyes of the Church, this refusal to settle down made them suspect; for it called into question the stability that was normal for existing orders, in particular the Benedictine monks. Even the prelates and clergy who were better disposed toward them viewed with a wary eye the excessive austerity of their way of life and their rejection of all ownership. When Bishop Guido I of Assisi, with whom Francis had remained in contact, one day reproached him about this, Francis responded: "My lord, if we had goods, it would be necessary for us to have weapons to defend ourselves. For it is over riches that arguments and court battles derive; it is this that creates so many obstacles to the love of God. Thus we do not want to possess any temporal good in this world."[22] In Francis' eyes, the real community of goods, characteristic for religious according to the juridical norms of the Church, was realized in dispossession. Francis strongly desired that he and his brothers might be no better provided for than the disadvantaged to whom they distributed, lacking anything else, pieces of their tunic or a portion of the resources that manual work and begging had procured for them. Thus these men, many of whom had been wealthy and honored before their conversion, seemed to have broken with civilization in order to return to the state of nature.

The brothers traveled two by two, gladly stopping before crosses and churches for which they bore particular devotion. Often they entered these churches and, if they found them poorly maintained, they might sweep the floor and ensure that the sacred vessels—the chalice and paten used during the Mass to offer the Eucharistic sacrifice—were in an appropriate place, according to the prescriptions of the Fourth Lateran Council (for at that time there were no tabernacles). These actions, worthy of a sacristan, can make one smile. But they are consistent with the piety of Francis, who venerated all tangible signs of the divine presence, like the leaves of parchment on which the name of God had been written: for he valued all forms of the Incarnation and mediation of the sacred. There is no hint of the magical or the superstitious here: only gratitude that God had used material things to reveal himself to human beings, from his body of flesh to the Eucharistic species of bread and wine which he had left to men and women in the memorial of his Passion. When the penitents of Assisi entered a town or village, they preached peace and comforted everyone by telling them to fear and love the Creator of heaven and earth, and to observe his commandments—a bare-bones catechizing, surely, but one intended to be effective and adapted to their public. Francis had no time for useless or idle words; he recommended to his brothers that they express themselves "in few words" and to live first by example what they were going to preach.

FRANCIS, INNOCENT III, AND THE ROMAN CURIA (1209–1210)

As long as the Penitents of Assisi were few in number, they could pursue their experiment without undue concern about ecclesiastical authorities. Once he had left the world, Francis was content to maintain contact with Bishop Guido I, who had taken him under his protection. But when the group had attained a certain numerical importance and its itinerant preaching campaigns began to reach regions where they were not known, he found himself confronted by new problems that forced him to define in a more precise manner the group's relationship with the Church. In the spring of 1209 (or 1210, according to some authors), the hagiographical sources tell us, the Twelve went to Rome. The number seems to have been purely symbolic: there were apparently only eleven, the priest Sylvester joining them only later. According to the Franciscan hagiographers, the Poverello presented to Pope Innocent III (r. 1198–1216) a kind of rule which described in general terms the form of life of the community. And Francis received the pope's approval.

In fact, the process probably was not quite so simple. First, Francis was unknown at the Curia and could claim for himself only the esteem in which the bishop of Assisi held him. This would have been insufficient to obtain approval by the papacy of such a new form of life. Furthermore, the Poor Man of Assisi, in spite of his protestations of submission to the Roman Church, had the conviction of having been called by God to propose to all men and women the evangelical ideal of which he and his followers were witnesses and disseminators. And this claim, on the part of an unlearned layman, had something shocking, indeed sacrilegious, about it. Finally, the text that Francis submitted to the pope for examination—which has not come down to us—seems to have consisted of Gospel passages, strung together, beginning with those he had read in the missal he had opened three times while searching for his own path. We find the substance of that path in the first chapters of what we can call the first rule of the order of Friars Minor, which dates from 1221.[23] Together, these texts constitute an exhortation to embrace the Gospel life, composed of the most concrete and demanding passages of the New Testament concerning poverty and fraternal charity, probably followed by a few elementary norms regulating a life in common. But this document had nothing juridical about it and was not in any way intended to define the organizational forms and observances of a new religious order. Thus it could not be approved as a rule by the "Lord Pope," as Francis called Innocent.

On the other hand, the form of life of the movement led by the Poverello presented to the Curia certain disturbing features. Francis certainly did not engage in any polemic against the clergy. But laity and clerics who soon came to join the movement found themselves on an equal footing with one another, contrary to all practice in existing religious orders. Innocent III himself, a few years earlier, had had to intervene in the affairs of a monastic congregation—that of Grandmont, founded in the twelfth century by Stephen of Muret, who had already claimed the evangelical ideal for himself—to arbitrate violent conflicts that were pitting the lay brothers or conversi against the choir monks whom the first group had excluded from the government of the order.[24] Even if a compromise had been found between those two antagonistic groups, did these difficulties not risk being duplicated elsewhere if one challenged the hierarchical principle by which clerics predominated over the laity?

But Francis of Assisi, even if one grants that he was inspired by God, was, at any rate, only a former merchant who had never gone to school and knew no Latin. If the papacy publicly approved his action and that of his brothers, might they not end up like the Waldensians and start preaching one day that it was better to obey God than men, having understood thus from a few isolated Scripture passages taken out of context? But the most serious reservations that the Curia could have had were probably related to the friars' refusal of all ownership. The bishop of Assisi had already been discomfited by this. For his part, Innocent III, who knew the weaknesses of human nature—he had devoted a whole treatise to them—and the demands of the common life, could only react negatively when faced with the claim of Francis and his companions to live without stable sources of income and fixed residences, even more so since the few

experiments in total poverty by religious communities during the twelfth century had all ended in failure.[25]

Francis had the good fortune to be dealing with a pope whose strong personality and intelligence were recognized even by his adversaries. Neither his aristocratic origins—he belonged to the family of the counts of Segni, in the south
of the Latium—nor his authoritarian temperament seemed to predestine him
to play a role of conciliator with respect to the religious movements that were
emerging from the world and aspirations of laymen and laywomen. But this
learned and energetic man who ascended to the pontifical throne at an early
age—he was thirty-seven years old in 1198—and who had attended the lessons
of great theologians and moralists (like Peter the Chanter) in the schools of
Paris had enough clarity of mind and energy to understand that the situation
of the Church, however serious it might have been, would become even more
desperate if it cut itself off from the lay elites of the Italian cities by systematically condemning all popular religious movements and pushing them into dissidence and hiding. Shortly after his ascension in 1199, Innocent had made a
significant gesture toward such movements, canonizing a pious layman, a cloth
merchant by trade, only recently dead, Saint Homobono of Cremona († 1197).[26]
During his lifetime, this penitent had, because of his charitable action, been
called "the father of the poor" in his native city and had energetically opposed
ascendant heretics there. By canonizing Homobono, Innocent III was officially
recognizing the positive elements in the religious aspirations of the popolo, the
class on the rise and soon to be dominant within the communes of Lombardy,
who were sympathetic to the discourse of the Patarines and bons hommes.

The Roman Pontiff, at the head of this battle, endeavored to distinguish
those currents that were clearly heretical, like Albigensianism (against which
he launched a crusade in 1209), from those whose doctrine seemed essentially
in conformity with the beliefs of the Church, even if some of their claims
clashed with the customs of the hierarchy and clergy. On the latter movements
he imposed certain conditions in order to obtain the assurance of the authentically Christian character of their way of life: a profession of orthodoxy, declara-
tion of obedience to ecclesiastical authority, acceptance of a way of life approved
by the Holy See, and finally renunciation of those calls to reform that would
have challenged the very structure of the Church. On the other hand, the pope
recognized that the search for evangelical perfection justified the creation of
new religious entities and authorized their members to live in poverty, without
making it an obligatory norm for the rest of the Church, and to devote themselves
to exhortatory preaching. Thus were the Humiliati of Lombardy reintegrated

into the Catholic Church. And as it was impossible to unite the different parts of this movement into a single entity, Innocent III promulgated no fewer than three rules, in June 1201, in order to organize the different elements of their *religio*. The unity of these three groups was assured by a common general chapter. The pope authorized their refusal to swear oaths, the obligation of their members to distribute to the poor all that exceeded their needs, and the custom of gathering together on Sundays to listen to the word of God and to exhort one another, on the condition that they not engage any doctrinal questions in their sermons. The experiment fully succeeded, at least at the beginning, since, according to the testimony of the French bishop and chronicler Jacques de Vitry, who encountered the Humiliati in Milan in 1216, they were the best defenders of Catholic orthodoxy in the town and did not hesitate to confront heretics in public disputations.[27]

In 1208 a disciple and admirer of Waldo, Durand of Huesca, who had returned to the Catholic Church with his followers after the Disputation of Pamiers, went to Rome, where he met Innocent III. Durand and his followers obtained the pope's approval for their proscription against accepting gifts of money beyond what was necessary to live on. Among these "Poor Catholics" (as they were called after their reconciliation with the Church), clerics and laity were united on an equal footing—but with different tasks—within the same religio. Their program of life (*propositum conversationis*), which Innocent III approved in writing, was not, however, a rule. And the Poor Catholics, whom the pope had placed under the protection of Cardinal Leo of Sainte-Croix, were not considered true religious by the Fourth Lateran Council and ended up being melded into the mendicant orders.

Finally, in 1209 or 1210—a short time before the meeting of Francis and Innocent III—another group of Waldensians from southern France, the "Reconciled Poor," who had come back to the Church under the direction of Bernard Prim, obtained from the same pope recognition of its legitimacy on the basis of a program of life similar to that of the Poor Catholics. The text approved by Rome authorized the group to engage in exhortative preaching (on the condition that they refrain from denouncing the abuses and vices of the clergy), as well as manual work. Measures were likewise taken to limit relations between men and women within the group, by forbidding them to sleep in the same house or to speak with each other except in the presence of other religious.

As interesting as these papal concessions were on the level of principle, they fell far short of resolving all the questions which the evangelical movements had raised. First, neither the Humiliati of Lombardy nor especially the Poor Catholics or Reconciled Poor were numerically very significant. On the contrary, the majority of Waldensians— who, in Italy, were called Poor Lombards— hardened their opposition to the Catholic Church after 1205 and set up their own ecclesiastical organization. Moreover, the reintegration into the Church of returning dissidents did not happen without difficulty. Numerous were the clerics who had nothing but mistrust and skepticism toward them. Thus the chronicle of the German Premonstratensian Burchard of Ursperg, who had been in Rome during the years 1210–1212, presents Bernard Prim and his companions in an unflattering light:

> They cut off the tops of their shoes and walked around practically barefoot; they wore the mantles of religious but they wore their hair just like laymen. But what really seemed to be the most reprehensible thing about them is that the men and women traveled together, lodged together most of the time in the same houses, and sometimes even, it is said, slept in the same bed! All these practices, they claimed, came from the apostles themselves.[28]

This testimony shows that the mixing together of these groups fed rumors and fantasies, as at the time of Robert of Arbrissel at Fontevraud. However, the major threat for the Church in Italy came not from these little groups but from the anticlerical opposition of those who were generically called "Patarines." It was impossible to say, in the majority of cases, whether these were Cathars, Waldensians, or simply political enemies of the Church and its followers. This oppositional current was particularly influential in Lombardy. In certain cities like Milan or Cremona, a veritable "anti-Church" was established, whose members claimed for themselves an evangelical radicalism and contested the role of the clergy and the sacraments. Faced with these movements, the Church was on the defensive and could respond only with various condemnations, spectacular but ineffective. For the autonomy of each city on the legislative and judicial planes complicated the application of constitutions mandating the death penalty for heretics, like the one Innocent III had had promulgated in 1212 by the young emperor Frederick II of the Hohenstaufen (r. 1212–1250), at the moment of his coronation at Saint Peter's in Rome.

It is thus at the very moment when the papacy was clearly moving toward a policy of violent repression of dissident religious movements, in Languedoc as well as in Italy, that Francis and his companions went to Rome to meet with Innocent III. According to the *Legend of the Three Companions*, which has probably borrowed the episode from Dominican hagiography, the Poor Man of Assisi made a strong impression upon the pope, who recognized him as the one he had seen in a dream, holding up a church—in this instance, the basilica of

Saint John Lateran—that was falling down.[29] This theme of the premonitory dream of Innocent III was widely diffused in iconography, especially in the basilica of San Francesco in Assisi, where it appears both in the frescoes of the lower church and in those attributable to Giotto and his workshop in the upper church. This account represents a rereading *a posteriori* of events: the "providential" character of the later success enjoyed by the two great mendicant orders having been projected backward onto the story of their founders. In fact, in the case of Francis, triumph was not so easy. According to the first *Life* of Thomas of Celano, the Poor Man of Assisi was first received by Cardinal John of Saint Paul, an austere Benedictine who had been papal legate in Languedoc and who had tried to wipe out the progress of the Albigensians, before being made bishop of Sabina. This man gave Francis a warm welcome but put a great deal of pressure on him to adopt an existing rule. Francis did not let himself be cowed. The matter was then brought to the pope, before whom Francis and his brothers now appeared. The spectacle of this little ragtag group and the conversations between the Poverello and Innocent III in the papal palace of the Lateran must have inspired more perplexity among the cardinals than enthusiasm—which caused them to stall for time. According to the English chronicler Roger of Wendover, the pope declared to Francis: "Brother, go look among the pigs with whom you are more comparable than among your fellow human beings! Roll around in the mud with them and fulfill your office as preacher among them by handing on to them the rule that you have prepared!" The Poor Man of Assisi went out into the streets of Rome and, coming upon a herd of pigs, rolled around with them in the mud, then went back to the pope and declared: "Lord, I have done as you have commanded!" Moved by Francis' humility and spirit of obedience, the Sovereign Pontiff acceded to his request.[30]

If we stick to the less dramatic version that Thomas of Celano gives of this encounter, Innocent III said to Francis and his companions, after giving them a few words of encouragement and counsel: "Go, brothers, and may the Lord be with you! Preach penance to all according to what the Lord will deign to inspire in you. And when the Lord will have multiplied you in number and grace, let me know of it. And so rejoice, for I will grant you more and, with greater peace of mind, be able to entrust more important missions to you."[31] In substance, the first part of the text probably corresponds to the reality whereas the second half ("I will grant you more . . .") probably constitutes a rhetorical amplification introduced by the hagiographer as a result of what occurs after these events. In the absence of any testimony from the Curia—for this meeting has left no written trace in the papal archives—we can conjecture that the question of the renunciation of all ownership by Francis was at the heart of the objections that had been brought up to him from the beginning by the pope and cardinals. Perhaps Innocent III finished by letting himself be touched by the fable which the Poor Man of Assisi recounted to him. With delightful confidence, Francis would have told him the story of a beautiful but poor woman whom a king espoused in the desert and from whom he had sons that he abandoned. Once they grew up, their mother led them to the palace. And the king, having seen them and becoming aware of their beauty, cried out: "If I feed strangers at my table, how much more should I take care of those who are my own children!" After this, he kept the children at his court in order that they might be raised there.[32] Under cover of humility and respect, Francis could not have urged the ecclesiastical hierarchy any more clearly to recognize in the marginalized brothers of Assisi the Church's authentic sons and true disciples of Christ.

Be that as it may, one has the feeling that in spite of an initial, rather negative reaction, the friars left a good impression on the Curia, as can be deduced from the positive attitude toward them of the Premonstratensian Burchard of Ursperg, who was then in Rome:

> There were others who had appeared after them [that is, the Waldensians who had been reconciled with the Church] whom the Lord Pope wanted to approve; they called themselves Poor Minors. They repudiated all the eccentricities and excesses mentioned above. But they traveled around barefoot, in winter as in summer, and accepted neither money nor alms except as food; they also accepted a habit when they absolutely had need of one and if someone suddenly offered it to them. For their part, they sought out nothing.[33]

When all is said and done, we can say that Francis won the blessing of Innocent III by impressing the pope with his trustworthiness and his attitude of submission to the clergy and the Roman Curia. The clear eye that the Poor Man of Assisi brought to the Church of his day was indeed devoid of animosity or disdain. And he assumed that, however mediocre the clergy might be, it still had an irreplaceable role in the life of Christians. As he will later write in his *Testament* about priests: "These and all others, I want to fear, love, and honor as my lords. I do not want to consider the sin in them, for I see in them the Son of God. . . . And all theologians and those who minister the holy divine words: we must honor them and venerate them as those who minister to us spirit and life."[34] It is probably because Innocent had intuited this attitude as he was talking with Francis and from the information he had gathered that he permitted Francis' initiative to develop even though it might have seemed unrealistic and doomed to failure.

We would, however, be on the wrong track to see in this conversation the official birth of the order of Friars Minor, as Franciscan hagiography later tended to do. In fact, the pope adopted a wait-and-see attitude regarding the little group which had come to find him, limiting himself to an oral approval of what these men were already doing: namely, preaching penance everywhere. But Innocent withheld immediate institutional recognition and even formal approval for their "program of life," as he had given the Reconciled Poor. Rather, he left to Providence—or rather to subsequent events—the test of whether the growing movement merited support. Only after the fact—and quite a lapse of time (for the theme is absent from Franciscan iconography before 1260)—was it asserted that Innocent III had approved the rule of the Friars Minor on this occasion (as Giotto depicted in a fresco in the upper church of the basilica of Assisi). On the contrary, it is certain that Francis made a profession of obedience "into the hands" of the pope (*professio in manus*): an action modeled on the feudal *commendatio*, which established a bond—his fraternity's submission to and dependence on the Roman Church, which granted it protection.[35] It also seems that Innocent III might have had the tonsure conferred on Francis and his companions on this occasion.

This question of the tonsure is one of the most tangled in Franciscan historiography; and the contemporary sources do not help us see our way through it. In the first *Life of Saint Francis*, Thomas of Celano does not write about it; and he mentions it only indirectly in the second. On the other hand, the author of the *Legend of the Three Companions* states that the brothers received the tonsure from the hands of Cardinal John of Saint Paul after their meeting with Innocent III.[36] It is essential to understand that there were two forms of tonsure in the Church at the time: the ministerial tonsure, conferred by a bishop on every man who asked to become a cleric and enter into holy orders; and the tonsure of conversion, which marked the entrance into religious life and which any religious superior, abbot or prior, could give to those who were dedicating themselves to God. Bonaventure, in the *Legenda maior*, states that the Poor Man of Assisi and his companions had received the first: that which, by making them clerics, licensed them to "preach the Word of God without hindrance."[37] One might doubt this account, for nothing attests that the lay brothers who entered afterward into the order and who gave themselves to preaching had been systematically tonsured. It appears more probable that the tonsure which they received consecrated their entrance into the religious state, as is confirmed by the fact that afterward Francis said, when he was having his hair cut: "And especially do not give me a big tonsure because I want to be on the same level as the simple brothers with my haircut."[38]

The tonsure did not immediately change the form of life of the members of this little community. But it was going to allow the transformation of this lay confraternity into a religious movement recognized by the Church (a *religio*), that was attached directly to the papacy through the person of Francis. It was only lacking a *titulus*, that is, a church to which the group would be canonically attached. Having requested such a place in vain from the bishop of Assisi, Guido II, and the canons of the cathedral of San Rufino (for the secular clergy were scarcely inclined to help him), Francis ended up obtaining in 1211, from the monks of Saint Benedict of Subasio, the concession—through an annual tax of a basket of fish—of the poorest church in their possession: Saint Mary of the Angels, or the Portiuncula. They settled right next to it, having been chased out of their hovel in Rivo Torto by the owner, who wanted to put his donkey there. This place, destined to become famous, was going to constitute their permanent base and the site of their periodic gatherings.

TO ANNOUNCE THE GOSPEL AND PEACE

Whether pleased or a little disappointed by the results of their journey to Rome, the friars seem to have experienced a real sense of satisfaction on the way home. And they demonstrated their joy in acts of mutual affection that constituted the principal glue of their little fraternity—something shown well by Roberto Rossellini in his film *The Flowers of Saint Francis*. While returning on foot to Assisi, they paused several times in places whose beauty and welcome were emphasized by the first biographer of Francis. In one of them, near Orte, where they remained for several weeks, they shared meaningful, profound conversation about their vocation, for papal approval had not resolved the problem of the identity of this group, which still had not yet clearly defined its aims. During one debate differing viewpoints surfaced: some brothers were probably leaning toward a form of eremitical life, based on a withdrawal from the world and the search for solitude; others showed themselves more sensitive to the needs of the apostolate and the necessity to proclaim the word of God to other people. Was it necessary to remain with Jesus on the mountain of contemplation or, "leaving God for God"—as Saint Francis de Sales later put it—descend with him onto the plain of fraternal service? Francis decided the debate: the life of prayer in the hermitages had to remain—and would remain while he was still alive—a spiritual requirement for the friars. But their principal mission was to win souls for God, following Christ, who had saved all men and women by the proclamation of his message and death. And once they had arrived back in the Spoleto Valley, the cradle of their fraternity, they resumed their itinerant preaching campaigns with renewed ardor.

Even if the approval they received from Innocent III remained purely oral and thus revocable, it facilitated the task of Francis and his companions, especially as the news of their approval rapidly spread. Henceforth, they could no longer be compared to the rebellious or dissident little groups. And the faithful, reassured by their orthodoxy, became more welcoming, while some clerics invited them to speak in their churches. But Francis was already looking beyond Italy. In 1211 or 1212, he tried to leave for the Holy Land, but contrary winds forced him to abandon his quest; indeed, he was fortunate to return safely to the port of Ancona on the Adriatic coast.

It was not from this coast—at least for the moment—that the broadening of his mission would come, but from Assisi itself. As humble as he may have been, "the Brother"—as his companions called him, according to Jordan of Giano— had a score to settle with his city. He had left there amid scoffing and taunts; now he was going to endeavor to conquer it spiritually, and with great bravado. Even before his departure for Rome, he had gone into the pulpit in the church of San Giorgio to exhort his fellow citizens to penance. Later he sought to make the most important places of the town his own—the gates of the city, the central piazza, the marketplace, the cathedral—and to gather attention to himself by eccentric displays. Thus, while he was recovering from illness and had eaten a morsel of chicken to regain some of his strength, he went into Assisi and asked a brother who was accompanying him to put a rope around his neck and parade him like a thief through the streets, while crying out all around him: "Come and see a glutton who, though you would not believe it, fattens himself up on the flesh of chicken."[39] This scene is normally interpreted as a provocation intended to awaken the religious zeal of his fellow citizens. In fact, this gesture corresponds to a famous ritual of humiliation, known north of the Alps under the name of *harmiscara* or *hachée*: in it, the guilty party simulated the sanction or punishment that his crime would have merited. In mimicking the penalty that he deserved, the penitent acknowledged his fault and accepted in advance his punishment, while at the same time he hoped to elicit the pity of his victim and thus eventually obtain his pardon.[40] While symbolically representing the punishment which God would be right to inflict for his sins, Francis was showing his fellow citizens the only way to escape it and to die in peace: complete surrender to God's will and becoming a "servant of God." The crowd ran to see the spectacle; aware of the ascetic life that Francis was leading, the people were deeply moved and said to one another: "Woe are we, wretched ones, who pass our whole lives well fed and who fill up our hearts and bodies with blood, luxury, and drunkenness!" Such theatrical moments were finally meant not to draw attention to Francis himself but to place within the urban topography the very figure of the suffering and humbled Christ, by becoming his living image. The ultimate goal was to restore the unity of the civil community—torn apart by rivalries between clans and party struggles—around a spectacle and meditation upon Christ's Passion.

But to win over Assisi was also to attract to himself eminent figures of urban society. Francis had an initial success in this domain with the entrance into the fraternity of a young man who belonged to one of the great aristocratic families, Rufino, grandson of Offreduccio. It is probably through Rufino that Francis met Clare, daughter of the nobleman Favarone of Offreduccio, whose family had returned from exile in 1210, having been banned during the struggles between the aristocracy and the popolo. The young woman, seventeen or eighteen years old at the time, was impressed by Francis, whom she had heard preach in the cathedral. Several secret encounters, in the presence of a few witnesses, demonstrated to Francis and Clare that there was indeed a real affinity between them; the young girl aspired to share the way of life of the brothers. In this relationship, which continued to deepen, Francis seems to have taken the initiative. Perhaps he had hoped that the conversion of Clare would produce a shock in the local aristocracy and constitute an example for other members of the ruling classes of the city. In any case, the decisive event occurred on March 28, 1212, on the night of Palm Sunday, when the young aristocrat fled from her family home with a companion, Bona of Guelfuccio, to join Francis and his companions at the Portiuncula. There "she surrendered her hair into the hands of the brothers," who welcomed her into their community as a new penitent.[41] But she could not remain with them. Her family, which had probably envisioned an affluent marriage for her, went looking for her. The Poverello placed her a few days later in a monastery of Benedictines in the area, San Paolo delle Abbedesse, and then, a little later still, in a community of recluses, Sant'Angelo in Panzo, near Assisi. There she was soon joined by her sisters Agnes and Beatrice, as well as by a few other young women of Assisi. Their uncle, Monaldo, tried to take them away by force, but they firmly persisted in their plan, and the family finally had to resign itself. Once passions had cooled, Francis settled this little group of women in the church of San Damiano, which he had restored with his own hands a few years earlier, having summarily created a dormitory, a refectory, and a tiny chapter room to accommodate them. They formed a community of penitents, subject to the authority of the local bishop like so many others during this period, which was marked in central and northern Italy by an extraordinary effervescence of female religious life. The earliest testimony which we have about them is that of Jacques de Vitry, a French cleric who had been named bishop of Saint John of Acre by Innocent III, and who had gone to Perugia in 1216 to meet the pope. He arrived, however, just after Innocent's death, which had occurred on July 16:

> In the midst of this corruption [at the Roman Curia], I nevertheless found consolation in seeing a great number of men and women who had renounced all their goods and left the world for the love of Christ: they are called Friars Minor and Sisters Minor. . . . The women live in different hospices and solitary places near the towns; there they live together in community from the work of their hands, without accepting any revenue. The veneration which clergy and laity have for them is a burden to them, embarrasses and vexes them.[42]

At first glance, Francis, by associating women with his fraternity, was placing himself in a direct line with certain religious movements of the twelfth century. One such example was the movement in western France launched and led by Robert of Arbrissel, whose spiritual influence had attracted to it laity of both genders, whom he brought together at Fontevraud into a collection of communities subject to the authority of an abbess. A little later, the new religious orders—in particular, the Cistercians and Premonstratensians—at first accepted the affiliation of a certain number of female monasteries. Rather quickly, however, the general chapters of these orders put an end to this practice, and the recruitment of new nuns was forbidden at the beginning of the thirteenth century. For neither the monks nor the canons regular wanted to be distracted from their vocations by the obligation to assure the care of nuns (*cura monialium*) on the temporal and spiritual level. Only in England did unique experiments continue in this domain. Saint Gilbert of Sempringham († 1189) had founded several double monasteries, where communities of men and women, living in separate buildings, gathered in the same church for certain liturgical offices; but development of the experiment was limited, in spite of a few attempts to establish, in Rome itself, a monastery of this kind at the beginning of the thirteenth century. Beginning in the 1170s, Waldo and the Waldensians emphasized the equality of men and women with respect to salvation and associated women to their apostolic ministry, while the bons hommes created enclosed places for virgins and widows to live together, some of whom became part of the "perfect," who consecrated themselves to prayer and sometimes even to the apostolate. From the beginning of his preaching campaigns in Languedoc, the future Saint Dominic had to confront this problem. This led him to found, in 1207, even before he established any convent for men, a female community

at Prouille, where he brought together a group of women who, under his influence, had come back to the Catholic faith from Catharism, and later, another
one at Rome at Saint Sixtus, at the request of the pope. Thus, at the beginning
of the thirteenth century, the question was being posed everywhere with a growing seriousness: how to welcome women, more and more numerous, who were
aspiring to lead a religious life without wanting or being able to enter into a monastery; the masculine orders remained uncertain as to how to respond to their
requests.

Francis, for his part, could not fail to be aware of these expectations. It seems
that he might have envisioned at the beginning a female community associated
in a complementary relationship with his fraternity, but no concrete evidence
survives. This ambition seems to have been abandoned quickly, and afterward
the hagiographical sources appear to have agreed to erase any trace of these
contacts. Different indications, starting with the text of Jacques de Vitry cited
above, make one think that at the beginning, the enclosure at San Damiano
had to be flexible to allow frequent gatherings and shared meals between the
Friars Minor and "Poor Ladies," who probably consecrated a part of their time
to charitable activities in the hospices and leprosaria. In 1212 Francis drew up
for Clare a form of life which we know about thanks to her inclusion of it in the
rule which Pope Innocent IV promulgated in 1253 for her community, on the
night before her death:

> Since, by the inspiration of God, you have desired to become daughters and
> servants of the Most High and Sovereign King, the Heavenly Father, and
> since you have given yourselves as spouses to the Holy Spirit by adopting a
> life conformed to the perfection of the holy Gospel, I want and pledge to al-
> ways have, myself and my brothers, a very special affection for you as [I have]
> for them.[43]

In 1214 or 1215 Francis persuaded Clare to assume the leadership of the community of San Damiano, which was taking on a rather familial character since
the blood sisters of Clare—Agnes and Beatrice—had come to join her there,
followed by their mother, Ortolana, after her widowhood, and two cousins,
Amata and Balvina. It did not take long for the community to grow. In 1218
Agnes took charge of the newly created community at Monticelli, near Florence. In the course of their preaching tours, Francis and his companions received into penance women—unmarried or widows—whom they directed
toward San Damiano or communities of the same kind that were developing
here and there. Thus we know from a deposition during the canonization process for Clare that Francis sent five "penitent" women to Monticelli; and that

she refused to accept one of them, Gasdia of Taccolo, whom she judged unready for religious life.[44]

It is difficult to have an exact idea of the life of the fraternity from the arrival of the first friars around Francis to the departure for Egypt in June 1219. The task of the historian is complicated by the absence before 1219 of legislative texts or documents showing the intervention of the Holy See on behalf of Francis and his brothers, as well as by the natural tendency of the hagiographers to idealize the foundational period. And in contrast to what was to happen a few decades later in England and Germany, no contemporary chronicler seems to have narrated the beginnings of the Franciscan movement in Italy and the manner of its settlement. If we credit the "pious traditions" handed down to us by Franciscan hagiography and local scholars, Francis visited almost all the towns and villages of central and northern Italy and founded the majority of the Minors' convents. Lacking authentic documentation, we are hardly in a position to judge the veracity of such an affirmation (similar to that found in the lives of many founders of religious orders). Umbria provides one possible exception: there the origins of some of the houses of the order are attested by both hagiographical and archival sources.

Thus we know that in 1213 the bishop of Gubbio, Villano, a Benedictine monk, authorized the friars to settle in town in an abandoned church, Santa Maria della Vittoria. There Francis converted a soldier by the name of Benvenuto, who afterward entered the order and was given the charge of taking care of the leper hospice of San Lazzaro. The same year, Francis preached at Terni, mounted on the top of an ancient column; at Foligno, where he was given lodging by a friendly family because the friars did not yet have any establishment there; and at Montefalco, where a few religious settled at Santa Maria della Salvetta. In 1215 he went to Trevi, which had been destroyed a little before by Duke Diepold of Spoleto; there he silenced a donkey whose braying was disrupting his sermon. The friars settled there in a little church situated outside the walls of the city. A little later, Francis spent the night in the abandoned church of San Pietro, at Bovara, where brother Pacifico had a vision of Francis bearing the sign of the Tau. In 1218 he was once again at Terni, where the bishop, Rainer, who liked Francis, characterized him in front of the faithful "as a simple and unlettered man" before allowing him to preach on the piazza of the cathedral and giving the friars the hermitage of Saint Cassian, near where they had settled. The only case where we might be able to go beyond these few factual indications is that of the little city of Gualdo (today Gualdo Tadino), situated along the Via Flaminia, around fifty miles north of Assisi; there the local Franciscan legendry, drawn up at the beginning of the fourteenth century from previous documentation, contains some interesting information.[45] We learn here that Francis had visited this town "while he was still wearing the clothing of a layman" (that is, before 1209), and exhorted its inhabitants "to obey the commandments of God and the precepts of our Holy Mother the Church." For this he was sprayed with mud and straw by his mocking listeners, forcing him to go wash his feet and shoes in a nearby stream. Later, at an unknown date but presumably around 1219, some Friars Minor went to Gualdo and there built a locus—a few huts with a garden—outside the walls of the city, in a craggy place called Valdigorgo where a stream of clear water bubbled up from the side of the mountain. Francis went back there in 1224 and was this time well received by the inhabitants, whom he urged to do penance and to place themselves at the service of God. His preaching converted a nobleman, the Count Saxo de'Brancheforti, governor of the city under Frederick II; Brancheforti later entered the Friars Minor as Brother Peter. For thirty years, he distinguished himself by his humility, serving as cook and porter, and enjoyed revelations on the joys of paradise and eternal punishments. The Poor Man of Assisi authorized a brother by the name of Fava to withdraw for some time into a cave to lead the eremitical life there; but Fava overdid his penances and privations. Thanks to a vision, Francis came to find him before he could succumb to the temptation of despair and ordered him to go back to the convent and to the life of the community—which he did.

Apparently, one of the problems that the Friars Minor encountered in this mountainous region was the fascination exerted by eremitism. During his sojourn in Gualdo, Francis exhorted them to "live in an ordered and discrete manner, by avoiding inflicting on themselves excessive penances." But a few decades later, a lay brother named Marzio, friend and companion of Brother Juniper, refused to follow the Franciscan community when it transferred inside the city to a new convent in 1245. He continued to live on the mountainous bank of the Serra Santa with a small group of hermits "imitating the blessed Francis and the holy fathers Antony and Hilarion" until his death.[46]

Other than this late chronicle and the writings of Francis (the majority of which are dated after 1220), we have for this period only a small number of testimonies, which, for the most part, are from outside the Franciscan movement and which, because of this, can hardly be suspected of bias. All indicate the stupefying rapidity with which the number of friars increased—"throughout the whole world," some sources say—and the success that their apostolate enjoyed among the laity of both genders. Among the reasons for this spectacular success, one must keep in mind the decline of the old religious orders, in particular Benedictine monasticism—victim of its own prosperity. At the very moment when Francis was journeying through Umbria with his companions, the monks of Santa Croce de Sassovivo, near Foligno, were finishing the construction of a splendid cloister decorated with mosaics which must have cost them a fortune.

A new form of religious life was being affirmed with the Friars Minor—one that was particularly attractive for young men. For while it was being approved by the Roman Church, it also satisfied aspirations that had scarcely been addressed except by dissident or clearly heterodox religious movements. The shock wave which ran through central and northern Italy at the time could be described rather as a great spiritual current, a kind of evangelical revival—*devotio* in medieval Latin—which touched every social milieu: men and women, couples and families, rich and poor, the educated and unlettered, ruling classes and the humble, clergy and laity.[47] At first, anybody could enter the fraternity without formalities or a novitiate, including married men who had obtained the agreement of their spouses.

Moreover, this religio did not yet have a precise name. It seems that in the beginning Francis and his companions might have called themselves Poor Minors and that they might have abandoned this name in favor of Friars Minor. We do not know when this might have happened, but it is well attested to already by the end of 1216 in the letter of Jacques de Vitry. Perhaps this modification was tied to the fact that, in the Christianity of the time, numerous contentious or dissident groups were claiming for themselves the name of poverty, beginning with the Poor of Lombardy, who constituted the wing most hostile to the Church among the Waldensians. Perhaps Francis and his companions judged it more prudent to distance themselves from the term. But this question of naming does not seem to have had great importance in their own eyes, since even in the rule that was elaborated in 1221 the expression "Friars Minor" appears only once.

We have often asked ourselves whether the word "Minors" (literally, *minores*, lesser, in Latin) refers to the social and political class of the city of Assisi, where, up to the peace treaty of 1210, the minores—that is, the social classes on the rise—were in conflict with the maiores, the aristocracy of feudal origin who had up to then governed the city. It is not obvious since the minores of Assisi—Francis knew it better than anyone, since he came from this class—were not the poor but people whose wealth had a different origin than that of the nobility.[48] More probably, the term, without being stripped of its social connotations, refers to *minoritas*—that is, to the condition and spiritual state of those who were deprived of power and influence by the fact of their poverty, but also to their lack of learning, their physical illness, or their marginality: in short, the neglected and little people who depended for their survival on Providence and the charity of others. However, for the friars, the essential was not the name, since every label risked engaging them in a process of institutionalization which a priori they distrusted.

At this time, the friars' way of life appears to have been marked by a great diversity, even if the fundamental principles which governed their existence were the same for all. Some of them lived at the edges of the cities and villages, while others—or the same men at different moments of their life—lived in little groups in distant places, grottoes, or hermitages. Some worked with their hands during the day among the peasants or for artisans, while supplying their own tools; others went begging to procure their food and that of the Sisters Minors; still others placed themselves at the service of lepers in hospices. It seems that a few friars lived as guests in various churches or monasteries where Francis came one day to find them in order to send them on mission.

The fraternal character of the early Franciscan movement was expressed with particular clarity at the moment of the periodic gatherings which bear the name of "general chapter." The majority of new religious orders had had institutions of the same type since the second half of the twelfth century. And in 1215 the Fourth Lateran Council obligated the superiors of monastic establishments to gather on the regional level at least once every three years. But in contrast to the Cistercian general chapter, which was a gathering of abbots, that of the Minors brought together all the friars at least once a year, up to 1222, and every one of the friars could freely intervene in the discussions that took place there. These meetings dealt with the concrete problems encountered in their daily lives and in the fulfillment of their missions. At the end of the time of collective reflection, the discussions concluded with the adoption of normative texts, later called constitutions and containing prescriptions imposed on all once they had been approved by the chapter.

The statistics concerning the number of participants at these gatherings that appear in the various contemporary sources have only a relative value, but they do reveal the rapid growth of the friars. One can already count three hundred at the chapter which gathered at a very early date (1215?) at the abbey of San Verecondo, at Vallingegno, to the south of Gubbio. The abbot and monks, who repented for having mistreated Francis when he had sought shelter with them after his conversion, demonstrated a great generosity toward the friars, providing "an abundance of barley bread, wheat, winter-barley and millet, drinking water, quince wine with water for the sick, and quantities of fava and green beans."[49]

There were already a thousand at the chapter which took place at the Portiuncula in 1218, in which Saint Dominic participated, according to Peter of John Olivi, and three thousand in 1222 at the Chapter of Mats, the last general chapter in which all the friars participated, lasting a whole week. But one would have a misleading idea of the Franciscan general chapter by considering it, above all, as a legislative moment. In fact, it was also the occasion for joyful reunions and an experience of companionship around Francis. It seems that those who participated in them had a lasting memory of them. Jordan of Giano, who joined the friars in 1219, has left us a really precious testimony of the atmosphere that reigned at the chapter of 1221, where he was chosen, against his will and after a misunderstanding, to be sent on mission to Germany:

> A bishop celebrated the Mass and it is believed that Francis read the Gospel and another brother the Epistle. Since the friars did not have a building [at the Portiuncula] to hold so many people, they camped out on the vast surrounding plain and slept in separate groups of twenty-three friars. At this chapter, the country folk took care to bring, rapidly and in abundance, bread and wine, for they were rejoicing at the reunion of so many brothers and of the return of Saint Francis. . . . Who could tell of the charity, patience, humility, obedience, the good fraternal humor that reigned among the brothers![50]

It is especially in and through prayer that this heterogeneous community found itself united. Whether they were clerics or lay, the brothers were all bound to the practice of the Divine Office—that is, to the recitation of the canonical hours every day, from Matins to Vespers as well as Lauds and Compline, and attendance at Mass. Those among them who did not know how to read replaced the reading of the Psalms with a certain number of Our Fathers and the Creed. In the beginning, the Minors attended the offices in the churches where they were passing. But since the texts varied from one region (or even one place) to another, after 1215 they adopted the Roman ritual "according to the usage of the Curia" and the breviary which contained the texts of this abridged office—except the Psalter, for which they kept what is called the Gallican version—whose diffusion throughout all of Christianity they themselves contributed to. Thus the friars, when they had been dispersed to the four corners of Italy (and soon of Europe), were able to recite and sing the same prayers at set times, which constituted a powerful factor of unity. Even more important was the celebration of the Eucharist, for which Francis had a wholly particular devotion, as it emerges from his *Testament:* "In this world, I see nothing bodily of the Most High Son of God except his most holy Body and his most holy Blood which they themselves [the priests] receive and which they alone administer to others."[51] For him, the Eucharistic sacrifice had to occupy a central place in the life of the individual and the community, for it was the celebration of the mystery through which God had taken on our humanity in order to offer men and women the possibility to be united to his suffering and humiliated body. It is in the sacrament of the altar that the link is established between the daily life of the friars and the ideal of mutual charity and peace toward which they had to strive with all their strength. The priests who had entered the fraternity were at its service and not the other way around. In his *Letter to the Order,* particularly addressed to the friar-clerics, Francis indeed asks them to say only one daily Mass in order to celebrate the Eucharist for itself and "not for any earthly thing, or through fear or love of any person, so as to please people." He was thus rejecting all proprietary usage and every appropriation of the Eucharistic sacrifice for private ends.[52]

At first glance, what seems to have most surprised contemporaries in the message of Francis and his companions is their impassioned engagement for peace, for they went from house to house repeating: "May the Lord give you peace!" or "Peace to this house!"[53] For those who heard this strange greeting, these were not just words or a pious vow that aroused perplexity or irritation among them. For the Poor Man of Assisi, it was an essential aspect of the Gospel message. Peace was not a new idea at the beginning of the thirteenth century, even if the people of this time were somewhat used to going to war or being the victims of war. From the end of the tenth century and throughout the eleventh, bishops and monks had taken the initiative to call together peace assemblies, especially in the southern areas of France, where royal power was so weakened that it was no longer capable of maintaining order and justice. The Peace (then the Truce) of God promoted by the Church was meant to assure to all those deprived of arms—women and children, merchants and pilgrims, clergy and religious—a minimum of security within the framework of feudal society, whose structures had been established in a climate of intensified violence. But in Italy, where imperial power continued to be exercised—albeit by delegation to counts and bishops—and where public jurisdictions continued to function, the peace movement was less developed than it was northwest of the Alps. Moreover, here the Church appeared, beginning in the twelfth century, less a factor of concord than a power in full expansion; it claimed for its members liberties and privileges, and it thus came into conflict with the Holy Roman Germanic Empire, and then—after the defeat inflicted on Frederick Barbarossa by the papacy and the Lombard League—with the cities that had gained autonomy within the framework of the communal regime. This regime rested upon free association and peace agreements between citizens, which must have made of the town a place where conflicts were resolved without resorting to violence and arbitration. But the social and political evolution of the majority of Italian cities soon gave the lie to this hope. Far from being harbors of tranquility, they were in the grip, especially after 1200, of endless dissensions among families and antagonistic clans, as even the history of Assisi illustrates at the time of Francis. It is the period when the upper levels of the bourgeoisie—the popolo—were struggling to wrest from urban patricians participation in power and when Guelfs and Ghibellines were giving themselves over to merciless fighting. The situation was no better in the countryside, where feudal lords tried to resist the encroachments of the neighboring communes, which were seeking to take under their control the whole of their contado.

In this profoundly troubled political and social context, the formula of greeting employed by Francis inevitably seemed incongruous or derisory. However, once the initial astonishment had passed, the meaning of this little phrase was better understood. To an urban society torn apart by struggles between factions and the vendetta, the Poor Man of Assisi and his companions were proposing what that society most desperately needed: peace.[54] Possessing no goods and being subject to all, the friars could have no quarrel with the people and became ipso facto *paciaires*—real peacemakers. Moreover, within the fraternity of the Minors, men who belonged to different social milieus peacefully coexisted: people who, in the world, would have been antagonistic to one another. This simple fact sufficed to confer on them a prestige that allowed them to intervene effectively in conflicts. And this probably explains the severity of Francis with respect to calumniating and disobedient friars. Finally, their action, if it was in line with the Church and was developed in connection with it, was not to be identified with that of the clergy, which then constituted an influential group, seeking to advance its own interests and to play a prominent role in society. For Francis' message of peace was a prophetic announcement devoid of any aim other than the search for peace for its own sake. We see this during the conflict which pitted the podestà Oportulo of Bernardo (and, through him, the commune of Assisi) against Bishop Guido II in 1225. When the bishop had excommunicated him, the podestà had it announced with a trumpet blast that he was henceforth forbidding the inhabitants of the city to have any economic dealings with the prelate. This was meant to virtually put Guido into quarantine and to sap the foundations of his power. Overcome by the climate of hate that was created in his own town because of this confrontation, Francis endeavored to put an end to it. To that end, he added an important verse to the *Canticle of Brother Sun* (or the *Canticle of the Creatures*), which he had composed a little bit earlier:

> Praise be to you, my Lord,
> For those who pardon for love of you,

And support illnesses and tribulations:
Happy those who will endure these in peace,
For by you, Most High, they will be crowned.[55]

After this, Francis called together the two adversaries, as well as their respective partisans, in front of the palace of the bishop, and the friars sang the verse which the Poor Man of Assisi had drafted for them. Immediately, they reconciled publically and put an end to their quarrel. In reality, things probably did not happen quite so simply, and the public ceremony must have been preceded by negotiations between the parties in which Francis probably had to be personally involved. But the reality of this arbitration has not been challenged by historians, and it is significant both that the commune accepted his mediation in a conflict which pitted it against ecclesiastical authority and that he called the representatives of the podestà in front of the bishop's palace, thereby placing the latter above civil authority.

Other contemporary witnesses attest to Francis' effective intervention in the internal quarrels of Italian cities. In Bologna, in 1222, a Dalmatian cleric, Thomas of Split (Spalato, in Italian), who was doing his studies in the city, reported Francis' words in this way: "During his whole discourse he spoke of the duty to extinguish hatreds and to conclude a new peace treaty. . . . God conferred such power on his words that they brought peace back into many aristocratic families torn apart up to then by old, cruel, and furious hatreds which had even led to assassinations."[56] We also know that he intervened to put an end to struggles between factions that were tearing apart the city of Arezzo in Tuscany. Medieval iconography has immortalized the scene where one sees Brother Sylvester, who was a priest, proceed to an exorcism that managed to evict a group of demons from the town. The episode remains obscure, but it is probably a matter of a hagiographical and clerical rereading of a mission of reconciliation between factions that Francis had come there to arrange. Another text shows us that gentleness and humility were not the only weapons that the Poor Man of Assisi employed and that, like the biblical prophets, he did not hesitate to use threats in order to try to reestablish concord between antagonistic groups. Thus did he address the inhabitants of Perugia this discourse devoid of all niceties:

You plunder your neighbors and you kill many of them! Therefore, I say to you: if you do not convert quickly and if you do not repair the damages you have done, the Lord, who lets no injustice go unpunished, will prepare a terrible vengeance, punishment, and humiliation for you. He will set one group against the other; discord and civil war will break out and cause you worse calamities than those that would come to you from your own neighbors.[57]

The warning announced by Francis was borne out: a little later, a violent conflict erupted between the popolo and the "knights." The knights, with the support of the Church, sacked the countryside surrounding the city and did a lot of harm to its inhabitants. This led to reprisals which were equally violent. And the hagiographer concludes: "Thus the inhabitants of Perugia suffered by punishment much more than the neighbors whom they had molested." This text perfectly illustrates the political and social reality in which the action of Francis is to be situated, in particular the threats to peace constituted by the tensions inside each of the cities as well as their conflicts with neighboring towns. It also, by the way, sheds light on his own feelings. For one senses coming to the surface the antipathy that this citizen of Assisi had vis-à-vis its rival Perugia, which had done him so much wrong. Had he not made war in his youth with the "popular" party of Assisi against the aristocratic families, like Clare's, who had found in Perugia both a refuge and military aid?

But beyond these memories, Francis was seeking to create a "culture of peace" in a climate of almost permanent and generalized civil war, founded on the considerations of justice and on a reminder of the duties the human person had toward God and neighbor. His discourse develops on three levels. First, he recalls to his listeners the fundamental relationship that exists between peace and penance: one who wants to make peace with another must begin by finding an interior peace which subjects the flesh (that is, all evil impulses) to the spirit, in such a way as to restore within oneself the divine order disrupted by sin. Only afterward will one be able to seek peace in this world; for that depends, before anything else, on the goodwill of people who establish, restore, and maintain it. It is that which the example of the inhabitants of Greccio had to experience *a contrario*, when, after being reconciled and living in peace for many years under the influence of Francis, they returned twenty years later to their quarrels and crimes. This led them to being struck by all sorts of catastrophes and to lose all their goods.[58] This peace, always precarious, was itself only a reflection of the eternal peace, which Christ had promised to humanity when he had said: "My peace I give you, my peace I leave to you." The establishment of this eschatological peace, which served to crown all human aspirations and hopes, would occur "in joy and exultation," as had been seen at the beginning of the Alleluia movement in 1233, when, following upon the actions of a hermit, Benedict of the Horn, the Friars Minor and Friars Preacher tried to translate this dream into the reality of the Italian communal society. As the Franciscan chronicler Salimbene, who had been a witness of these events in Parma during his youth, describes it: "A time of quiet and of peace where the weapons of war were completely put aside; a time of sweetness and happiness, of praise and jubilation." Thirty years later, again he evokes with emotion "the songs and praises of God that were sung by knights and burghers, citizens and peasants, young people and virgins, the old and the young in all the towns of Italy."[59] The friars had to be not only witnesses of this messianic peace coming down from heaven through the actions of men and women, but also its artisans: the avant-garde of a reconciled humanity. As the Franciscan Alexander of Bremen wrote in the middle of the thirteenth century, "Francis brought peace back to men and women who had found themselves in a situation of conflict, so that his order might show forth Jerusalem." For Jerusalem, according to the traditional etymology of the Middle Ages, meant in Hebrew "vision of peace."[60]

"WHY YOU?"—THE CHARISM OF FRANCIS

At the center of the new community was Francis, who seems to have exercised a kind of fascination and genuine attraction on the majority of those who met him. From 1210 on, he had become a significant person in his city and in the neighboring regions, as is evident from the dedicatory inscription on Saint Mary Major of Assisi, dated 1216 and visible today, where one reads that the apse had been restored "at the time of Bishop Guido and Brother Francis." Indeed, during the first phase of its life, the Franciscan movement was fully in the hands of the Poor Man of Assisi; everything revolved around him. To enter this *religio* was not to adhere to a rule; it was to respond to Francis' call to conversion and to follow him in this quest for Christian perfection.

Francis was certainly the most prominent figure and the leader of the brothers, but everyone lived together on an equal footing. According to his own words, he conceived of his role as that of a mother toward her children or of a mother hen with her chicks. This implied on his part both a gentleness and vigilant firmness. More than the head or the founder, he was a kind of moderator exercising an uncontested authority, calling from the Friars Minor a "holy obedience," immediate and joyful, which would ensure that the group could function without disciplinary norms or sanctions. Structures barely existed, but a personal bond united each friar to Francis, who, until the creation of provinces in 1217, was the only hierarchical superior of the Friars Minor; until 1219 he himself received all those who desired to lead an evangelical life in his manner. The friars whom he placed at the head of the provinces were called "ministers," that is, servants. In the beginning, at least, they were simply the personal representatives of Francis. Their sole disciplinary prerogative consisted in granting (or not) to the friars of their territory an obedience—that is, the permission to leave the group to journey to specific destinations, lest they wander the world in a haphazard manner. Indeed, this situation does not reflect any desire on the part of Francis for power or centralization. He absolutely refused to be called Father or Master and remained until the end the Brother par excellence. But all were convinced—and he especially—that the form of life of the Minors and the ideal of minoritas that inspired him had found their origin in God, who had revealed these things to him which the pope had afterward approved. Francis' way of living and acting constituted the foundation and criterion of the life of the Friars Minor, and his personal holiness was the guarantee of the legitimacy of their existence vis-à-vis the Church and the surrounding society.

One of the favorite companions of Francis, Masseo of Marignano, asked him the question three times: "Why you?" And as his interlocutor was astonished by this insistence and sought to understand the meaning of the question, the brother became more specific: "Why does the whole world run after you and why does everyone seem to want to see you and hear you and obey you? Physically, you are not a handsome man; you do not have great knowledge; you are not high-born. How does it happen that everyone is running after you?"[61] In the *Fioretti*, this account is destined to highlight the humility of the saint, who responds that the Lord used him precisely because of his unworthiness. But this manifestation of modesty does not in any way detract from the relevance of the question. For one cannot understand the success of the Friars Minor and the wave of enthusiasm that they aroused in central Italy without coming back, in the last analysis, to the person of Francis. This leads us to ask ourselves about the nature of his charism. As Brother Masseo had said, Francis was not distinctive because of the beauty of his features or his physical bearing. The Dalmatian cleric Thomas of Split, who met Francis when he came to preach in Bologna in 1222, has left us a realistic and candid portrait of him: "He was wearing a nasty-looking habit; his whole bearing seemed unremarkable; his face was not handsome."[62] Indeed, all contemporary sources concur in recognizing that he was of stunted appearance and hardly elegant. According to Thomas of Celano, who surely is drawing upon the portrait of Saint Bernard while adapting it to the physical reality of Francis, whom he had stood next to several times between 1215 and 1221, he was "small rather than tall. He had a round head and of medium dimensions; the forehead small and straight; medium-sized eyes of the color black, the beard black and thin, the neck skinny." Nothing noteworthy, nothing a priori impressive. But once Francis began to speak, his body became animated and one immediately noticed "his voice vibrant and soft, clear and sonorous, his lips fine and thin, out of which came a word soothing, burning, and penetrating" and his way of "making his whole body a tongue."[63] However, he was neither a great preacher nor a born orator; and the testimony of Thomas of Split, who had seen him in the heat of action, allows us to clearly understand that the prestige that surrounded him was due as much to the indefinable aura that surrounded his person as the magic of his speech. In any case, he inspired expressions of general enthusiasm in the places where he went, as indicated by the account of his entrance into the town of Ascoli Piceno in the Marches: "The people had such faith in him that one considered oneself happy to have been able to touch his clothing. . . . The clergy were pleased [with his coming], bells were rung, people had a festive air, women expressed their joy, children were jubilant; people tore branches off trees and ran out to meet him singing psalms."[64] But far from clarifying, such texts, strongly marked by a rhetorical cast, only blur things further by applying clichés to Francis borrowed from the Bible, in particular from the Gospel account of the triumphal entry of Jesus into Jerusalem on Palm Sunday. Moreover, they generally concern events that occurred after 1220, after he had acquired a great renown that preceded him everywhere he went. On the contrary, much less numerous are testimonies concerning the first years of his itinerant apostolate which might allow us to understand how and why public opinion, at first mistrustful if not hostile, had swung quickly in his favor, to the point of feeling an enthusiasm for him that would only grow. Even if the approval given by Innocent III played a role in this turnaround, it is not enough to explain this immense popularity whose source was based on the very personality of Francis, bringing the charism close to home. His contemporaries saw in him a living saint who was responding to their hopes but who was nonetheless inimitable.

In the religious mindset of the laity at the start of the thirteenth century, a saint was distinctive by his or her ascetic behavior and by the ability to perform miracles. Francis fulfilled the first of these requirements, treating his body with severity. Multiplying fasts and privations, deliberately seeking out the most mediocre foods, and sharing the little that he had with the disadvantaged, he incarnated in the eyes of the crowds who saw him the very model of a man of God (*vir Dei*). To the end of his life he endeavored to put an end to the veneration directed at him by revealing to his listeners the rare infractions that he had committed to the privations which he was inflicting on himself. Thus one day he declared in Assisi: "You think I am a saint. Well, I confess to God and before you that during this illness I ate meat and ate stew!" But far from disappointing them, this public confession only doubled the fervor of his listeners, now touched with pity and compassion:

It was winter. It was really cold and he had not yet recovered from his quartan fever. They were striking their breasts, accusing themselves and saying: "This holy man is accusing himself with great humility of having pampered his health, whereas he so obviously needs it. We who know his life well, know that it is because of his excessive abstinence and austerity that, since his conversion, we see him living in a body barely alive."[65]

We touch here the very heart of the reputation of the holiness of Francis. For these Italian crowds who were acclaiming him, a saint was not a great personage—an abbot, a bishop, or a sovereign—one who would be famous in the exercise of his functions. The Church has venerated so many of them. Rather, Francis was a simple and poor man who had willingly accepted privations and suffering in order to "follow naked the naked Christ." This was no Saint Thomas à Becket, the archbishop of Canterbury, assassinated in his cathedral († 1170), or Saint Cunegunda, the spouse of the Emperor Henry III († 1040), canonized in 1200 by Innocent III. Francis was an ascetic, full of goodness and fervor to whom God, precisely because of the sacrifices which he had embraced while he was alive, had granted a supernatural power over the forces of evil under its various forms: bad weather, illnesses, conflicts, and wars, but also anxiety, despair, and pride. Others before him—hermits, recluses or pious pilgrims, but also Cathar bons hommes or Waldensian preachers—had been able to impress people by their austerity or their edifying lives. But in Francis, they vaguely perceived something more: his strength of conviction fascinated them, but even more so did his total sincerity, his constant refusal to allow the least distance between the exterior and the interior, between word and action aimed at making it real in this world.[66]

The other dimension of holiness had to do with miracles. On this point, it is difficult to get an exact idea of the reality because the Franciscan hagiographers had a tendency, from the 1240s to the 1250s, to present Francis as a champion of Christian perfection, gifted with all the charismata, in the context of a polemic that was pitting them against the secular clergy and of the rivalry that was developing with the Friars Preacher. In this perspective, the majority of his biographers, desirous of presenting their subject in every way conformed to Christ, attributed to him many of the miracles that appear in the Gospels: healings of the blind and paralytics, multiplication of loaves, and even resurrection of the dead. Indeed, Francis seems to have maintained a prudent reserve with respect to the thaumaturgical power given to him. We know of only two cases—the paralytic of Narni and the scrawny and limping child of Toscanella—in which he was said to have touched a sick person in order to heal him.[67] Even in the first case he intervened only at the request of the local bishop, tracing a sign of the cross on the body of the sick person. During an inquiry by the Curia just before Francis' canonization in 1228, witnesses spoke of miracles which had occurred through him by means of objects that had touched his body (a piece of cloth, for example, or a cord) before or after his death. Certain miracles reflected the needs of the society of the time and especially of the rural world. Thus the cattle of the village of Sant'Elia on the plain of Rieti were healed of the bovine plague after being sprinkled with water in which the saint had washed his feet; not far from Greccio, Francis delivered villagers from the scourge of wolves and from hail which had been devastating their vines and fields every year; finally, at the abbey of San Verecondo, he cursed and "condemned to death" a ferocious sow which had killed a newborn lamb: a little later, the beast fell ill, dying after three days.[68] In this last instance, the objective of the hagiographer was less to recount a miracle than to illustrate the performative power of the word of Francis, who immediately made happen what he was saying. He who had feared the effect of personal curses from his father at the time of his conversion and had sought to neutralize them through the blessings of an adopted father whom he had recruited for the situation did not hesitate to use this weapon against the perpetrators of crime, even when they belonged to the animal kingdom.

Other accounts which aim to illustrate Francis' prophetic gifts tell of predictions whose precision later events were to demonstrate. It is thus that he announced the wholly unexpected conversion of a nobleman of Lisciano who had been abusing his spouse; and terrible calamities befell the city of Perugia after his preaching had been disrupted there by knights galloping noisily around him.[69] The gift of clairvoyance, which a number of testimonies attribute to him, fits into the same perspective: no one had more capacity than he to penetrate consciences and read hearts. This profound lucidity made a strong impression on his followers. Thus we see, in the *Legend of Perugia*, Francis refusing entrance into the fraternity of a postulant who apparently was presenting all the signs of devotion but who remained at root attached to his goods; or exposing a brother who enjoyed a great reputation of holiness among his companions because he perpetually kept silence. Having discovered that the friar was refusing to go to confession, Francis declared to an incredulous Brother Elias that this religious was in fact possessed by a demon; indeed, the brother left the order a little after that and died miserably.[70] At this level, the supernatural intersects with spiritual experience or simple clairvoyance, with no need for the hagiographers' miraculous interpretations.

Francis, for his part, seems to have done everything to discourage veneration of him. He warmly thanked those who spoke of him without kindnesses, like the bishop Rainer of Terni, who had presented him to his flock, in 1218, as "a poor man, humble and unlettered," or the peasant who, while accompanying him to La Verna, declared with a certain harshness: "Try to actually be as good as people say you are, for many have put their trust in you. It is important not to disappoint them!"[71] But the Poor Man of Assisi had not been expecting this warning. Since the people held him up as a saint, since the friars themselves argued over his nail-clippings and were distributing among themselves the water that he washed with: well, he would play the game and align himself to the model to which others wanted him to conform, if that could be useful for the good of souls and contribute to getting those who met him to see the power and goodness of the One who, in his eyes, was the only saint.

Because the contemporaries of Francis were impressed by the integrity and authenticity of his witness, they were similarly prone to lend an ear to his novel manner of preaching. Actually, the term scarcely describes the exhortations that he addressed to his listeners in a familiar and expressive language. In the first years after his conversion, when he was working to restore churches in the environs of Assisi, he uttered to no one in particular his naïve appeals, which made one think of nursery rhymes or childish singsong: "The one who will give me a stone will receive a reward; the one who will give me two will receive double; the one who will give me three, triple!"[72] Sometimes, he even addressed his listeners in French—which, at first glance, was not the best way to be understood. But love never expresses itself better than through the obscurity of a foreign language, and Francis probably wanted to show by this that God was beyond words and intelligible language. Later the content of his discourse grew richer, but without ever becoming complicated or abstruse, as is clear from the eyewitness reaction of Thomas of Split to his preaching on the piazza in Bologna, August 15, 1222: "He spoke so well and with such perfect clarity that the developments of this unlettered man plunged even the scholars in his audience into boundless admiration. His discourses, however, did not result from the great genre of sacred eloquence; they were rather like harangues."[73] The Latin word which the chronicler uses to describe this kind of speaking (*concionare*) goes back to the vocabulary of the most elemental political eloquence, that of civic assemblies (*concio*) of the towns of communal Italy, where improvisational and poorly educated orators endeavored to win popular support thanks to gestures, vocal effects, and a direct and colloquial language appropriate for getting the attention of the crowds. Francis was speaking like the layman he was and did not employ an elevated style or the flowery rhetoric that clerics learned in the schools. In Bologna, according to Thomas, he chose as the theme of his preaching "angels, humans, and demons." And he knew how to draw out the concrete implications for his listeners. In other instances, he was content to simply mention in a few words the vices and virtues or to expound on a few sharp contrasts: "pleasure is brief/everlasting the punishment/the suffering modest/the glory infinite."[74] Francis knew how to adapt to different audiences and was also capable of reaching a courtly public. Arriving one day at a castle where the nobles of the area were gathered for a knighting ceremony, he addressed them by beginning not with a verse from Sacred Scripture, as was the custom of clerics in his day, but with a few verses from a courtly ballad in Italian that he knew by heart and which was probably known to his audience:

> So great is the good that I expect,
> That every pain is my delight.[75]

Having recourse to this language of love which expressed the emotions of a smitten heart, ready to endure the worst sufferings in the expectation of the joy that the companionship of his beloved was going to win for him, he applied it to the spiritual life in order to impress upon the knights and ladies who were listening to him the relationship between the sufferings and penances that the saints inflicted on themselves here below and the ineffable reward with which God would grace them in the hereafter.

The majority of his hearers were recruited, however, from among citizens, especially the bourgeoisie, whose mindset he knew particularly well. This is what allowed him to create images of gripping realism for them, like the one he used in his *Letter to the Faithful* about the last moments of a rich man. This was certainly a written text, but we can deduce that he would have used this type of hard-hitting *exemplum* in his oral catechizing:

> The body is sick, death approaches; his family and friends come, telling him: "Get rid of your goods!" Then his wife and family members begin to feign crying. And, seeing them weeping, he is moved by a bad thought and, thinking to himself, he says: "Here is my soul and my body and all my goods. I give them over into your hands . . ." And they immediately send for the priest. The priest says to him: "Do you want to receive forgiveness for all your sins?" He responds: "I do." "Do you wish to make satisfaction as much as you can with your fortune for what you have committed and for the fraud and deceits which you have done to people?" He answers: "No." And the priest asks: "Why not?" "Because I have already handed everything over to my family and friends." And he begins to lose his voice and thus the wretched man dies.[76]

Francis himself defined for his brothers, in the normative text of 1221 known
under the name of the *First Rule*, what the proclamation of the Kingdom of
Heaven consisted of that was at the heart of their mission:

> And all my brothers, whenever it pleases them, can announce this exhortation
>   and this praise or something similar, among all people with the blessing of
>   God:
> Fear and honor, give thanks and adore
> The Lord God Almighty in Trinity and Unity,
> Father, Son, and Holy Spirit, creator of all things.
> Do penance, produce fruits worthy of penance,
> For we will soon die.
> Give and it will be given to you.
> Forgive and it will be forgiven you.
> Happy are those who die in penance
> For they will be in the Kingdom of God.
> Woe to those who do not die in penance
> For they will be sons and daughters of the Devil
> Whose works they do,
> And they will go to the eternal fire.[77]

The word of Francis had so much success because it contrasted with the silence of numerous prelates and the majority of priests of the period, who were,
according to the expression of one of their own, Jacques de Vitry, "like dumb
dogs who do not know how to bark." And it was a truly positive message, as
Francis did not lose himself in recriminations and carefully avoided all fruitless
polemic. In contrast to his contemporary Saint Dominic, his primary objective
was not to defend the Church against its adversaries or even to proclaim sacred
doctrine by refuting the errors of the heretics, but to communicate to all men
and women of his day the fundamental certitudes that animated him: God is
good and full of love; we must praise him for having sent into this world his Son,
who has suffered for us and who wants to save us; the human person has the
obligation to respond with such care by changing his or her life without delay,
for the day of judgment approaches.

This announcement was not one activity among others but was the very essence of his mission:

> Since I am the servant of all [he writes in his *Letter to the Faithful*], I am
> bound to minister to you the fragrant words of my Lord.[78]

But in his eyes, preaching—even the spontaneous kind that he preferred—was
not an end in itself. It was a simple reminder that God alone could make fruit-

ful. And the witness by example appeared to Francis to be at least as important as that of the spoken word. Thus did he ask his brothers to "preach by their actions" while proclaiming the Gospel. And he could not preach what he had not yet discovered and experienced for himself. When he exhorted the faithful, "impassioned gestures and movements punctuated his words and swept up his listeners toward the celestial mysteries"; and gesture often replaced the word.[79] Man of the spoken word, Francis communicated equally with his body, which was constantly in motion. Sometimes he translated the sufferings of the Crucified into mime, sometimes he stripped himself publicly to represent the nakedness of Christ on the cross and shocked his audiences so as to lead them, in their own way, to "follow naked the naked Christ," having wept for themselves and their sins. More than just a sermon, it was a veritable performance during which the body of Francis became the very place where the sacred representation of the Crucified was being played out, a kind of living emblem of Christ. Different witnesses who had had the privilege of seeing and hearing him affirmed that they would not have been capable of repeating afterward exactly what he had said to them but that they had been fascinated by this encounter, in which the man absorbed the message and seemed to be identified with it. For his aim was less to inculcate in his listeners the Christian faith through explanations than to implant it in their memory. To remember Jesus Christ, to ceaselessly recall in one's heart (*recordatio*) his sufferings or the prescriptions of the rule, to make a joyful or sorrowful mystery come alive in the "one who ruminates": such was, in his eyes, the best way to get the message heard and for each one to live it. Thomas of Celano, moreover, says that "his memory served him like a library."[80]

From the very beginning of the fraternity, the custom had been that when a brother thought or said something bad of one of his companions, the offender would ask the one offended to put his foot on the offender's mouth in the manner of a punishment. But the most remarkable example of Francis going beyond words happened near the end of his life after he had gone to San Damiano at the request of Clare and her sisters, who were complaining for a long time of being deprived of his presence and his conversations:

> Lifting up his eyes to heaven, he began to praise Christ. Then he had some ashes brought to him. With them, he drew a circle around himself on the ground and then sprinkled the rest over his head. All the sisters were expectant; surprise filled every heart. Finally, he stood up and the stupor was at its height when they heard him recite the *Miserere* psalm as a kind of sermon. When he was finished, he did not wait around any longer and left.[81]

By having recourse to the "rationale of gestures" and even to a kind of magical ritual more than to discursive reasoning, Francis took his distance from preaching as it was practiced in his day.[82] He certainly did not want to pass for a sacred orator. Moreover, had he not called himself, at the beginning of his religious life, "the herald of the Great King," which got him beaten and thrown into the snow by brigands who had asked him who he was? He could not indicate more clearly that he intended only to be a spokesperson, a messenger, whose sole merit was to faithfully transmit to its receivers the message he had been entrusted with. Thus when the brothers arrived in a village, the one who was the most gifted with words issued a call to conversion in a few colorful and vibrant words. After this, everyone began to sing the praises of God, leaving to the preacher the task of concluding with these words: "We are the *jongleurs* of God and the true reward that we desire is to see you lead a truly repentant life."[83] The expression *jongleurs de Dieu* can appear colorful to us; but in the social and cultural context of the period, it was frankly provocative to the extent that it associated two concepts—*jongleur* and *Dieu*— from two cultural worlds that were foreign and, in some respects, antagonistic to each other.

LEAVING ITALY AND ENCOUNTERING ISLAM (1217–1220)

At the general chapter which met at the Portiuncula on Pentecost in May 1217, two important decisions were made: provinces were created, led by ministers, and several groups of friars were sent beyond Italy to the Holy Land, England, Germany, and Hungary. It was a decisive turning point for the fraternity, which, by expanding geographically beyond the Peninsula, affirmed the universal character of its message and its vocation to transmit it to the whole of the known world. At first, things went fairly poorly and the missions on the whole suffered failure, except in England. Indeed, the enthusiasm of the friars was matched only by their lack of preparation, especially in languages. And their lack of any written endorsement from the papacy made it easy to reject their message. In certain cases, especially in Germany, they were even viewed as heretical preachers and expelled from the region. We shall return in more detail to these misadventures and their consequences.

When the friars began to move beyond Italy, Francis, who saw himself as the model for his brothers, chafed at the suggestion that he remain behind in Italy, where he would run no risk. So he left for France (the term used, in the texts of the period, to describe the country where the *langue d'oeil* was used— essentially the northern half of present-day France). Francis was especially drawn to this country, especially "because France loved the body of Christ"; he "desired to die there because of the respect they had for the holy sacrament."[84] This reasoning can seem strange. It can be understood only in the context of both the intense Eucharistic piety of Francis and the special place that this devotion had north of the Alps. Indeed, since the end of the twelfth century, the bishop of Paris, Maurice de Sully, had ordered the practice of genuflection before the consecrated host, and in the northern regions—Artois, Flanders, and Brabant—Beguines like Marie d'Oignies († 1213) and Ida of Nivelles († 1231) were leading an intense spiritual life, rooted in the humanity of Christ and his "real" presence in the species of bread and wine.

Francis thus left for France after the general chapter of 1217, but he did not get far; arriving in Florence, he ran into Cardinal Hugolino, who discouraged him—even, according to some sources, forbade him—from making this journey. Francis submitted himself to the prelate's will and returned to Umbria; a small group of friars soon reached Paris under the direction of Brother Pacifico, who became the first minister of the new province of France.

What exactly happened in Florence during this encounter, historic in every sense of the term? If its truth is incontestable, its real significance is difficult to gauge, for the hagiographical sources—the only ones we have on this subject—give us three different versions of it. We should note first that, if not the first encounter, this probably is the first important conversation between Francis and the cardinal-bishop of Ostia, one of the most influential members of the Sacred College, who was to play such an important role afterward in Francis' life and that of the Friars Minor. In 1217 Hugolino had no institutional responsibility with respect to the fraternity, and there is no reason to think that he might have succeeded in the role of protector of this movement to the Benedictine cardinal John of Saint Paul, who had died in 1214 or 1215, having given a kind welcome to Francis in Rome. Hugolino had just undertaken a peacemaking mission among the towns of central and northern Italy, which he was seeking to reconcile among themselves under the aegis of the Holy See and from which he sought contributions to the expenses of the upcoming Crusade. Since his entrance into the Sacred College in 1198, Hugolino had been charged by Innocent III with several delicate missions, especially in relation to the Empire; but he was not a pure diplomat. Even if he was not on the same level as Francis, he was nonetheless a deeply religious man who did not hesitate to recall the counsels of a Cistercian spiritual master, Rainer of Ponza, who had been a disciple of Joachim of Fiore. His encounter with the Poor Man of Assisi is thus not to be reduced—contrary to what Paul Sabatier imagined in his famous *Life of Saint Francis*, which appeared in 1893–1894—to a confrontation between an authoritarian prelate, charged by the pope to transform the Franciscan fraternity into a religious order subject to the Roman Church, and a simple and evangelical man who was seeking to preserve the free and enthusiastic spontaneity of the movement which he had launched. The most believable interpretation of this episode is the one that the *Legend of Perugia* gives to it, according to which Hugolino gave Francis advice which was judicious and to be ignored at his peril: he should not leave Italy before the stability of his foundation was assured. In this instance, the threat was coming particularly from the Roman Curia and from bishops who, at the Fourth Lateran Council, had adopted a canon that severely restricted new orders: "We strictly forbid the founding in the future of any new order. . . . Whoever intends to devote him or herself to the religious life must choose an approved order."[85] On this point, the situation of Francis and his fraternity was very precarious, for having received only oral approval of their way of life by the pope, they possessed no proof—neither rule nor papal letters of privilege—of that endorsement. The following hypothesis has recently been put forward: Honorius III approved, in 1216 or 1219, a little rule, different from the text which Innocent III had verbally ratified in 1209, in order to shield the Minors from the conciliar decision. But in the absence of any document that would have preserved any evidence of this, this is just speculation. The danger which threatened the work of Francis was not at all imaginary; Hugolino was right to order him to remain in Italy.

At one point during the discussion which undoubtedly took place in Florence with the cardinal, Francis reportedly exclaimed:

> Do you think, my lord, that the Lord has sent the Friars Minor only into our own provinces [Italy]? Quite the contrary: God has chosen them for the salvation of souls throughout the whole world among not only Christians but unbelievers as well. And provided that they observe what they have promised the Lord, the Lord will provide them with everything they need, among unbelievers as among believers.[86]

Thus at the very moment when the survival of his foundation was under challenge, the Poor Man of Assisi clearly and publicly affirmed its universal character and its vocation to move beyond the frontiers of Christianity. In fact, Francis is probably the first Christian saint in the Middle Ages to have sought contact with the Muslim world—and to have achieved it. According to his first biographer, Thomas of Celano, he had been planning to go to Syria since 1212 "to preach penance to the Saracens and other nonbelievers," but the ship on which he had embarked in Ancona was forced by a storm to turn back. This was the year when bands of young men who were called the Pastoureaux (Shepherds) left in great numbers from France and Germany in order to go to the Holy

Land. Some of them traversed central Italy. Perhaps the aborted attempt of Francis was similar to this collective departure, which ended in resounding failure.[87] A little later, probably in 1213, Francis may have tried to go to Morocco, by land, "to preach the word of Christ to the Miramolin"—that is, the emir al-Mumenim ("leader of the believers") of the Almohad dynasty, who ruled at Marrakech at the time—as well as to his coreligionists. But Francis fell ill on the road in Spain, which forced him to interrupt his journey and return to Italy.[88] In 1217 he sought to justify his departure to Cardinal Hugolino by referring to the universal mission of his fraternity and its vocation of announcing the Gospel. Regardless of the exact words of the appeal, we can have no doubt that the Poor Man of Assisi had conceived by this time a truly ambitious project of a missionary apostolate that would not be limited to the Christian world. After the general chapter of the Friars Minor at the Portiuncula on Pentecost the same year, had he not sent several groups of friars toward different countries of Europe but also dispatched Brother Giles to Tunis and Brother Elias to Palestine, each with a few companions?[89]

Francis finally realized his dream in 1219. Departing from Ancona in the month of June with Peter Cattani, he disembarked at Saint John of Acre, where he met up with Elias and the handful of friars already there. From Acre, around the end of July or beginning of August, he reached Damietta, an important port located on the Nile Delta and which was then being besieged by the Crusaders' army. For on April 12, 1213, Innocent III, in the bull *Quia maior*, whose purpose was to invite the prelates of the Church to gather together in council at Rome in 1215, had also addressed to Western Christians a passionate call to the Crusade. Indeed, having sketched an unflattering portrait of the founder of Islam, he announced the final and imminent defeat of the Saracens:

> A certain son of perdition, the pseudoprophet Muhammad, has arisen. Through worldly enticements and carnal delights, he has seduced many people away from the truth. His perfidy has prospered until this day. Yet we have faith in God, who has already given us a good omen that the end of this Beast is drawing near. The number [of the Beast] is 666, according to the Apocalypse of John, of which almost six hundred years have already passed.[90]

The initiative for this new Crusade—the fifth, according to the traditional list—has to be viewed in the context of the great victory that the allied kings of Castile and Aragon had won in 1212 at Las Navas de Tolosa over their Muslim adversaries of al-Andalus, which led, over the next decades, to the conquest by Christians of the southern part of Spain, except for the extreme southeast, which was to become the kingdom of Grenada. In the climate of exaltation and euphoria created by this success, the pope probably had the impression that the moment to strike a decisive blow against Islam had arrived. This would lead him to order a series of measures aimed at hastening its end: organization of a Crusade to reconquer Jerusalem, taken from the Christians in 1187 by Saladin; legal restrictions for Muslims and Jews living in the Holy Land in order to differentiate them better from the Christian faithful and to protect Christians from their influence; strict limitations on relations, starting in the sexual realm, between Christians and the "blasphemers of Christ," and so on. Part of this program was set in motion at the time of the Fourth Lateran Council, especially with the canon *Ad liberandam*, which anticipated a mobilization period of three years, accompanied by a Truce of God putting an end to warfare within Christianity, in order to prepare for the new Crusade. The Church called all Christians of age to take up arms to participate in this venture, by reason of the fidelity they owed to Christ humiliated and outraged by the loss of the Holy Land. After the death of Innocent III, prosecution of this Crusade was taken up by his successor, Honorius III (1216–1227). A fleet transporting several thousand Crusaders left Italy for Egypt in the spring of 1218. The purpose of the expedition was the taking of Damietta, principal economic market of Egypt on the Mediterranean. The troops landed before the city on May 29, when the Ayyubid sultan, al-Malik al-Kamil ("the Perfect King," r. 1218–1238), nephew of Saladin, had just succeeded his father, al-Adil. The Crusaders were wholly ignorant of the country, and their leaders were exhausting themselves in vain quarrels, especially after the arrival of a papal legate, the Spanish cardinal Pelagius, who, wanting to control everything, sowed disorder in the Christian camp. The poorly conducted siege dragged on, but the difficulties which the new sultan encountered in imposing his rule prevented him from taking advantage of the Crusaders' mistakes.

This is the context into which the arrival of Francis of Assisi in Damietta during the summer of 1219 has to be placed. His presence for several months here and his attempt to convert the sultan to the Christian faith are fully documented facts. All the hagiographers, from Thomas of Celano, who wrote his *Life* in 1228–1229, a little after Francis' death, to Bonaventure of Bagnoregio, author of the *Legenda maior* at the beginning of the 1260s, mention them. Other contemporary testimonies also exist, outside the Franciscan order. The earliest is that of the French prelate whom we have already mentioned, Jacques de Vitry, bishop of Saint John of Acre since 1216, who participated in the Crusade and who mentions the presence of Francis at Damietta in two of his writings: a letter that he addressed from Egypt in 1220 to Honorius III and a passage in his *Historia occidentalis* drawn up in Acre in 1226, in which he expatiates at length on the origins of the Friars Minor. Moreover, two chronicles of lay origin written in the Holy Land a little after the events add some important elements to the story. The first is the *Chronicle* of Ernoul, squire of Baliol II of Ibelin, who left us an account in French of the Third, Fourth, and Fifth Crusades, extending the Latin chronicle of William of Tyre. This text has come down to us through the edited version and summary made by Bernard the Treasurer (between 1227 and 1229). A little later, probably around 1229–1231, the anonymous author of the *Legend of Heraclius* (from the name of the Emperor Heraclius, who figures in the first paragraph)—a Frank of the Holy Land who also draws upon Ernoul—provides critical information about the encounter between Francis and the sultan. Within the framework of an expansion of that account, he attributes the final defeat of the Fifth Crusade to the sins of the Crusaders. The testimony of these chroniclers who belonged to the entourage of John of Brienne, king of Jerusalem, present at Damietta in 1219, is all the more precious since they were well informed on questions having to do with the Near East and the Crusades. Moreover, they considered the action of Francis foolhardy because, in their eyes, there was no agreement possible between Christianity and Islam. For that alone, in any case, the existence of this collection of contemporary documents, as discordant as they can be on the details, precludes our viewing this encounter as fictitious, even if the memory of it was later embellished or deformed.[91]

What were Francis' aims when he arrived outside of Damietta, and what did he do during the months that he spent in front of the town under siege, between July or August and November 1219? He certainly never thought about joining the Crusade as a combatant—his status as a religious prohibited him from taking up arms no less than his personal approach, founded on the rejection of violence; nor could he serve as a military chaplain. He seems rather to have seen here an opportunity to test the Gospel ideal of the Friars Minor. In fact, Jacques de Vitry complains bitterly, in his letter of 1220 to the pope, that several members of his entourage, clerics as well as laymen, fascinated by the personality and example of Francis, abandoned the bishop during the siege of Damietta in order to follow Francis and enter into his order.[92] Once on site, it did not take the Poor Man of Assisi long to realize that the situation was at a stalemate from a military point of view and that the use of arms was leading nowhere. The siege of the town had lasted for more than a year without decisive results, and an offensive launched by the Crusaders on August 29, 1219, against the troops of the sultan, who had feigned a retreat, ended in a bloody defeat. It is at this moment that Francis took advantage of a truce to leave the Christian camp and cross over to that of the sultan. Taking a single companion,

Brother Illuminato of Rieti, Francis first alerted the legate Pelagius, who refused him any safe passage and who did not hide his disapproval of the plan.[93]
Francis cried out, "Sultan, Sultan!" while approaching enemy lines, and was
soon stopped by the Egyptian soldiers, who led him to their master.[94] None of
the authors of sources close to the event who were outside the Franciscan milieu indicates that he suffered any mistreatment. This fact is not surprising in
itself: from the sultan's perspective, this Christian might have been a renegade
wanting to change sides and religions, or an emissary of the Crusaders charged
with a diplomatic message—which was all the more possible since negotiations
for a truce were already under way between the two camps.

On this famous episode, reported by numerous chroniclers and hagiographers and immortalized by Giotto in the cycle of frescoes that he painted
around 1300 in the upper basilica of Assisi, at least two traditions exist. For the
chroniclers outside the Franciscan order, Francis sought—in vain—to convert
the sultan and his people. Thus Jacques de Vitry, witness to the event, writes on
this subject in his letter of 1220 to the pope: "Burning with zeal for the Christian faith, he was not afraid to cross over to the army of the enemy and, after
having preached for several days the word of God to the Saracens, he obtained
few results [*modicum profecit*]."[95] Returning in a more expansive manner to this
important event in his *Historia occidentalis* in 1226, the prelate affirms that the
simple presence of Francis had transformed the sultan of Egypt from the ferocious beast which he was initially into a docile listener who heard his guest out
for several days. But fearing that Francis might convert his subjects, he had him
led back with honor to the Crusaders' camp, while at the same time asking him
to pray "so the Lord deigns to reveal to him the law and the faith which might
please Him more."[96] The basic idea is the same in all the accounts outside the
Franciscan tradition, even though in the meantime the Crusade had failed and
Francis was now considered a saint. Thus does the second account of Jacques
de Vitry amplify and dramatize the event by underscoring that the sultan had
been shaken by his words and nearly converted to the Christian faith.

For Franciscan authors, by contrast, the Poor Man of Assisi went to the sultan animated by the desire to suffer martyrdom at his hands. Thus in the *Vita
prima* of Thomas of Celano, the tragic end which Francis logically expected is
prefigured by ill treatment inflicted on him by the soldiers who arrested him.
But al-Kamil treated him kindly and listened to him defend Christianity against
the Muslim doctors of the law who surrounded him. After this oratorical joust-
ing, the sultan tried to win over Francis by offering him opulent gifts, which he
refused, declaring "that he despised them as dung"—and this aroused the admiration of the sovereign. Not wanting to tarnish the image of his hero by

mentioning the setback, the hagiographer concludes his narrative by explaining the refusal of God to grant him martyrdom by the fact that "a singular grace," much more painful and glorious, was being reserved for him: an allusion to the stigmata of the Passion which Francis was going to receive in 1224.[97] In the *Legenda maior*, Bonaventure claims to have an authentic account of that discussion from Brother Illuminato, Francis' companion that day. In this telling, having been roughed up by the soldiers who arrested them, both friars were dragged into the tent of the sultan, who welcomed them with kindness and asked them the reason for their coming. The Poor Man of Assisi responded "that he has been sent not by any man but by the Most High God in order to show him—him and his people—the way of salvation and to proclaim to them the Gospel which is the truth; then, he preached to the sultan the Triune God and Jesus as savior of the world with great strength of soul and fervor of spirit."[98] Seeing that the sultan was hesitant to convert, Francis proposed that they submit themselves to the judgment of God by undergoing the ordeal: the judges (*qadis*) and scholars (*ulama*) as well as he himself would enter into the fire. Thus would be shown, according to the result of the test, which of the two religions was superior. The Muslim clerics having rejected this test, which they considered an act of foolishness, Francis then proposed to the sultan that he would enter the flames alone. The sultan would not allow this but gained a real admiration for him and even a certain desire to convert to Christianity. He did not, however, act on this for fear of the reactions of his people. He offered gifts to Francis, who did not accept them. He returned to the camp of the Crusaders, because he did not see the signs of authentic piety in al-Kamil. This version of the episode has been immortalized by Dante in a few famous verses of the *Divine Comedy*:

> He had gone to preach Christ and his apostles by a thirst for martyrdom
> In the presence of the proud sultan.
> But finding this people too difficult to convert
> And not wanting to remain unproductive,
> He came to harvest other fruits on the soil of Italy.[99]

Thus, whereas at first glance hardly an episode in the *Lives* of Saint Francis appears to be "legendary," in the negative sense of the term, the encounter of the Poor Man of Assisi with the sultan of Egypt is probably one of the best attested episodes, historically speaking, even if its exact significance is not obvious. It occurs in a period in which each camp was wary of the other, for neither force seemed capable of carrying the day. It is well known, moreover, that al-Malik al-Kamil had a tolerant and open mind in matters of religion. A German cleric and future cardinal, Oliver of Paderborn († 1227), taken prisoner by the Muslims at the time of the final defeat of the Crusaders in August 1221, sang the praises of the sultan's magnanimity and goodness, in a letter which he sent to him after his release.[100] There is nothing unbelievable about the sultan of Egypt's desire to show this unexpected Christian visitor that Muslim hospitality was not just a word, and to place Francis under his protection.

The behavior of Francis, as Bonaventure describes it, is more surprising at first glance. The proposal to undergo the ordeal by which he challenged the Muslim doctors of the law can seem especially strange coming from such an evangelical man. But we should not forget that Francis was nourished on biblical passages and that certain ones could have influenced his behavior, like the incident in the first Book of Kings (1 Kings 18:20–48) in which the prophet Elijah confronts the priests of Baal to prove to King Ahab the superiority of the God of Israel over the god worshiped by Queen Jezebel. In spite of all the efforts deployed by the priests, they did not succeed in setting fire to the sacrifice that they had prepared, while that of Elijah immediately ignited, after which the priests of Baal had their throats cut by the crowd of converts to the God of Israel. If he did not know this text, the Poor Man of Assisi could not have been ignorant of the Canticle of the three children in the furnace (Dan 3:1–30) or the story of Daniel in the lions' den (Dan 6:1–24), often cited in the liturgy: accounts of martyrdom that ended in the confusion of persecutors and the recognition of the true God by kings Nebuchadnezzar and Darius. Furthermore, recourse to the ordeal by fire to prove the righteousness of a cause was not unknown in the popular religious movements that had been flourishing in Italy during the eleventh and twelfth centuries and of which Francis was both heir and exponent. It suffices to mention the story of a man named Peter known as Igneus, "man of fire": a Tuscan hermit who, in the middle of the eleventh century, walked barefoot on coals to convince simoniac priests to rally around the partisans of the reform of the Church. They were obliged to do so after he had survived this test. Finally, we also have the testimony of an Arab author of the fifteenth century, Ibn al-Zayyat, who evokes an epitaph on the tomb of the great mystic Fakhir al-Din, spiritual counselor of al-Kamil (which one could then see in the cemetery of Cairo) and where it was written: "He was a person of virtue known to all. His famous adventure with Malik al-Kamil and what happened to him because of the monk: all this is very famous." According to Louis Massignon, who was the first to draw our attention to this text, the Christian monk (*rahib*) to whom this refers would be none other than Francis of Assisi. And it would be fitting to identify Fakhir al-Din, who died a nonagenarian a little after 1219, with the sage who, according to the account of Bonaventure, distanced himself when Francis proposed the ordeal of fire, probably less from fear than because he disapproved of the recourse to such a barbarous procedure in matters of religion.[101]

Did Francis really go to the sultan with the intention of suffering martyrdom there, as all the Franciscan sources indicate? Some commentators are doubtful today, fearing to attribute to their hero a suicidal attitude or irresponsible behavior. For my part, I tend to think that martyrdom did enter into his perspective, keeping in mind what we know of his mindset and his cultural formation. Were not the majority of saints that one heard about in the liturgy and whose images one could contemplate in the churches of Umbria martyrs, beginning with Saint Rufino, the first bishop of Assisi, whose relics had been the object of a solemn translation into the cathedral of his native city? Moreover, was not Francis' vocation and that of his order marked by the desire to follow the example of the apostles who had given their lives to witness to their faith and to diffuse it throughout the world? Contrary to what is sometimes affirmed, the search for martyrdom was not in contradiction with his desire to follow Christ, who died on the cross to open to humanity the way to salvation. To face tribulations and dangers, including the loss of life, in order to spread the Christian faith was, from the beginning, a constitutive element of Franciscan sensibility. Jordan of Giano recounts that when volunteers were sought to go to Germany at the time of the general chapter of 1221, "almost 90 friars, enflamed with the desire of martyrdom, stood up and offered themselves up to death," and that he himself, "assuming that he was going to immediately suffer martyrdom there," sought to know the names of these heroes—which led him, after a combination of incredible circumstances, to leave with them.[102] Finally, we know that Clare of Assisi, who was very close to Francis in many regards, when she learned of the tragic end of five Franciscans who had been executed at Marrakesh in 1220, wept because her condition as a female recluse impeded her from going to be martyred in Morocco.[103]

Upon his arrival in Egypt, Francis quite probably shared the prejudices of Christians of his time against Islam. He probably knew only Muslims from the *chansons de geste*, where they were presented as idolaters—adoring statues of Muhammad and of a mysterious god called Termagant, lustful and fanatical. Nor is there any possibility that he might have had access to the translation of the Qur'an in Latin, which had been done around 1140, on the order of the abbot of Cluny, Peter the Venerable, desirous to refute the errors of these "sons of Hagar," or *agarènes*, whom many Western clerics still considered to be heretics. This text is known only through a small number of manuscripts and does not seem to have penetrated into Italy. In leaving to meet the sultan, Francis was thus sincerely convinced that he was going to be martyred for his faith; but he accepted this risk. In fact, this danger was not fanciful. Among the Friars Minor who had been sent on mission at the time of the general chapter of Pentecost 1219, just before Francis' departure for Egypt, five were going to go among the Muslims of Spain. Having reached Seville, they succeeded in getting into the Great Mosque, where they started to preach against Muhammad. After being arrested and imprisoned, they were sent on to Marrakesh, where Don Pedro—brother of the king of Portugal, who led an army of mercenaries at the service of the Almohad sultan Abu Ya'qub Yusuf al-Mustansir (r. 1213–1224)— was able to get them freed. But disregarding the counsel of prudence by their Christian protectors, they began to preach once again in Marrakesh. This led the sultan to ban them from the city. They soon returned and were again imprisoned. As soon as they were released, they went back to publicly attacking the beliefs of Islam, which finally earned them decapitation on January 16, 1220.[104] A few months later, their remains were brought back to Portugal, where they spurred numerous miracles. And it was in seeing their remains pass by the abbey Santa Cruz de Coimbra that the young canon regular Anthony—the future Saint Anthony of Padua—decided to enter the Franciscan order.

Unlike the friars executed in Morocco, Francis would have been unlikely to have personally attacked Muhammad in front of the Muslims who were present; if he had, he would have been interrupted or chastised quickly. The sultan seems to have feared no such attack, since he allowed Francis to speak. It did not take al-Kamil long to realize that this unarmed and oddly dressed person was not a Crusader but a man of God; and Francis did not find in the sultan the persecutor of the Christian faith he had expected. Everything seems to have occurred in a manner surprising for both men. The encounter ended by challenging the received ideas of each man about the other and the other's religion. And that is probably why this face-to-face engagement has taken on historic importance and has continued to fascinate people across the centuries.[105]

It is probably futile to try to know "what really happened" between Francis and the sultan on that day in September 1219. But the simple fact that such an encounter even took place already constitutes in itself a novelty—at least for the West, since public religious controversies in the presence of a sovereign were not unknown in the East. Al-Kamil presided over one such meeting in Egypt in which participated, on the Christian side, the Coptic and Melkite patriarchs. What remains unknown—most unfortunately so—are the topics of the conversation in the sultan's camp. The eyewitnesses and those close to the event all mention a "preaching of the word of God" by Francis, which would have taken the form of an exposition of the principles of the Christian faith and a call to conversion.[106] This discourse inspired in the sultan esteem for the preacher, and an appreciation of his courage if not his beliefs. Accounts from the entourage of John of Brienne, however, portray a confrontation, indeed a contentious debate, between the Poor Man of Assisi and the doctors of Islamic law ("We will show you . . . by correct reason that your law is bad"): something that appears quite astonishing on the part of Francis, who had mastered neither the language nor the arguments of theologians.[107] Bonaventure introduced in his *Legenda maior* the account of the ordeal as Brother Illuminato had described it so as to underscore the necessity of a supernatural intervention in order to come to the faith.[108] All of this remains in the realm of hypothesis, and we must recognize that there is no reason to choose one of the "readings" of the content of this encounter over another.

However, according to the Chronicle of Ernoul, close to the event and well informed, Francis declared to Cardinal Pelagius that he wanted to go among the Saracens "only if a great good would come from it."[109] But what could be the "great good" which justified such a difficult initiative? A conversion of the sultan to Christianity, which would have as a consequence the conversion also of his entourage and his people, as had been achieved with the barbarian kingdoms in the Early Middle Ages? Certainly, but the Poor Man of Assisi was not naïve or presumptuous enough to believe that he was going to obtain this miracle right away. And the question of war and peace was no doubt also a subject of this conversation, as a text of Franciscan origin—unfortunately not dated—titled *The Words of Brother Illuminato*, gives us to understand, according to which Francis declared to the sultan: "It is right that Christians have invaded the land that you live in, for you blaspheme the name of Christ and you turn from his worship all those whom you can. But if you would recognize, confess, and adore the Creator and Redeemer, Christians would love you as themselves."[110] We can assume that Francis would have suggested to the sultan that in granting Christians free access to Jerusalem, he would be freeing them of the moral obligation that they had to conquer the city militarily. The Crusade would then lose one of its fundamental motivations: the claim of the right of Christ's faithful to go there peacefully and without being subject to financial exactions in their holy places in Palestine. Perhaps we find an echo of this in the proposition which the sultan would make to the Crusaders a few weeks later, when they had seized Damietta: to cede Jerusalem to them in exchange for a quick withdrawal from Egypt. This compromise, which had the support of John of Brienne and the majority of the Frankish barons, was rejected by Cardinal Pelagius, who wished to continue the all-out fight against Islam and who was finally forced to capitulate after the defeat of Mansourah on August 30, 1221. The idea was taken up again by al-Kamil and Frederick II during their negotiations in 1229, which resulted in the Treaty of Jaffa. Thanks to the latter, Jerusalem—except the esplanade of the mosques—Bethlehem, and Nazareth, as well as a corridor to the sea, were given back to the Christians. This allowed Frederick II to crown himself king of Jerusalem in the church of the Holy Sepulcher without having to spill a drop of blood. Had the excommunicated emperor realized the dream of Francis or, in any case, answered one of the requests that he had addressed to al-Kamil ten years earlier? It does not seem absurd to me to at least ask the question.

The behavior of Francis vis-à-vis the sultan, as much as we can gather from contemporary sources, prompts us to reconsider the question of his attitude toward the Crusade. It has become commonplace to contrast the violent and intolerant attitude of the papacy—which, in Innocent III and his successors, saw in Islam above all a threat to Christianity and dreamed only of breaking its power through the Crusade—with that of the Poor Man of Assisi, partisan of the mission to and peaceful dialogue with Muslims. This thesis is especially founded on a passage in the *Memorial* (*Memoriale*) of Thomas of Celano, where we see Francis trying to dissuade the Crusaders from throwing themselves into an attack against Damietta, which, as we have seen, took place on August 29, 1219, and ended in bloody defeat. But in the hagiographical account, this exemplum serves above all to illustrate the gift of prophecy of the saint, who had predicted that the Christians would suffer defeat if they joined the combat that day. It would be incongruous to see there the sign of an opposition in principle on his part to the use of arms against unbelievers, because the text specifies that Francis had had a particular grief in observing the enormous losses suffered by the Spanish contingent, "of which he saw few survivors, so great was their enthusiasm during the fighting."[111] The Poor Man of Assisi was not *a priori* an adversary of the Crusade, if only because it was an institution of the Church, promoted by the papacy to which the order of Friars Minor had been closely tied from the beginning. We also know that Francis did not hesitate to hold up for his companions the mythical memory of "the Emperor Charles, Roland, or Oliver: those holy martyrs who died fighting for the faith of Christ."[112] Finally, we should not forget that, in the spirit of Christians of the time, the Crusade was not—as we often imagine it in our own time—a religious war or a kind of colonial expedition. It was first of all an armed pilgrimage whose purpose was the defense or recovery of the Holy Places: a new exodus of the people of God on the way to the Promised Land and the holy city Jerusalem, where the conversion of unbelievers and the reconciliation of humankind had to happen with the approach of the peaceful kingdom of the Messiah.

Francis did not challenge the Crusade; he uncovered and fulfilled its profound meaning, which was a search for fraternity between Christians of the West and the East in which Muslims and Jews could find their place. Indeed, Judaism and even Islam appeared to clerics at the beginning of the thirteenth century less as religions in competition than as imperfect and particular revelations: steps toward the universal religion, Christianity.[113] Far from simply wanting to fight "the infidels," Crusaders sought to convert them to that which was for them the true faith, as attested by various papal bulls from the beginning of the thirteenth century, which provide the first examples of this orientation toward proselytizing and conversion. We find the same tonality in the letter addressed to al-Kamil by Oliver of Paderborn in 1221 after the failure of the Crusade; the German cleric emphasizes the points of agreement between Islam and Christianity and asks the sultan to at least grant free access to Jerusalem for Christian pilgrims. In this perspective, the Crusade was above all a means for leading Islam to listen to the Christian message, instead of immediately putting to death all those who were challenging its foundations.[114]

The missionary preaching of Francis therefore does not present itself as an alternative to the military enterprise launched by the papacy against Islam, but develops along a parallel logic. Without question, for his contemporaries, the founder of the Minors belonged to the contingent of Crusaders and participated, on the level of emotions, in the achievements and failures of the Christian army. But without any kind of angelism, he seems to have sought, by his personal witness, to offset the negative image of Christianity which this recourse to violence could give to Muslims. For a relationship of force (which could be inevitable at any given moment but which constituted in his eyes only an exception), he sought instead to substitute a witness of weakness and submission—pushed all the way to martyrdom, if that failed—which was addressed to pagans and to Christians alike, while inviting them to turn toward the All-Powerful God whom both enemy camps were claiming for themselves at every opportunity. In his eyes, there was no more contradiction between the search for martyrdom and the desire to convert unbelievers than there was between Crusade and mission. As G. K. Chesterton rightly saw it, the Poor Man of Assisi "began from a principle that it was better to make Christians than defeat unbelievers. It was not *a priori* absurd to imagine that one could convert by the blood of missionary-martyrs those that one could not defeat militarily."[115]

It seems, however, that Francis' attitudes evolved after his encounter with the sultan al-Kamil. Damietta was finally taken by the Crusaders on November 5, 1219, and this long-awaited conquest was accompanied by massacres and acts of violence. According to the author of the *Eracle*, who was a witness to these events, Francis "saw the evil and the sin which began to grow among the members of the army and this displeased him. Thus, he left and went directly to Syria before returning to his own country."[116] Disheartened by the conduct of his coreligionists, far from what should have been, in his eyes, the behavior of a "knight of Christ," he preferred to distance himself from the expedition that was evolving in a direction contrary to the idea that he had of the Crusade. It is hardly possible that he went afterward to Jerusalem—the pope had forbidden Christians to make the journey during the time of the Crusade to avoid providing the Saracens who collected taxes on pilgrims with financial resources—but he passed some time with his brothers in what remained of the Latin States. It is probably this sojourn in the Holy Land and the good impression Francis had left with the Muslims which explains why the Minors were, in 1333, the first—and for a long time the only—Latin religious authorized by the sultan to return to Jerusalem, and that they saw themselves entrusted, at the request of the king of Naples, Robert of Anjou, with watching over certain Christian Holy Places, a trust they still maintain today.

THE PAINFUL INSTITUTIONALIZATION OF THE
FRANCISCAN MOVEMENT (1220–1223)

According to the Franciscan chronicler Jordan of Giano, informed by an eyewitness, a prophetess living in the Holy Land who was known as "the Tongue-that-Proclaims-the-Truth" declared to the friars: "Come back, come back, for the order is troubled by the absence of Brother Francis; it is divided and in the process of destroying itself."[117] Thus in the spring of 1220, the Poor Man of Assisi returned to Italy, where problems had been multiplying in his absence. A certain number of unfortunate initiatives had indeed been taken by the "vicars"—in the strict sense of the term, "those replacing" him—to whom Francis had delegated his powers during his absence: Matthew of Narni, who remained at the Portiuncula, and Gregory of Naples, who visited the communities throughout Italy. During a general chapter gathering the "eldest" religious (*seniores*), Matthew and Gregory had promulgated statutes or constitutions that increased the number of days during which the friars were obliged to fast (which tended to align their fasting practices with those of monks). On the other hand, Phillip the Tall, to whom Francis had entrusted the care of watching over the Poor Ladies of San Damiano, took his mission too much to heart and obtained from the Roman Curia measures of protection on behalf of the Poor Ladies, thus openly contravening the injunctions of the Poverello, who had strictly forbidden the friars from soliciting privileges in high places. Finally,

Brother John, called "de capella" ("of the hat") or "de Campello," who was particularly responsible for providing care for the lepers, got it into his head to organize them into a kind of religious order whose approval he requested from the Holy See. All these initiatives had created within the fraternity a certain turmoil that subsided once Francis returned to Italy and took the situation back in hand.

But these events revealed the existence within the Minors of a real uncertainty over the very meaning of their vocation. Were they called to involve themselves in charitable activities at the service of the sick and poor; or rather to live like monks or hermits, far from people and the world; or even to dedicate themselves to pastoral activities while seeking to make up for the insufficiencies of the secular clergy with their penitential preaching? Obviously, the question had not been resolved, and the refusal of Francis to let his brothers specialize in tasks defined with any precision began to cause problems.

Just back from the Holy Land in May 1220, and even before returning to Assisi, Francis went to Viterbo to meet with Honorius III. Since 1209 contact between Francis and the papacy had never been interrupted, as is shown by the testimony cited from Jacques de Vitry. But since the death, in 1214 or 1215, of Cardinal John of Saint Paul, Francis no longer could rely on the support of a prelate who could serve as a go-between in case of difficulties. For its part, the Roman Curia seems to have decided upon a wait-and-see policy toward the Minors, for no document attests that it intervened in the life of the fraternity before 1219. With the rapid growth of the order during these years, and after the tensions which had surfaced during Francis' sojourn in the East, such a situation could not continue much longer. Francis obtained the annulment of the papal privileges which had been granted without his permission to Brothers Philip and John; and once he reached Assisi, he abolished the statutes regarding fasting adopted in his absence.

At the end of September 1220, on the occasion of a general chapter of Saint Michael, he announced his intention to abandon the direction of the order. To justify this unexpected decision, which astonished and disheartened the friars, he pointed to the state of his health. He had indeed come back sick from the East, where he had, it seems, contracted trachoma, which was eventually to make him virtually blind, and malaria, which racked him with violent pains of the spleen and liver. But the real reason for his unexpected withdrawal was probably his desire to avoid putting himself into conflict with the papacy or with those friars who were calling for a more precise definition of the mission of the order. A few days earlier, on September 22, 1220, a bull of Honorius III had imposed on those who wished to become Friars Minor a novitiate of one year before they could make profession; and it also prescribed canonical sanctions against those brothers who "would wander outside of obedience," measures that tended to transform the fraternity into a structured religious order. Thus did Francis designate to succeed him Peter Cattani, a lawyer from Assisi who had been one of his very first companions and who had accompanied him to the Holy Land. But Peter died in March 1221, and he was replaced by Brother Elias.

This rush of events and measures in the year and a half after Francis' return to Italy reveal serious problems within the fraternity which the successes of the previous years had masked but which now erupted into the open. The anarchy which had reigned in his absence demonstrated the excessive dependency on the Poor Man of Assisi by his foundation, while the misplaced initiatives taken by some of his companions raised the question of just how the Friars Minor were going to play a role in Church and society. The very growth and extension throughout Christianity of the fraternity of Minors made inevitable a process of institutionalization for which Francis was not prepared, even if he was not contesting its necessity. Evidently, the Poor Man of Assisi felt overwhelmed by the expansion of a religious movement which he had expressly not willed, even though he had joyfully welcomed its birth and development. According to the *Legend of the Three Companions* and the *Memorial* of Thomas of Celano, Francis saw in a dream a little black hen with countless chicks who were ceaselessly chirping for her to protect them but whom she was having trouble gathering under her wings. And Francis said to himself:

> I am this hen with my small stature and my dark color. . . . The chicks are my numerous and virtuous brothers that my poor forces are not able to shelter from calumnies and persecutions. I will thus go and entrust them to the Holy Roman Church. She has the power to chastise our enemies and to also guarantee to the children of God full freedom to allow for a much greater number to be saved.[118]

Even if these words are not authentic, they seem to reflect the mind of Francis after his return from the East and his attitude toward his foundation. It is possible—but not certain, since the testimonies of his biographers on this subject are not clear: this step might in fact have taken place one or two years later—that he then asked Honorius III to put the Friars Minor under the protection of a cardinal. The pope acquiesced to his request and named Hugolino. The two men knew each other fairly well, having met in Florence in 1217 and perhaps on other occasions as well, and liked each other, even if they did not share the same vision of religious life.

But it is inside the fraternity that the situation was changing at an especially rapid pace. Since 1219 Francis had given up the authority to admit new recruits into the order, delegating this power henceforth to the provincial ministers. And the General Chapter of 1221 would be the last in which all the Friars Minor would participate. In addition, among the novices who were pouring in, and whom Francis no longer personally knew, were many noble and educated men, clerics as well as priests, like the young canon regular Anthony of Coimbra, the future Saint Anthony of Padua, who had joined the order in 1220. Thus the group of Friars Minor that was sent to Germany after the general chapter of Pentecost 1221 included twelve clerics and five laymen. We really do not know how to extrapolate from these numbers about the canonical status of the members of the order at this date. These friars of the second Franciscan generation were probably not less generous or less pious than their predecessors, but they were introducing into the communities new habits and a less spontaneous style of life. The reasons that had impelled them to enter the Minors were not always the same as those of the first companions, who had been attracted by the project of the evangelical life and the absolute poverty of Francis. Indeed, certain newcomers considered the entry into the fraternity above all as the surest means of salvation. One sees this in the account of the conversion of the English priest and preacher Haymo of Faversham, future minister general, who had exhausted himself with penances to the point where he saw a cord appear which he seized and which allowed him to go up to heaven, after which he assumed that the choice of being a Friar Minor was the most worthy one.[119] This kind of motivation was foreign to the mindset of the Poor Man of Assisi, who did not concern himself with meriting salvation, something he considered a free gift of God. There were also among the newcomers men who were less mature and younger men animated by an enthusiasm which sometimes seemed excessive to their contemporaries. A prelate like Jacques de Vitry, who, though he really esteemed the Minors, did not hide his concern about the evolution under way when he wrote in 1220, a little before the establishment by the papacy of the obligatory novitiate:

> This religious movement appears really dangerous to me because it admits into its group not only mature men but even adolescents and unprepared individuals. And whereas they should have begun by exercising for a time a regular discipline and by demonstrating their worthiness, here these brothers are sent two by two throughout the whole world![120]

In the first years, Boncampagno of Siena, a lay master who taught rhetoric in Bologna, noticed some disturbing deviations among the brothers:

A good number of Friars Minor are young people and children. Whence it happens that because of the fragility proper to their age, they are inclined, as nature would have it, to instability and lack of balance. These, indeed, have reached such a degree of foolishness that they wander about without any discernment throughout the cities, towns, and remote places, while putting up with horrible and inhuman suffering which makes martyrs of them.[121]

Thanks to this massive and unchecked influx of postulants admitted with no formality other than a simple promise of obedience and the taking of the habit, individuals were also introduced into the order who, once past the initial enthusiasm, found themselves restless and practiced a kind of unsupervised wandering. Certain ones left the order after some time to return to the world or to enter into another religious congregation without permission—which was in contradiction with the canonical norms that then regulated consecrated life. Others were reproached for their laziness, even for moral deviations or uncertain beliefs. Even some among the most seasoned friars who had participated in those poorly prepared missions in Germany and Hungary came back disappointed and sometimes bitter. From experience, it became obvious that enthusiasm alone was not sufficient and that the Franciscan message could not be propagated in the regions north of the Alps without the support of ecclesiastical authorities.

Some authors misread the meaning of the resignation of Francis, seeing in it a reaction of deep disappointment or of protest against the decisions that had been imposed on him by the papacy against his will. In fact, the reality is both simpler and less dramatic. In asking the help of the papacy in 1220, the Poor Man of Assisi was not throwing himself into the mouth of the wolf with the cleverness of an innocent lamb; he was acknowledging that his personal action and energy were no longer sufficient to assure the direction of his fraternity, which was passing through a crisis of growth tied to its change of status. In fact, in the Church of his day—like today's—a charism could not be recognized and authenticated by the hierarchy unless it resulted in the creation of a religious order:

From the moment when the dream of the founder is shared with others— however purely spiritual one might imagine it to be—a discipline is imposed and soon the rigor of law. To be established, the religious family needs a formal recognition by the hierarchy. To live, it has to have rules of admission, temporal resources, status of members, governance. The acceptance of the rule, under the governance of a leader: such is the principle of unity of every religious family.[122]

Francis did not feel that he was the person for this new situation. It is for this reason that he preferred to voluntarily let go of the direction of a movement which had been, up to then, totally his. No founder or leader of an order in the Middle Ages had had such a power. But he did not, for all that, give up influencing the order or orienting its future. On the contrary, it is in leaving to his "vicar" and to the Roman Church the care of making decisions of a normative or disciplinary type that he could hope to preserve a superior authority, of a spiritual type, that would only have been diminished in the heat of daily administration. Aware of the changes which had become inevitable, the Poor Man of Assisi was going henceforth to limit their extent by proposing himself as a model: certainly not to put himself forward but in order to provide the friars a living illustration of the way to be and live as a Friar Minor. To the hierarchy of authority he would henceforth juxtapose a hierarchy of example through his own personal witness.

Francis' choice to withdraw from the leadership of his order did not depend on simple tactical considerations. For him, example was worth more than words, because it does not widen the gap between what one is and what one ought to be, unlike words of counsel, which are usually disheartening or lacking relevance. Example speaks without saying anything; it attracts without forcing, and it goes forward without blocking anything else from happening afterward. Thus was the Poor Man of Assisi going to try, even more than before, to educate others by his deeds. But not content to "give good example," he especially sought to create actions capable of shocking and imprinting themselves on individual and collective memory—whence the often theatrical character of his public interventions during the last years of his life. When he appeared, disguised as a beggar, before his brothers comfortably seated at table on a feast day to ask them for an alms, he offered not a single word of reproach; but this little drama was enough to provoke within them a feeling of guilt and shame that pushed them to question their behavior.[123] Wanting the Minors, after his death, to "serve as an example to the world," he forced himself to live the life of a saint, for he knew that what he said or did was immediately followed and imitated by his disciples.[124] Thus did he feel himself bound, as long as he was alive, to be equal to his reputation: "If they believe me to be a saint and I do not lead the life appropriate to a saintly man, I will be a hypocrite," he declared.[125] At the same time, he endeavored to destroy the reputation of holiness that surrounded him. For when he heard it said about him by the crowds: "He is a holy man!" he cried out: "Do not praise me as if it was an accomplished fact! For I can still have sons and daughters! One must not praise anyone as long as one is not certain of his or her end."[126] Nevertheless, unlike some of his predecessors, like

Bernard of Clairvaux who "played the saint" on certain great occasions and involved himself with more zeal than charity in ecclesiastical and theological quarrels of his day, Francis wanted to behave in a holy manner in all his actions and to make of his life a continual exemplum, so that he might remain after his death always alive in the minds of his companions. Whence the extreme tension in which he lived during the last years of his life and which did not ease up until the approach of his death.

For his part, Cardinal Hugolino, who seems to have experienced a certain uneasiness at that time in the face of deviations that were threatening the Franciscan movement, took a series of measures to orient its evolution in the direction desired by the papacy. On June 11, 1219, the Curia had intervened through the bull *Cum dilecti filii* to reassure the prelates of the regions north of the Alps on the orthodoxy of the Friars Minor and the exact nature of their way of life. Although the friars told the bishops of their papal approval, they could not produce any official document to support their words. This text is important because it constitutes the first official document emanating from the papacy on behalf of Francis and his companions, of their life and "religion of the Friars Minor," according to the expression used therein to describe them. Another letter of the same type was sent by Honorius III, on May 29, 1220, to the bishops of France, where the brothers had begun to settle while Francis was in the East.[127] A little after his return, as we have seen, the bull *Cum secundum consilium* was promulgated to institute a novitiate of a year before admission into the order. It was addressed significantly to "Brother Francis and to the priors and custodes of the Friars Minor," which testifies to the difficulty that the Curia had in defining the structures of this totally new kind of religious movement. Behind all of these pontifical documents, we obviously see the intervention of Hugolino, whose biographer did not hesitate to write, around 1240, that "he took in hand the order of Friars Minor, which at the beginning was wandering without any specific boundaries, by giving it a new rule, thereby conferring a form onto this formless movement."[128] Even if the author exaggerates the role of the future pope Gregory IX a bit, there is no doubt that the institutional genesis of the order was the result of a close collaboration between Francis, the provincial ministers, and the cardinal, at the end of which the papacy vouched for the order of Friars Minor by means of a more intensive introduction of the brothers into pastoral activities.

The 1220s also marked a painful turning point in the life of Francis, as he was led to distance himself from Clare and San Damiano. The situation of women who had entered into religious life in the wake of the Friars Minor was particularly disturbing, since they did not have a rule beyond the brief "form of life" which Francis had drawn up for them in 1212: a simple commitment to be of service to them which included no specific statement on their way of life. But the Roman Church allowed "religious women" only a cloistered life of the monastic kind and of Benedictine inspiration which the community of San Damiano had to accept or disband. This process of regularization ultimately ruptured the unity of the Franciscan movement which Francis had wanted at the beginning: fully open to Christians of both sexes.

We are poorly informed on this period. In recent years, a controversy has arisen over the authenticity of the "privilege of poverty" which Clare, in her *Testament*, claims to have received from Pope Innocent III. This privilege would have guaranteed to the community of San Damiano, in complete contradiction with canonical legislation, the right to live without having landed or immovable properties. The authenticity of this document has been contested but more recent arguments have supported it, without definitive resolution of the question.[129] On the basis of the latest research, we can accept that Francis intervened on behalf of Clare with the pope at the end of 1215 or the beginning of 1216 and convinced him that San Damiano could live without possessing any goods, with the support of the Friars Minor, who committed themselves to beg alms for the "reclusive Poor Ladies" who resided there. Whether the privilege might have remained purely oral—like the approval of the "form of life" of the Friars Minor by the same pope in 1209—or whether it was committed to a written document makes little practical difference.

In any case, from 1218 to 1219, the situation of Clare and her companions deteriorated in the sense that, in order to respond to the requirements of Lateran IV, Cardinal Hugolino created a new female congregation, which he first named the Poor Ladies of the Valley of Spoleto and of Tuscany. The community of San Damiano then had to accept the "form of life" of Benedictine inspiration, which he imposed on the houses that were assimilated into the new order. Francis may then have taken his distance from Clare and her companions, and after his return from the East, this distancing may have been translated into decisions which broke with previous practices. Thus in the first rule of the Minors, in 1221, he formally forbade his brothers from "receiving women into their obedience" and asked them to content themselves to giving them spiritual counsel, "after which they will do penance wherever they wished."[130] These dispositions, which are found integrated into a chapter consecrated to "evil looks" and to the danger of frequenting the company of women, seem at first glance tied to considerations of morality, even more so since they immediately precede a chapter consecrated to fornication and the sanctions to be taken against brothers who gave in to this vice. But such motivations might have been neither the only nor even the most determinative: in fact, Francis probably wanted to distance himself from the "Poor Ladies" when he understood that Hugolino had very specific ideas about San Damiano.

In this regard, it is appropriate to dispel a misunderstanding concerning the relationship between Francis and Clare. As Jacques Dalarun has clearly demonstrated, their relationship was neither reciprocal nor exclusive. Whereas Francis' name is cited thirty-two times in the writings of Clare, hers is never mentioned in those of her master and friend.[131] The vision of a mystical couple, idealized and inseparable—having become classic to the point of banality as a result of certain biographies and films that have been devoted to them—no longer holds water. The *Assisi Compilation* and the *Treatise on the Miracles* of Thomas of Celano devote a lot of space to other women in the life of the Poor Man of Assisi, like Jacoba de' Settesoli—"Brother Jacoba"—his Roman disciple who had the privilege to be present at his death, and Praxedes, whose spiritual director he was. And if there is no doubt that Clare considered Francis a model and an absolute point of reference, Francis did not have the same solicitude for her. Rather, his was an affectionate attention due to a profound esteem as well as to the responsibility which he had undertaken in her regard when he had inspired her to leave the world and to join his fraternity. Thus, once he obtained from the papacy the assurance that the community of San Damiano would continue to live in accord with evangelical poverty and that it would maintain its spiritual bond with the Friars Minor, could he then consider that he had fulfilled his obligations toward her, while at the same time maintaining a profound connection with her which was to lead him to return to San Damiano when he felt his end approaching.

Other factors also contributed to his decision to stand back from Clare and her companions. Obviously, his companions were divided on the issue. Some, under the influence of a monastic tradition grounded in the "Lives of the Fathers" (of the Desert), which conveyed a fundamentally misogynous message, probably were reluctant to maintain the fairly close relationship between men and women which must have characterized the life of the fraternity in the early days. Francis, for his part, quickly realized that the process of the regularization of the *mulieres religiosae*, on which the Cardinal had taken the initiative, was irreversible and that the Roman Church would not tolerate for long the survival of a community that lacked a rule and did not observe a cloistered life. To try to reverse or slow down this evolution was to throw himself into a losing battle and to run the risk of endangering the unique status enjoyed by the Friars Minor in the eyes of the papacy. It is probably in this context that Francis took the liberty to correct the wording of Hugolino, who spoke to him about the "sisters" of San Damiano, telling the pope that it was better to describe them as "ladies." By using this term, the Poor Man of Assisi translated, on the level of terminology, the process of courteous distancing which allowed him to dissociate the destiny of his own order from that of the community directed by Clare.

Did he later regret having been too tough in her regard and having deprived himself of her presence for too long? The fact remains that we see him, during the last months of his life, again seeking contact with San Damiano and addressing different messages to the Poor Ladies. In his "last will," he urged them to remain faithful to what had been their common intention, namely the practice of full poverty lived as a total dependence on God and other people, with a hint of emotion and even compassion in the face of the sacrifice which they had made on the demands of the papacy but also at his request. After his conversion, Francis did not call Clare by her actual name but referred to her as *christiana*: the Christian. Some have wanted to see in this word the sign of the attention he brought to the spiritual dimension of the life of this woman, to the exclusion of all personal attachment. Certainly: but I would be rather inclined, following Jacques Dalarun, to see in this term a reference to the *pauperes christiani*, an expression which at that time described lepers and which went back, ultimately, to an image of suffering and self-denial.

THE FRANCISCAN PROJECT BETWEEN UTOPIA AND CODIFICATION: THE YEARS OF THE RULES (1221–1223)

The other that needed urgently to be addressed was the redaction of a rule. The question of Franciscan rules is so complex that even today specialists are far from reaching any agreement on certain points. In 1209 Francis had had a text approved by Innocent III that seems to have comprised a series of Gospel passages one after another. It was not a rule but a simple program of life (*propositum vitae*), lacking any juridical force, not having been promulgated by the papal chancery in an official document provided with a lead seal (in medieval Latin: *bulla*, whence the English word "bull"). Over the next years, the fraternity had lived in a kind of institutional vagueness since, even though the majority of bishops authorized the friars to preach in their diocese and the brotherhood had the support of the papacy, it did not constitute, juridically speaking, a religious family approved by the Church. In the *Legend of the Three Companions*, we read that Francis had written "several rules" before 1223, and some modern authors have supposed that Pope Honorius III had issued normative texts relative to the Minors in 1216 or in 1218. This is not impossible, but since no trace of such things has come down to us, this is not the place to dwell on these hypotheses.

In fact, the general chapters had been the occasion to carefully elaborate statutes or constitutions meant to resolve this or that problem. Until 1220 Francis had probably hoped that these "amendments" added to the text of 1209 would allow the Minors to avoid having to write an actual rule which, in his eyes, would fossilize the spirit within a text and align his movement with other religious orders. But after his return from the East, it did not take long for him to understand that he could no longer evade the pressures from the Curia. Canon 13 of Lateran IV, promulgated in 1216, effectively obligated all new orders to adopt one of the existing rules: either that of Saint Benedict, which governed the life of monks, or that of Saint Augustine, followed by canons regular. When he was reminded of this requirement by the ministers provincial and Cardinal Hugolino, Francis opposed them with a clear, even staunch refusal, since he was convinced that God had revealed to him a new form of religious life—a life according to the Gospel—which had nothing to do with those rules which had preceded it. He declared:

> My brothers, my brothers, God has called me to walk in the way of humility and showed me the way of simplicity. I do not want to hear any talk of the rule of Saint Augustine, of Saint Bernard, or of Saint Benedict. The Lord has told me that he wanted to make of me a new fool [*novellus pazzus*] in the world, and God does not want to lead us by any other knowledge than that.[132]

The cardinal did not insist; but the Poor Man of Assisi, having learned from the incident, undertook with his companions to draft the text known as the "first rule," which was finished in 1221.[133] It appears as a mélange of exhortations, spiritual reflections, and norms of behavior, enriched by numerous biblical citations. Indeed, Francis thought of it not as a juridical document but as a reminder of fundamental principles of a life in minoritas, accompanied by a few indications on the means of putting them into practice and the errors to avoid. Thus this rule, completely atypical and unsatisfactory in the eyes of canonists, was not acceptable to the papacy, which refused to promulgate it. This explains the name of *regula non bullata* (nonpromulgated rule) which is sometimes used to designate it. Refusing to be discouraged, Francis went back to the task and ended up with a more concise and rigorous text, which Honorius III approved on November 23, 1223, in the bull *Solet annuere*—whence its name of *regula bullata*—whose original is kept today in the lower basilica of Assisi. it is often referred to as the second rule, and it has remained, through the centuries, the rule of the Friars Minor.[134]

The bull *Solet annuere* conferred on the Franciscan order the juridical foundation that it had lacked, by dint of a pious subterfuge. It presents itself as a simple confirmation, banal and anodyne, of the text that Pope Innocent III had approved in 1209 (for the papacy did not wish to contravene the measures taken by the Fourth Lateran Council to prohibit the creation of new religious orders). In fact, this was only a face-saving fiction, because the *regula bullata* of 1223 had little in common with the text of 1209. But it also differed appreciably from the rule of 1221, a certain number of measures of which had been eliminated. Evidently, this official document, which represented the maximum of what the Curia could accept, was far less than what Francis wanted, even if it remained faithful to its fundamental intuitions. Up to the end, he endeavored to realize all its possibilities, both through his personal witness and especially through the precise indications that he gave to this subject in his *Testament* of 1226. The rule which reflects the intention and program of the Poor Man of Assisi is thus not the *regula bullata* of 1223 but that of 1221, which can be considered the "foundational document" or charter of the fraternity.[135]

It is indeed from this text that one can attempt to reconstitute the project of Francis in its profound coherence, for he expresses himself here with total freedom and great spontaneity. Let us note first that the Poor Man of Assisi did not seek to attain moral perfection or the summits of asceticism. In some respects more detailed and much broader, he aimed rather to define what one might call a Franciscan utopia (in the sense that one speaks of the utopian socialisms of the nineteenth century). That is to say: a collective project certain aspects of which can seem barely realizable, but whose profound inspiration has continued to inspire fertile experiences even up to our own day. Francis indeed sought to create among the Friars Minor a kind of human and Christian existence characterized by alternative behaviors in relation to those of the surrounding society and designed to establish a strong and authentic relationship between men and women, in the light of what exists between them and God.

THE POVERTY OF CHRIST AND HUMAN MISERY

In the first chapter of the rule of 1221, the fundamental principles of the life of the Minors are defined in the following way: "The rule and life of these friars is this: to live in obedience, in chastity and without anything of one's own, and to follow the teaching and the footprints of Our Lord Jesus Christ, who said: 'If you wish to be perfect, go and sell all that you have and give it to the poor, and you will have treasure in heaven; and come and follow me.'"[136] From the beginning, the Franciscan fraternity defined itself as an "upside-down world," a community of poor and chaste men subject to others (*minores, subditi*), whose way of life is founded on the refusal to possess anything whatsoever. Indeed, for Francis, the root of evil, from which neither individuals nor groups escape, resides in an egocentric vision of the world and human relationships. The quintessential sin for the human person consists in appropriating to oneself one's own will and to "rejoice in the good that the Lord says and does in oneself."[137] It is precisely here that one can locate the rejection of God and, at the same time, the obstacle that renders the existence of a fraternal society impossible here below. Indeed, possession and the spirit of property or money are at the origin of the violence in relationships between human beings. And the "foundational document" rightly underlines the relationship that exists between cupidity in its various forms (*avaritia*) and evil (*malitia*)—that is, between evil passions and all forms of oppression. To be converted to the Gospel thus consists in walking this same road in the other direction, entering into a process of disappropriation by following Christ, who, having nothing other than his life here below, became a being totally possessed by God, the "son of God." For the less a human being possesses, the more he or she belongs to God: the sovereign Good who is at the origin of all goods, to whom it is proper to give back these goods in a prayer of praise and gratitude. To live in poverty is to thus return to the perfection of the beginning—that of Adam before the Fall—and to rediscover the only true wealth, which is that of shared love.

To a society in expansion profoundly attached to the notion of profit, Francis opposes a dynamic myth: that of the poverty of Christ. The term "myth" must be understood here in its etymological sense: not a more or less far-fetched invention but a founding narrative that accentuates certain traits of the reality which it describes in order to clarify its meaning. Thus, for Francis, Jesus was not only a wanderer who, according to his own words (Matt 8:20; Luke 9:58), "had no place to lay his head," and who lived with his disciples in frugal simplicity. Both he and Mary were poor people who asked for hospitality and lived from alms.[138] To expand on what was for him a proof, Francis culls, selects, and juxtaposes all the passages of the Gospels that move in the direction of these affirmations, from the rejection of the newborn babe of Bethlehem, whom no hostel owner wanted to welcome, to the tragic end of Judas—the only companion of Christ who worried about the morrow, whose tragic fate clearly illustrates what happens to one who places his or her trust in riches. This is the perspective we must embrace if we are to understand the disdain and even the profound repugnance that money inspired in Francis. The radical purity of the popular religious movements and the mistrust of the Church of his day toward ill-gotten money are renewed, but are transposed into another key in Francis' attitude toward coins and money: "If by chance we find some in whatever place, let us not value it more than the dust that we trample under our feet!"[139]

What does he dislike about money? It both stirs up an evil desire in individuals and distorts relationships between human beings by conferring on those who possess it an illusory security. At the end of his life, as knights of Assisi were bringing him back to his native city to die, they went through a town where they wanted to buy some food but no one would agree to sell them anything. This made the Poverello say to them: "If you have found nothing, it is because you place your confidence in your flies [this is what he called *denarii*] and not in God. But return without blushing into the houses where you have gone; instead of asking the merchants to buy, ask an alms for the love of God. The Holy Spirit will act in them and you will find everything in abundance."[140] The anecdote nicely illustrates the project of Francis, which was to give birth in the heart of the world a society without money and without goods, where an "economy of poverty" would prevail, characterized by liberality and the redistribution to disadvantaged persons of all that was not strictly indispensable to the survival of the community. At the base of this kind of life were primarily work and, secondarily, begging, which would allow the group to address its needs. The very word "mendicants" which, beginning in the 1240s and 1250s, served to describe the Friars Minor as well as the Friars Preacher, attests to the fact that it is one of the aspects of their behavior that struck their contemporaries the most. For the first time, they were dealing with religious who refused to be owners! But the rapid evolution of the Franciscan order soon blurred the exact meaning of this notion: for the Poor Man of Assisi, alms ought not constitute a recompense given to friars equivalent to a religious service, like the more or less fixed offerings that the faithful made to priests or monks on the occasion of certain cultic actions. Rather, "It is the inheritance and justice due to the poor and which has been procured for us by Our Lord Jesus Christ."[141] Indeed, it constitutes a right for those who are in need, for they are asking for justice and not charity. In this perspective, to have recourse to "the table of the Lord" is not at all shameful or humiliating. The one who begs for the love of God must be, on the contrary, at ease and joyful, for he is claiming only what is his due: that part of the inheritance which God has reserved for the poor and of which all those who possess goods should be its "ministers." If shame there is, it is a good thing, since the one who refuses an alms, by his or her action breaks the bond of fraternity between human beings; and the one who begs is the truly rich person, since he or she offers in exchange for an alms the love of God in comparison to which all things of the earth are nothing.

In the mind of Francis, the recourse to alms was only a palliative for the brothers, who ought not rely on them unless they were incapable of providing for their own needs by working. Those who knew a trade were permitted to keep their tools, but it was forbidden for them to receive a salary in money or to devote themselves to a professional activity which would have given scandal.[142] Most of them probably put themselves at the service of a farmer—doing day labor in exchange for a piece of bread and some fruit—or worked with an artisan. Here again, the novelty was considerable. Surely, the monks had never forgotten the demands of the rule of Saint Benedict in the matter of work; and the Cistercians in the twelfth century had revived the practice of manual labor in their own monasteries. But for them, it merely constituted one ascetic practice among others. And the duty of providing for the community, in fact, fell upon the lay brothers who were given the material tasks to do, especially agricultural production and the raising of animals. Francis' perspective was completely different: to work with one's hands was certainly to avoid laziness, the enemy of the soul, but especially to earn one's bread by the sweat of one's brow and to share the condition of the vast majority of the people of his day, the workers, since the nobles and clerics were dispensed from this obligation.

If Francis rejects money with such vehemence, it is also because, in line with the economic ideas of his time, he was convinced that the quantity of money available in the world was constant and that by enriching oneself and especially in storing up coinage—but also in stocking foodstuffs, as merchants were then doing, while waiting to be able to sell them at the best price—one was depriving others of such things. He also criticized money for reducing objects to their exchange value—that is, to the price which it was necessary to pay in order to acquire them. But this reduction of everything to its monetary value constituted in his eyes a distortion, because everything has its uniqueness and its own dignity. By using monetary coinage as a gauge of value, the human person was taking the place of God, who had created them, leading to a kind of diabolical transubstantiation. Whereas wealth divides and separates, the renunciation of every form of possession, on the contrary, renders love possible, for the one who has nothing of his or her own does not hesitate to open the door to all, to the good and the bad alike. For Francis had chosen to place himself at the sides of the poor, the disinherited and the marginalized of every kind: lepers, thieves, vagabonds—all those who then constituted the dregs of society were for him objects of preference. Not in virtue of any kind of messianic idealization of the working man or of a theology of liberation *avant la lettre* that would have led him to choose the camp of the oppressed in order to save them from their condition by any means; rather, because in each one of them, more than in every other human being, he found the face of Christ crucified.

> When you see a poor person, he said, you must consider that person in the name of the one who comes, that is, the Christ who took upon himself our poverty and our infirmity. Thus the poverty and infirmity of this person are the mirror in which we must contemplate in love the poverty and infirmity that Our Lord Jesus Christ suffered in his own body in order to save humankind.[143]

To share the life of the poor constituted the best way to come close to Christ, whose representatives and "lieutenants," according to Francis, they were on this earth. Thus did he want his brothers not just to distribute their goods to the indigent at the time of their entrance into the order, but to lead a life identical or at least comparable to theirs. Indeed, no one was more aware than he of the ambiguities of religious poverty: voluntary and not lived on a daily basis. So many orders and movements that claimed this ideal for themselves had betrayed it within the space of a few generations! This was the case, for example, of the Cistercian monks, whose stunning economic success had, at the end of a few decades, seriously encroached upon the ascetic austerity and fervor of the early days. But also groups of lay origin and from a more modest social class like the Humiliati of Lombardy, who, by dint of emphasizing the evangelical value of manual work, fairly quickly came to grief in commercial ventures and the accumulation of goods. Thus did the Poor Man of Assisi show himself to be more rigorous on the subject of lived and concrete poverty than previous reforming currents or dissident groups had been. Among neither the bons hommes nor even the Waldensians does one find a requirement of such an absolute abnegation. Numerous anecdotes illustrate the concern which Francis had to not lose contact with the realities of misery and to experience need and nakedness for himself. Thus when he encountered some raggedly clothed poor people on the road, he offered them his habit or his cloak and experienced a feeling of shame in seeing a beggar dressed more poorly than himself. To allow the mother of a young man who was coming to enter the fraternity to live on something after the departure of her son, he sold the only copy of the New Testament that he possessed and gave her the sum of money thus obtained; for nothing—not even the holy books and objects which were used for liturgy—was more sacred for him than the poor. Finally, we know that he frequently visited the lepers, not hesitating to share their meal and to serve them, while calling them his "Christian brothers."[144]

But it was not sufficient to just give the example personally. It was even more necessary to define the norms pertaining to life in community and for the future. Thus does the "foundational document," just like the official rule of the order promulgated in 1223, put the accent both on the refusal of settling down in all its forms and on the precariousness which had to reign in their establishments: "Let the brothers beware, wherever they are, in the hermitages or in other places, of appropriating to themselves any place and of defending it against anyone."[145] The giving up of ownership was, however, only one aspect—even if the polemics that developed around this within the Franciscan order have illustrated it more than the others—of a search for insecurity, which was translated in Francis as much by a great mobility as by the concern to abandon oneself to Providence. It is in this spirit, for example, that he forbade his companions from soaking the vegetables the night before that were going to be eaten the next day or to gather more alms—under the circumstances, offerings of food—than was necessary to survive that same day. These scruples can appear excessive to modern minds, familiar with abundance and with the wasting of food. They illustrate the constant concern of the Poor Man of Assisi to renounce all prudence or foresightedness in order to count only on God. The kind of evangelical life that he was recommending was not one of abstract principles: Francis did not prepare a case against ownership, as Proudhon did in the nineteenth century. He preferred to set forth unequivocal gestures intended to strike the mind of his companions and disciples. This explains why one day he refused a cell that was prepared for him because a brother had described it as "your cell" and also why he asked to die naked, laid out on the ground, after being stripped of his clothes.[146]

THE RENUNCIATION OF POWER

To live in community, without money or goods, was a foolish undertaking. Cardinal John of Saint Paul and Pope Innocent III had advised Francis, at the time of his coming to Rome in 1209, that his ideal was too demanding. They had probably thought in the depths of their hearts that once the early fervor had passed away, the friars would grow tired of such an austere life, especially the permanent precariousness which could become traumatizing. In fact, such criticism of the Franciscan notion of poverty was to appear again later in ecclesiastical circles. Would not the absence of even minimal fixed revenues lead these religious of a new sort, paradoxically, to be constantly preoccupied with temporal things, like food and lodging, instead of consecrating themselves to their spiritual concerns or pastoral tasks? Thus their desire to practice a fully evangelical way of life—an aim that was in essence praiseworthy might end up imposing on them an even more "carnal" way of life than that of laity out in the world . . .

This risk was not imaginary, as the history of the Franciscan order demonstrated afterward. But Francis had provided an antidote which was going to render the demands of a life in "minority" manageable. The compensation for poverty, the assurance against the anxieties of daily life and the uncertainties of the morrow, was life in fraternity. The Friars Minor did not have to feel abandoned or left to their own devices, for they could rely totally on one other. The fraternal and communitarian aspect of the Franciscan movement fits effectively into a logic of disappropriation. To live in "minority" was to refuse wealth and power, which implied being subject to all and to giving up every form of violence, even legitimate violence, in human relationships. But the more one is *minor* (small, humble), the more one is a brother of others and, first of all, of those with whom one lives. The ideal is thus not to seek to be sufficient unto oneself but to share what one receives and to accept that one needs others in the smallest details of daily life. The absolute poverty desired by Francis set up a new type of relationship—to goods, but also between persons, founded on genuine solidarity. The care of the other was indeed fundamental in the early community, as attested by the fact that the "foundational document" of 1221 suspends the most severe prohibitions with respect to sick brothers or those in difficulty. If a brother found himself in a situation of distress, he could, in order to get out of it, receive and use money and even, in the case of need, travel on a horse, all things absolutely prohibited by the rule, for "necessity knows no law."[147]

The fraternity constituted, moreover, an indispensable foundation for the friars from an economic point of view. It was really necessary to eat, cook for oneself, wash the dishes and the clothes. To assure these functions while at the same time allowing the community to devote itself to prayer and preaching, Francis and his companions distinguished three kinds of friars: preachers, contemplators (that is, those who pray), and workers.[148] This threefold division is reminiscent of the division that governed feudal society and whose importance Georges Duby and Jacques Le Goff have brought to light at the level of mentalities and collective imagination.[149] According to this normative schema, society was organized on the basis of three hierarchical "orders": clerics, fighters or lords, and the mass of workers (*laboratores*), rural as well as urban, who assured the productive functions and survival of the social body in the alimentary realm. Had Francis been influenced by this ideology of the three functions? Only superficially: for within the three categories of friars enumerated in the rule of 1221, there was no hierarchical distinction among the Minors—not more than between clerics and lay brothers—and, especially, the same people had to devote themselves in their turn to preaching, prayer, and manual work according to the needs of the community. In practice, only the friars authorized by their minister had the right to preach by words, but the text of 1221 adds immediately after: "Let all the brothers, however, preach by their actions and let each minister or preacher not appropriate to himself the office of preaching," that is, not arrogate it to himself as if it belonged to him and could never be taken away.[150] We find confirmation of this in the *Rule for Hermitages*, composed by Francis around 1223, which provides that those who want to live for some time a solitary experience of religious life will go off "into the desert," in little groups of three or four. Some, whom the text calls "the mothers," will lead "the life of Martha"— that is, take care of the material tasks and relations with the exterior world—while the others, "the sons," will lead "the life of Mary" (the sister of Lazarus, not the mother of Christ) by giving themselves to prayer and contemplation. But it is assumed that, after a period of time, "the sons will take on the office of the mothers in their turn."[151] We sense through these directives that Francis and his companions wanted above all else to avoid falling back into the distinction, prevalent in the religious orders of their day, between the choir monks, who gave themselves to spiritual and liturgical tasks, and the lay brothers, who were responsible for material needs. In their eyes, on the contrary, all those who had entered into the order had to live there on an equal footing and to make the good functioning of the community possible by their activity.

The Franciscan fraternity also distinguished itself from all forms of religious life at the time in the exercise of authority. The "foundational document" of 1221 is clear about this: it is designed to make of the community of brothers a society without power and thus without violence, a place where hierarchical relations of an authoritarian type would have no reason to exist. That does not mean at all, as is sometimes suggested, that Francis was devoid of organizational gifts or that he sought to create informal groups, as one would say today. On the contrary, we have seen that from the outset he had promoted certain structures, like the general chapter, and that he took the initiative to create provinces, directed by ministers, from 1217 forward. But the very title of "minister," which the Poverello gave to these authorities, is revealing: "minister" signifies "servant," and the function of the minister was conceived, before all else, as a service rendered to others, exercised within the context of the fraternity and under its control. We cannot fail to be struck by the measures which, in the rule of 1221, were meant to impede every deviation toward the individual exercise of power on the part of superiors and in particular by the passage that specifies, "Let no one be called prior but let all universally be called Friars

Minor and let them wash each other's feet."[152] In addition, it is specified that all the functions that implied the use of authority will be temporary and that, when those who have been charged with it will have done their duty, they will then return to the ranks and take their place once again alongside the others. All is done to avoid that a distinction be introduced which, before long, will create a gap between a hierarchy and a base, between leaders and subjects. A brother even had the right to refuse to carry out an order given by a superior if he judged the order unjust or contrary to the rule, and even to denounce the superior publicly if he persisted in his transgression: "And if they saw one of them [the ministers] walking carnally and not spiritually with respect to the righteousness of our life, if he will not have amended himself after the third admonition, let them denounce him to the minister and servant of the whole fraternity at the time of the Pentecost chapter, notwithstanding any obstacle."[153] As we have seen, nothing could be more different from feudal society, where noble power was exercised over dependents in an often arbitrary manner—but also from the monastic conception of authority by an abbot elected for life whom the monks were bound to obey as to God himself. Among the Friars Minor, born in the Italian communes where aspirations to a certain democratic life were beginning to appear, all had the same rights and the same duties; for the foundation of their unity was not the cenobitic or conventual life but a freely chosen poverty and a mutual charity. From their side, the superiors, at whatever level they are found, had to, before all else, behave toward their companions as mothers toward their sons, on the model of "Jesus our mother": a theme which some spiritual writers of the twelfth century had emphasized and which Francis largely took over.[154] But we should not be deceived! In the mind of the Poor Man of Assisi, the maternal relationship implies not only kindness and affection but also a vigilant attention on the part of authorities to the needs as well as the deviations of those who had been entrusted to them.

The counterpart of this extraordinary freedom of the friars in their relationships consisted in obedience. If the community could be allowed to exclude every relationship of force within it, it is because its cohesion rested on the willingness of a perfect obedience. On this point, Francis demonstrated a real stubbornness, for it was a fundamental necessity for the survival of his work and an essential dimension of "minority." To live under obedience was indeed to listen to the other—and first of all to the superior, minister, or guardian—rather than to act on one's own initiative and through one's own means. That implied, on the part of all, an attitude of mutual kindness which Francis called "the obedience of charity": "Through charity of spirit, let them serve one another willingly and obey each other mutually."[155] Let us note in passing that this attitude

really defined the obedience of the Poor Man of Assisi himself vis-à-vis the ecclesiastical hierarchy and the clergy, whom he always refrained from lecturing,
"even if sometimes the subject sees better and more useful things to his soul
than those ordered him by his superior."[156]

Here again, we would risk giving an incomplete picture of the early Franciscan fraternity if we restricted ourselves to a few abstract principles. It was first of
all an environment of life, even if, at the time of their voyages, it was limited to
one companion, the *socius*, because the friars were not authorized to journey
alone. One coexisted in sincerity, "each one manifesting his need to the other,
so that the other might find what was necessary for him and administer it to
him. And let each one cherish and nourish his brother, as a mother cherishes
and nourishes her son in all that God will give him grace to do."[157] Has a
brother gotten up during the night crying out that he is dying of hunger? Francis hurries to prepare him a meal in which everyone participates in order to
ensure that the famished brother might not be ashamed because of his hunger,
and in order to respect the diversity of characters and temperaments: "Let not
the one who does not eat judge the one who does eat!"[158]

Contemporary observers have been struck by the harmony that character-
ized the first years of the fraternity, as witnessed by the enthusiastic remark of
Jacques de Vitry when he had encountered the Minors for the first time in 1216:
"Their manner of living is like that of the early Church of which it is written:
'The community of believers were of one heart and one mind.'"[159]

But the demonstrations of unanimity, as touching as they might have been,
did not suffice to resolve all the problems that coexistence in a single community of clerics and unlettered laymen, rich and poor, young and old, came to
pose. The first of these distinctions was probably the most difficult to overcome,
for it did not have a cure. Francis, convinced that each one ought to remain in
the state in which he had heard the call of God, was firmly opposed to the taking up of studies by the friars who did not know how to read or who did not
know Latin. He showed himself equally rigid on the question of the equality of
clerics and laity within the order, which constituted one of the most original
characteristics of his foundation. The only difference that he allowed among
them was on the level of the liturgy. The clerics, who knew Latin, recited the
office and said the prayers for the living and the dead "according to the custom
of clerics"; the laymen contented themselves to reciting a certain number of
Our Fathers, as well as the Creed at each of the canonical hours, as was the
norm in lay confraternities.[160] But that did not involve any segregation or distinction of a hierarchical type. Moreover, the lay brothers who knew how to

read—which was the case with Francis—could have a breviary like the friar-clerics, thus privileging a cultural criterion over a canonical distinction.

On the level of daily life, the most difficult divisions to overcome were probably those that had to do with social birth and wealth. Although the Franciscan texts of the thirteenth century are rather discreet on this subject, they sometimes allowed some interesting remarks to filter through, like this anecdote reported both by Thomas of Celano and in the *Assisi Compilation*. Francis was making his way, sick, on a donkey next to a brother probably Leonard, who was from an aristocratic family of Assisi:

> The brother, tired from his journey, began to complain and to say to himself: "His family could not be compared to mine and now he is the one who sits in a saddle and I am the one who am walking, dead tired, prodding the beast." Thus was he in his thoughts when all of a sudden the saint got off his donkey and said to him: "Brother, it is neither just nor fitting that I ride mounted whereas you go on foot, for in the world you were more noble and wealthy than I."[161]

As this exemplary account shows, Francis was not unaware of the differences and did not contest the foundation of social distinctions, as his attitude with respect to Brother Leonard shows. But to the rich as well as to the humble who had joined him, he was proposing a unique model: that of Christ, who "came from the celestial thrones into the womb of the Virgin," as Francis put it in an arresting phrase.[162] The logic of the imitation of Christ had to permit the Friars Minor to overcome the tensions arising from their social differences. "Let all the brothers strive to follow the humility and poverty of Our Lord Jesus Christ!"[163] In practice, humility did not always come quite so easily. And the time when Francis was the only superior to whom all the friars were tied by a personal bond of obedience had already passed by the years 1221–1223. By this time, local superiors—ministers provincial, custodes, guardians at the level of each community—were in place, and their role was only to be strengthened; for, at first simple personal representatives of Francis in the faraway regions, they now became—as the "foundational document of 1221" attests—pastors and spiritual authorities of the souls of their brothers, with juridical power over them. But the massive influx of new recruits had permitted entry into the order some unstable or unmotivated individuals, who were having difficulty with the demanding life of the Minors and who were contesting, sometimes violently, the authority of their superiors. This is attested to in the famous *Letter to a Minister* which Francis had sent, probably in 1221, to one of the ministers who found

himself confronted by difficulties within a community which had been entrusted to him. He shared his anxieties with Francis. The text is so extraordinary that it deserves to be extensively cited:

> To Brother X, . . . minister: may the Lord bless you! Concerning the state of
> your soul, I say to you, as I can, that whatever impedes you from loving the
> Lord God and whoever would be for you an impediment, friars or others,
> even if they beat you up: you must consider all these things as a grace. . . .
> And love those who do these things to you and do not desire anything other
> than that which the Lord will give you. And love them in this and do not
> even desire that they be better Christians. And this may be better for you
> than the hermitage! And I want to know in this whether you love the Lord
> and me, his servant and yours: if you act in such a way that there is no brother
> in the world who may have sinned as much as he will be able to sin and who,
> after having seen your eyes, will never go away without your mercy, if he asks
> for mercy.[164]

Evidently, the unknown superior in question here was having a hard time of
it and was on the verge of despair when he solicited Francis' help. Francis, first
having comforted him in the terms which appear in the letter, told him that he
was going to submit, at the next general chapter of Pentecost (we do not know
which year), a new normative text laying out the path to follow in cases such as
this. He formulates it like this:

> If one of the brothers, at the instigation of the enemy [the Devil], has sinned
> mortally, let him be bound by obedience to have recourse to his guardian.
> And let none of the brothers who would know that he has sinned, shame him
> or criticize him, but let them have great mercy toward him and let them keep
> the sin of their brother hidden. . . . Likewise, let them be bound by obedi-
> ence to send him to his custos with his companion. And let the custos come
> to help him with mercy, as he himself would want someone to come to his
> aid if he were in a similar situation.[165]

In fact, this proposed statute, so full of humanity, must have come up against
some resistance, for it was not adopted. Be that as it may, the *Letter to a Minister* shows that obedience—such as Francis had conceived and defined it—now
constituted too weak a bond to assure the good functioning of the fraternity;
and it also shows that superiors were deprived of the means to force those who
were refusing to comply. There was no choice but to introduce into the rule
disciplinary and even repressive measures. The "foundational document" of
1221, which contains an article anticipating the immediate and definitive expul-

sion of brothers from the order who committed the sin of fornication (in other words, sexual relations) testifies to this. Another addition prohibited them from frequenting the company of women.[166] These sanctions or precautions could, moreover, find justification in certain passages of the Gospels. Had not Christ said: "If your hand or your foot is the cause of your scandal, cut them off and throw them far away from you; better to enter the Kingdom of God with one limb or lame than to be thrown with both hands or feet into the eternal fire" (Matt 18:8)?

THE SALVATION OF "INFIDELS"

The rules of 1221 and 1223 both present two of the measures relative to "those who go among the Saracens and other nonbelievers." This constitutes an absolute novelty. For the first time in the Middle Ages, the conversion of non-Christians figures among the objectives assigned to a religious order; and the relationship with Islam is especially envisioned in a perspective that is not one of confrontation. Certainly, by the beginning of the thirteenth century the propagation of the Christian faith among pagans—specifically, peoples living on the banks of the Baltic—had begun to be mentioned in certain papal texts. But it is with the founders of the mendicant orders, Dominic and especially Francis, that concern for the evangelization of "the infidels" became an essential object within Western Christianity, in a perspective that we can characterize as missionary before its time.

In the Franciscan "foundational document" of 1221, chapter 16 is exceptional in this regard: the text begins by citing the passage of the Gospel in which Christ declares to his disciples: "I am sending you as lambs in the midst of wolves; be, therefore, patient as serpents and simple as doves" (Matt 10:16).[167] Obviously, Francis wanted to put his brothers on guard against a naïve or over-enthusiastic approach to the mission. The simple fact of going among the Muslims to announce the Gospel could only invite hostile reactions, because with the exception of merchants, Christians who were willingly going into these countries were already suspected at best of religious proselytizing, and at worst of being equivalent to Crusaders: thus aggressors and enemies. Fortified by his own recent personal experience, Francis reminds the brothers that leaving on mission into Islamic lands assumed on their parts the conscious and willing acceptance of the risk of losing their lives for Christ, like the Apostles. To these "missionaries"— the word is not used because his call to conversion concerned Christians as well as pagans—Francis proposed two kinds of possible behavior, according to the circumstances and the context:

The brothers who go thus [among the Muslims] can envisage their spiritual role in two ways: either by not making accusations or disputes, but being subject to every human creature for the sake of God and simply confessing that they are Christians; or, if they see that such is the will of God, by proclaiming the word of God so that the pagans believe in Almighty God, Father, Son, and Holy Spirit, creator of all things, his Son, redeemer and savior, [and] they have themselves baptized and become Christians.[168]

This innovative text, which disappeared from the chapter of the rule of 1223 consecrated to mission, represents the final stage of the thought of Francis on the question—after the experience he had had in Egypt in 1219 and the tragic end of the five Friars Minor martyred in Morocco in 1220.[169] He had probably understood that the "indiscreet" seeking of martyrdom, which had pushed these men to attack the beliefs of Islam publicly and head-on, could be an ambiguous approach, for it risked looking like the desire for an individual exploit more appropriate for moving Christians than for drawing unbelievers to the true faith. A contemporary English cleric, Thomas of Chobham, moreover, underlined in the same years the excessive and ineffective aspect of such preaching among the Saracens and severely judged the religious who were going among the pagans "to tempt God rather than to preach."[170] For Francis too, it was better to adopt behavior founded on discretion and humility, without seeking doctrinal confrontations, which could only lead to persecution and violence. For, as Jacques de Vitry noted a few years later:

The Saracens willingly listen to the Friars Minor when they preach about faith in Christ and the teaching of the Gospel. But when the brothers openly oppose Muhammad as a liar and an unbeliever, then these impious people strike them with blows and chase them from their towns; if God was not miraculously protecting them, they would have killed them.[171]

What the friars ought rather seek in their relations with Islam was "to be subject to every creature for the sake of God," though without hiding their identity: that is to say, to be of service to the Muslims in a spirit of divine adoration while at the same time not hesitating to confess before Islam, if need be, that this attitude was mandated to them by their Christian faith. This notion of submission (*subditi*, in Latin) has its roots in the Bible, where it is applied to Abraham and among the prophets of the Old Testament. It had found an echo in the Qur'an, where Abraham, Moses, and Jesus are all described as "servants," in conformity with the etymological meaning of the word "Islam": the verb *aslama* has, in Arab vocabulary, the meaning of "submitting oneself to the law of God" and thus being saved. At the time of his conversation with the sultan and thanks to contacts in the Holy Land, Francis perhaps had been aware that the two antagonistic religions possessed a common substratum and that, from this fact, there existed a possibility of dialogue among them.

The rule of 1221 adds that, under favorable conditions, the brothers could adopt another attitude: to preach one's faith in Almighty God—the divine attribute par excellence for Islam—without hesitating to underscore the differences that separate Islam from Christianity. And it is obviously not by chance that the text evokes the Trinitarian nature of God and the role of Christ as redeemer and savior of the human race, both of which the Muslims deny. It does not, however, include any criticism of Muslims' beliefs, and it ends with an evocation of the Kingdom of God and of the return of Jesus at the end of time, which is not in contradiction with the Qur'an. One can thus summarize the position of Francis by saying that in 1221 he has recommended a dialogue without concession with Islam—for he recalls that Christ "will be ashamed in heaven of those who on earth were ashamed of him"—but a dialogue led in peace and humility, with martyrdom being nothing more, in this perspective, than a passage to the end, a risk that one had to accept but not to seek out.[172]

We can go a little farther and wonder whether the experience which Francis had had of Islam in 1219–1220 had not had other repercussions for him. He had encountered in the East true believers; and he was probably struck by the call to public prayer launched several times a day by the muezzin, as certain passages of two of his letters that are dated after his return from the Holy Land seem to indicate. In his Letter to the Leaders of Peoples, he addresses himself to civil authorities throughout Christianity:

> And among the people who have been entrusted to you, render such honor to the Lord so that, every evening, it might be announced to all the people, by a herald or by another signal, that all must render praise and thanksgiving to the Almighty Lord. And if you do not do this, know that you will have to render an account before the Lord your God, Jesus Christ.[173]

Likewise, in his *First Letter to the Custodes*—that is to say, to the local superiors of his order—he specifies: "And concerning one's praise [of God], proclaim and preach to all people that at every hour and when the bells sound, praise and thanksgiving always be rendered to Almighty God by all the people over the whole earth."[174] In the treasury of the Sacro Convento in Assisi, one can still see today an ivory horn as well as two batons which were reportedly offered to Francis by the sultan of Egypt in 1219. On the silver finish that was added in the thirteenth century onto the Oliphant, we can read the following inscription: "With this bell [!], Saint Francis gathered the people together for preaching and with these batons he imposed silence on them." Even if it was a full century after the events, perhaps this little phrase preserves the memory of the encounter of the Poor Man of Assisi with al-Kamil, who had probably made more of a mark on Francis than we usually think. Moreover, we know that in 1221 Francis, perhaps impressed by the inscriptions celebrating the name of Allah which he had been able to see in the mosques, had wanted to introduce into the rule a measure intending that every writing that contained the name of God be gathered up from the ground and honored, even if it might be the writing of a pagan. As some people were astonished by this and asked him why it was necessary to gather up even these last, he responded: "The reason is that one finds there the letters which make up the most glorious name of the Lord God. All that is good in these writings belongs neither to the pagans nor to anyone but to God alone from whom all good things come."[175] In the end, he did not obtain the agreement of his companions, and his proposal was not acted upon. But he came back to the subject in his *Testament* in 1226—which shows how close this issue was to his heart—where he says concerning God: "His most holy names and written words, I want them gathered up wherever I find them in inappropriate places, and I wish that they be gathered up and put in a proper place."[176] Perhaps it is not too far off the mark to see, in the extraordinary respect shown by the Poor Man of Assisi toward the divine name, the idea that there might exist a kind of supernatural power proper to the divine names of God, which is the basis of the Kabala, where each of the divine names contains within it its own power. In any case, it is in Franciscan milieus where the devotion to the Holy Name of Jesus developed during the last centuries of the Middle Ages. This is probably not a coincidence.

One of the most innovative aspects of the Franciscan utopia is that it puts the propagation of the Gospel in a universalistic perspective. In the eyes of Francis, all men and women, whatever they might be—pagans, unbelievers, and Christians—need to do penance and to turn themselves toward the divine love. Thus the relationship with Islam, such as it is expressed in the rule of 1221, is marked not by a sentiment of superiority or of combativeness but by the certitude that sinful humanity is called to move forward together toward the knowledge of the true face of God. On this point, the message of Francis was scarcely accepted. In the bull *Vineae Domini custodes*, which Pope Honorius III issued on October 7, 1225—while the Poor Man of Assisi was still living—concerning the Franciscans and Dominicans who were going to the Maghreb, it is stated, right from the start, that their principal objective should be the conversion of the infidels and the return of apostates to the Catholic faith. To do this, the pope granted them the right to preach freely and to baptize the

Saracens as well as the power to excommunicate those who had passed over into "heresy"—a term which in this context could only refer to Islam.

Since the rule of 1221 had not been followed for a long time by the Minors, it is not easy to clearly discern whether the negative reactions that it sparked came from within the order or from the papacy. In fact, this prolix collection of exhortations and norms, enriched with numerous long biblical citations, was difficult to apply, and the Poor Man of Assisi had to go back to work to draw up a text of a more statutory character. He devoted himself to this task during the winter of 1222 and spring of 1223, at the hermitage of Fonte Colombo, with Brothers Leo and Bonizo, the latter known for his knowledge of canon law. He then went down to Rome to present his project to Cardinal Hugolino, after which the text was discussed with the ministers, who made numerous modifications to it during the general chapter of June 1223. The final version was probably not the work of Francis, for it was drawn up in excellent Latin—not that of the Poor Man of Assisi!—and includes certain juridical expressions totally foreign to his vocabulary and mentality. Finally, Honorius III promulgated the rule on November 29, 1223, in the bull *Solet annuere*. It was addressed to "Brother Francis and to the other brothers of the order of Friars Minor"—a term which was becoming the name of this new "religio," now officially recognized.[177]

The rule of 1223 offers a much shorter text than that of 1221—twelve chapters instead of twenty-four—stripped of a good part of the biblical references which abounded in the "foundational document"; and its tone especially is much more legislative. Francis remains here the point of reference: it is he who promises obedience and that of his brothers to the pope, while the pope states that the brothers are bound to obey Francis and his successors. Moreover—and this is unique in the rule of a religious order in the Middle Ages—the founder of the Minors interjects himself several times into the rule in the first person singular in order to give injunctions or denounce behavior contrary to the spirit of the Gospel: "I counsel, I warn and I exhort the brothers . . ." (LR 3:10); "I strongly forbid all the brothers . . ." (LR 11:1). On the whole, the text tempers the rigor and the creative innovations of the rule of 1221. Certain prescriptions disappear completely, like the reference to the two manners of comporting oneself among the Saracens, while manual work is presented here no longer as an obligation imposed on all but as a grace received by certain brothers. Other things are added, like the absolute prohibition for the Minors to accept money, except through the intermediary of "spiritual friends" in cases where necessity would have made itself felt. In a general way, the rule of 1223 puts the accent on the hierarchical function of the minister general, the ministers, and custodes who become veritable superiors provided with a canonical authority within the order, as well as an absolute obedience owed to them by the friars. The brothers like-wise are prohibited to enter the convents of women, in conformity with con-temporary legislation, and the different sanctions envisioned by the previous text against friars who became fornicators or heretics are now replaced by the general norms of the Church in this domain. The conditions for the admission of postulants are defined for the first time with precision, and the obligation is also specified for the friars to ask the pope for a cardinal protector, so as to maintain a constant bond between the order and the Roman Church. In sum, however, the rule of 1223 preserves the essence of the message of Francis but without the evangelical radicalism of the "foundational document" of 1221.

TRIALS AND TEMPTATIONS: THE TIME OF DOUBT (1223–1224)

The years 1223 and 1224 were, for Francis, a time of trials. His biographers, beginning with Thomas of Celano in his first *Life*, reveal that he was assailed by pessimism and even by great temptations, without specifying their nature. In fact, the Poor Man of Assisi seems to have experienced a growing malaise, finding himself as he did in an awkward position with respect to the movement which he had started. The problem was not an institutional one; officially he was no longer its leader, since he had given up directing it in 1220 and because, since March 1221, Elias, faithful companion and excellent administrator, was running the daily affairs of the order. But Francis remained the indispensable point of reference, as shown by the place that he occupies in the very text of the rule of 1223 and the role that he had played in its redaction. However, the cli-mate was no longer that of the early years. For numerous friars now, the founder was an unknown quantity whom they had at best perceived from a distance, on the occasion of a general chapter. Moreover, the number and role of clerics trained in the schools and universities, as well as the number of priests, had continued to increase within the order. Francis feared, not without reason, that they might force his foundation to undergo an evolution which, in the end, could threaten his fundamental ideas, especially the spirit of evangelical sim-plicity. This is what one senses in the response, both positive and reserved, that he made, probably at the end of 1223 or in 1224, when Anthony of Padua asked him for permission to give lessons in theology to the brothers of his convent: "To Brother Anthony, my bishop, Brother Francis, greetings. It pleases me that you teach the friars holy theology, provided that in studying, you do not extin-guish the spirit of prayer and devotion, as stated in the rule."[178] Francis was neither unlettered nor an enemy of learning. He knew how to read and write and had acquired a good understanding of the Latin of the biblical and liturgical texts. Several times in his writings, he testifies to an esteem for theologians thanks to whom the word of God could be better understood. But it did not take him long to understand that an excessive infatuation with intellectual work and knowledge was putting his foundation in danger. At a time when books were expensive, precious objects, did not the simple fact of possessing them risk placing the friars in the company of the rich and threaten their close contact with the uninstructed masses? Thus we often find in Francis' words and writings an invitation to keep their distance as much as possible from a culture of book-learning to which so many temptations were tied. Apprehensive that his friars might have books, he declared: "If my brothers had listened to me, no one would have possessed anything other than the habit allowed by the rule with a cord and britches."[179] And to a novice who wanted to have a psalter with him, he sharply answered:

> "When you will have a psalter, you will want a breviary; and when you will have a breviary, you will install yourself in a throne like a great prelate, and you will command your brother: 'Bring me my breviary!'" Carried away by passion, he took some ashes from the hearth, sprinkled them over his head and rubbed them in, all the while repeating: "I'm a breviary, I'm a breviary!"[180]

In the same period, it seems that Francis was also subjected to intense pressure by the provincial ministers and some of his companions to attenuate the rigor of his requirements. We have seen that certain proposals that he had made at the time of the redaction of the rule of 1223 had been rejected by such friars as being too idealistic and impossible to live out. To speak in this way about a slackening or the beginning of decline among the friars, as some hagiographers and chroniclers have done, especially the Franciscans of a "spiritual" tendency at the beginning of the fourteenth century, is surely exaggerated and anachronistic. To incriminate the papacy for its lack of understanding of Francis is no longer an adequate explanation, even if it is certain that Cardinal Hugolino and the Curia were striving to "normalize" the order of Minors so as to make it an effective instrument at the service of the Roman Church. In fact, what really rankled Francis was the feeling that his own creation was starting to slip away from him. Sociologists have often analyzed this phenomenon; and it has merit not just in the realm of religion. Every organization that attains a certain size necessarily undergoes a process of evolution which is translated into a need for institutionalization and is accompanied by internal tensions. New feelings are manifested—the search for identity, the affirmation of an esprit de corps, the desire to see visible successes—and certain deficiencies in the legislative realm that were completely acceptable within the small group at the beginning, where affective relationships prevailed, rapidly become intolerable.

This is what happened to the Friars Minor, whose numbers, in these years, seem to have jumped from three thousand to around five thousand—to be sure, an unverifiable approximation—and who had settled in most of the countries of Western Christianity. This evolution certainly fits into the logic of what Francis had wanted; for since 1217, and especially in 1221, he had sent small groups of friars throughout Europe and even to the East so as to give a universal echo to his message. But he probably had not anticipated the repercussions of this missionary expansion. North of the Alps, the friars could present themselves only with difficulty as wandering apostles, close to those on the margins by their dress and style of life, without being mistaken for heretics or vagabonds. The harsh climate no longer allowed them to simply be content with precarious shelters—to sleep under the stars or in simple branch huts. In these regions, they had to beg their food rather than to try to find work because initially no one knew who they were. People expected them to preach at least as much as to give the witness of a humble and poor life. All these elements involved a rapid evolution in the forms of presence and the conditions of the life of the brothers. In northern Italy as much as in France, Germany, and England, they accepted rather quickly the provision of living spaces (*loca*), and soon chapels or dilapidated churches—modest, certainly, but already different from the simple shelters or shacks in which Francis and his companions had lived during the first years. And even if Jordan of Giano tells us that the Minors whom Francis had sent to Germany in 1221 had not allowed anyone to construct a cloister for them, asserting that they did not even know what the word meant, there is mention, for the first time (in 1225–1226, in an official letter of Brother Elias), of a Franciscan "convent" in Valenciennes. This marks a significant step in the process of the settling down of the movement.

Francis was not fundamentally opposed to this evolution, but he dreaded that it might lead the Minors to distance themselves from poverty. Going to Bologna, he heard someone speaking about a "house" (*domus*) of the brothers and, scandalized by this terminology, which suggested the possibility of an appropriation, he ordered them, including the sick, to immediately abandon the locale where they were living. Even in Assisi, he had a house destroyed which the commune had arranged to be built for the friars at the Portiuncula. Thus did the rule of 1223 include a firm prohibition of ownership, which does not appear at all in the rule of 1221, as if the Poor Man of Assisi wanted to eradicate the process of the friars' settling down in the towns or on their periphery. Moreover, although the rule of 1223 did not expressly forbid the lay friars from preaching, the ministers had a tendency to choose preachers who were going to exhort the faithful from among the clerics who knew Sacred Scripture and were capable of explaining it. Francis was thus witnessing the return in force of the distinction, which he had endeavored to transcend, between, on the one hand, friar-clerics trained in preaching who no longer had the time to work with their hands and who risked letting themselves get overwhelmed by studies and pastoral tasks and, on the other hand, the lay brothers whose "lack of learning" tended to confine them to low-ranking chores or domestic needs.

Finally, the papacy had more and more of a tendency to rely on the Minors to put into action its policy of reform of the Church and the winning back of souls. Beginning in 1222, we see Honorius III relying upon the friars to take disciplinary measures against abuses committed by certain elements of the high clergy of Lyons, whose conduct had aroused numerous protests. In October 1225 the same pope granted to the friars who had left as missionaries for Morocco the right to absolve excommunicates and heretics and allowed them in March 1226 to carry money. Even more serious, several papal bulls, between 1222 and 1227, authorized the Minors to have their own oratories and soon their own churches where they could celebrate Mass and recite the office, even in case of interdict, with a cemetery to bury their dead. Finally, in December 1224, they obtained the privilege— exceptional for the time—to say Mass on a portable altar when they were moving about without having to ask the consent of the bishop. All these measures were designed to remove them from the authority of the local ecclesiastical hierarchy, contrary to the recommendations of Francis. The action of the Friars Minor was no doubt gaining in immediate effectiveness, but, in being given the ability to "go around people" with the support of the Holy See every time that they ran up against resistance to their apostolate, they risked making themselves appear suspicious to the secular clergy, who might consider them the vanguard of the intrusive actions of the papacy in a Church where numerous prelates remained legitimately attached to their ecclesial prerogatives.

In 1223 and 1224 the uneasiness of Francis only increased and seems to have become for him a nagging suffering aggravated by problems of health. In his eyes, his foundation was every day being further transformed into a religious order concerned above all with apostolic effectiveness in the short term, at the risk of giving up certain aspects of their early form of life which were now appearing useless and bothersome. But nothing was more foreign to his mind than this "culture of results," which risked fostering among the friars a sense of self-importance and ambition. The Francis of these difficult years looks like an uncomfortable person, refusing to be confined to the role of the creator of an order marked by success while waiting to remain peacefully among his own. He who had always shown himself sociable and courteous now avoided the company of the brothers and spent long periods in hermitages accompanied by a few companions, like Rufino and Leo, his faithful secretary. He was irritated to see that some within the hierarchy of the order had begun to consider him with a certain condescendence when he reminded them that their real vocation was simply to follow the poor and suffering Christ. The text titled "On Perfect Joy"—whose author and date of composition we do not know but whose authenticity is not contested—shows Francis imagining that he would one day be rejected and disdained by his own. According to this story, arriving one night at the Portiuncula, Francis knocked at the door and urgently asked that someone open it and let him in. After Francis had identified himself, the friar-porter answered: "Go away! You are only a simpleton and an ignoramus; in any case, there are many of us here and so we do not need you."[181] Certain hagiographical texts of the thirteenth century are similar. Thus the *Assisi Compilation* reports a dream in which Francis saw the friars rebel against his authority because they found him too simple and too humble to be a good superior.[182] Even if such accounts somewhat dramatize the contrast, they nonetheless reflect the hidden thoughts of some friars for whom the order could finally move on from its founder. According to the author of *On Perfect Joy*, Francis concluded by saying: "If I keep patience and am not shaken, I tell you that true joy and true virtue and the salvation of the soul consist in this."[183] But he did not always manage to keep this serenity, and he seems to have suffered a great deal from the hypocrisy of some of his companions, who were friendly when with him but criticized him behind his back. As a result of the betrayal, Francis lost his joyfulness and was assailed by doubts. According to Thomas of Celano, one day when he was lying sick on his bed, he vehemently cried out: "Who are these who have ripped my order and my brothers out of my hands? If I live until the general chapter, I will really show them what my will is!"[184]

We do not know the exact nature of the "great temptation" that some of his biographers talk about. Perhaps Francis even thought about taking back power within the order to put it back on the paths that it should not have strayed from, by relying on a trusted group of friars against those ministers who disapproved of his orientations and negotiated underhandedly with the Curia. This is what Mao Zedong did in our own time—*mutatis mutandis*—at the moment of the Cultural Revolution, vis-à-vis a part of the direction and cadres of the Chinese Communist Party, to avoid the transformation of his movement along bourgeois lines, at the risk of having the political system which he had put into place implode and at the price of innumerable victims. But the parallel stops there.

The Poor Man of Assisi, unlike the Great Helmsman, was not animated by any desire for power and had renounced the recourse to violence in all domains: "I do not want to become an executioner who punishes and tortures," he declared when a brother urged him to respond vigorously against the evolution under way.[185] Indeed, he did not consider himself a New Moses come down from the mountain with the Tablets of the Law who could impose his views on his companions. The legislative texts of the fraternity had always been elaborated and discussed collectively, and when he felt as if he was not being followed, Francis softened his demands to take account of the concrete possibilities and limits of his brothers. He who had always prized fraternal charity would have been in contradiction with himself if he had sought to use his personal prestige in order to impose his desires and make his own views prevail. Up to the end, however, he never stopped making his voice heard or, rather, bearing witness: having formally abdicated all position of power on the institutional level, he wished at any rate to give the best example of the evangelical life according to the rule and perfect humility, thus creating within the order, parallel to its official hierarchy, a hierarchy founded on holiness, allowing him to offer to his brothers a model to follow and, later, a memory which they would not be able to betray.

FROM THE STIGMATIZATION TO THE *TESTAMENT* (SEPTEMBER 1224–SEPTEMBER 1226)

It is in this troubled context that Francis' withdrawal into solitude during the summer of 1224 with a few companions, among whom was Brother Leo, is to be situated. We should pause for a moment on his choice of this site. La Verna, or Alverna—a translation drawn from its Latin name (Alverna)—is a wild area in Tuscany, northeast of Arezzo, right in the heart of a mountainous plateau which rises to more than four thousand feet. Not far from there were (and are still today) the abbey and hermitage of Camaldoli, centers of a monastic order, that of the Camaldolese, established in the eleventh century and strongly marked by the eremitical ideal. This uninhabited area belonged at the beginning of the thirteenth century to an admirer of Francis, Count Rolando de Chiusi, who had offered its use to him and may even have been willing to give it to him. However, this tradition is uncertain, since the act that contains this donation, dated 1213 or 1218, was drawn up only in 1274 and mentions no precise territorial limit.

La Verna is not only a solitary and wooded place. We also find there an extraordinary conglomeration of twisted rock formations that look like the witnesses of the last convulsions of the creation of the world and that abound in caverns and natural shelters offering ideal conditions for a small group of hermits. But eremitism comprises—as we often forget since, with the exception of the *Assisi Compilation*, the Franciscan sources of the thirteenth century scarcely mention it—a fundamental dimension of the life of Francis, who, following Jesus, alternated preaching campaigns with times of solitude devoted to meditation and prayer, out in nature, far from every populated area. From the time of his conversion, his life had been marked by frequent sojourns into such isolated places: the Carceri (not far from Assisi, on the slopes of Mount Subasio), Poggiobostone, la Foresta and Fonte Colombo (in the mountains which surrounded the basin of Rieti), the Sacro Speco ("Holy Cave") of Saint-Urban above Narni, the Isola Maggiore in the middle of Lake Trasimeno, Le Celle in the mountains rising above Cortona, Montecasale, and so on. Indeed, in this part of the Apennines, the limestone relief favored the formation of countless grottoes which, in bad weather, served as shelters for shepherds and their flocks but were usually deserted. Well before Francis and his companions journeyed there, some of these had welcomed hermits, alone or in small groups, who had, with their own hands, widened these natural crevices in order to make them habitable, creating little sanctuaries, often dedicated to Saint Michael the Archangel, which attracted the surrounding populace. In several places, beginning with the Carceri and Monteluco, near Spoleto, the brothers took over this preexisting eremitical tradition, and a certain number of solitaries joined them, which forced Francis sometimes to take measures to lighten the excessive rigor of their ascetic practices, incompatible with the form of life of the Minors.

Francis went to La Verna to observe there, in solitude, the Lent of Saint Michael, a time devoted to fasting and prayer from the feast of the Assumption (August 15) to that of the Archangel (September 29). This ascetic practice has left no trace in the rule of the Friars Minor, but Francis, like many Christians of his day, had a great devotion to Saint Michael, about whom one day he declared that "everyone ought to offer to God praise or a special sacrifice in honor of so great a prince," whose principal role was to lead the souls of the dead into paradise.[186] The hermitage of La Verna, where Francis dwelled with a few companions in August and September 1224, had been conceived and set up for long sojourns; and the conditions in which they lived reveal at least some organization. The texts from the period which refer to the episode mention a hut where the brothers ate together, a cell where Francis prayed, and an altar on which he opened three times a small book containing the text of the Gospels. Moreover, he had with him something to write with, since he drafted the *Praises of God*, which he gave to Brother Leo with a blessing written in his own hand. It is during this period that the Poor Man of Assisi received in his body the stigmata—

that is, the five wounds of Christ: two on his hands, two on his feet, and the wound on his right side. According to Franciscan tradition, the event occurred on September 14, 1224, the feast of the Exaltation of the Holy Cross, but this precise dating comes at a later time. Indeed, the earliest sources—Brother Elias in his *Encyclical Letter* of 1226 and Thomas of Celano in his *First Life of Saint Francis* (1229)—kept to more vague indications: "a little time before his death" in the former, "two years before his death" in the latter—which suggests that the coincidence with the liturgical feast of the Holy Cross was the fruit of a later theological elaboration. Concerning the place of the miracle, Thomas of Celano is categorical and, like Brother Leo, who was the only witness to it and does not contradict him on this point, there is no reason to doubt the traditional account.

What exactly happened on La Verna on an undetermined day in September 1224? It is difficult to say with any precision, for Francis did not mention it in his writings, and he forbade from speaking about it those rare persons who, while caring for him during the two years that followed, came to observe or touch the traces of the wounds. It is thus only after his death and before he was buried that a certain number of witnesses, in particular the friars, were able to actually see them on his flesh. As "vicar" of the founder who had just died, Brother Elias immediately sent to the whole order an *Encyclical Letter* announcing the great news, but he limited himself to merely describing the stigmata and affirming their miraculous character, without giving any indications of the circumstances in which these wounds, which rendered the Poor Man of Assisi akin to the Christ of the Descent of the Cross, could have been produced.[187] Beginning in 1229, with the first *Life of Francis* by Thomas of Celano, a detailed account was available, which was later going to serve as a framework for most of the other hagiographers. According to Thomas, Francis saw in the sky a man with six wings (two gathered above the head, two extended out as if for flight and two covering the bottom of the body), which had the appearance of a seraph as described in certain Old Testament passages, but suspended from a cross. Francis fell to the ground filled with joy, but he did not really understand what meaning this vision might have. He then rose and reflected. It is then that the stigmata began to appear on his own body.[188] According to the *Assisi Compilation*, written after 1250, Francis, having arrived at La Verna, was praying for God to let him know his will when he saw birds of every kind come and perch on his little cell, each singing in its turn, which he greatly admired and which consoled him. And as he was wondering about the meaning of this miracle, he was answered interiorly that God would give him many consolations in this place. After which: "Among other graces, hidden or manifest, which the Lord

sent to him is the vision of the Seraph which filled his soul with consolation
and brought him extremely close to God for the rest of his life."[189] We will return later to the stigmatization of Francis and try to shed a little light on this
extremely delicate and complex matter. But it is fitting here to place this episode in the context of his spiritual journey. Indeed, from the beginning of his
conversion, he had not ceased praying before crucifixes—especially the one at
San Damiano—and to meditate on the mystery of the Passion of Christ. He often wept while invoking the torments that the Savior had endured on the cross
out of love for the human race. It thus seems possible that he might have understood, once confronted with this strange supernatural apparition, that he
could be united to Christ Crucified through his own personal passion: that, in
the perspective of the life he had been living for several years, his suffering and
disappointments had taken on a meaning which in his eyes they previously had
not had. If we accept this interpretation, we understand better that the first reaction of Francis had been to put down in writing a prayer in Latin, the *Praises
of God,* where he enumerates with emotion and thankfulness all the attributes
of God, the "All Powerful" as well as "Merciful Savior," and whose text, accompanied with a personal blessing, he gave to Brother Leo.[190] Having kept the
small piece of parchment on his person as an amulet for several decades, Leo
gave it as a gift in 1258 to the abbess who had succeeded Saint Clare as head of
the convent of the Poor Ladies of Assisi. It then later passed to the basilica of
Saint Francis, which has kept this autograph of Francis, illustrated with a mysterious design and rendered authentic by the sign of the Tau, which he added
with his own hand. In this short message, the Poor Man of Assisi, without making the least allusion to what he just lived through, limits himself to reproducing
a passage from the Book of Numbers (Num 6:24–26). But the choice of this text
from the Old Testament is not without significance, since it evokes the manifestation of God to a person: "May the Lord bless you and keep you! May he show
his face to you and show mercy to you. May he turn his face toward you and give
you peace!"[191] Destined for Leo, this formula probably gives us an echo of the
spiritual experience that Francis had just lived through and which had transformed him. The hagiographical sources indeed agree in stressing that the revelation which he had had of the infinite grandeur of God, as well as the
assurances that he had received about his own salvation and the destiny of the
Friars Minor, allowed him to find inner peace once again, in spite of the ongoing tribulations inflicted on him by demons who, according to Thomas of Celano, "sent him stronger and stronger temptations to the extent that his merits
grew . . . while they struggled to lead him to mediocrity."[192] Everything seems
to have happened as if the reception of the stigmata had constituted for Francis

the culmination of his giving up control over the future of his order. That did not impede him from reaffirming up to his death with a steely serenity the fundamental points of the Gospel life whose observance appeared essential to him. But he did it finally without animosity toward those who did not share his views, for he understood that his suffering and tribulations were the price to pay for joining himself to Christ in his kingdom of glory: he who had been abandoned by the Apostles in Gethsemane, denied by some of them, and crucified.

During the two years before his death, Francis seems to have wanted to reconnect with the beginnings of his spiritual adventure and to start again to serve the Lord and other people as he had done after his conversion. In spite of the numerous illnesses that he was burdened with, which continued to get even worse, he did not remain passive but continued to witness to a poor and humble life, founded on an intense personal relationship with God in prayer and meditation. Between the end of 1224 and February 1225, mounted on a donkey, he made a preaching tour in Umbria and in the Marches. But in springtime the ophthalmia, from which he had suffered cruelly since his return from Egypt, worsened; and he accepted to stay some time at San Damiano, where Clare and her sisters took care of him. It is at this time that he began the redaction of the *Canticle of Brother Sun* or *Canticle of the Creatures*—the title varies according to the manuscripts which have come down to us—which he was to finish only a few days before his death. Then, on the insistence of Brother Elias, he agreed to submit himself to medical treatment, which only made things worse. At the hermitage of Fonte Colombo, a doctor cauterized his temples with a branding iron, which only made him suffer more and brought him no comfort. A few months later, at San Fabiano near Rieti, he had his ears punctured without any result. In April 1226 he was led to Siena in order to consult some famous doctors, but he was seized by all kinds of illnesses and vomited so much blood that it was thought he was going to die. It was then that he had his first testament written down, brief and moving; there, having blessed the brothers, he declared:

> Since, because of my weakness and the pains from my illness I am not able to speak, I am briefly making known my will in these three words; that is, as a sign and a remembrance of my blessings, let them mutually love one another, let them love and always observe our lady, holy poverty, and let them show themselves always faithful and subject to the prelates and all the clerics of holy mother the Church.[193]

However, he survived this crisis and was brought back to the hermitage of Le Celle, near Cortona, where he rested for some time and drew up his actual *Testament*, in May or June 1226.

This text is one of the most famous and most important among the writings of Francis, and even though he strictly forbade the addition of any glosses to it, few other writings have been as commented on and discussed over the centuries within the order of Friars Minor and the Church. The word "testament" appears there only one time, but its author defined its meaning and significance in three expressions: remembrance (*recordatio*), admonition, and exhortation.[194] A few years later, Gregory IX spoke about it as a "commandment (*mandatum*) which is called testament"—the characterization that highlights the document's significance and the stakes in the debate about it immediately after the death of the Poor Man of Assisi. Indeed, the *Testament* is especially aimed at the internal orientations of the order of Minors and denounces a certain number of deviations which could threaten the essential intuitions upon which it had been founded. Francis, who had overcome the temptations of the preceding years, wants to give witness that he believes, both for himself and for his brothers, that full fidelity to their original vocation within the institutional framework defined by the rule is possible. In the first part, he writes of himself as if he had never done this and retraces his spiritual steps since his "turnaround" and conversion to the Gospel. This was not a matter of giving himself over to a narcissistic exercise of "ego-history," or of giving free rein to a nostalgic emotionalism by evoking the first years of his fraternity. Rather, it was a last attempt to leave his mark on the order of Friars Minor by bequeathing, on the eve of his death, a testimony on the meaning of its vocation and a "how-to" of the rule. Aware that after his death discordant commentaries might appear regarding the real intention that was at the heart of the rule, he preferred to give it its only authorized commentary—his own—which the friars henceforth had always to keep in mind so as to refer themselves to it for all decisions. This demand is directly in line with the culture of exemplarity that Francis had practiced since he had given up the direction of the order, in order to attempt to preserve the ideal of this "minority" from all deviations by underscoring the exemplary and normative character of his own life. This claim, which can at first appear overblown, is justified by his charisma: since his conversion, he recalls, he has acted under the divine impulse, and the form of life which he created and diffused among the friars had been inspired in him by God, for all comes from him and constitutes a gift on his part ("the Lord gave me, Brother Francis, to do penance"; "after which the Lord gave me some brothers, no one showed me what I ought to do but the Most High revealed to me that I ought to live according to the Holy Gospel").[195] This is what allowed him to give himself as an example, as Saint Paul had done with certain churches that he had founded, without, for all that, falling into boastfulness.

Francis' mention of his conversion and of the fraternity of the first years, moreover, recalls the desire that he expressed in the last years of his life to return to the humility of the early days—to serve lepers, to work with his hands, and to rely on alms only in cases of necessity, to obey superiors without hesitation or murmuring, to announce peace—not to idealize this past but to try to give back to it a reality that it was in the process of losing. It is striking that Francis does not present poverty as a determining element of his vocation. In fact, the fundamental experience he emphasizes is the encounter with lepers, which had shaken up his life by getting him to enter the world of the excluded. These certainly included the indigent; but in letting it be understood that neither the desire to become poor nor the refusal of ownership constituted the decisive factors of his vocation, he was reminding his brothers that at the center of the project of the Minors is the desire to follow the footprints of Christ and to fully embrace the logic of the Cross, which leads, here and now, to a reversal of values.

Francis, however, does not make of the origins an absolute. He is aware of the intervening changes in the life of the Friars Minor, who have now become a religious order, while at the same time recalling that their churches and the places where they were residing had to remain in conformity with poverty (verse 24). In the second part, he admonishes his brothers by asking them not to betray the primitive ideal whose essential elements he is recalling: fidelity to the Roman Church because it perpetuates the reality of the Incarnation through the religious buildings, sacred vessels, and especially the Eucharist, and thus renders visible the presence of God among men and women; and submission to priests, whose very purpose is to consecrate the body of Christ and whom it is necessary to respect, whatever might be their unworthiness and weaknesses. This reminder of obedience due to the Church at all levels is the occasion for Francis to urge the brothers not to abuse their growing popularity and not to absent themselves from the authority of bishops or pastors by seeking to obtain privileges and exemptions from the Holy See, as certain friars had already begun to do. The tone of the text, tense and impassioned, becomes violent in verses 31, 32, and 33, where we find a detailed and unexpected description—let's be frank—of the repressive process to implement toward those friars who "do not wish to say the office according to the rule or who want to modify it in another way or who would not be catholic."[196] The formulation is rather vague, but it certainly alludes to deviations which were happening before Francis' eyes and which other sources mention: friars preferring the ease of the hermitage to the apostolate or refusing to confess their sins, wanderers removing themselves from community discipline, heretical infiltrations, and the like.

This danger was not at all imaginary. In 1224, for example, at Colle Val d'Elsa, a little town in Tuscany located halfway between Florence and Siena, a veritable tempest had been unleashed by the preaching of a Friar Minor named Paul, who had just given up his vocation and been excommunicated as an apostate and heretic by the local archpriest. Furious about the judgment, which they believed to be unjust, the mayor and numerous inhabitants of the town supported the religious and invited him to preach in the palace of the commune. At the conclusion of this sermon—the exact content of which we unfortunately do not know, but which must have consisted of attacks on the secular clergy and its wealth and power—he and his supporters were grabbed by the crowd; a cleric was severely injured.[197] This friar Paul had probably given up the habit of the Minors after the promulgation of the rule of 1223 whose content, it seems, might have disappointed the proponents of a radical evangelicalism within the order; and he had engaged, in the name of absolute poverty, in a struggle against the local ecclesiastical hierarchy. This earned him the support of the municipal authorities of the little Tuscan town.

Against such wayward friars, Francis issues a veritable penal code, which is striking in its severity. Indeed, it asks that they be denounced and led away to the custos of their region, who will hold them as prisoners under his watch before sending them on to the minister provincial, who will in turn hand them over to the Cardinal of Ostia—that is, to Hugolino, who will impose on them the sanctions envisioned in this case by the Church. Such harshness surprises because although in previous texts, like the "foundational document" of 1221 and especially the *Letter to a Minister*, which must be dated around 1221, grave faults committed by friars, like fornication, were denounced with severity, but the envisioned sanction—which could be as severe as expulsion from the fraternity in the case of recidivism—was left to the discretion of the local superiors, who were urged to demonstrate patience and mercy.

By 1226 Francis seemed disposed to abandon the loving tone. The number of these deviating or disobedient brothers must have been increasing, and their behavior probably risked jeopardizing the future of his order. But the procedure established for such difficult brothers, completely new for religious of the time, also constituted a way for Francis to urge his brothers to offload onto the Roman Church the disciplinary dimension which the life of every human group of a certain size includes. By underlining the role of the papacy as authoritative point of reference and as guarantor of the respect of the laws, he urged the Minors to accept among themselves a hierarchy founded on the holiness of their life. This division of roles can seem foreign to the modern mind, but we should not forget that it was familiar to the Christians of the Middle Ages, for whom the Church had two faces tied to the two different aspects of its presence in the world: on the one hand, emperor and king, charged with establishing order and peace in Christian society, and, on the other hand, pope and bishops, who had responsibilities of a spiritual and pastoral order with respect to the faithful. At the time and in the area where Francis was living, the Holy Roman Emperor only occasionally played the role which had been his at the time of Charlemagne or the Ottonian sovereigns; the papacy had largely substituted itself for him in the exercise of temporal power. It is thus not surprising, in this context, that Francis might have seen in the Church, above all, a structure of power and a coercive force to which the friars should not hesitate to run in times of difficulties and troubles.

In the last paragraphs of his *Testament,* Francis emphasizes that this text must not be considered in any case like another rule but that it simply allows the friars to observe the rule of the order "in a more catholic way" (*melius catholice*). The expression is difficult to translate because the translation "in a more catholic way"—as it is sometimes rendered—does not take into account his thought, to the extent that this word has taken on today a confessional connotation which it could obviously not have had in the thirteenth century. In fact, by this phrase the Poor Man of Assisi urges his brothers to live in the most total fidelity to Christ and to the Church that represents him in this world. Moreover, he absolutely forbids the glossing of this text: first of all by the hierarchy of the order which might believe itself authorized to interpret it; but especially by the friar-clerics, those intellectuals who, according to the felicitous phrase of Grado Merlo, were able to "modify the genetic code of Franciscanism through their commentaries."[198] He asks all to observe the rule and the *Testament* "simply and without gloss" and to put it into practice until the end of time.[199] The text ends with a final blessing of the Father, Son, and Holy Spirit which Francis transmits to all his brothers—and which sounds like a final farewell.

Part II

Death and Transfiguration
of Francis
1226–1253

3

BECOMING SAINT FRANCIS

1226–1230

At the end of June 1226, Francis asked to go back to the Portiuncula, the cradle of the fraternity, which ought to, in his eyes, remain a place for the Gospel life and an example for the whole order. But he was so weakened and the heat was so terrible in the middle of the summer that he was taken to Bagnara, a cooler place situated in the middle of the mountains, near Nocera Umbria. At the end of August, his condition worsened even further and he had to be brought back to Assisi, escorted by knights sent by the commune fearful above all that his body would fall into the hands of the people of Perugia or another town if he happened to die on the way. These fears were not without foundation, for the same year as Francis' death, the inhabitants of Bettona, a little village near Assisi, seized the relics of Saint Crispolto, a legendary martyr who had become their patron saint and in honor of whom they had built a lovely church, to which his remains had been transferred. By a terrible irony of sorts, the founder of the Minors, who had during his lifetime refused to be venerated as a saint and who had believed that nothing had been definitively achieved before death, was in the process of becoming a living relic and was henceforth going to be treated as such!

THE DEATH OF A MAN, THE BIRTH OF A SAINT

The Poverello remained for a short time in the palace of Bishop Guido II, where he added a verse to his *Canticle*, inviting the prelate and the podestà, who had been engaged in a test of wills, to reconcile; they did not wait long to do so. As the *Assisi Compilation* would have it, Francis then asked two brothers to sing out in his presence the "Praises of the Lord," that is, the *Canticle of the Creatures*, which they did throughout the night for him and those who were keeping vigil around the palace. But Elias asked them to put an end to this, saying that those who heard this singing could be scandalized by it and think to themselves: how is it that he can show such joy when he is so close to death? Should he not rather be thinking about his death?[1] Francis would not let himself be swayed by this argument, and up to the end he would not stop singing the praises of God or having them sung. Obviously, his entourage was fearful that his lyrical excesses might damage his reputation of holiness, because singing had not yet entered into the classic image of a saint getting ready to leave this world! In the hagiographical texts of the period, the manner of dying was an important element of the process which elevated a person to the rank of servant of God, destined to become the object of a cult after death. A founder of an order in particular ought to leave this world in reflection and prayer, while blessing his spiritual sons who were pouring out abundant tears. This is the image that emerges from the account of Francis' last moments as Thomas of Celano describes them in his first *Life*. Feeling his end approaching, Francis asked to be taken back to the Portiuncula, where he wanted to die and be buried. During his last days spent in the little convent, he added to the *Canticle of the Creatures* a final verse about death:

> Praise be you, my Lord,
> For our sister, bodily death
> From whom no living person can escape
> Woe to those who die in a state of mortal sin,
> Happy those whom it surprises doing your will,
> For the second death can do them no harm.[2]

The "second death" that he was referring to in this last verse is the one that will follow the Last Judgment for those cast out, whereas the elect will be called to eternal life with God. Having blessed the brothers who were around him—Brother Bernard, who was probably the closest to him on the spiritual plane, but also Brother Elias and a few others—he asked for bread and gave a small piece to each one of them, then had the passages from the Gospel of John read out in which Jesus mentioned the imminence of his Passion. Two or three days later, Francis asked that he even be placed on the ground; a little after, dressed in a hair shirt and covered with ashes, he gave up his spirit during the night of October 3 and 4, 1226, at the age of forty-four or forty-five years old.

There is no reason to doubt the account of this edifying end. As he had endeavored to make of his life an exemplum, Francis wanted to dramatize his own death in order to make of it a sacred drama by reliving the final steps of the life of Christ, from the Last Supper to Gethsemane, by leaving his brothers an unforgettable image. The *Assisi Compilation* nonetheless adds an episode which contributes a note of humanity to this beautiful scenario. A few days before his death, Francis was visited by a high-ranking widow, Jacqueline de' Settesoli, who belonged to the Roman family of the Frangipani, for whom Francis had a deep friendship and who had been very important to him. Even as he had been thinking about writing to inform her of his condition, she had, of her own accord, gone to Assisi in order to bring him what he was lacking in order to traverse this last stage: a tunic of ash-colored cloth in which he could be buried, some wax to make candles, and some incense to perfume the place where he was going to surrender his soul. But Francis was not yet dead and Jacqueline also brought him a *mostacciuollo*, a cake of almonds, sugar, and honey, which he loved and which she had let him taste during a previous encounter. He was able to swallow only a single mouthful.[3] The episode adds a picturesque note to Francis' exemplary death; it significantly concludes the account of the life of Francis with a double transgression. First, as a woman, Jacqueline would not have been allowed to enter the Portiuncula, inside the cloister; but he overcame the hesitations of his entourage by giving her the title of "Brother Jacopa": the one whom Franciscan tradition was soon to celebrate as "another Christ" had need of a new Magdalene. Moreover, a saint worthy of the name does not die while eating sugared cakes! This is probably the reason why this incident appears in the hagiographical texts only after 1250, when the reputation of the holiness of the Poverello was solidly established.

Once Francis had given up his spirit, his body was stripped and the witnesses present were finally able to see the stigmata. According to the description which Elias gave of it a few days later, Francis' tortured and bleeding flesh had "miraculously" recovered its softness and the beauty of a child's body; in the sensory conventions of the time, this was considered a sign of holiness. At dawn, his corpse was taken back to Assisi. The procession paused for a moment at San Damiano, where the coffin was opened so that Clare and her sisters could gaze one last time upon the face of their master and friend. This was the occasion of funereal weeping, the *pianto*, that women customarily performed during the funeral of a family member, and which was answered by the *lamento* of the now-orphaned Friars Minor. These groans of sincere grief contrasted with the joy of the inhabitants of Assisi, who could not hide their satisfaction in having a new patron saint. It is for this reason that the desire expressed by Francis of being buried at the Portiuncula was simply forgotten: this convent at a distance from the walls of Assisi was too vulnerable to the greed of neighboring cities. Thus his corpse was transported into the town and provisionally buried in the church of San Giorgio, located at the place of the present-day basilica of Saint Clare, which had been his parish during his youth.

The death of the Poor Man of Assisi created an entirely new situation for his brothers, and for the papacy and the commune of Assisi as well: the three entities having the vocation of managing his memory. On the institutional level, strictly speaking, Francis did not leave a great void, since he had officially given up all practical leadership of the order. But it was necessary to find a successor to him. Brother Elias had assured the interim in some manner, since Francis had entrusted the direction of the order to him in 1221. But against all expectation, at the time of the general chapter, which was held for the first time without Francis on Pentecost of 1227, it was not Elias who was elected to succeed him but John Parenti, a jurist educated in Bologna who was then minister of the province of Spain. By this choice, the authorities in the order probably intended to put an end to the tenuous leadership roles which had prevailed while the founder was still alive, but it also provided the occasion for the friar-clerics, who had received some kind of academic or university training, to have their voices heard within the order even more by ousting the layman Elias.

Devotion toward the Poverello, in any case, did not take long to express itself. His companions, as well as those who had been close to him at one time or another in his life, were safeguarding and passing on his bodily or physical relics (hair, clippings from his fingernails, water that had washed his wounds . . .), as well as objects having belonged to him, like fragments of his tunic or the pillows on which he had laid his head during his illness. One such relic ended up in France between 1227 and 1228 and became the object of great devotion on the part of Blanche of Castille and the future Saint Louis. But after the replacement of Elias by John Parenti, who was general minister from 1227 to 1232, the Franciscan order seems not to have taken the initiative to seek Francis' canonization by the pope: the only one capable, since the end of the twelfth century, to confer on a servant of God the honors of the liturgical cult and an official recognition of sanctity.

THE CANONIZATION (JULY 1228)

In fact, the papacy had taken the initiative at the moment when Cardinal Hugolino, who had personally known the Poverello well, was elected pope, on March 19, 1227, taking the name of Gregory IX. He was to lead the Church until 1241. And it is he who built the foundation for the cult and legend of Francis, while at the same time watching closely over the future of the order. It was necessary to act quickly so as to publicly demonstrate his admiration, which we have no reason to think insincere, for the Poor Man of Assisi; but especially because this death was going to allow him to transform a complex personality— which could be pulled in different directions and toward very different ends— into an exemplary figure in conformity with the Christian tradition. In itself, this approach was legitimate because Francis had always affirmed and shown in his behavior that holiness could be lived only in fidelity to the Church. But it is not certain that Francis would have appreciated the way that his personal renown and the evangelical witness that he had left behind were being orchestrated by the papacy. Make no mistake: Gregory IX, as cardinal, had supported Francis' project and, unlike some other prelates, had believed it to be realizable. Several times he had served as an intermediary between Francis and the Roman Curia, faithful to his role as protector of new religious movements and orders (*religiones novae*) that were proliferating throughout Christianity at that time. But he saw above all in the Franciscan movement a means of advancing the reform of the Church set forth by the Fourth Lateran Council, of which he had been one of the organizers. During the last years of the life of Francis, Cardinal Hugolino had exerted increasing pressure on the Friars Minor in order that they might become more integrated into the life of the Church and contribute to its renewal. Now that the Poor Man of Assisi was dead, the new Pope Gregory was going to use the considerable prestige that surrounded him as a weapon against all those who, in Italy and elsewhere, were obstructing the action of the papacy.

The steps of the canonization process of Francis are not known in any detail, and the description, both indirect and grandiloquent, given of it by Thomas of Celano, who was an eyewitness, does not always give us a very precise idea of it. Franciscan hagiography explicitly relates it to the troubles that were occurring in Rome beginning on Holy Thursday of 1228, after the excommunication by Gregory IX of Emperor Frederick II, who had not kept his promise to leave on Crusade. The pope, believing himself no longer safe, left Rome to take refuge first in the region of Sabina, in Rieti, and then in Umbria. From Spoleto, he went on to Assisi, where he prayed at the tomb of Francis and visited Clare and her sisters. It is there that he began the process of canonization, which was still in its embryonic stages. It proceeded more quickly when the pope considered that, as he and a certain number of cardinals of the Curia had known Francis well, it was needless to open an investigation on his merits and virtues, which were already well known.

We do not know whether the stigmata figured into any of this. Gregory IX later said that the phenomenon had been one of the principal reasons for the canonization. But this seems doubtful, since there is no explicit mention of the stigmata in the pontifical documents of 1228, or in any official papal document before 1237.

In May–June 1228, witnesses were heard, according to the procedure that had been in force for a few years. But these testified only to the miracles that were occurring in great numbers over the tomb or at a distance from it, which resembled those of any saint of the time. These were mostly healings of the lame, the blind, and paralytics, as well as the freeing of "demoniacs" and other possessed persons through the intercession of Francis after his death: all conformed to the typology of the miracles of Christ as reported in the Gospels. All those healed were from central Italy. This shows that the renown of the Poor Man of Assisi had not yet gone beyond the zone where the greater part of his life had unfolded. The examination of the dossier was entrusted to a few cardinals. Their report, favorable to the canonization, was discussed in consistory at the beginning of July and unanimously approved. The reading of the miracles followed, during a public consistory in which the prelates present at the Curia were gathered, and a certain number of them spoke in praise of the new saint. At the end, the pope fixed the day and place of the canonization. It occurred on July 16, 1228, on the piazza of the church of San Giorgio in Assisi. Gregory IX pronounced the ritual formula by which he entered Francis into the catalogue of saints; he then celebrated Mass inside the church in an ambiance of great fervor and popular rejoicing. Through this ceremony, which Thomas of Celano describes with many details (for the first time in a *Life* of a saint), the sanction of the Roman Church made of this person, dead for only a short time and scarcely known beyond the region, a universal saint for all of Christianity.[4]

A certain number of significant historians, beginning with Ernst Kantorowicz, have assumed that the canonization of Francis constituted a response by Gregory IX to the plotting of Frederick II, who was in open conflict with the papacy; and that this opportunely provided the pope with a weapon against the partisans of the emperor, the Ghibellines, very influential in the Italian communes.[5] Formulated in these terms, the hypothesis is certainly exaggerated, for no text relevant to the canonization of Francis—not even the *Life* that Thomas of Celano composed immediately after the event—mentions the excommunicated emperor. But the ceremony and the repercussions that it had had in Italy contributed without any doubt to reinforce the prestige of the papacy at a particularly difficult moment in its history and to increase its influence in Umbria, where Assisi had rallied to it as a political ally in 1226. In fact, the papal decision was a real opportunity for Gregory IX to affirm the supremacy of the Roman pontiff in the Church and in Christian society. Thus there was a positive trade-off for both groups: as "vicar of Christ"—a title that the papacy had claimed since Innocent III—the pope was granting extraordinary support to the Friars Minor by testifying to the sanctity of their founder, who was still little known at that time. But the canonization also reinforced the papacy's own legitimacy with respect to its adversaries—the emperor and his partisans, of course, but especially the numerous "heretics" and "Patarines" in northern Italy, who were accusing the Church of having betrayed or blurred the Gospel message—by raising to the altars Francis, advocate of a wholesale evangelicalism lived within the Church.

With Gregory IX, the papacy began to give to the canonization a solemnity that it had never previously had.[6] The two bulls promulgated in July 1228 on the occasion of Francis' canonization are not mere stereotypical formularies of the chancery; they are, rather, elaborate texts whose purpose was to inscribe the figure of the new saint into a theological perspective and a veritable renewal of the notion of holiness. The first (*Sicut phialae aureae*), addressed to the bishops of France, shared the good news with them. Not that the Friars Minor were particularly numerous in this country, but they had been favorably welcomed there and were benefiting from the sympathy of the Capetian monarchy, whose kindly dispositions toward the Church Gregory was cultivating. The second (*Mira circa nos*) constituted a veritable programmatic manifesto of the "good use" of the holiness of Francis. Military metaphors abound here. The pope gives an enthusiastic interpretation of the holiness of Francis, comparing him to the worker of the eleventh hour sent by God into his vineyard devastated by the Philistines—that is, the heretics and other adversaries of the Holy See. The founder of the Minors is presented as a "new Samson," a man full of spiritual fervor who, with the jawbone of an ass—that is, simple preaching, without affectation—has, while still living, led the battle against the world and the flesh and whose intercession is now going to support the Church in its battle against the forces of evil. In addition, Gregory praises Francis for not simply having been concerned with his own salvation, but for having brought together the active and the contemplative life and for engaging in a new evangelization of the Christian world. The virtues and personal merits of Brother Francis do not draw the attention of the pope. He says nothing about his love of poverty or his desire to "be subject to every creature for the sake of God," preferring to underscore Francis' providential role, which consisted in "supporting the house" and "fortifying the temple," as the high priest Simon, son of Onias, had done of old (Sir 50:1–4). This rather rare biblical reference is probably at the origin of the image described by the hagiographers after 1245 and then illustrated by painters, where one sees Francis appearing in a dream to Innocent III holding up the crumbling basilica of the Lateran. Gregory IX canonizes not a man whom it was necessary to imitate or follow but rather a function: that of founder of an order who appeared at an especially opportune historic moment for the Church in order to permit it to accomplish its mission in the world.[7] The canonization of Francis constitutes both the first metamorphosis of his identity and a decisive step in the integration of the Franciscan movement into the institution.

To be fair, it is nonetheless appropriate to stress that if the papacy took advantage of the sanctity of Francis, the latter acquired, thanks to the canonization, a notoriety that he had lacked outside Italy. It is striking to note that some contemporary chroniclers who were interested in the beginnings of the Friars Minor failed to mention the name of the founder. This is the case with Jacques de Vitry in 1216. Even in 1219, when he encounters the Poor Man of Assisi in Damietta, "a simple man and without learning, beloved of God and others," he gets the name wrong, calling him Francinus! It is the same with Boncampagno of Signa and Burchard of Ursperg, who were contemporaries, as well as for the authors of the *Chronicon Montis Sereni* (Lauterberg) and of the Chronicle of Saint-Martin of Tours, who seem not to know his name.

But the most significant avowal of ignorance comes from within his own order: Thomas of Celano, while addressing Francis in his first *Life*, does not hesitate to say: "Your dying is the just punishment for not having adequately sought to know you when you were still living among us!"[8] And the chronicler Jordan of Giano, who was part of the mission sent into Germany in 1221, naïvely recounts that, having brought back from Italy in 1230 a few relics of the Poverello which Thomas of Celano had given him, he was welcomed with great solemnity by his confrères in Eisenach; surprised by this great unexpected show of piety, "he had, from that time forward, a great devotion to Saint Francis, whom he had already known while he was alive; but this display of affection prompted him to esteem him even more."[9] This passage makes us think that, though admiring him, he had not up to that point really considered him to be a saint.

But things changed quickly after his canonization. The *Histoire d'Éracle*, which around 1228–1230 mentions the sojourn of Francis in Egypt, already calls him a saint, and near the end of 1228, Elizabeth of Hungary, princess of Thuringia, having become a lay penitent, dedicates the hospital for poor and sick which she founded at Marburg in Thuringia to Saint Francis. Thanks to Gregory IX, the quip that the young knight of Assisi had thrown at his companions when he found himself in prison in Perugia—"What do you think of me? Know that one day I will be venerated throughout the whole world!"—was now in the process of becoming a reality.[10] Thomas of Celano quotes Francis even more specifically—"the whole world will venerate me as a saint" (2Cel 4)—but undoubtedly wrongly, for at the time that he was speaking, Francis was certainly not dreaming about the glory of the altars!

THE FRAMING OF THE IMAGE: THE LIFE OF
SAINT FRANCIS BY THOMAS OF CELANO (1228–1229)

Since the end of the twelfth century, a canonized saint had to have a *Life* approved by the Curia, from which "lessons" of the liturgical office were drawn and which were to be sung or recited in his honor on the day of his or her feast. It was thus an important text, since it defined for a long time the figure and the principal traits of the servant of God whom one wished to honor and celebrate. In the spring of 1228, as the canonization approached, the Franciscan Thomas of Celano was chosen by Pope Gregory IX and by Brother Elias to write this *Life*. He was a friar-cleric from the little town of Celano in the Abruzzi, who entered the Minors around the year 1215. He had been sent on mission into Germany in 1221, during the general chapter of which Jordan of Giano has left us a colorful description, becoming custos in the Franciscan province of Teutonia in 1223. He was not a close companion of Francis, whom he had simply met during certain gatherings after his return from the East, and his information is sometimes lacking, particularly about Francis' youth and on the period of the beginnings of the fraternity, about which certain companions of the Poverello felt obliged afterward to fill in the gaps. But his work—which we have often cited—is not lacking in merits: far from it. Indeed, Thomas knew well the writings of Francis, the rules and the *Testament*, as well as the *Encyclical Letter* of Brother Elias regarding the stigmata. His brothers in religion must not have been dissatisfied with him since they later asked him to write a choral legend of their founder for liturgical use; then, at the end of the 1230s, a text which today has been given the title of *Umbrian Legend*; and, finally, in 1246–1247, a second *Life* of Francis titled *Memorial* [or *Remembrance*] *of the Acts and Virtues of Saint Francis*, which was especially meant to complete the first *Life* and to which is attached, before 1253, a *Treatise on the Miracles*.[11] Far from repeating himself, he endeavored throughout his lifetime to enrich his *Lives* with new elements and to bring to his subject a testimony that was on the whole honest and balanced. He died around 1260, and his work was eclipsed in the following years by the *Legenda maior* of Saint Bonaventure, a veritable official biography of the Poor Man of Assisi, whose redaction entailed, beginning in 1266, the disappearance of almost all those which had preceded it.

The *Life of Saint Francis* by Thomas of Celano, approved by Gregory IX in February 1229, is a fundamental text because it fixes in an almost definitive manner the steps of the saint's earthly life; and we are still the beneficiaries of it today.[12] Since the end of the nineteenth century, when the renewal of Franciscan studies began, the work of this "organic intellectual" of the order of Friars Minor has been the principal victim of the "historiography of suspicion," inaugurated by Paul Sabatier, who wanted to see in Thomas an official writer merely seeking above all to please those who had commissioned him; Sabatier and his followers thereby exaggerated the role played by Gregory IX and Elias in the story of the Franciscan movement. Others have reproached Thomas for the excessively literary character of his work, where one finds numerous borrowings from previous hagiographical texts, like the *Life of Saint Antony* by Athanasius of Alexandria, the *Life of Saint Martin* by Sulpicius Severus, or even the *Lives of the Fathers of the Desert*. But recent works have questioned these prejudices and have shown that it was both excessive and unfair to see in Thomas only a compiler without originality or a partisan author. For example, the respect that he shows Brother Elias does not impede him from disagreeing with the description which the latter had given of the stigmata of Francis in his *Encyclical Letter* of October 1226, or from underlining the essential role played within the order by the four "pillars"—probably Angelo, Bernard, Leo, and Rufino—whom he presents as "spiritual men" especially faithful to the message of their master.[13] If he remains relatively silent on the subject of Saint Clare—which is normal since she was still alive (Thomas wrote her *Life* after her death and canonization in 1255)— he does not fail to point out the close bonds that united her to Francis and his first companions and the eminently Franciscan character of the religious experience of the Poor Ladies of San Damiano.[14] In fact, Thomas of Celano is a rather mainstream author who celebrates, in a sometimes vivid manner, the radical "newness" introduced by Francis, while at the same time being careful to situate his experience of life and holiness within the tradition of the Church.

What especially interests us here is to grasp the objective that Thomas of Celano set for himself. Indeed, in this work, he strove to take account of the personal charism of Francis, in understandable terms, while at the same time showing what his sanctity owed to the pope and to the Roman Church. These two perspectives, which today can seem to us to be different if not contradictory, were in his eyes closely associated, revelatory of the mindset of a good part of the brothers in these years immediately after the death of the Poverello. Unlike the bull of canonization, where Francis is presented as an indispensable reinforcement for the Church against its enemies from without, Thomas of

Celano emphasizes that the Church found in him a force for the renewal that it needed. Thanks to the new interpretation which Francis had given to the Gospel, the cleavage between the Church and world, which the hagiographer denounces at the beginning of his *Life of Saint Francis*, was in the process of being reduced. This was enough to assign to Francis a providential and determinative role in the history of salvation. By this very fact, all previous forms of religious life were becoming obsolete, and the only model of Christian life which responded to the demands of modernity—that of its period, of course—consisted in following the life of Christ in poverty and humility. But the holiness of Francis would not have had any meaning if it had retained a purely personal character. His ability to integrate the value of minority into a fraternity, then an order, gave it its real fruitfulness. This is all the more important because it constitutes the first attempt aiming to establish a link between Francis and Franciscanism. In this line of thought, his stigmatization constitutes for Thomas not only a great miracle, as Brother Elias had declared, but the confirmation by God of the exceptional character of his ideal and of the vocation of his order.

The problem, for Thomas of Celano, was to find the means to protect the evangelical radicalism of Francis and his companions against the criticisms or attacks of their detractors, as well as against the risks of slackening inside the order, to which it seemed susceptible. This, in his eyes, could be done only within the framework of a strict collaboration with the Roman Church, by following the example of Francis and of Hugolino, who, in spite of some misunderstandings, had sealed a sincere and durable alliance. But the accession of the cardinal to the papal throne made this alliance considerably more significant, helping to usher in, throughout the whole of Christianity, a "Franciscanized" Church under the direction of the papacy. We understand better, in this perspective, the extremely long and detailed development which Thomas of Celano devoted to the canonization ceremony of Francis, of which he was an enthusiastic witness. For this account allowed him to present Francis as the "pope's saint," in the double sense of a holiness ratified and authenticated by the Holy See and a profound and sincere adhesion of the Roman pontiff to the Franciscan message.

JEWEL BOX AND MAUSOLEUM: THE BASILICA OF SAN FRANCESO IN ASSISI

The day after his death, the body of Francis had been buried in a church in Assisi, San Giorgio, but as we have seen, this was only a temporary solution. Beginning in 1227, the idea took shape in the mind of Gregory IX and Brother

Elias of building a great basilica in Francis' honor, where his relics would be offered to the veneration of the faithful. When Brother Elias was ousted from the direction of the order, during the general chapter of Pentecost of the same year, the pope entrusted him with the task of realizing this church, and he gave himself to it with all the energy he was capable of.

The lands where the sanctuary was going to be built were acquired quickly thanks to the generosity of two Assisi citizens who made a gift of them to the Holy See and to the support of the commune. As the bull *Recolentes qualiter* of Gregory IX attests (April 29, 1228), the construction had been projected a little bit before the canonization process and the acquisition of land made by Elias on behalf of the pope on March 30, 1228. The place where the basilica was to rise was situated outside the walls, just beyond the western gate of the city, in a place called the "lower hill" (or "hill of hell," since it had sometimes been used for capital executions); but not long after it was to be renamed and become the "hill of paradise." The expenses, which had to be considerable (for it was an enormous construction site, where work went on for almost half a century), were covered at the start by the papacy, which alone had the ability to meet them. In April 1228 it granted indulgences to all those who would make a financial contribution for the realization of this grandiose building. Private benefactors probably responded to this appeal, like Jacopa de' Settesoli, this great Roman woman whom Francis called "Brother Jacopa" and who became the only layperson privileged to be buried there. Later, the commune of Assisi also participated in the expenses, instituting in 1232 a grain tax levied on all the inhabitants of the city under pain of banishment—which had to upset the population. Finally, when Elias became general minister of the Friars Minor in 1232, he decided that the order also had to contribute to the costs by organizing begging and collections in Assisi itself and within all the Franciscan provinces, which were heavily taxed in 1237 for the production of bells for the bell tower.

Elias' initiatives aroused protests by some of the companions of Francis, who believed that an order of poor men ought not throw itself into such costly endeavors. This resistance did not impede Elias from realizing his projects in record time. The most urgent was to construct a double church, comprising two structures imposed one on top of the other. The construction began with the lower church, a kind of immense crypt destined to harbor the relics of Saint Francis. The pope laid the first stone the day after the canonization, and the lower church was completed for the most part in 1230—which allowed the remains of the Poverello to be transferred there. On the latter occasion, in order to decorate the church, Gregory IX offered a crucifix embellished with precious stones and containing a relic of the True Cross. While the lower church was destined for the use of friars and laypeople wanting to approach the tomb of the founder, the upper church, more narrow and slender, was built on top of it, between 1232 and 1239, destined for solemn rituals and to serve as the papal chapel when the pope was in residence in Assisi. The ensemble was completed by a bell tower in 1239.

The structure was oriented toward the west, like Saint Peter's in Rome or the Holy Sepulcher in Jerusalem, and its porch opened out onto the town. Built in a Gothic style—modern for the period, especially in central Italy, where the Romanesque forms were maintained until the end of the thirteenth century—by highly qualified masons who had probably worked on the cathedrals of Reims and Angers, the basilica of Assisi anticipates the great church halls that were to be built by the Friars Minor everywhere in Europe after 1250. An adjacent convent was soon added. More than a hundred friars could reside there at the same time, and the general chapters of the order were henceforth to take place there. In addition, Gregory IX wanted to make Assisi one of the residences of the papacy, which led him to build, on the western extension of the convent, a veritable palace—the Franciscan chronicler Salimbene calls it the "Gregorian Palace"—where several popes stayed during the thirteenth century.[15] Indeed, after 1230 all the lands were exempted from the jurisdiction of the bishop of Assisi and transferred to the papacy. In less than thirty years, an enormous complex of buildings thus arose out of the earth in this place. It comprised the basilica of Saint Francis, which a papal bull of April 1230 defined as "the head and mother of the whole order of Friars Minor," on the model of the title of Saint John Lateran, "mother of all churches"; the Sacro Convento, where Brother Elias resided during his generalate; and an imposing palace which allowed the Holy See to affirm its authority over Umbria. It is in this fortress that the pontifical treasury was to be placed under careful guard in the second half of the thirteenth century.

We find at this level all the ambivalence of the attitude of Gregory IX, who certainly had intended to give homage to Saint Francis in building a grandiose church in his honor but who had also sought, by drawing on the memory of the Poverello and the prestige of the order of Minors, to make of Assisi one of the centers of papal power in central Italy. Turning his eyes from the East, where Frederick II had "profaned" the Holy Sepulcher by crowning himself king of Jerusalem in 1229, the pope was creating in Assisi a new sanctuary under his direct control, which he was probably hoping to make one of the great centers of pilgrimage in Western Christianity. His successor, Innocent IV (r. 1243–1254), finding the structure too austere, ordered the embellishment of the "basilica" of Assisi—the first appearance of the term—in 1253 with stained glass and paintings. This would make of it, between 1250 and 1320, one of the most important places of artistic creation in the West.

BETWEEN CIVIL RELIGION AND THE DEVOTION OF THE FRIARS MINOR: THE SCANDAL OF THE TRANSLATION OF THE RELICS (MAY 25, 1230)

At the beginning of 1230, with work on the lower church nearing its end, Gregory IX gave the order to transfer the relics of Saint Francis there, for this construction was going to serve as its special container. The ceremony took place on May 25, on the eve of Pentecost, without his being able to preside over it as he had hoped. But he was represented by three papal legates, granted new indulgences to those who participated in it, and offered numerous gifts as well as a large sum of money for the continuation of the worksite. The general minister John Parenti had called a general chapter, which had gathered a few days earlier. Nearly two thousand Friars Minor met in Assisi for this occasion. The gathering was marked by disruptive incidents: the partisans of Elias, having broken into the hall where the provincial ministers were meeting, claimed for him the right to participate in this gathering, from which he had been excluded since he was at that time neither a minister nor a custos. They were not necessarily wrong, for if the rule of 1223 had provided that only the provincial ministers and custodes had the right to participate in the election of a new minister general, it was not expressly forbidden for other friars to be present as well. In any case, according to the English chronicler Thomas of Eccleston, many inhabitants believed that the friars were in fact arguing because Elias had already proceeded in secret to transfer the relics of Francis in order to prevent them from being damaged during the course of the ceremony.[16] This fear was not at all imaginary. When Saint Anthony was to be buried at Padua in 1231, fervor became so overheated that an intervention of the bishop and the police of the podestà were needed to ensure that the body of the illustrious preacher arrived intact in the church of the Friars Minor, where he was to repose. Likewise, during the translation of the remains of Saint Elizabeth of Hungary, at Marburg in 1235, popular enthusiasm was so intense that the garments with which her corpse were dressed were torn to pieces, as some of the devout sought to procure relics for themselves and to touch the remains of the saint. The hypothesis of a clandestine translation of the relics of Saint Francis organized by Elias with the complicity of certain influential families of Assisi thus cannot be dismissed, even if in the bull that Gregory IX addressed on this subject with an extremely harsh tone a few weeks later, his criticisms are addressed to the Friars Minor and to the communal authorities of Assisi, without any particular reproaches being made against Elias.[17]

In this extremely agitated and tense climate, the ceremony presided over by John Parenti quickly took a catastrophic turn. The triumphal cart carrying the sarcophagus containing the remains of the saint left from San Giorgio winding its way through the narrow streets toward the new basilica, situated on the other side of the town; soon, however, serious shoving in the crowds necessitated the intervention of the communal militia. According to the papal bull, certain citizens seem then to have grabbed the relics and "profaned" them. Even if the term is vague, it probably signifies, as the pope detailed it in the rest of the text, that laypeople had upset the good order of the ceremony as the brothers had planned it, and had tried to take it over. Finally, to avoid having the tumult degenerating into a riot, the podestà and Elias forbade the crowd—as well as the Friars Minor and the general minister!—from going into the basilica, whose doors were hermetically sealed and access into it guarded by armed men. The relics of Saint Francis were then laid in a small vault dug into the rock, located at the intersection of the nave and transept, which one could reach only through a narrow corridor coming from the brothers' choir and closed off by a locked door.

Many questions have been asked about the role of Elias and his motivations in this affair. Some think that when he saw the procession turning into a riot, he simply did his best to preserve the integrity of the relics and to prevent certain people from taking advantage of the confusion in order to seize them. But others, like Richard Trexler, envision far more serious stakes. In this telling, Elias, by having the relics of the saint transferred a few days before the official ceremony, intended to prevent discovery that Francis' corpse lacked evidence of the stigmata, which either was never found on him—this is the thesis of the American historian—or had quickly disappeared, as certain contemporary chroniclers, like the English monk Roger of Wendover († 1236), stated.[18] These statements contradict the testimony of Thomas of Celano, according to whom the body of Francis bore the stigmata when he was buried, for it was a gift that God had made in him and that was reserved for him. But this has not stopped some from stressing that Thomas' legend was an official text, and as such can be suspected of embellishing a more prosaic reality.[19] Given the information that we have at our disposal, it is difficult to choose among the different interpretations, but we can reasonably deduce that Elias had the remains of Francis transferred to the basilica before the solemn ceremony in order to prevent the criticisms of the brothers who remembered that Francis had expressly wished to be buried at the Portiuncula.

In any case, this episode reveals strong opposition between the inhabitants of Assisi and the Friars Minor, who had not given sufficient consideration to their expectations. Thus the laity felt frustrated during this feast, from which they had hoped to reap great advantages for themselves, beginning with the miracles that were generally produced on the occasion of the translation of relics. In their eyes, Francis—Ciccu or Cicco in the vernacular—was first of all the new patron saint of the city and their official protector: thus an eminent figure of civil religion, over whose cult they hoped to exercise a right of supervision. But the friars made of it their own affair and, by hiding his body in a place difficult to reach, Elias was determined to prevent the development of a popular devotion around the tomb. In fact, the pilgrimage to the basilica of San Francesco was to conserve, until the nineteenth century, a local (or better, regional) flavor, but soon came into competition with the success of the pilgrimage to the Portiuncula. Moreover, women were not authorized to go beyond the grill of the choir, as attested by Angela of Foligno, who went there in 1300 and therein had a vision.

Whether the friars had desired it or not, this magnificent jewel box built to house the relics of the Poverello never became a great thaumaturgical sanctuary. Paradoxically, the miraculous side of Franciscan holiness was tied not to the charismatic figure of the founder but to that of an austere—but great—theologian-preacher: Saint Anthony of Padua, who died five years after Francis. Indeed, by the end of the fourteenth century, the burial place of Francis seems to have become rather inaccessible to most; and after the work done upon the orders of the Franciscan pope Sixtus IV during the 1480s to make the crypt inviolable, no one had been able to see his remains, whose very placement was kept secret, thus fostering more or less fantastic speculations about their posthumous destiny. In the middle of the sixteenth century, the Franciscan chronicler Mark of Lisbon went so far as to claim that Francis' remains were to be found in a richly decorated subterranean chapel, where the incorrupt corpse reposed upright on a chair, looking to the east, illuminated by light surrounding his stigmata—a belief lacking all foundation. When the remains of Francis were rediscovered in 1818, they were found in a stone sarcophagus protected by an iron grate.

Through the bull *Speravimus hactenus* of June 16, 1230, Gregory IX reacted very strongly against the translation debacle, for which he held the Friars Minor and the commune responsible. Having mentioned his generosity and gifts, without which the new basilica could not have been built so quickly, he reproached the podestà for not having ensured that the translation of the relics was effected under good conditions; and he announced his intention to withdraw from the basilica of San Francesco its privilege of exemption in order to place it under the authority of the bishop of Assisi. Moreover, he threatened the municipal authorities with excommunication unless they repaired their wrongs toward God and the Holy See within fifteen days by offering the latter "sufficient guarantees." He was no less severe with the Friars Minor, whose divisions and intrigues had been at the origin of this fiasco; he struck their convent with the interdict. After some time, as no one had any interest in seeing the situation get worse, things calmed down. And as to Elias—in spite of the accusations of abuse of power levied against him, which forced him to withdraw for some time into a hermitage to do penance—he soon returned into the good graces of Gregory IX. But the vehemence of the pope, as it was expressed in the bull *Speravimus hactenus*, is enough to illustrate the importance of what was at stake.

Barely deceased, Francis thus had his most cherished desire ignored. He had wanted to be buried at the Portiuncula, which the people of Assisi instead called Saint Mary of the Angels, for it was there that he had had the revelation of the Gospel form of life to which he and his brothers were called. He had wanted to make of "this place that was truly holy and where God lived," a kind of "mirror of the order," the place of an exemplary community leading the "angelic life" under the direct authority of the general minister.[20] At the moment of his death, the friars of the Portiuncula were still working there with their hands and were bringing aid to the poor peasants of the area, who, in return, were giving them bread for the love of God. It was also there that the Minors had gathered in general chapter up till 1227. But the times had quickly changed, and the little church lost its role to the basilica of San Francesco beginning in 1230: with the risk that the Franciscan movement would be identified with all that the new basilica—one of the most ambitious architectural and artistic projects of its day in Italy—signified in the eyes of the world.

4

THE "SECOND DEATH" OF FRANCIS

1230–1253

THE DISTORTION OF THE FRANCISCAN PROJECT

We have seen that, just before the unfortunate events of the translation, the Minors had held a general chapter in Assisi during which numerous perplexities and doubts on the way the rule ought to be interpreted were expressed. Were they bound to observe all the evangelical counsels which were found within the text, and did they have to keep in mind, in their daily behavior, the injunctions that were contained in the *Testament* of Francis? The general minister, John Parenti, was of the opinion that the rule was clear enough and that it sufficed in itself. But the debates were marked by such confusion that it was determined that a small group of representative personalities of the different tendencies which had come to light would go and find the pope in order to ask him to decide. After receiving the petitioners and hearing them out on this matter, Gregory IX promulgated the bull *Quo elongati* on September 28, in which he responded to their questions.[1] The pope affirmed that the *Testament* of Francis, however pious may have been the intention of the saint when he composed it, had no juridical value, for it had not been approved by the ministers gathered in the general chapter, and that the friars were bound to observe only the evangelical precepts expressly mentioned in the rule. Giving a posthumous lesson in democracy to the Poor Man of Assisi, he reiterated that, in the law of the Church, "what concerns all must be discussed and approved by all"; this had not been the case for the *Testament*. And since "an equal cannot bind an equal," Francis who, at that time, had been exercising no function of authority within the order, did not have the right to prescribe anything to his brothers without their consent. Gregory could not have made it clearer that if the Poverello had enjoyed, while he was still living, a charismatic prestige which had allowed him to take certain liberties with canonical norms, this was no longer the case after his death.

Moreover, this setting aside of the *Testament* helped to make the rule less a form of life, as Francis had conceived of it, than a collection of authoritative statements whose observance was virtuous and whose violation a source of sin. In responding as he did, the supreme pontiff was probably hoping to put an end to the discussions and differences that were beginning to manifest themselves within the order. In fact, just the opposite occurred. For a long time, the *Testament* of Francis remained a subject of division. The friars began to write commentaries on the rule—henceforth the only point of reference having an indisputable authority—in order to try to grasp what might have been the intention that animated its authors when they had stipulated a particular measure. This was at the origin of—as Francis had already predicted in his *Testament*—a great number of glosses and commentaries, often in disagreement with one another, if not directly contradictory, which only increased confusion in the minds of the friars.

Simultaneously, Gregory IX tried to resolve another difficulty: as the order developed more and more, the question of the ownership of goods was raised in an even more pointed manner. In conformity with the will of their founder and the rule, the Friars Minor refused to possess anything as their own or in common. But what about the houses, lands, and churches that people gave to them? And how to gather together the funds necessary for the construction of their residences, however modest they might be, without having any money? The pope believed that he had found a solution by proposing a distinction between ownership and use—a distinction that was to profoundly mark the life of the order for a century. For everything having to do with immovable goods and alms or gifts given as money, the brothers would be aided by persons chosen from among their benefactors or friends who were asked to receive and manage these resources on their behalf, while at the same time procuring for them what was strictly necessary for their upkeep and ministry. The solution appeared ingenious but, in practice, it soon posed more problems than it had resolved. Indeed, either the *nuntii* and "spiritual friends"—as the papal text calls them—were completely devoted to the brothers and, in this case, risked being substitutes in name only who simply relieved them of the cares of the management and the uncertainty of the morrow; or they maintained, with respect to the Minors, a real autonomy, in which case it would not be long before conflicts erupted between them. In fact, the system functioned so poorly that in 1245 the bull *Ordinem vestrum* eventually had to give Franciscan superiors the right to use money! In addition, this text specified that the ownership of the order's goods, both movable and immovable, now devolved to the Holy See, which put at the disposal of the Friars Minor all that could be "useful" for their lives: a notion that was much more elastic than that of "necessity" in the text of 1230, and that risked transforming their refusal to possess into a purely legal fiction.

In *Quo elongati*, Gregory IX also stated that only the provincial ministers and one custos per province (chosen from among their fellow custodes) would henceforth have the right to participate in the general chapter. As there were at that time thirteen Franciscan provinces, this resulted in a group of twenty-six people who were empowered to give counsel to the general minister and to elect his successor. The decision of the pope was intended to favor an evolution of the structures of the order in an oligarchical direction, quite far from the warm ambiance of the previous general chapters, where all the Minors gathered so as to be together around Francis, to share their experiences, and eventually to agree upon measures for living in greater fidelity to the Gospel.

Concerning the relations of the friars with the local ecclesiastical authorities, the first years of the pontificate of Gregory IX accentuated an evolution which had already begun at the end of Francis' life and which he had tried in vain to erase in his *Testament*. From 1227 on, a torrent of papal bulls rained down on the order, endlessly conferring upon it ever-expanding privileges: power given to ministers to absolve brothers who were under excommunication; exemption from compelling such friars to appear before an ecclesiastical judge; the right to a special cemetery next to their residence and to bury there some of their dead as well as their benefactors; special protection of the Holy See for new convents founded in Italy. The culmination of this process was the bull *Nimis iniqua* of August 21, 1231. In it the pope—claiming he was indignant that the Friars Minor, "who, in great denial of themselves, have decided to follow the poor Christ in the greatest poverty, are being persecuted by those who were criminally fattening themselves up on the patrimony of Christ" and that "certain prelates are demanding the tithe on their gardens and the hundredth on their houses just as on the houses of Jews"—solemnly affirmed the order's exemption from episcopal jurisdiction and threatened violators with heavy sanctions.[2] And so that these measures did not remain a dead letter, Gregory instituted throughout different regions of Christianity "apostolic conservators," chosen by the members of the clergy who were known to be favorable to the Franciscans, to ensure that this new law was respected. All these measures found their justification in the desire of the papacy to render the ministry of the friars more effective by conferring on them broad autonomy within the ecclesiastical structures and by transforming them into a clergy of elite. But as Francis had predicted, such privilege was sure to provoke negative reactions on the part of the secular clergy, who soon felt marginalized by these assistants who were in the process of becoming competitors.

In yet another domain, the Minors drifted rapidly from the ideal of their founder: the place within the order given to learning and to learned people, the clerics—who were not necessarily all priests. Beginning in the 1220s, students and soon masters coming into the order from the schools and universities had entered in rather large numbers, especially in the regions north of the Alps. Quite naturally, these educated brothers were promoted to positions of responsibility, at the head of the provinces and also within the realm of the teaching of theology and preaching. In *Quo elongati*, Gregory IX stipulated that the brothers who had studied theology would be exempted from the examination and approval of the general minister, who alone had the authority, according to the rule, to grant the right to preach. Moreover, among the objects whose use was permitted to the Minors, Gregory especially mentions books, in such a way as to favor the study of Sacred Scripture within the order. Since many of the secular clergy, lacking training, were incapable of proclaiming and explaining the word of God, the pope intended to confer this task on the Friars Minor and Preacher. Beginning in 1236 he fostered the creation of schools of theology (*studia*) at Padua and Bologna, where friars would go in order to be formed as "lectors" destined to teaching in the principal convents of these provinces. It was the same in Paris, where, after the entry into the order in 1231 of the regent master of the university, Alexander of Hales, the convent of the Cordeliers—the name that was given to the Friars Minor in France—became an important center of studies, where were formed and taught persons as important as John of La Rochelle, Eudes Rigaud, future archbishop of Rouen and counselor of Saint Louis, and Haymo of Faversham. Likewise in Oxford, where the chancellor of the university and future bishop of Lincoln, Robert Grosseteste, came to give public lectures in theology beginning in 1229 at the convent which he had had built for the friars. These men quickly left behind the approach of penitential exhortation that their founder had set for them and gave themselves more and more to preaching of a spiritual type, centered not only on morality and behavior but also on dogma and the sacraments. They also threw themselves into the ministry of confession, although Francis had explicitly desired that they leave to the secular clergy the care of reconciling to the Church sinners who had converted. Nevertheless, in the beginning, only the professed of the order who had received the authorization to do it from their minister provincial could administer the sacrament. The popes, cardinals, and princes favored this evolution by choosing their own confessors and their chaplains from among the Friars Minor. And thus the convent-churches became centers of religious and sacramental life frequented by numerous laity.

In this new context, the position of the lay friars became delicate within the order. Not knowing how to read or not knowing Latin, they could not do studies. Between 1232 and 1239 Elias, who himself was not a priest, defended them from the exclusive prerogatives claimed by the clerics and entrusted them with functions of responsibility, notably at the head of the provinces whose number he multiplied and which he had ordered inspected by visitators, thus creating within the order a kind of administrative hierarchy devoted to him. But these authoritarian practices ended up exasperating the friar-clerics, especially the theologians who engineered his fall from grace. It is surely not by accident that the general minister who succeeded Elias, after the brief interregnum of Albert of Pisa (r. 1239–1240), was an English scholar, Haymo of Faversham (r. 1240–1244), who had not known Francis and had been formed at the *studium* of Paris. In reaction against the excesses that had marked the generalate of Elias, the general chapter of 1239 decided that the lay friars, even educated ones, would henceforth be excluded from functions of authority (as ministers, custodes, guardians). Moreover, their admission into the order was subject to restrictions so severe that their recruitment soon dried up, to the great satisfaction of the Italian chronicler Salimbene of Adam, who frankly declared, a few years later, that he did not see what usefulness the presence of such unlearned people could have.[3] In this context, we can better understand the lamentations and invectives of the Franciscan poet Jacopone da Todi against the "Paris which has destroyed Assisi"—that is, against the clerical and university mindset which had made of the fraternity created by Francis an order of doctors and priests.[4] But even more than the university, had the papacy played a decisive role in this extremely rapid process of distancing—or rather of "estrangement," to take up an old medieval French word which has survived only in English—at the end of which the religio of Francis was transformed into a mendicant order very close to the Friars Preacher of Saint Dominic and became a particularly effective instrument at the service of the Roman Church.

FRANCIS OF ASSISI "SUPERSTAR": ALLEGORICAL AND ESCHATOLOGICAL INTERPRETATIONS

In these same years, we see within the Franciscan order an exaltation of the role of Francis in Christian holiness and salvation history: a development which facilitated the disappearance of the concrete historical figure of Francis from sight. Brother Elias had already given the signal for this the day after the death of the Poor Man of Assisi by announcing to the brothers the news of the stigmatization and the miraculous transformation of Francis' body, which, though stiff and covered with wounds borne before his death, became soft and shining with innocence at the moment when he gave up his spirit. If this latter miracle, often evoked in the Lives of the saints, seems relatively banal, the same does not apply to the stigmata, whose miraculous novelty was emphasized by Elias and whose manifestation was, according to him, "without precedent in previous centuries, except in the Son of God, Christ our Lord."[5] In the wake of this miracle, Elias described Francis as "a crucified man bearing on his body five wounds which are truly the stigmata of Christ." His account contains no explanation of this mysterious phenomenon, limiting himself to a description: in the hands and feet wounds as if brought about by nails which would have pierced through the flesh on both sides; and, for the side wound, blood flowing from a tearing as if from the thrusting of a lance. One could not state more clearly that Francis was a living image of the Crucified.

Returning to the subject two years later in his *Life of Saint Francis,* Thomas of Celano was more nuanced than the minister general. Not hesitating to contradict the description which Elias had given of the stigmata in his *Encyclical Letter,* he stated in effect that the wounds were not gaping cuts but rather—at least for the hands and the feet—protrusions of flesh in the form of nails, signs of the ardent desire of Francis to identify himself with Christ on the cross, mysteriously realized at the time of the apparition of La Verna. The hagiographer continues with his comparison: for him, Francis bore the trace of the wounds of the Crucified "as if he had been hung from the cross with the Son of Man," at the end of a kind of play of mirrors between the physical sufferings of Christ and those of his own body.[6] God had filled him by granting in him this prerogative of a love superior to martyrdom and a singular grace. From this subtle and respectful analysis of the mystery of the stigmata which Francis had wanted to keep hidden while he was alive thus comes the image of an exceptional saint in whose body the divine and human were mingled, and about whom Thomas does not hesitate to declare that "his life throws off a greater light than that of the saints who had preceded him."

News of the stigmatization quickly became widespread throughout Christianity, and iconographical representations of it seem to have appeared almost as rapidly. In the early 1230s Raoul of Villedieu, abbot of Mont-Saint-Michel, had a stigmatized Francis depicted on one of the capitals of the cloister. A contemporary enamel from Limoges, today preserved in Paris in the Musée de Cluny, depicts the scene with precision. Henceforth, at least north of the Alps, by far the most widespread image of Francis was to be as a stigmatized saint, to the detriment of other aspects of his life and holiness. In rare cases—we know of a few—where artists had depicted him without the stigmata, a miracle came later so as to rectify the deficiency, as Thomas of Celano recounts in his *Treatise on the Miracles.*[7] Such imagery prompted negative reactions from some prelates, like the bishop of Olomac, Robert the Englishman, who, in 1236 or 1237, prohibited every iconographical representation of the stigmata of Saint Francis by stating that "only the Son of the eternal Father had been crucified for the salvation of humanity and that Christian religion must only give to his wounds a suppliant devotion." But he was severely contradicted and sanctioned by Gregory IX, who clearly took a position in favor of the authenticity of the bleeding wounds of the Poverello.[8]

Parallel to this evolution, we begin to see certain ecclesiastical milieus exalt the figure of Francis within an eschatological perspective. Indeed, beginning in 1229, Gregory IX seems to have been definitively convinced that Emperor Frederick II, who had not hesitated to negotiate with the enemies of Christianity and to strike at the authority of the Apostolic See, was the Antichrist, that "son of Belial" whose appearance at the approach of the Last Days the Apocalypse had announced. Historians have scarcely taken seriously the words that were spoken by the pope and cardinals at the time. At best, they have seen them as grandiloquent formulas crammed full with obscure scriptural allusions which could affect but a small number of learned individuals. This is not accurate; for when Gregory IX, in the liturgical hymn which he composed for the canonization of Saint Francis, evoked the "last head of the dragon" (*Caput draconis ultimum*), it was not, for him, a simple allegory but a specific reference to the seven-headed dragon that the Apocalypse depicts and to the commentaries which had recently explained its historical meaning. Indeed, according to Joachim of Fiore, the sixth of these heads was Saladin, who had taken Jerusalem from the Crusaders in 1187; the seventh and last could only designate Frederick II, who had just "profaned" the Holy Places in crowning himself king of Jerusalem in the Holy Sepulcher. This is confirmed by the great encyclicals of 1239–1240 against Frederick, whom the pope describes as the "beast rising from the sea."

But against this monster and tyrant with whom Gregory had begun a struggle that was to last until his death in 1250, the Church was not without resources. In another liturgical hymn of the period (*Proles de caelo prodiit*), the Poor Man of Assisi is identified with the prophet Elijah, who was to return at the end of time, according to the words of Jesus himself (Matt 17:10–13). Francis is presented in the hymn as a "new legate sent on behalf of Christ, who carries the banner of the cross in his own body," emphasizing once again that the stigmata had confirmed his sanctity and that his life had recapitulated and "represented" the life of Christ for his contemporaries.[9] He is the one who led into battle a triple army (trina acies, a clear allusion to the Friars Minor, the Poor Ladies—the recluses at San Damiano—and the lay penitents within the Franciscan ambit) which was going to put to flight the troops of the impostor seated in Jerusalem. Opposite the new incarnation of the Beast of the Apocalypse— the excommunicated emperor—Francis appears as the artisan of a reconciliation between God and the human race "in the time of anger," a new Enoch "who pleased God and was translated into paradise" (Sir 44:16), after strengthening the faith of the people by penance.

The Franciscan tradition later took up this theme and popularized it through a collection of exempla composed around 1270 by Thomas of Pavia, based on the memories of a companion of Francis, Brother Stephen.[10] According to this account, the Poverello went to Apulia, at Barletta, to preach against the extravagance and sensuality that was prevalent in these places. Court personnel revealed his presence to Frederick II, who invited him to his palace—probably Castel del Monte—and offered him a festive meal, in the course of which the saint ate hardly anything. The emperor then tried to tempt him. He led him into a vast and well-heated room where there was a soft bed, and sent him a young girl whose mission was to seduce him. But Francis slept on a bed of embers, where he invited the temptress to join him. Terrified by this unexpected proposal, the woman ran to recount the story to the sovereign, who allowed the Poor Man of Assisi to leave, having declared: "This man is truly the friend of God!" The anecdote, however improbable on the historical level, must have had a certain success, for it was taken up again almost as is in the Actus and Fioretti in the fourteenth century. In these texts, though, the tempter is not Frederick II but the sultan of Egypt.[11] Even within the order, the wonder that surrounded the saint of Assisi only increased. Certain brothers affirmed that Francis, while yet alive, had miraculously appeared to them while they were gathering in a provincial chapter in Arles. Others declared that they had seen him in the sky on a chariot of fire, like the prophet Elijah. These episodes were immortalized by Giotto at the beginning of the fourteenth century in the frescoes of the upper basilica of Assisi.[12]

POCKETS OF RESISTANCE AND CENTERS OF FIDELITY: THE COMPANIONS AND CLARE OF ASSISI

We would be going down the wrong road, however, if we believed, on the strength of the recriminations that figure in certain hagiographical sources of the end of the thirteenth century or the writings of the Spiritual Franciscans of the fourteenth century, that the majority of Friars Minor rushed to betray the message of Francis after his death. This pessimistic view constitutes a flagrant anachronism, as attested by the fact that, after the bull *Quo elongati* in 1230, the ruling authorities of the Minors carefully avoided consulting the papacy on the interpretation that ought to be given to specific points in the rule and that they now led this discussion among the friars themselves. On the other hand, it is well established that most of them avoided rushing into the breach that Innocent IV had opened in the practice of poverty with the bull *Ordinem vestrum*. Moreover, in 1251, the general chapter of Genoa even decided to cease applying this text, so many abuses had it generated.

THE COMPANIONS AND THE *SACRUM COMMERCIUM*

Beginning in the 1230s, however, differences were starting to become evident among the brothers over the interpretation of the poverty required by the rule, and these resulted in attitudes which oscillated between withdrawal and open conflict with the hierarchy of the order. Indeed, the rapid marginalization of the first companions led them to withdraw into the hermitages, which afterward remained among the principal centers of opposition to the deviations, real or imagined, with respect to the rule introduced by the successors of Francis. Thus Brother Giles († 1262) withdrew to Monteripido, near Perugia, where he quickly acquired a reputation of great sanctity, as attested by his *Life*, and by the assertion, totally lacking any historical foundation, that Saint Louis visited him dressed as a pilgrim. It is Giles who asked Brother Leo to go to Assisi and break the stone vase which Elias had set up in front of the entrance to the basilica of Saint Francis in order to collect the offerings of the faithful intended to finance its construction; this he did to the great scandal of the friars present and the furor of the minister general. Elias brutally repressed what he considered to be unacceptable forms of disobedience: Caesar of Speyer was put under house arrest and killed by his jailer in 1238 or 1239; Simon of Collazzone († 1250), who enjoyed a great reputation of holiness and was to be the object of a canonization process in Spoleto in 1252, was confined to his convent; and even Bernard of Quintavalle, the first disciple of Francis, seems to have been persecuted at this time.

It is in this climate that one must, with all probability, situate the redaction of a text that is both beautiful and somewhat mysterious: the *Sacrum commercium beati Francisci cum domina Paupertate*.[13] This work, whose surprising title can be translated as "The Sacred Covenant [or Contract] between Saint Francis and Lady Poverty," constitutes the first theological reflection on the meaning of poverty for the Franciscans and presents itself under a form both poetic and dramatic. Anonymous and undated, it has inspired much perplexity. And among its recent editors, some have situated its redaction at the end of the 1220s; others have pushed the date toward 1253–1255. It seems more likely placed in the last years of the generalate of Elias (1232–1239), since the text alludes to the multiplication of provinces to which Elias had proceeded to reinforce his control over the Franciscan order, as well as to his indifference with respect to spiritual matters and piety. This matches well what we know about the behavior of this minister general: an excellent administrator and able manager, but poorly attentive, it seems, to properly religious realities. If we accept this dating, the author could have been Caesar of Speyer, who had helped Francis in the redaction of the first rule, for the numerous biblical citations or references that we find there are similar to those which figure in the "foundational document" of 1221. Caesar, a ferocious opponent of Elias, would have drafted it a little before his death, that is, between 1235 and 1238.

The *Sacrum commercium* is not a biography of Francis but the courtly account—filled with allegories without, for all that, losing its simplicity—of an encounter and dialogue between Francis, accompanied by a few companions, and Poverty, represented as the spouse of Christ and a Lady whom the brothers had the duty to faithfully serve. The depiction is thus one not of mystical nuptials, as has too often wrongly been stated, but of a contract of an economic sort (for such is the primary meaning of *commercium* in medieval Latin) between two parties, metaphorically transposed into the realm of religious life. At the beginning of the work, Francis is alone and the author describes for us his impassioned quest for Poverty, understood both as a form of self-denial and as a social choice, in terms that remind us of those used in the Graal, which had just come to find its definitive literary form in French. The persons whom he asks to point out to him the place where he could meet this lady are surprised by this strange request; but one ends up telling him that she resides on a high mountain. The Poor Man of Assisi takes himself there with a few faithful companions; and there he does find the queen of virtues, "now a widow, abandoned and despised by all."[14] The group of brothers of which Francis is now a part addresses Poverty with a request of an alliance inspired by their desire to be saved ("for one cannot enter into the eternal kingdom unless marked with her seal"). She responds to this with a long evocation of her historical destiny, from paradise up to the time of the martyrs and that of the monks, by way of the passion of Christ and the life of the apostles.

After this the narrative focuses on contemporary events depicted as an opposition between the "true" and "false" poor—the latter presented as "bad religious" who are persecuting the former. And the false poor use as a pretext the usefulness of the Friars Minor and their apostolate to win over the good graces of the powerful in order to relax the rigor of their observances.[15] The author then gives himself over to a fiery attack on the new orientations of the order which have broken the "sacred covenant" concluded by Francis with Poverty, her state likened to the powerlessness of Christ on his cross. Without evoking any name—but the allusions are transparent—he develops a veiled critique of the construction of the basilica of Assisi, whose sumptuousness sits poorly with "Poverty who lives alone and without honor." At the end, the friars who are present renew their pact with their "lady" and conclude this encounter with a "feast" of bread and water. And when Poverty asks them to show her the cloister where they reside, they lead her to a hill—probably the hill of paradise where the basilica of San Francesco was being built—and turning their back to the church under construction, they have her admire the splendid panorama out on the plain while saying to her: "Lady, here is our cloister!" implying a refusal on their part to settle in the city and to consecrate themselves to purely pastoral tasks.[16] After this, Poverty announces tribulations and difficult struggles for the friars who will want to remain faithful to her and cautions them not to let themselves become discouraged, for God will give them the strength to persevere until the end and the final reward. It could hardly have been said more clearly that the spirit of Francis and especially his demanding and concrete conception of poverty were being betrayed at the very center of his order, and that the friars were obliged to oppose with all their strength the elimination of an essential aspect of his message.

CLARE OF ASSISI AND SAN DAMIANO:
GUARDIANS OF THE MEMORY OF FRANCIS

The opponents of the ongoing normalization did not, however, constitute a homogeneous group, for they did not all have the same adversaries. If the group of friars who had expressed themselves in the *Sacrum commercium* seemed to be aiming at the ruling circles in the order, and especially Elias, then Clare of Assisi, for her part, kept up excellent relations with Elias but entered into conflict with the papacy, which she criticized for distorting the project to which she had dedicated her life with the support of Francis and in conformity to his will. In the 1220s the community of San Damiano was already gaining in importance; by 1238 it had around fifty religious and had, in the interim, spread out to several foundations in central Italy (Monticelli near Florence, Monteluce in Perugia, Vallegloria in Spello, Arezzo, and so on). But the conditions of life for the sisters had been appreciably modified. Beginning in 1218–1219, as we have seen, Cardinal Hugolino had undertaken to standardize the feminine religious movement that was then spontaneously developing in central and northern Italy under different forms (recluses, penitents, amorphous groups, and the like) whose common denominators were the attachment to poverty and the desire to lead a life of penance.[17] Thus did he draw up for these communities a "form of life" which transformed them into monasteries directed by abbesses, all placed under the patronage of the Virgin Mary. In 1220 Hugolino, having spent Holy Week at San Damiano, where he was edified by the life of the community, imposed his regime on Clare and her companions. But the "Poor Enclosed Sisters," as they had begun to be called in pontifical documentation since 1225, did not yet constitute a structured religious order. And up to 1228, the Curia seems to have taken account of the uniqueness of San Damiano. In the bulls that were addressed to them at the time, Clare is never identified as abbess, and the women are called "servants of Christ" and not nuns. Moreover, while Francis was still alive, Clare had felt protected by him. For in spite of the distance that he had taken from the "Poor Ladies," as he preferred to call them, he had always believed that they had to maintain a privileged relationship with the Friars Minor. He had, moreover, encouraged them to resist all the pressures to change by addressing to them, a little before his death, a brief exhortation known as his *Last Will*:

> I, Brother Francis, wholly humble, wish to follow the life and poverty of our Most High Lord Jesus Christ and of his most holy mother and to persevere in this till the end; and I ask you, my ladies, and I counsel you to always live in this most holy life and poverty. And guard yourselves well from ever distancing yourselves from it in any way upon anyone's teaching or counsel.[18]

This last recommendation was not unnecessary because, once he became pope in 1227, Gregory IX increased his pressure on the female communities and established a veritable religious order which he endowed with a rule of Benedictine inspiration. His initiative was perfectly logical, for the traditional religious orders which, like Cîteaux or Prémontré, had accepted nuns into their communities in the twelfth century, were now refusing to receive any more new monasteries in order not to be too weighed down by the obligations which the spiritual direction of these ever more numerous feminine communities entailed. To ensure the success of his operation, which he held close to his heart, the pope needed the backing of Clare, whose movement was enjoying an undeniable spiritual expansion. Thus did he seek to make of San Damiano the head of a new structure that would bear its name. In July 1228 the supreme pontiff, who was then staying in Assisi, went to San Damiano in order to meet with Clare a few days before the canonization of Francis. The conversation had to have been particularly difficult. In any case, it seems to have left both protagonists with a bad taste in the mouth: Gregory IX never returned to San Damiano for the rest of his pontificate, even though he often resided in Assisi afterward. And Angelo Clareno, at the start of the fourteenth century, even claimed that Gregory had excommunicated Clare! This claim appears dubious, but it is certain that, from that time on, she was mistrustful of and ever vigilant with respect to the projects and undertakings of the pope.

In fact, Gregory IX's foundation and San Damiano had things in common as well as appreciable differences. The rule which he had imposed on the Poor Ladies claimed to follow poverty, but it was the type of religious poverty being practiced in Cistercian monasteries, which was then the template for the Roman Curia. The accent there was on the contemplative life and strict enclosure verging on reclusion. This constituted a novelty within Benedictine monasticism. Such an option had as a corollary the obligation for female religious to have landed properties so as not to be inconvenienced by the concern for daily survival or led to seek out contacts with the outside world in order to procure resources for themselves. Finally, the twenty-four monasteries that made up the new congregation were exempt from diocesan authority and directly attached to the Roman Church in the person of a cardinal protector who was, beginning in 1228, Raynaldo of Jenne, the future Pope Alexander IV. But far from being agreeable, Clare seems to have chafed at the idea of being imprisoned in the feminine order created by the pope. She did not accept, then or later, any compromise of absolute poverty, which was the only common point that she maintained with the Friars Minor. Thus she could not allow her monastery to have landed possessions or fixed revenues. Only by continuing to live in precariousness and in covering their daily needs through manual work and the recourse to charity could the Poor Ladies of San Damiano hope to keep a link with the real poor and remain faithful to the Gospel message which Francis had given to them. Between these contradictory demands, it was necessary to find a compromise. And we can imagine that the compromise that emerged from this conversation—or series of conversations—satisfied neither of the two protagonists. Clare had to take the title of abbess, which she found distasteful, and to accept that her community must become a part of the new feminine congregation created by Gregory IX as the order of San Damiano. But she asked the pope to guarantee a particular status to the monastery of San Damiano as well as to a few religious houses which she herself had created, namely, the privilege of not being forced to accept immovable goods. This is what we call the "Privilege of Poverty," which has been widely discussed by historians in recent years: the question being to know whether the privilege granted to Clare by Gregory IX was new or simply a confirmation of a similar document which had been granted her in 1215 by Innocent III. In either case, we need to underline the paradoxical character of the situation that was now created: the community of San Damiano, finding itself promoted to the rank of motherhouse and with the official name of a congregation whose way of life, on one essential point, it did not share and whose effective direction was now in the hands of the pope or his representative.

This first crisis was soon followed by another when, in 1230, Gregory IX promulgated the bull *Quo elongati.* Among the points of the rule which the Minors had asked the pope to clarify was the question of the prohibition of entering into the monasteries of women, "except those to whom a special permission has been granted by the Holy See."[19] Until then, the brothers had assumed that this regulation did not apply to San Damiano, which was considered a kind of extension of the Franciscan order, whose minister general put at the disposition of Clare and her sisters two or three friars to go out begging food for them (since they could not leave the convent), as well as chaplains who celebrated the Mass there and administered the sacraments to them. But the pope responded by distinguishing feminine monasteries in general, where the friars could go for tasks of spiritual direction, and those of the enclosed Poor Ladies, access to whom was now prohibited to the Minors for any reason whatsoever. Evidently Gregory IX meant thereby to cut the last remaining ties between San Damiano and the companions of Francis. Clare rose up against this decision and sent away all the Franciscans who were associated with the convent, "refusing to keep the begging friars who were bringing them bread for the body, since she could no longer keep those who were provisioning it with food for the soul."[20] Probably alerted by Elias and faced with the threat of a hunger strike which would have surely created a scandal, Gregory IX reversed course and entrusted to the minister general the care of finding a palliative solution.

Matters thus returned to the *status quo ante,* and on this point the situation scarcely evolved further for the rest of Gregory's pontificate. But skirmishes continued between the pope and Clare, a charismatic personality both venerated and feared, whose personal prestige was reinforced by her inflexible fidelity to the demands formulated by Francis in the matter of poverty. Her intervention in the conflict which opposed Gregory IX to Agnes, daughter of the king of Bohemia, founder and abbess of the "Damianite" convent of Saint Francis in Prague, gives eloquent witness to this. Indeed, in 1238 she had asked the pope that her community might be able to live according to the Privilege of Poverty, granted to Clare and her sisters, and not according to the "form of life" of the order of San Damiano which he had created. He bluntly refused her this authorization and urged her to mistrust the advice of "a person who has more zeal than reason." This vicious little phrase probably refers to Brother Elias, since Clare had written a little before to Agnes:

> Do not entrust yourself and do not devote yourself to anyone who would take you away from your vocation, hinder your course, and prevent you from being faithful to the Most High in the state of perfection in which the Spirit of the Lord has called you. In order to walk more surely in the way of the commandments of the Lord, follow the counsel of our very reverend father, Brother Elias, minister general. . . . And if someone says to you or suggests to you other things contrary to our form of perfection or opposed to our divine vocation, do not follow his counsels, even if they come from a very highly placed person.[21]

We might be surprised to see Clare make such a big deal of a man who, in the eyes of the author of the *Sacrum commercium*, was in the process of striking a fatal blow to the evangelical message of Francis. But no trace of hostility can be found in her toward the basilica of Assisi, whose construction was at the center of the activity of Elias from 1229 to 1239, owing to the profound attachment that she bore to the one who had been her guide in the spiritual life. She probably considered that this sumptuous edifice was not contrary to poverty to the extent that the friars had no ownership of it and the pope ruled there as master. Moreover, the resources for the financing of the worksite came essentially from alms and gifts, which was in conformity with the rule of the Friars Minor. Besides, Elias, as minister general, seems to have played a role of protector toward the feminine religious movement of Franciscan inspiration. Indeed, after being forced to resign from his charge in 1239, he withdrew "into the places of the Poor Ladies"—without authorization of the pope, who thereby excommunicated him.[22] In 1241 Gregory IX levied sanctions against "sisters minor," "female Cordeliers," or "discalced," who had probably survived in the shadows thanks to the protection of the minister general and had been placed outside the reach of the law.[23] These measures were aimed at "religious women" who, unwilling to submit themselves to a strict cloister and to sequester themselves into a purely contemplative life, had maintained apostolic or charitable activities, especially in hospices and leprosaria, and sometimes gave themselves over to preaching. The Franciscan sources are very discreet on this point, but various testimonies outside the order allow us to think that this was an important matter indeed. Beginning in 1224, the "sisters minor" (*sorores minores*) of Sant'Agatha, on the edge of Verona, who took care of the lepers of the hospice of San Giacomo, were commanded by the Franciscan visitator, Leo da Perego, future archbishop of Milan, to adopt the rule of San Damiano and the cloistered life. A part of the community refused this "enclosure" and chose to remain at the service of the lepers by founding a small congregation for this work subject to the local bishop.[24] Moreover, the English chronicler Matthew Paris recounts that in Burgundy, around 1225: "A young girl went to the residence of the Friars Minor where, at her request and after having been duly instructed in the requirements of the order, she put off her shoes, put on a sackcloth and hair shirt, and for many years she devoted herself to preaching the Gospel of peace in the cities and towns, especially to the feminine sex."[25] Similarly, the young Rose of Viterbo († 1251), who was not able to obtain admission into the community of the Damianites of her city, had her hair cut like a cleric, put on a hair shirt tunic tied by a little cord, and began to preach to the women of her neighborhood, then systematically went about the streets of the town, a cross in her hand.[26] Evidently, a certain number of "religious women" did not easily give up an engagement in the world and were then pursued for this reason by ecclesiastical authorities.

All these calls to order and the sanctions of the papacy strengthened Clare in the conviction that absolute reclusion was being imposed on her and her companions and that she had to renounce every form of wandering and active life. Henceforth, she lived enclosed in her monastery of San Damiano, of which she endeavored to make a model and exemplary community for the female Franciscan movement, as Francis had tried to do with the Portiuncula for the Friars Minor. It is with her that Brother Leo placed the mysterious parchment scroll where he had put in writing the memories which he had preserved of the Poor Man of Assisi, with whom he had been very close; and it is to the abbess Benedetta, who succeeded Clare as the head of the community of San Damiano, that he passed on the personal breviary of Francis, after keeping it for a long time in his own possession. Ill for twenty-nine years, Clare no longer participated in exterior events except through visions, like the one of Christmas night in 1252, when she was transported in spirit to the basilica of San Francesco, where the friars were gathered to sing the office of the Nativity. Significant in this respect is the dream that she had, at a date which might be 1230, and which she reported to some of her companions in the following terms, according to the testimony of Sister Filippa di Messer di Gislerio at her canonization process in 1253:

> Lady Clare recounted again that she had seen herself carrying to Saint Francis a basin of hot water to wash his hands. She climbed up very high on a ladder, but she did it with so much ease and nimbleness as if she was walking on flat ground. When she reached Saint Francis, the latter brought out of his chest a breast and said to her: "Come, take and suck!" She did it. Then Saint Francis asked her to suck a second time. And what she thus tasted seemed to her so sweet and delectable that she was unable to express it in any manner. And after she had sucked, this tip or end of the breast from which the milk was coming out remained between the lips of the blessed Clare; she took with her hands what had remained in her mouth, and it appeared to her like gold that was so clear and brilliant that she saw herself in it as in a mirror.[27]

This text, which was not repeated in the *Life of Saint Clare* written at the end of the 1250s by Thomas of Celano or in the later hagiographical texts, will obviously give joy to psychoanalysts, who will not fail to note the inversion of sexual differences that it implies: the man nourishing the woman with maternal milk and not the opposite. But we will truly grasp the significance of it only by placing it within the spirituality of the period—where the theme of "Jesus our mother" had held an important place since the end of the twelfth century—and in the psychology of Clare. Every dream or vision—the two terms were pretty much synonymous in the Middle Ages—is a means to know the secrets of God. It is both enigmatic (to the extent that it asks for an interpretation in order to be understood) and prophetic (since it announces things that are going to occur)— here, the fact that Clare aspires to soon be reunited with Francis in the afterlife.

But perhaps the most important point is the role played here by food. When Francis was still in this world, Clare did not have any greater desire than to eat in his company and with his companions; and the *Fioretti* has given us the memory, probably embellished with a strong dose of the marvelous but very real, of a meal that they had together at Saint Mary of the Angels and which resulted in a mystical ecstasy of the two protagonists communing in the Holy Spirit.[28] In general, food has a fundamental place in the life and religious experience of Clare. Francis and the bishop of Assisi, moreover, once had to intervene to obligate her to mitigate the rigor of her fasts and those that she was imposing on her community, which was endangering their health. And in 1230, as we have seen, she did not hesitate to begin a hunger strike, dangerous for bodies already weakened by fasts and vigils, in order to force Gregory IX to abrogate a measure concerning San Damiano which she judged unacceptable.

Like many "female religious" of her time, Clare associated extreme asceticism with holiness, in line with the eremitical movement and penitential spirituality. Without going so far as thinking about her in terms of "holy anorexia," as has been done, one must recognize in her an expert in the privation of food for whom the fast—which she considered a form of the stripping of oneself, not as a quest for suffering—held the same place that disappropriation had for Francis. Thus the maternal milk in the text expresses a fundamental relationship: it is spiritual food, taking us back to the teachings of her guide and friend. And the dream of Clare probably expresses her fear of being cut off from the living forces which he was bringing to her, by losing contact with the Friars Minor, from whom the pope wanted to separate her. Finally, it underscores all the preciousness which she attached to the "form of life"—the milk that is transformed into gold—which Francis had given to the sisters of San Damiano, whom he had urged, in his *Last Will*, never to abandon. For the struggle of Clare to remain faithful to the teachings of Francis was not simply the expression of a personal sensibility harmed by the evolution under way, it found support also in the adhesion of her community. The sisters indeed seem to have constituted with her one body, whose unity was founded on shared intentions and ideals with their superior, in whom they saw "the holiest woman since the Virgin Mary"; she, for her part, the "first mother and mistress of the order," as her companions called her, considered them as the protagonists of her own spiritual experience.[29]

Clare, isolated after the fall of Elias in 1239 and ignored by the new rulers of the order, who had little in common with her, enjoyed a better fate under the pontificate of Innocent IV (1243–1254). This pope, desirous to unify the two "souls" of the feminine religious movement—its Franciscan origins and the Benedictine orientation which Gregory IX had given to it—and to entrust its spiritual direction to the Friars Minor, promulgated in 1247 a new rule for the Damianites. It presents itself as a "rule of Saint Francis," even if the holding of immovable goods by the monasteries was explicitly anticipated therein. Clare was not duped by this new label and obtained from the pope an exemption for San Damiano by virtue of the Privilege of Poverty. Meanwhile, she got down to work and composed a "form of life" herself, which she submitted in 1251 to Cardinal Raynaldo, protector of the order. Long negotiations were again necessary in order for this text to finally be approved and promulgated by Innocent IV—on the eve of Clare's death, which occurred on August 11, 1253.[30] We should note in passing that this is the first rule written by a female religious for her own community, other than that which Heloise had composed in the twelfth century for the Abbey of the Paraclete, which was used nowhere else. In this regard, it marks an important step in the recognition of the particularity of the religious experience of women. We find here both an explicit reference to the "form of life" which Francis had drawn up for Clare in 1212 and the confirmation of the Privilege of Poverty. Moreover, the name that she gives to her group was not Sisters Minor, as might have been expected, but rather Poor Sisters (*sorores pauperes*)—an expression that goes back to the beginnings of the early fraternity. It took no less than twenty years of struggle and five successive rules to arrive here; and we can only admire the tenacity and passion which never ceased to animate Clare during this combat and allowed her to write at the head of her rule of 1253 these few simple but essential words:

> The form of life of the order of Poor Sisters, which Saint Francis has instituted, is this: to observe the Holy Gospel by living in obedience, without anything of their own, and in chastity. . . . And just as, since the beginning of her conversion, she, as well as her sisters, has promised obedience to blessed Francis, she likewise promises to observe the same inviolable submission to his successors.[31]

This victory was not long-lived, however. The papal bull was addressed to Clare as "abbess of San Damiano" and was valid only for this "proto-monastery" and, later, for that of Prague; for Agnes of Bohemia had petitioned the pope to allow them to follow this rule as well. More than a rallying to the views of its saint, who was to be canonized in 1255, it was a last homage rendered by the ecclesiastical hierarchy to the "old combatants" of evangelical poverty, as if to signify that this page in the history of the Church had had its hour of glory, but that it was now definitively turned. All other feminine monasteries of the Franciscan movement indeed kept the rule of Innocent IV or had recourse to another which authorized them to possess immovable goods, as that which Alexander IV—the former Cardinal Raynaldo—had granted in 1254 to the female convent of Longchamp, near Paris, which Isabel of France, sister of Louis IX, had just founded.

In 1261 the nuns left San Damiano in order to settle inside the walls of Assisi, in an immense convent connected to the new church just built in honor of Saint Clare, canonized six years earlier by Alexander IV. And in 1288 they gave up the Privilege of Poverty with the encouragement of Pope Nicholas IV. But in 1263 Urban IV promulgated a new rule which was going to be imposed on all the feminine communities of Franciscan inspiration, united into one group to which he gave the name "the order of Saint Clare." By a cruel twist of fate, the one who was described as "the little plant of Saint Francis," and who died surrounded by some of his first companions (Leo, Angelo, and Juniper), had to push the meaning of abnegation—albeit posthumously—to the point of giving her name to a text which explicitly granted to the Clares the right to own the goods that she had refused her whole life long!

From the death of the Poor Man of Assisi to that of Clare, San Damiano was probably the principal center of resistance to the profound changes that were affecting the Franciscan movement in all its forms and, as a result, the very image of Francis. But did the admirable tenacity of the Poor Ladies imply on their part a flawless fidelity to the heritage that they intended to preserve? The question is not sacrilegious because the kind of monastic life and the constraints imposed by the Roman Church could not fail to have repercussions on their way of interpreting the message which they had received from their master. Indeed, over the years, we see intensified in Clare two tendencies—neither of which would go so far as to be considered deviations—characteristic of her spirituality. On the one hand, because of the enclosure to which she and her sisters were now subjected, she was led to reduce the notion of minoritas to the poverty which she had had to fiercely defend, to the detriment of other aspects of the Franciscan charism, and to identify it with the refusal to own goods in common, which was for her the only way to be distinguished from the nuns of a Benedictine obedience. On the other hand, she emphasized the mystical implications of poverty which she saw, first of all, as a spiritual condition to live in relationship with the mystery of Christ. These distortions with respect to her model do not detract from the value of her witness but oblige us to temper the assertion, fairly widespread these days, according to which she would have been the only authentic heir to the life of Francis and the most faithful interpreter of his thought.

FORGETTING FRANCIS?

By examining the writings redacted inside the order of Minors during the first decades after the death of Francis, we are struck by the rapid disappearance of every concrete reference to his form of life and to the economic and social aspects of poverty as he had lived it. Certainly, this kind of observation generally has little place in the hagiographical texts, but it is the same in the other sources that were not subject to the same constraints. Sometimes even reference to the Poor Man of Assisi is completely absent. Thus Anthony of Padua († 1231), who had known Francis personally, does not cite him a single time in his sermons. And even when certain Franciscans, like John of La Rochelle in Paris in 1230, made him the object of their preaching, it was to affirm, in an abstract manner, that God had created the man Francis in the image of the divinity of Christ and a resemblance to his humanity. Thus we might sometimes wonder whether the person they are talking about is really the author of the rule of 1221, for whom poverty consisted in living in the midst of the needy poor and the lepers. Similarly, his seeking contact with people on the margins, with brigands whom he endeavored to reintegrate back into the surrounding society, is evoked only fleetingly and with some embarrassment. This process of standardization had already begun in the last years of the life of the founder, as one sees it in the important difference that exists between the dictates of the rule of 1221 regarding manual work—presented as an obligation for all—and those of the rule of 1223 on the same subject, where manual work appears as only one possible option and as an ascetic exercise. The very fact that one might have soon given to the Franciscans and Dominicans the name "mendicant orders" clearly signifies that they were drawing the majority of their resources from begging and alms, not from manual labor. In the meantime, the question of poverty had evolved in the direction of a debate within the order of Friars Minor, as we already noticed in the *Sacrum commercium*; and the "intention of the rule" was the object of long discussions and theological and juridical controversies. This sliding toward abstraction and ideology was even accentuated by the fact that the Friars Minor—because their role within the Church was hotly contested by certain elements of the clergy—were obliged to affirm their specificity by putting the accent on poverty to the detriment of other aspects of "minority," like the renunciation of power or simplicity. And they had a tendency to define this notion, in a much more narrow manner, as the refusal to possess goods in common.

Along similar lines, we can situate the tendency, obvious since the death of the Poor Man of Assisi, to hide his relationships with women during his lifetime. Even if, as we have seen, he was led to take a little distance from Clare and San Damiano after 1219, their relationship was never interrupted, as his *Last Will*—the warm exhortation which Francis addressed to them a little before his death—shows. However, when Thomas of Celano wrote his *Life* of the founder of the Minors in 1228, he mentions Clare only twice: once—albeit, in a laudatory manner—at the moment when he speaks of the activity deployed by Francis to restore San Damiano, and, after Francis' death, when he recounts the stopping of the funeral cortege in front of the convent and the moving farewell of the "Poor Ladies" to their spiritual father.[32] We will have to wait until the 1250s to see Franciscan hagiography mention the existence of "Brother Jacopa," to whom Thomas of Celano, in his *Treatise on the Miracles*, will devote a long exposition, as well as that of the Roman hermit Praxedes, who also had been very close to Francis.[33] This conspiracy of silence seems calculated to make of him not the instigator of a movement of evangelical revival open to all, independent of every consideration of gender or state of life, but rather the founder of a purely masculine religious order. This adds to the dehumanizing of the figure of Francis, which was considered a necessary counterpart of the recognition of his sanctity by the Church and which renders so difficult every undertaking to rediscover his real face today.

Another aspect of the life of Francis which seems to have been rapidly eclipsed or poorly interpreted is his engagement on behalf of peace. On the earliest image that we have of him, a fresco at the Sacro Speco of Subiaco which is dated to 1227 or the beginning of 1228, the saint is depicted holding in his right hand an unrolled parchment leaf—or cartoon—where one sees the inscription, in large letters, "Pax huic domui!": "Peace to this house!" This echoes the greeting he often used. In later iconography, this image was quickly replaced with a book—which could be the Gospel or the rule of the Friars Minor—as was fitting for a founder of an order, or more frequently still by the stigmata. One will also note that the bull of Francis' canonization does not mention his actions on behalf of peace and is, on the contrary, filled with military images. On this point, the bull contrasts singularly with that by which Innocent III had announced in 1199 the canonization of a lay saint, Homobono of Cremona († 1197), who was praised for the zeal that he had displayed in reestablishing peace in his city and is called a "man of peace" (*vir pacificus*).[34] That probably implies not any disavowal of the action of Francis in this area but rather a lack of understanding of the connection which he had established between poverty and peace. Starting from the assertion that the majority of acts of violence and conflicts are tied to ownership and to the desire for power, Francis had wanted to carry, with his brothers, the witness of what could be a gathering of poor people united in mutual affection and the refusal of every aggressive claim. At the same time, he had urged those who remained in the world to be reconciled to their enemies, without neglecting the social and collective dimension of evil, as the very concrete tonality and style of his preaching testify to, as much as we can know it. But these efforts toward the reestablishment of peace could only lead to results that were precarious and always had to be renewed, since they were tied to the "conversion" of individual people and to the persistence within them of peaceful dispositions. It is in this line that, once again, is to be placed, at the end of the 1220s, the preaching of an Anthony of Padua, who endeavored to reestablish peace between the political forces in conflict in the Marches of Treviso—failing, moreover, in this undertaking.

A few years later, in 1233, the Friars Minor, together with the Preachers (actually following their lead), threw themselves into a great campaign of peacemaking on the plain of the Po River. The movement, which had started with the call of a popular preacher and became known by the name of the "Alleluia," marks the grand entry of the mendicant orders into the regions extending from Lombardy proper up to Bologna and the Marches of Treviso, by way of Verona and Vicenza.[35] The popular aspiration for peace, as much within the cities as between them, was at that time so strong that the ruling classes, in some of the cities, were obliged to give up power for a few weeks or months to these mendicant religious. This attests to the popularity which these orders had acquired in just a little time. Their entrance onto the scene was translated into modifications in the communal legislation whose specifics varied from town to town but which was inspired by the same concerns. If at Bologna and Verona the role of the Dominicans was preponderant, in Parma, Milan, and Vercelli it was to Franciscans like Gerard of Modena and Leo da Perego that this task was entrusted. It is unnecessary to go into the details of the measures which were passed or abrogated, but the principal ones aiming to reestablish peace in the cities were a general amnesty to wipe out the traces of previous violence, the return of the banished who were reintegrated into communal life, and the concluding of peace treaties between warring families in order to preempt reprisals and a recourse to the vendetta. Moreover, citizens who had been imprisoned for debts were freed. In Parma, Gerard of Modena was able to put into the communal statutes the obligation for the commune to remunerate four lawyers to serve as advocates and counselors for the poor, widows, and orphans. The religious took advantage, moreover, of the power which had been conferred upon them in order to introduce into the communal legislation the statutes promulgated by the Holy See in 1231 against heretics, who would be subject to the death penalty. On the other hand, measures which the majority of these cities had established for about fifteen years to restrict the privileges of the clergy, especially in the fiscal and judicial domains, were abolished, while sanctions were provided against usury, sorcery, luxury, and prostitution in order to enforce the demands of Christian morality upon the daily life of citizens. All things considered, besides the measures which undeniably aimed to bring peace to the city and to protect the weak, the mendicants were concerned with preserving the interests of the clergy and enlisting the cities in the papacy's antiheretical program. But the majority of these reforms were short-lived, for after a few months, the attempts of the mendicant preachers to bring peace back into the region ended in a fiasco and the whole movement was discredited. Once the euphoria had faded, the traditional political games reemerged, and the statutes which had been promulgated were abolished or fell into obsolescence.

It is useless to wonder whether Francis, had he not died seven years earlier, would have approved or not of those friars who had invested themselves in this peacemaking campaign and sometimes played a determinant role in it. He was not *a priori* hostile to an intervention of civil authority in the religious realm; he had, after all, addressed a *Letter to the Rulers of the Peoples* asking them to take measures to give honor and thanksgiving to the Lord every evening through a herald or some other signal.[36] But this was a simple invitation to increase piety and devotion in the cities or states in the rulers' domain. And Francis would probably have had difficulty imagining that his brothers, whom he wished to be humble and subject to all, would one day take power and seek to modify communal legislation. Indeed, for him, to have recourse to the law in order to change customs and behaviors demonstrated an impatience and a desire to solve problems in an authoritarian fashion; this contradicted his personal approach to conflicts. The Poor Man of Assisi did not undertake peacemaking campaigns; he proclaimed peace. In his eyes, only an act of penance was capable of opening the way to a true reconciliation. To preach peace was not, for him, a means of disciplining or preaching at society but the occasion to actualize, through people and groups who accepted to forgive each other grievances and wrongs, a new world reconciled to God and to one another.

In a few years, the remembrance of Francis (as he had been in life) thus began to get blurred, and whole parts of his personality began to be lost from view. Within the order, certain people, like Albert of Pisa, minister of the province of Germany, then England, and finally minister general in 1239, saw Francis first of all as an ascetic. To believe the testimony of the Franciscan chronicler Thomas of Eccleston, Albert claimed that Francis, a year after the promulgation of the rule, had added a constitution prohibiting the friars from eating more than three morsels of food offered to them—a ruling of which there is not a single trace![37] Others, outside the order, did not hesitate to present Francis as someone who was a little naïve and too kindly disposed toward those who were evil. This is the stance of the French cleric Henry of Avranches, who, having been a part of the court of Frederick II, joined that of Gregory IX, who commissioned him to adapt in Latin verse the *Life of Saint Francis* of Thomas of Celano: a task which he fulfilled around 1232. This text hardly presents anything original, except where the court-poet rails against the Italians whom he reproaches for being heretics who rebel against every superior authority, and for being quick to violence in their social relationships. Something astonishing three or four years after the canonization of Francis, this diatribe full of bitterness ends with a few verses in which the author openly mocks the pious simplicity of the Poor Man of Assisi and criticizes as blameworthy the indulgence Francis had shown toward the Italian communal world and its aspirations for freedom:

> Francis whose soul is simple and pious,
> Supports everything and everyone
> and is aware neither of vices nor faults;
> And in spite of the malice of his fellow citizens,
> he sees in them wise men
> and does not believe that the Italians have any need of a master.[38]

As it is scarcely possible that Henry of Avranches would have personally known Francis, it is not beyond reason to find in this development the echo of certain statements that he had heard about Francis at the Curia. Indeed, Henry probably would not have brought this unkind judgment upon the saint if he had thought it would risk shocking Gregory IX, the one who commissioned the work and who, to believe the *Assisi Compilation*, had once, when he was still only Cardinal Hugolino, called Francis "a little simple-minded brother."[39] This critical attitude, nevertheless, seems to have been less widespread than a rather dull depiction of the Poor Man of Assisi that one finds, for example, at a slightly later time (around 1260–1270) from the Franciscan Salimbene of Adam, who had met some of Francis' first companions, like Bernard of Quintavalle or Leo. This prolix chronicler mentions several times the founder of the order which he belonged to and praised his kindness (*benignitas*) and patience in suffering. But if he sees in him a saint whose virtues and miracles he is proud to be able to mention, beginning, of course, with the stigmata, he does not, for all that, feel himself obligated to follow his example nor even encouraged to do so.[40] Hostile toward the lay brothers, for whom he shows a profound disdain, Salimbene believes that a good Friar Minor is first of all an educated preacher charged to direct the spiritual life of the faithful from the pulpit and in confession. And he does not imagine that poverty can be anything but the absence of ownership which characterized the convents to which he belonged.

   At this level, one could speak of a "fading image" of Francis (Théophile Desbonnets). Friars were not ignorant of his life or of his historic role, but some had lost connection with him on the spiritual level. But let's not paint too dark a picture based on Salimbene, who perhaps constitutes an extreme case. During the same period, the English Franciscan Thomas of Eccleston, who had drafted his *Treatise on the Coming of the Friars Minor to England* between 1232 and 1258, recalled that his provincial, William of Nottingham (r. 1240–1254), said to him, concerning poverty, that two things must not be forgotten: the spirit of Francis and his intention on this subject such as it is expressed in the rule. The chronicler himself does not hide his disapproval regarding the debates and controversies that were developing at that time over this matter within the order. He notes that Saint Francis supposedly appeared to a brother who was asking himself questions about this very thing. And Francis said to him: "Go to the lay brothers; they will explain the rule to you!"[41] The Poverello thus remained for some of his spiritual sons a living touchstone. But for the greater number, who had but a vague image of him, he was already nothing more than the author of the rule to which they had adhered and the founder of the order into which they had entered.

Part III

IMAGES AND MYTHS OF FRANCIS OF ASSISI

FROM THE MIDDLE AGES TO TODAY

5

Medieval Interpretations of Francis: Thirteenth to Fourteenth Centuries

Even if some aspects of the personality and behavior of Francis of Assisi were quickly lost from view, his figure enjoyed, during the century after his death, a growing popularity as a result of the extraordinary expansion by the order of Minors. Around 1300 the number of friars is estimated to have been more than three thousand, scattered among several hundreds of convents in Western Christianity and in the East. Each of these convents was a center for the diffusion of the cult and image of the holy founder, who thus attained in a short time a renown which no Christian saint had known since Saint Martin. At the same time, Lives of Francis multiplied. Between 1230 and 1263, we see no fewer than a dozen Latin legendae devoted to him, without even mentioning their translations and adaptations in most vernacular languages of Europe. This sudden flourishing of hagiographical texts constitutes in itself a historic event whose significance and importance merit a moment's pause to try to understand.

ON THE PROPER USE OF LEGENDS

Let's ask ourselves: why so many Lives or legends? It is sometimes believed today that in the Middle Ages it was impossible to speak of a great person, whoever he or she was, without placing him or her in a religious perspective. Nothing is less true of the thirteenth century, when chronicles abound whose authors were perfectly capable—especially in Italy, where a strong record-keeping culture existed—of writing historical works without recourse to supernatural explanations. Indeed, no one at the time considered writing a legend in honor of Philippe Augustus or the emperor Frederick II; even the *Life of Pope Gregory IX* (around 1241) resembles the biography of a sovereign more than that of a servant of God. In other words, the distinction between hagiography and history was clear in the medieval mind. Legends were written only about saints or persons who were reputed to be saintly.

The chroniclers of the thirteenth century had not completely ignored Francis; and some of them mention him in their writings. Normally, however, these testimonies do not tell us very much about their subject since their authors—with the exception of Jordan of Giano and Salimbene, both Franciscans—limited themselves to mentioning his name and origins, while adding that he had founded the Friars Minor and that he had been canonized by Pope Gregory IX in 1228.[1] In fact, what especially struck historians of the period is the success of Francis' order and its extremely rapid diffusion throughout all Christianity. But other than the testimony of Thomas of Split, who had seen Francis preach in Bologna in 1222 and who has left us an arresting description of this episode, these notices are too quick and general to constitute a substantial contribution to the understanding of the person.

Since Francis was considered a saint even while he was still alive and was canonized less than two years after his death, it is not unusual that the principal sources that mention him would be the legends (*vitae, legendae*) or miracle collections—that is, the texts which fall under the genre of hagiography. Indeed, at this time, every man or woman recognized as a saint by the Church was given a Life—or even several Lives—written in Latin, recounting his or her great deeds and celebrating his or her virtues, followed by a more or less inflated list of miracles attributed to the saint's intercession. It was supposed to be read (in the etymological meaning of the Latin word *legenda*: read out) on the day of the feast, during the office which clerics and religious recited or sang. But the proliferation of legends with Francis as their subject during the forty years that followed his death went beyond liturgical necessities. It resulted especially from the fact that those who had known him and wanted to extol his memory recognized that he had been not a political figure or theologian but rather a true disciple of Christ, thus a subject for a legend rather than a mere historical personage. Indeed, the hagiographical texts are distinguishable from biographies or narrative accounts in that they were written not to recount the life of a man or woman from birth to death—which they do only in a summary or selective manner—but above all, in presenting their subjects as models of Christian perfection, to incite their hearers or readers to lead better lives. In this sense, the medieval legend is closer to the epic or *chanson de geste* than to the chronicle, because it is aimed at producing an effect of personal involvement. It calls to mind acts or words that, within the context of salvation history, render present and alive once again the holiness of a man of God and thus prolong the effects of his creative dynamism. Whereas the rules and constitutions tended to fix and thus freeze Francis' spiritual experience and whereas the bulls of canonization betrayed it, the hagiographical account of his deeds calls for a creative assimilation of his message. In this sense—and in this sense only—can one adhere to the formula of the Bollandist Hippolyte Delehaye, according to whom "the legend is an envelope which hides a treasure of higher truths."[2] This affirmation in no way means that the legendary accounts or miraculous phenomena which they describe are to be taken literally as factual or objective realities. It simply indicates that the legend—and hagiography in general—not only reflects the taste for the miraculous which would have marked the medieval spirit, but drives a theological truth which goes beyond the historical truth by laying out the hidden thread of the presence and intervention of God within a human life. The legendary is thus not less real but more than real, and this explains the seductive power which it has exerted over hearts and minds in every age.[3]

But if the legend is not a writing that is true in the sense that we use today, it must—in order to take account of a higher reality—utilize schemas and accounts that are believable in the eyes of the public to which it is intended. Thus the historian would be wrong to deprive him- or herself of this evidence and to consider the hagiographical dimension as an element added to the biography of the saint, a superficial overlay that must be removed in order to recover the lived reality. To insert Francis, as did his first biographer Thomas of Celano, into a tradition whose most prestigious models go back to Late Antiquity—the *Life of Saint Antony*, the hermit of the desert of Egypt, by Athanasius of Alexandria, and the *Life of Saint Martin of Tours* by Sulpicius Severus—is not to willfully falsify the image of the Poor Man of Assisi but rather to show that Francis was equal in virtue to the greatest saints of Christianity and followed in their wake. The hagiographical texts come from a rhetorical genre—the literature of praise—whose pitfalls we must avoid by identifying the standardized elements within it. The Lives of Saint Francis are not exempt from this. And they present to us the major inconvenience of being for the most part indifferent to chronology. Except in matters of his youth and conversion, where authors are obliged to lay out the facts successively, they have difficulty situating some of the events in relationship to others and scarcely bother trying to date them. For, in fact, the man interests them less than his work; and for them, the important events of his life were those that could have an influence upon the future of their order. More than the personality or the steps in the biography of the Poor Man of Assisi, the legends which were devoted to him allow one to grasp the impact which he exercised on the minds and hearts of his contemporaries. It then falls to the historian

to detect the vestiges of truth which each testimony contains and to clearly ar-
gue for the interpretation to be given it. He or she can do it better since the hagiography, in the thirteenth century, had changed in relation to previous periods
and was beginning to claim a certain historical truth, by employing direct testimonies and sometimes even the writings of saints or documents about them.
This evolution is particularly acute in the case of Francis, to the extent that numerous witnesses who had known him personally were still alive when these
legends were composed and they could be enlisted against unlikely or erroneous
affirmations—which sometimes did occur.

HAGIOGRAPHICAL LIVES AND COMPILATIONS

THE FRANCIS OF THE FIRST LIVES (1228–1260):
CONTRASTING IMAGES

In the first *Life of Saint Francis*, that of 1228, Thomas of Celano sought to illustrate the significance which the life and message of Francis had for Church
and society by presenting him as the holiest man of all time and as a "seraphic"
figure. At the same time, he underscored that this "new evangelist" had been
sent by God to repair the Church and reform religious life. This interpretation
allowed him to justify the passage from the early fraternity to the order of Friars
Minor and to affirm that only a close association of the order with the papacy
could guarantee the preservation of the spiritual message of the Poverello. But
this synthesis, all in all fairly successful, did not enjoy a monopoly for long. The
legend, abridged in 1230 into nine lessons which Thomas of Celano drew from
it for liturgical use, was soon rivaled by the versified, that is to say rhymed, office which the Franciscan Julian of Speyer constructed from the hymns composed in honor of Saint Francis by Gregory IX and certain cardinals at the time
of his canonization. Julian's text was to be mandated for the recitation of the
office within the order of Minors, though it was modified several times. Thus
in 1263 the general chapter ordered that the verses that evoked in stark terms
the conflict of Francis with his family ("He behaved with great insolence toward his parents who had nourished him") be replaced with a much more
neutral expression ("God in his mercy showered him with divine gifts"); a great
saint like Francis could not be shown to be insolent towards his parents![4] On
the other hand, between 1232 and 1234, Henry of Avranches put into Latin
verses the *Life of Saint Francis* by Thomas of Celano, not without adding—as
we have seen—a few developments of his own. Julian of Speyer wrote another
Life during these same years. On the whole, however, this first wave of hagio-

graphical texts remained fairly consistent: each of them adding only nuances or corrections of detail to the portrait of Francis as it was borrowed from his official biography. But during this period, the authors of these Lives conserved only those elements of Franciscan origins compatible with the status of a religious order which the fraternity had ended up adopting; they voluntarily obscured certain aspects of the life of their founder that had become useless, or even dangerous, to mention.

By contrast, from 1240 forward, we see a rupture in the hagiographical tradition of the Poor Man of Assisi related to the profound transformations that the order had undergone after the forced resignation of Brother Elias in 1239, in particular, the accelerated process of clericalization within it. The authors of these later works, all Franciscan, sought above all in the life of Francis either confirmation or rejection of the innovations which had been introduced among the Minors after his death. If they were interested in this past, it was to justify or deplore recent developments. This explains the occasional polemical tone of these accounts, which remain, nonetheless, marked by a demand for fidelity to the message of the Poor Man of Assisi. We generally date from 1240 or 1241 a writing titled *On the Beginning of the Order of Friars Minor*, attributed by its first editors to the "Anonymous of Perugia," who was in fact Brother John of Perugia, disciple and confessor of Brother Giles, one of the first companions of the Poverello.[5] Different from previous texts, it was not, properly speaking, a Life of Francis because it was as closely associated with the companions with whom he discovered his vocation of evangelical preacher in a church of Assisi. Rather, it was a chronicle of the beginnings of the order that emphasizes the collective character of the Franciscan experience and underlines the essential role played by Cardinal Hugolino in the approval of the Franciscan movement. This writing reflects the mentality of the clerical element which came into prominence in the order following the fall of Elias. For its author, the Minors certainly proceed from Francis, but the founder appears framed from the beginning within a religious order called to be the privileged ally of the Roman Church through its pastoral engagement. Moreover, careful to eliminate all that might make Franciscanism appear to be a subversive social movement, the author reports with particular insistence words through which the founder cautioned his brothers not to judge the rich and powerful over their appearance and to avoid in their preaching every form of opposition to or criticism of the established order.

A more marked and decisive turning point in the hagiography occurred around 1246. During the generalate of Crescentius of Jesi (1244–1247), the Minors, at that time strongly rivaled by the Friars Preacher and contested by certain elements of the secular clergy, felt the need to raise the value of the profile of their founder. As a result, in 1244 the general chapter of Genoa urged the friars to gather up all the memories that could yet be collected about "the signs and wonders of the most holy Francis." This call seems to have hit home, for several new works resulted from it. The first is the *Legend of the Three Companions,* so called because it is preceded in most of the manuscripts by a letter sent from Greccio, on August 11, 1246, by three of the closest companions of Saint Francis: Brothers Leo, Rufino, and Angelo.[6] In this letter, these friars remind their readers that miracles do not constitute sanctity but are only manifestations of it. This was undoubtedly a warning against the temptation to give too much of a role to the supernatural wonders attributed to Francis and a protest against the oblivion into which the memory of his life and virtues was currently falling. Indeed, the *Legend of the Three Companions,* a work, in spite of its name, by a single Friar Minor (perhaps Brother Rufino, cousin of Clare, but certainly not Brother Leo), constitutes first of all the response from Assisi to the appeal launched by the general chapter. The author, who knew quite well the customs of the town where Francis had grown up, did not hesitate to fill in the gaps of the *Life* of Thomas of Celano and sometimes even to contradict it regarding the early life of the Poverello, on the details of which he was particularly well informed. As in the text of the *Anonymous of Perugia,* the discovery by Francis of his vocation to the Gospel life is here placed after—not before—the arrival of his first companions, and in the church of Saint Nicholas in Assisi, not at the Portiuncula. It is here also that for the first time we read of the episode of the crucifix of San Damiano that spoke to Francis, and the account of the dream which enabled Innocent III to identify him without hesitation during their first meeting in Rome.

The *Legend of the Three Companions* closely associates the personal journey of Francis with that of his companions and presents him as the twelfth member of the early fraternity, thus as the closest of the apostles to Christ. For its author, Francis was a prophet of God, predestined for holiness during his life and a visionary of the future. The fable of the little black hen with the wings of a dove that ends up understanding that she is incapable of protecting all her chicks by herself allows the author to explain the willingness of the Poor Man of Assisi to place his order in the hands of Cardinal Hugolino and the Roman Church so that they might care for it and help it to grow. The detailed account of the order's origins is interrupted around 1210, and the work concludes with two chapters devoted to Francis' stigmatization and death. These chapters were long thought to have been added at the beginning of the fourteenth century. Today it seems more probable that the author of the *Legend* did not intend to compose a new exhaustive biography but was trying only to respond to the call of the minister general by completing the existing Lives as needed. This would explain the chronological gaps in the text. And this is accentuated by a certain number of "prophecies" *post eventum* intended to legitimate the order as it was at the time of writing. In concluding his work with the account of the canonization of the Poor Man of Assisi, the author was seeking to anchor the legitimacy of the Friars Minor in the exceptional personality of a founder to whom the papacy had granted its supreme recognition. When all is said and done, this text, very detailed in its emphasis of the historical and human figure of Francis, is situated in the same line as the *Anonymous of Perugia*, from which, moreover, it borrows many points; for one finds there a dithyrambic elegy of Cardinal Hugolino, and the Poor Man of Assisi is presented as a devoted son of the Roman Church.

The *Legend of the Three Companions* is not an isolated text. It seems to be part of a group of writings and documents designated under the name *Florilegium of Greccio*, which has been, since the end of the nineteenth century, at the center of the research and polemics tied to what began to be called the "Franciscan Question." Without entering into the details of these erudite controversies—which have been fruitful to the extent that they have helped to progressively clarify this debate—we can summarize the terms of the controversy in a schematic manner in order to better grasp what was at stake.

To the letter that Brothers Leo, Rufino, and Angelo sent from Greccio to the minister general Crescentius of Jesi on August 11, 1246, they added a "packet" of accounts and testimonies whose precise contents unfortunately elude us. In addition to the *Legend of the Three Companions* were certainly also the reminiscences of Brother Leo, who had been the secretary of Francis and sometimes his confidant. This was not a structured hagiographical text but pages and notes which were later gathered together to form rolls. Leo had consigned there a whole series of biographical episodes about Francis and some words—or *logia* (sayings)—taken down from his lips. This collection escaped the destruction of the previous Lives of the founder ordered by the general chapter of 1266, since it was not a biography but an unedited dossier of documents. Leo gave it to San Damiano after the death of Clare, and later it entered into the archives of the Sacro Convento of Assisi. Given the proximity of Leo, Angelo, and Rufino to the Poor Man of Assisi, these documents are obviously of capital importance. From Paul Sabatier in the years 1890–1928 up to Raoul Manselli, and particularly in the works of Rosalind Brooke and Jacques Cambell, a number of historians of early Franciscanism have endeavored to reconstitute this florilegium in the hope of finding there the "real" Saint Francis: the one known by those who called themselves in these texts "We who were with him" (*Nos qui cum eo fuimus*), intending by that to mark their testimony with the seal of absolute authenticity.[7] Unfortunately, all attempts made to reconstruct its exact content inevitably are undermined by the fact that this florilegium is known only through passages which contemporary (and especially later) authors have extracted from it in order to insert them into compilations. And the undertaking is all the more arduous since Brother Leo, who lived until 1271, never stopped reworking these writings and adding new elements to them until he died.

In fact, in the beginning, the documentary material gathered in 1246 by the companions especially helped to establish or enrich new biographies of Francis. Thomas of Celano, who had never stopped writing on the life and holiness of Francis since 1228, composed a new *Life* in 1246–1247, at the request of the minister and the general chapter.[8] This was not strictly speaking a biography, but rather a "memorial" (*memoriale in desiderio animae*) built around the virtues of Francis (poverty, asceticism, love of prayer), in which the author sought to recast the figure of Francis within a theological perspective. Thus, regarding his youth, Thomas writes that he was predestined for holiness and emphasizes the knightly and courtly aspirations of the Poor Man of Assisi, whereas he had presented Francis in his first *Life* as a merchant blinded by the thirst for gain. Francis is no longer a sinner-become-penitent but an exceptional person to whom God has entrusted the mission to call the people of his time to conversion by his word and example. In a significant way, it is no longer the encounter with the leper that marks a decisive turning point in Francis' spiritual itinerary but a miraculous event—the conversation with the crucifix of San Damiano—that confers a divine seal on his evangelical project. In a context now marked by opposition over the role of the Mendicants in the Church, it was necessary to rethink the figure of the Poverello by emphasizing the importance of the Friars Minor and their holy founder in the history of salvation. In the second part of his work, Thomas of Celano utilizes the elements placed at his disposal by the companions and, in particular, by Brother Leo in order to launch his warnings, both passionate and polemical, to the friars of his day, many of whom, according to him, were neglecting the teachings of Francis and losing sight of his example. The work thus testifies both to the regret of having lost Francis as an incomparable guide and to a real anxiety about the evolution of the order, whose unity is being threatened by rivalries between individuals and internal conflicts.

We find the same concerns, but with a stronger and often more polemical tone, in the collection of exemplary accounts and logia relative to Francis, inspired by the second part of the *Florilegium of Greccio* attributed to Brother Leo, that is referred to under the name of the *Assisi Compilation*.[9] Again it is necessary to be clear that we know this text only through a manuscript dated in

1310 conserved in Perugia (whence the name *Legend of Perugia* that was long given to it), which surely contains additions to the original version. All trace of the early text of the *Compilation* is lost, but its redaction must probably be put in relationship to the new call launched at Padua in 1276 by the Franciscan general chapter urging the Minors again to take up the search for "the works of blessed Francis and of other holy friars." As its title indicates, it is not a biography but a collection devoid of any coherent plan, in which the edifying anecdotes follow one another without any logical connection. We find here episodes which Thomas of Celano had borrowed from the *Florilegium of Greccio* in order to insert them into his *Memorial,* but also texts probably from the pen of Leo. The emphasis is on the person of Francis and on the fact that he had to remain a model for his friars who had known him poorly after his death, when God had judged him worthy to occupy the throne left vacant in heaven by Lucifer after his revolt. For the author, the Poor Man of Assisi was above all a simple and unlettered man who cultivated humility and who energetically opposed every form of pride, especially the "knowledge that puffs up." His whole life, beginning with his conversion, had unfolded under the sign of poverty, and he had not hesitated to engage in begging. As Jacques Dalarun has rightly noted, the image of the founder which emerges from this text is hardly consistent. Indeed, the author highlights the humanity of Francis, especially the evangelical freedom which he manifested in his attitudes and actions, but also the harshness that he showed with respect to his own body and in his relationships with his brothers. It is difficult to know whether these contradictions reflect those of Francis himself or the desire of the disciples to root his person in the spiritual and ascetic tradition of monasticism which could not fail to have influenced them.[10]

The most original aspect of the *Assisi Compilation* resides in the stress put on the torments endured by Francis during the last years of his life. Thomas of Celano had already mentioned this in his *Memorial* of 1247; but here the narrative is more insistent and dramatic. Confronted by the process of the institutionalization of his fraternity, the Poor Man of Assisi was unable to find inner peace and to get beyond the contradictions in the midst of which he was struggling—to the point of becoming mistrustful of his entourage and avoiding all contact. The man Francis is omnipresent in this text, but he appears here above all as a living reproach addressed to his brothers, for the mention of some aspects of his life seems to have an essentially accusatory role. The heart-wrenching account of the sufferings which the lack of understanding by his closest companions had inflicted on him and the denunciation of the oblivion into which all memory of him was in danger of sinking constitutes as much a criticism of the impasse into which the papacy and its own leaders had led the Franciscan order as it was a vigorous reminder to the order. When all is said and done, what emerges from this text is a pessimistic vision of the situation of the Minors and an oppositional discourse whose real significance escapes us. Lacking the ability to date with any precision the various elements of the *Compilation*, we are left to discern whether some of the diatribes which are attributed to Francis—for example, those against vast and sumptuous constructions into which the friars had settled, or against their ambition to become "savants"— were actually spoken by him or whether these are later additions tied to another chronological and institutional context.

The rapid success of the hagiographical texts about Francis in the forty years after his death does not merely reflect his popularity. It also corresponds to a series of successive efforts by his spiritual sons to establish the image of their master: efforts that were inconclusive in that these texts evoked and diffused contrasting interpretations of Francis. Searching for an identity which was not given at the start, they had tried to find answers by rereading the life of the Poor Man of Assisi. Indeed, far more than any other religious order, the Minors were tied to the person of their founder, to his words and his deeds. For most monks, Saint Benedict was only a name: that of the author of the rule which they were striving to follow. As for Saint Bernard, if he had strongly marked the whole Cistercian tradition with his spirituality, it was especially his writings, in particular his admirable biblical commentaries, which held the attention of his disciples. It was wholly otherwise for Francis: first, because he had left only a small number of writings, which, except for the Rule of 1223, were quickly forgotten, but especially because of the charism which he had claimed for himself in his *Testament. Franciscus forma Minorum* (Francis, the "form" of the Friars Minor): this Latin expression found in the liturgical texts is difficult to render into English since the word "form" is too abstract, and "model" would be inadequate as a translation. *Forma* suggests, rather, conformity, or a mold into which one must be poured. From the moment that the reference to Francis and his message was experienced by his disciples as a vital necessity, it was logical that these men might seek in his deeds and acts the key for their own history. At the time, a fundamental question predominated: how was the Order of Friars Minor going to be able to develop without distancing itself from the spirit which had marked its beginnings and from the example of its founder? These impassioned efforts to capture the Franciscan newness and define it in terms acceptable to the Church and the society in which they were living reflect both the formidable impact which the message of the Poverello had had on his contemporaries and the tensions which soon manifested themselves inside the order claiming him for itself.

Indeed, beginning in the 1240s, two principal orientations in the hagiographical realm, corresponding to different interpretations of Franciscanism, began to be affirmed. On the one hand were those who saw in the ideal of "minority," as the Poor Man of Assisi had lived it and proposed it, an evangelical catalyst for human history whose specificity must be preserved at all cost; on the other hand were those who, convinced that the principal aim of Francis had been the reform of Christianity, especially sought to make of the order an effective institution, well integrated into the ecclesiastical organization and endeavoring to attain the pastoral objectives given to it by the papacy. The first group put the accent on the break between the charismatic example of the Poor Man of Assisi and the way that the order had developed after his death, as well as on the steady decline of its fervor, having distanced itself from the purity of the origins and the intentions of its founder. As a result, the recourse to hagiography was essentially a way of escaping from the process of evolution which religious orders know all too well, by emphasizing the radical nature of the early Franciscan project.

The second group, by contrast, endeavored to demonstrate the fundamental continuity that existed, in spite of necessary adaptations, between the will of Francis and the institutional line followed by the order during its brief history. And as these two tendencies did not take long to enter into conflict, Franciscan hagiography took on, from the beginning, a militant and sometimes even polemical character, each biography responding to the previous one in order to fill in its gaps or to dispute the validity of certain assertions figuring therein.

The divergences between these hagiographical sources have sometimes led to their outright rejection, with some authors going so far as to state that, in order to know the life of Francis, it was better to rely on the contemporary witnesses outside the Franciscan order—accounts published under the title of *Testimonia minora* by Leonhard Lemmens in 1926—than on the biographies. But would we deny the reality of the Passion of Christ because the four evangelists have provided narratives which on certain important points are different if not contradictory? On the contrary, the diversity of interpretations of the person of Francis which had marked the hagiography of the Minors up to 1260 constitutes such a richness that allows us to recall episodes in the life of the Poor Man of Assisi whose understanding would be significantly impoverished had only one version of them come down to us. This constant work of revision, correction, and the search for an increasing precision in the recall of the events of his life has not been the simple manifestation of a "duty to remember," as is said today. For more than a century, this process has maintained a fruitful dialogue across the miles with the figure of the founder.[11] In this sense, the Lives of Saint Francis previous to that of Bonaventure and the documentary materials accumulated during this period by his companions constitute, in spite of the problems which their interpretation poses, a privileged field of observation for the one who seeks to know the foundational orientations of the early Franciscan fraternity and the beginnings of the order of Friars Minor.

THE *LEGENDA MAIOR* OF BONAVENTURE (1263):
THE OFFICIAL LIFE OF FRANCIS

A few years after his election as minister general, Bonaventure of Bagnoregio, who led the Friars Minor from 1257 almost until his death in 1274, believed that it was necessary to write a new Life of Saint Francis in order to put an end to the disagreements that were manifesting themselves in the order around the figure of its founder. In 1260 the general chapter of Narbonne entrusted him with this task, which he did with great care, since he wanted to personally meet eyewitnesses who were still alive, like Brother Giles or Brother Illuminato, who had accompanied the Poor Man of Assisi to the sultan of Egypt. Bonaventure's work was approved in 1263, and in 1266 the general chapter of Paris ordered

> that all the legends previously written about the blessed Francis be destroyed and that, where they could be found outside the order, the friars endeavor to suppress them, since this legend which has been written by the general has been compiled according to what he himself had from the lips of those who were almost always with the blessed Francis and who knew all things with certainty and that the things thus attested have been scrupulously written down.[12]

The injunction seems to have been followed with great zeal, for very few manuscripts of the biographies before that of the minister general have survived in Franciscan convents. Fortunately for us, the renown of the saint of Assisi was such that the libraries of a number of houses of other religious orders preserved a few copies of these texts henceforth prohibited among the Minors. Thus were they preserved and, much later, recovered. The consequences of this order to destroy, however, were severe: the *Legenda maior,* soon followed by a *Legenda minor,* was now the only written source from which the friars could draw information about their founder.[13] The Bonaventurean legend is "major" in every sense of the term: its author has tried to fix once and for all the image of the Poor Man of Assisi, and he has largely succeeded.

Although born in central Italy, Bonaventure was educated in Paris, where he had followed the lessons of Alexander of Hales and where he taught theology. He had known neither the Poor Man of Assisi nor the milieu of the first companions. And it is no exaggeration to say that he had received Francis from the Church and even from the papacy, as is clear from the fact that he never refers to the *Testament*. His legend gives us hardly any new elements; on the contrary, some episodes that appear in the previous Lives are not found in Bonaventure's or are interpreted in such a way so as to attenuate their significance. Thus the manual work to which the Poor Man of Assisi had attached well-known importance is nothing more than a simple antidote to idleness. The legend presents itself, moreover, not as a true biography but rather as a compilation of two historical sections corresponding to the beginning and end of the life of Francis, separated by long expositions devoted to his virtues, which are manifestations of his life in Christ. Unconcerned with chronology, the author proceeds by the association of ideas and spiritual themes, and lays out a kind of mosaic assembled from textual fragments borrowed from previous Lives, scrubbed beforehand of the harsher aspects and polemical or nostalgic affirmations which they could have had. However, as fastidious as his interpretation can appear to a reader today, the work possesses a real coherence and a certain freshness. Bonaventure was the first to give a global spiritual interpretation of the figure of Francis, by emphasizing his providential role in the history of salvation and by assigning him a prime place in Christian eschatology.[14]

Indeed, beginning in the 1240s, the ideas of Joachim of Fiore († 1202) had found a certain echo within the Franciscan order. For the notion was disseminated that a great persecution was going to be inflicted upon the Church by a person described as the first Antichrist, identified with the excommunicated Emperor Frederick II, who would seek to destroy it. In this combat, which, according to the Calabrian prophet, was going to mark the transition from the second to the third age of the world, the Age of the Spirit, two groups of "spiritual men" would be called to play a decisive role. It was tempting to identify these battalions destined to victoriously confront the Antichrist and his minions with the two mendicant orders, the Minors and Preachers, whom God had sent at the appropriate time to save his Church. None of this went beyond an orthodox framework, and, as we have seen, Gregory IX had been the first to confer upon Francis an eschatological status by presenting him as the worker at the eleventh hour of the Gospel, come to bring a decisive support to the Church in its struggle against the forces of evil, doubling in strength at the approach of the Last Days. But certain friars, convinced that their order was called to play a decisive role in the coming of this new spiritual age, which, according to Joachim, was going to occur around 1260, went even farther. One of them, Gerard of Borgo San Donnino, did something imprudent by writing and diffusing in Paris, in 1253, an *Introduction to the Eternal Gospel,* in which he did not hesitate to suggest that the ecclesiastical hierarchy had served its purpose and that the Friars Minor had to take up the direction of the new spiritual Church, which was in the process of being established in order to lead it to the full understanding of the "Eternal Gospel." The reaction of the University of Paris and the secular clergy was violent: Gerard was imprisoned to the end of his days, his book was condemned, and the Minors were deprived for a time of their pastoral privileges by Pope Innocent IV. The minister general, John of Parma, held responsible for these deviations, had to resign from his functions in 1257. It is in this dramatic context that Bonaventure was elected to succeed him, and he immediately endeavored to reestablish peace within the Franciscan order and in its relations with the Roman Church.

One of the means of doing this was the redaction of the *Legenda maior,* which profoundly renews the interpretation of the figure of the Poor Man of Assisi within the order by supplying it with a perspective that was both theological and mystical. Francis is presented here as a man who, having gone on the search for Christ and having found him, had become assimilated to him. To demonstrate this "journey of the mind toward God," which culminates in the vision of La Verna, where Francis had mounted like Moses on Sinai, Bonaventure punctuates that journey with successive appearances of Christ crucified, in order to signify that the Poor Man of Assisi had kept his eyes fixed on the cross throughout his life. At the end of this process, he had become a living image of Christ, and this conformity to the Savior had been concretized through the impression of the stigmata in his flesh: a privilege which he was the first and only person to have received. Thus is Francis, who was not a saint like all others, raised above humanity in order to accede to an eschatological status: "Charged with mission like the Angel, wholly burning with the fire with which the seraphim were burning, carried by a chariot of fire after having climbed all the rungs of holiness (*homo hierarchicus*), he came to us with the spirit and power of Elijah."[15]

New Elijah, new John the Baptist, he is the Angel who rose up from the East, while bearing the seal of the living God (namely, the stigmata) mentioned in the Apocalypse (Rev 7:2), after the opening of the sixth seal. By placing on the forehead of the faithful the sign of the Tau (τ)—the nineteenth letter of the Greek alphabet, which, like the Roman capital T, evokes the cross—he had inaugurated a new era in the history of salvation for the Christian people, whose vanguard was constituted by the order of Friars Minor. This grandiose vision is put in the context of a specific eschatological perspective: far from seeing in Francis, like some holders of the joachimite teachings, the one who had undertaken to challenge the clerical structures of a framework that had become obsolete and superfluous, the author of the *Legenda maior* presents him, rather, as the originator of a mystical Christianity which was going to enable the establishment of new relationships between the Church and the human race. But at the same time that he exalts and renders the figure of Francis sublime, as none of the previous biographers had dared to do, Bonaventure deprives his charism of all historical dimension and endeavors to reformulate it in impersonal terms. For him, what is of the divine in the Poor Man of Assisi is not his life but the rule of his order as it was approved and interpreted by the papacy. Through the *Legenda maior*, the minister general has obviously sought to turn the attention of his readers or hearers away from their founder's deeds and actions—but also his words and writings—which they were still scrutinizing in search of a justification for their behavior. To exorcise this fundamental anxiety, Bonaventure presents himself as the champion of a living and intelligent fidelity to the Franciscan spirit, while underlining that the experience of the early years was only the initial phase of an evolving process which could go in a direction that Francis had not necessarily foreseen:

> I vow before God that the reason why I have loved the life of Saint Francis so much is that it resembles the beginning and the growth of the Church, which began with simple fishermen, then was later enriched by illustrious doctors and scholars. Thus, the order of Saint Francis has not been established by the prudence of human beings but by Christ . . . and the best proof of its divine character resides in the fact that the people reputed for their wisdom have not been afraid to mingle with the company of simple men.[16]

It could not be said more clearly that the experience of the first time of the fraternity could no longer constitute an absolute reference and paradigm for the Franciscan order and that it was no longer right to accord it a privileged attention. Whereas the previous hagiographers, beginning with Thomas of Celano, had had a tendency to see in the rapid increase in the number of friars a factor of decadence or, at the very least, of relaxation, Bonaventure reverses the perspective: the historical context having evolved, certain practices or recommendations of Francis, like the prohibition against the friars' possessing books or the obligation to do manual work, no longer had meaning at a time now marked by the growth of studies and universities, a time when well-formed preachers were needed. In Bonaventure's eyes, adapting the rule to new conditions was not the sign of decline but, on the contrary, a necessity, and the presence within the Minors of an ever-growing number of bishops and doctors in theology was a testimony to the assistance which God had continually accorded this order, which was his work and not that of Francis, the simple instrument of his will. In the last analysis, it was thus the growth of the order and its ever-more-intense incorporation into the structures of the Church that constituted the proof and guarantee of the divine grace that was working within it.

Bonaventure, who was, with Thomas Aquinas, one of the great intellectual figures of the thirteenth century, believed that the order of Friars Minor had to dissociate itself from the history of its founder. But instead of clearly assuming this break, he tried to resolve the problem by dehumanizing the figure of Francis. Indeed, in the *Legenda maior*, poverty is reduced to an interior virtue deprived of all human contact and social repercussions. When Bonaventure reports the episode of the encounter of the Poor Man of Assisi with the leper, he says that the latter disappeared in a miraculous way at the moment when Francis embraced him, as if the leper had been a phantom or a simple occasion offered to the saint to manifest his charity.[17] Forty years after the redaction of the rule of 1221, the spirit that had animated the "foundational document" of the early fraternity was reversed! Francis has become an ascetic and a mystic. He is no longer the initiator of a religious movement founded on the practice of *minoritas*, and the friars could at the very most be inspired by his example in the matter of mortification and obedience. In the last analysis, we can say that with the *Legenda maior* of Bonaventure, we see at work in the hagiographical domain a process comparable to that which had led, after 1239, to the clericalization of the Franciscan order and which was profoundly distorting the original spirit. In every sense of the term, it was a matter of a "misadventure"—according to the expression used by Jacques Dalarun in another context—which will have a difficult life and grave consequences, since, up to the nineteenth century, the *Legenda maior* has been the principal source, if not the only biography, through which it was possible to have access to the figure of the Poor Man of Assisi, and the one which inspired artists, beginning with Giotto, in their representations of the saint and the principal episodes of his life.

THE FRANCIS OF THE COMPANIONS AND THE SPIRITUALS: THE RETURN OF THE MARGINALIZED AND VISION OF THE SILENCED

During the generalate of Bonaventure (who, after becoming a cardinal, died in 1274), calm returned among the Minors, and the interpretation that he had given of the holiness of Francis does not seem to have been openly contested. It is true that the threats that weighed heavily at that time upon the role and very survival of the order, increasingly criticized by the secular clergy and attacked by some bishops at the Second Council of Lyons in 1274, fostered a kind of solidarity within the order. In the long run, the brothers emerged as victors over these trials, and the conception of Franciscan poverty elaborated by Bonaventure was, in some way, "canonized" by Nicholas III in 1279. In his bull *Exiit qui seminat*, which was immediately inserted as a decretal into canon law, this pope affirmed in effect that the rule of Saint Francis was no longer to be the subject of criticism, and that the renunciation, for the sake of God, by the friars of the possession of goods in common was holy and in conformity with evangelical perfection. The same text dispensed them from doing manual work and authorized them to have books. Their pastoral privileges were even widened in 1281 through the bull *Ad fructus uberes* of Martin IV, which granted them the freedom to preach and hear confessions everywhere without having to ask permission from bishops or pastors. This decision, in contradiction with the thought and words of Saint Francis, who, in his *Testament*, had asked the Minors not to seek to impose themselves where priests were not disposed to welcome them, again increased the hostility of the secular clergy.[18]

After the death of Bonaventure, tensions soon reappeared and became exacerbated within the Franciscan order, to the extent that the favors and privileges which it had received from the papacy had accentuated the tendency toward relaxation and abuses. Beginning in the years 1275–1280, an oppositional current arose in the Mediterranean countries—from Italy to Catalonia and including Provence and Languedoc—among friars who came to be referred to as "Spirituals." In fact, this was not an organized faction but comprised individuals and groups who, while sometimes differing on remedies, deplored the evolution which the order had undergone during recent decades and who aspired to live in poverty in all its purity. One of their principal spokespersons was the great Spiritual and theologian Peter of John Olivi († 1298), who recalled that the friars, not content to possess anything either individually or in common, also had to have the "poor use" (*usus pauper*) of goods that were placed at their disposition. These ideas were condemned in 1297 by the Franciscan hierarchy, in whose eyes the essential criterion was the usefulness that the order had for the Church. These ideas expanded throughout central Italy, in particular in Florence, where Olivi had resided and taught for some time, as well as in southern France, where his writings in the vernacular had influenced numerous "Beguines," some of whom belonged to the Franciscan Third Order.

Beginning in the 1290s, the conflicts between the Spirituals and the Community—that is, the majority of the Order that was pleased with the current situation—had become violent, and the dissidents soon saw no other way forward but to ask the papacy and the hierarchy of the order to recognize the existence of two distinct currents within Franciscanism and to allow them to live in accordance with their ideas, without being disturbed or molested. They believed that they had obtained justice for their cause when, in 1294, a hermit from the Abruzzi renowned for his simplicity and austerity, was elected as Pope Celestine V, whom they immediately called "the angelic pope." Celestine authorized the petitioners to establish a congregation of "Poor Hermits of Pope Celestine." But he resigned after only a few months. His successor, Boniface VIII (r. 1294–1303), annulled without delay this decision of his predecessor and placed the Spirituals once again under the authority of their superiors within the convents of the Community, where they were roughly treated. Some of them, in particular Angelo Clareno and Ubertino da Casale, refused to submit themselves and fled to Greece and Armenia, while the great Franciscan poet Jacopone da Todi (1230–1306), who had heaped sarcastic criticisms upon Boniface VIII and supported the revolt of the Colonna in 1298, was thrown into prison. The conflict arose again at the Council of Vienne (1311–1312), called by Pope Clement V, who tried in vain to reconcile the two camps after examining the grievances and dossiers set forth by both camps. His successor, the jurist John XXII (r. 1316–1334), exasperated by these struggles, put an apparent end to them by condemning the Spirituals and unleashing against them and their supporters a bloody persecution that created numerous victims, particularly in southern France.

This stormy context, which climaxed during the period 1328–1340 in a major crisis in the relationship between the papacy and the Franciscan order, had historiographic and hagiographic repercussions. Beginning in the last decades of the thirteenth century, the efforts deployed by Bonaventure to minimize the significance of the example constituted by the life of the Poor Man of Assisi came under attack, and some Spiritual friars accused him of having deliberately betrayed Francis' message.[19] Even if everyone did not go as far, we see being affirmed from various sides, between the last quarter of the thirteenth century and the middle of the fourteenth, efforts to propose an image of Francis different from that which had been laid out by the *Legenda maior.* In the camp of the Spirituals, a certain number of writings were drawn up, without official recognition and sometimes circulated secretly, which reflected the malaise within the order as well as a real desire to reconnect with the spiritual climate of early Franciscanism through the example of the founder. Their authors were indeed animated by the conviction that the uniqueness of the holiness of the Poor Man of Assisi resided in his way of life and that it was indispensable to emphasize the aspects of his life which were capable of inciting the friars and the penitents to imitate his virtues. The majority of them were inspired, in different degrees, by the dossier compiled in 1244–1246 by the first companions and especially by Brother Leo, who had embellished it up to his death in 1271. Added to it was a collection of *Words of Francis* (*Verba Francisci*) and considerations on the interpretation of the rule (*Intentio regulae*). Two Friars Minor from the region of the Marches, which was the refuge of the Spirituals, Conrad of Offida and James of Massa, handed on this heritage to Angelo Clareno and Ubertino da Casale, leaders of the dissident movement from the end of the thirteenth century and beginning of the fourteenth. Ubertino had recovered the "rolls" that Leo had given to the abbess of the monastery of Saint Clare of Assisi and used them to feed the polemic against the Community at the Council of Vienne, by referring explicitly to the words of Francis transmitted therein. It is in this context that was elaborated, in 1310 at the latest, the final version—the only one which has come down to us—of the *Assisi Compilation*. In the same line, an anonymous author drafted in 1317–1318 the *Mirror of Perfection* (*Speculum perfectionis*), an important text in which Paul Sabatier, at the end of the nineteenth century, believed that he had found the "real" Life of Francis of Assisi, which, according to him, had been concealed and kept hidden by the authorities of the order.[20]

In these writings of the Spiritual tendency, Francis is presented as a "mirror"—a perfect reflection—of the poverty and sufferings of Christ, whence the title given to some of them (*Speculum minus*, after 1276; *Speculum perfectionis* in 1318). The aim pursued by their authors was not to draw up new biographies but to trace an ideal portrait of the Friar Minor by way of exemplary accounts drawn from the life of the Poor Man of Assisi and his first companions. Contrary to the interpretation of Gregory IX taken up by Nicholas III in the bull *Exiit qui seminat*, they declared that the rule had to be read in the light of the *Testament* and followed to the letter. For them, poverty—which was not limited to the renunciation of ownership but had to be translated into a particular style of life in terms of clothing and dwellings—constituted the essential if not exclusive criterion of authentic Franciscanism. Thus had they taken up with insistence in their writings the criticisms which the founder had formulated while he was still alive against excessively comfortable houses, huge churches, and the possession of books. Finally, these texts exalted the "little flock" which, within the order, had remained faithful to the intuition and will of Francis, as well as the particular affection that he had had for humble and simple religious, whom he presented as his "knights of the Round Table." The Portiuncula, to which it was believed Pope Innocent III had granted in 1215 a plenary indulgence at the request of Francis, is presented here as the spiritual high point of Franciscanism, in opposition to the basilica and Sacro Convento, which had become symbols of power and luxury.

This focus on the myth of origins marks the return, front and center, of everything that the work of Bonaventure had tried to roll back. But the moving evocation of the beginnings of the order that one finds in these works is situated now in a polemical context, the aim pursued by the authors being to breathe life again into an ideal which they believed to have been betrayed. Since this line of thinking was in the minority among the Friars Minor, and as its adherents were soon marginalized or eliminated, the contrasts became radicalized. Faced with a reality that was more and more disappointing for them, the Spirituals called prophecy to the rescue and laid particular emphasis in their writings on the revelations which Francis had received from God. Bonaventure had mentioned them in his *Legenda maior*, but had emphasized that the saint had never wished to divulge their content and that it was thus useless to consider them. For the Spirituals, by contrast, the substance of these messages, which included the prediction of imminent tribulations in the order, had to be revealed in order to give courage to those who found themselves in the midst of trials: the "remnant" that was maintaining the bond of fidelity uniting the Friars Minor to their founder and who were suffering veritable persecutions by the Community and the "carnal Church." But thanks to the support of an angelic pope and to the coming of a Restorer, who would lead the Friars Minor back to the purity of their origins, the persecuted minority was to end up triumphing over its adversaries and regenerating the order and Christianity.

The image that the Spiritual Franciscans sought to give to Francis reflects what we can call "the vision of the silenced," intended to compensate, through an escape into eschatology, for the disappointments that the evolution of the order and the growing hostility of the papacy in their regard were inflicting on them. As their contemporary Dante Alighieri has Bonaventure say in the *Divine Comedy* of two emblematic figures of the Franciscan order (the intransigent defender of absolute poverty Ubertino da Casale and the cardinal Matthew of Acquasparta, concerned above all with putting the Minors at the service of the Church):

> But such will come neither from Casale nor from Acquasparta
> for those from there who read our Rule
> are given either to flee from it or to make it too strict.[21]

The author of the *Divine Comedy* intended by this to underscore the irreducible opposition between the friars: on the one side, those for whom obedience to the Church was an end in itself which justified abandoning rigorous application of the rule; on the other side, those who, considering poverty the heart of the Franciscan message, identified it as Christian perfection itself. But the verses of Dante can equally mean that, in his eyes, the "reading" which the Spirituals were making of Francis and his rule was not necessarily more faithful to his authentic spirit than that of their adversaries.

FROM THE *ACTUS/FIORETTI* TO *THE BOOK OF CONFORMITIES*: THE FOLKLORIZING OF FRANCISCANISM AND APOLOGETIC DETOURS

After 1330 the principal leaders of the Spiritual currents within the Franciscan order were scarcely able to make themselves heard, condemned as they were to flight and clandestinity; and they soon disappeared. But the form of religious sensitivity that they incarnated survived them and continued up to the end of the fourteenth century to impregnate writings relative to Francis, of which certain ones have profoundly contributed to the construction and diffusion of his image. Between 1327 and 1337, Ugolino di Montegiorgio, a Friar Minor who was living in the Marches of Ancona—a region to the east of Umbria and rich in hermitages where the memory of the Poverello remained very much alive—composed a work in Latin titled *The Deeds of Saint Francis and His Companions (Actus Beati Francisci et sociorum eius)*, which was completed after his death by a continuator.[22] This obscure religious, who lived in the little convent of Soffiano and seems to have had a modest level of education, knew the writings of Brother Leo as well as those of Angelo Clareno and was familiar with the community of La Verna, renowned for its rigorous observance of the rule. In this collection, he reports the "notable facts and admirable deeds" of Francis, as well as those of some of his companions "omitted in the legends but which are greatly useful and precious," while adding developments relative to the life and miracles of a few saintly Friars Minor who had lived in the Marches of Ancona. The *Actus* was translated into Italian (Tuscan) between 1370 and 1390 by an anonymous Franciscan, who put a little order into this composite work and markedly abridged it (from seventy-six chapters to fifty-three), while appending to it five "Considerations on the Stigmata." The ensemble which results from these alterations bears the name of the *Fioretti di messer sancto Francesco e d'alquanti suoi santi compagni* and presents itself in fact as a sprig of "little flowers" *(fioretti)*—that is, as exemplary episodes and accounts that follow each other without logical link.[23] Unlike the *Actus*, the *Fioretti* was widely diffused and constitutes one of the signal vernacular texts of Italian literature of the fourteenth century. It is a work of edification that aims to increase the prestige of Francis and the Friars Minor. Historical exactitude is not its strength, even if its authors have been able to integrate into their accounts known stories worthy of faith transmitted by oral tradition or in writings which have not come down to us. But their principal interest lies in the expression of a popular Franciscanism that constitutes a mindset more than a program of action or claims.

The *Fioretti* displays a marked increase of the marvelous by comparison with previous hagiographical writings. As Frédéric Ozanam noted in the middle of the nineteenth century, "to the extent that the memory [of Francis] becomes more distant, the imaginations which do not want to detach themselves from him delight in reviving him by way of new traits; wonder is added to wonder, without lying and only for this need that we have to believe and to admire."[24] Thus the meeting of Francis with the sultan of Egypt ends, as in a fable, with the baptism of the latter as death approaches. The conversion came after the Poor Man of Assisi had demonstrated his holiness by proposing that a beautiful Saracen woman, who had come to his room to seduce him, sleep with him on a bed of coals where he was lying without any harm. This prompted the repentance and conversion of the temptress as well.[25] Similarly, we find in the *Fioretti* a moving account, though purely legendary, of a visit by Saint Louis, king of France, to Brother Giles in Perugia. In the course of this meeting, the two men embraced without exchanging a word, so much had each understood at first glance the depth of their spiritual agreement.[26] And here is recounted for the first time in detail the famous episode of the wolf of Gubbio, already mentioned in general terms in certain sermons at the end of the thirteenth century.[27] Through this process of the folklorizing of the Franciscan deed is expressed both the nostalgia of a lost paradise—the time of the beginnings of the early fraternity which, at 140 years' distance, still remained an essential reference point—and the desire of the authors to exalt the greatness of the spiritual revolution introduced by Francis. Sometimes the evocation of the fusion of the human and divine, so characteristic of the work, is particularly successful, as in the account of the meal taken in common at the Portiuncula by Francis and Clare, surrounded by a few of their companions:

And, during the first course, Saint Francis began to speak about God with such eloquence, with such elevation, so marvelously was the divine grace descending upon them in abundance that they were all caught up in God. And while they were thus raptured, their eyes and their hands lifted up to heaven, the people of Assisi and Bettona and those of the surrounding countryside, saw that Saint Mary of the Angels and the whole convent and woods which was at that time next to the convent were in the process of being completely consumed by flames, and it seemed to them that a single fire was occupying the place of the church and convent. Thus the people of Assisi ran there in great haste in order to extinguish the fire, firmly believing that everything was burning up. But having arrived at the convent and seeing that nothing was burning, they entered there and found Saint Francis and Saint Clare and all their companions caught up in God in contemplation, and seated around this humble table. Whence they understood with certitude that this was a divine and not a material fire that God had made appear miraculously to show and represent the fire of divine love with which the souls of the holy friars and sisters were burning. Thus did they leave, their hearts filled with a great consolation and spiritually edified.[28]

Through such imagined accounts, the authors of the *Actus* and the *Fioretti* also emphasize, as is natural, what is closest to their hearts. If they show themselves attached, like the Spirituals of the preceding generation, to the exaltation of material poverty and humility, they especially value ascetic rigor and the search for perfection through the practice of a strict observance of the rule culminating in the mystical life. The friars whose virtues and miracles they celebrate—like Bernard, the first companion of Francis, Giles, and different holy men of Umbria and the Marches—are presented here as contemplatives living in hermitages where one came to find them in order to solicit their spiritual help or intervention, not as religious concerned above all with pastoral action. Francis himself, whom the *Actus* and *Fioretti* place at the side of and yet above the group of the first twelve companions—like Christ surrounded by his twelve apostles—is exalted here as a fully evangelical man; but he is also depicted as the holder of mysterious secrets and certain promises concerning the future of his order. God assures him during his stigmatization that it will endure until the end of the world, that its adversaries will perish, and that every person who loves it will have a good end. Such rigorist and "corporatist" (institutional) inflections, already present in some hagiographical texts of the second half of the thirteenth century and in the writings of the Spirituals, had an important growth the farther behind one leaves the period when the Poor Man of Assisi and his companions had lived, about whom one had, by 1230, only an indirect and largely mythical knowledge.

One of the major themes of this whole literature is that of the conformity of Francis to Christ. The theme is not strictly speaking a novelty, for it was already assumed in the *Legenda maior* of Bonaventure, and, toward 1300, the Franciscan poet, Jacopone da Todi, had given this relationship an admirable formulation in one of his *laude*: "O Francis beloved of God, Christ showed himself in you" ("O Francesco da Dio amato/Cristo en te s'ene mustrato," *Lauda* 62, 1–2). But it is in the *Actus* that Francis is explicitly presented as "a second Christ given to the world," an expression which will be taken up again in the *Fioretti* and later still will be the object of lively polemics.[29] To maintain, as numerous Franciscan authors did in the fourteenth and fifteenth centuries, that Francis was "another Christ" or a "second Christ"—*alter* in Latin means the other, the second in a relationship between two people—was in effect the same as saying that Francis was so far along in the following of the Savior that he was in some way identified with the life and person of the latter. But this affirmation was not lacking in ambiguity. Was it simply a matter of qualifying his extraordinary spiritual experience by underscoring that the Poor Man of Assisi had been the renewer of the evangelical life in the world and that he had by his renewed witness to the message of Jesus the impact and actuality that it had lost in the course of centuries? Or did it mean that he was truly the reincarnation of Christ, *Christus redividus*, which raised theological difficulties, since the Church considered the Son of God as the sole Mediator? Franciscans of the Spiritual orientation began to incline toward this interpretation. Ubertino da Casale speaks of a total assimilation of Francis to Christ; in the same years, Angelo Clareno evokes the perspective of a glorious resurrection of the Poor Man of Assisi once the corruption and decadence of the Franciscan order attained their culmination point. In the *Actus*, the interpretation of the theme of conformity is literal, since Francis is presented here as a "conformed copy" of the Son of God. In the "Considerations on the Stigmata," which follows the *Fioretti*, the account of the stigmatization is enriched by a number of specific details about the place, the hour, and the circumstances of the phenomenon, which aims to render it fully believable but brings no new element to its understanding and, on the contrary, accentuates its supernatural character.

The last step of this process of exaltation was attained with the *Book of Conformities*, composed between 1385 and 1399 by Bartholomew of Pisa (*De conformitate vitae Beati Francisci ad vitam Domini Iesu*), approved by the Franciscan general chapter in 1399, and afterward diffused widely throughout Christianity, especially after the invention of the printing press.[30] The work parallels the life of Francis with that of Christ. The author lifts up no fewer than nine conformities between them, explained within the context of forty "fruits" which structure his laborious demonstration. It is a wordy synthesis which, in the effort of establishing at all cost a relationship of perfect identity between the two persons, sinks into artifice and fable, for their conformity is manifested only under its most external aspects. Thus, according this work, Francis came into the world in a stable and was placed by his father in a manger in order that the circumstances of his birth might be similar to those of the birth of Christ. This mechanism—an empty, awkward effort to divinize the founder of the Minors and exalt in the same breath these same friars above all other religious orders—tragically illustrates the incapacity of the Franciscans of the end of the fourteenth century to grasp the spiritual experience of their founder in terms adapted to the cultural demands of their day. With this book, the alienation of the friars from the figure and message of the Poor Man of Assisi reached such a degree that one can say that, with it, a period of Franciscanism came to an end. The thread of the connection to the first generations having been broken, the search for the true image of Francis through the redaction of hagiographical texts was going to be interrupted, for the problems were now elsewhere. After 1400 the polemics and conflicts between the different branches and reforming movements within the order of Minors, all claiming to be the legitimate heirs of Francis—Observants against Conventuals in the fifteenth century, then, after 1530, Capuchins against Friars Minor—were to monopolize all energies. Indeed: so thoroughly that the Middle Ages, which had been so rich in stimulating interpretations of the saint of Assisi, would transmit to the modern age only an impoverished and schematic image of him.

FRANCIS IN IMAGES

In a paradoxical manner, specialists of Franciscan studies, who are passionate about hagiographical texts regarding the Poor Man of Assisi and who have argued among themselves for more than a century, have become interested in the iconography only since the 1980s. This fundamental gap probably results from the fact that historians have long considered images as mere reflections of the writings which had inspired their creators. For several decades now, we have been more aware of the uniqueness of the iconographical sources, which must not be considered simply as illustrations and which, even when they have been inspired by well-known texts, maintain broad autonomy in relation to them. In this perspective, the Italian historian Chiara Frugoni has played a pioneering role by studying the evolution of the iconography of the stigmata of Saint Francis in the Italian and European art from the thirteenth century and the early fourteenth. She has shown how these representations give us information as valuable and original as do the Lives and miracle collections.[31] Even if we do not share all the conclusions she has drawn from her inquiries, we must recognize that she has opened a way on which many, since then, have been engaged, and that many questions have been posed anew.

At the time when Francis died, portrait art was just in its infancy. Since the end of Antiquity, the human figure had disappeared from Western art. And when it reappeared in the course of the twelfth century, it kept for a long time a stereo-typical and hieratic aspect in mural painting as well as in sculpture. Thus we possess no realistic portrait of the Poor Man of Assisi before the last quarter of the thirteenth century, whereas his first biographer, Thomas of Celano, has left us a precise description of his physical appearance, largely from direct observa-tion.[32] Beyond this hagiographical text, we have a testimony that confirms that Francis was no Adonis. The chronicler Thomas of Split, who had seen him preach in Bologna on August 15, 1222, tells us, "He was wearing a nasty habit; his whole person seemed without significance; his face was not handsome." At a time when effigies were being painted and sculpted of only a few sovereigns or great ladies, there was no place for a realistic portrait of the Poverello. By contrast, we do possess an idealized representation of him that was painted a few months before his canonization (July 16, 1228), since the name that figures there is that of Brother Francis, and not Saint Francis. This fresco is found in the Saint Gregory chapel of the Sacro Speco, in the great abbey of Subiaco, where he had gone in 1222; an effigy of Pope Gregory IX painted in the same place opposite that of Francis and serves as its pairing.[33] The Poor Man of Assisi is represented facing out, without nimbus or stigmata, with a beard and a monas-tic habit, the waist belted by a cord of seven knots (possibly added later, for the image has often been touched up over the centuries), and holding in his hand a square scroll bearing the inscription "Peace be to this house!" But however interesting it might be, this representation of the founder of the Minors as a person of tall stature—whereas we know him to be short—dressed in a Benedic-tine habit, with blond hair and the emaciated physiognomy of an ascetic, tells us more about the monks' admiration for him than about his real appearance. We can say as much of the first tableaux which appeared in central Italy, a *pala* or *dossale* in wood, which typically bore a painted image of the Virgin or of a saint that a devotee placed behind the altar, like those of Bonaventura Berling-hieri at San Miniato (1228?) and at Pescia (1235). These works where Francis is depicted alone reflect the reverential attitude of the friars and of the faithful toward the founder of the Minors and the stigmatic of La Verna, but they tell us little about his life and actions. That was about to change, though, as the fame of the Poor Man of Assisi became diffused in hagiographical texts and preach-ing. Francis had so struck his contemporaries that the emotions which animated his presence, the originality of his relationships with people and animals, and the newness of his message all contributed to the individualization of the image that evolved over several decades. Let's note in passing that the same phenomenon occurred in the case of the emperor Frederick II, another marvelous character (*stupor mundi*) of this era, who was the first medieval sovereign whose iconographical depictions—mostly sculptures, in his case—were meant to reconstitute the physiognomy of the person.

With the success of his order and the multiplication of convents that constituted so many mediators of his memory, Francis became, in a few decades, a figure of major importance in Italian art.[34] Beginning around 1250, we see images of the Poverello being diffused, like those of Margarito of Arezzo, which, while conserving a certain stiffness or awkwardness, depict him as a living person, small in stature and with an expressive face, whose whole body seems animated by a very definite movement, in conformity with the memory of the friars who had known him, which oral tradition passed on. But it is not before 1275–1280 that we witness the full and entire recovery of the person of Francis in painting, with the realistic portrait—a man small and homely, with an emaciated face but still beaming an extreme gentleness—which the Florentine Cimabue made of him on the right side of the north transept of the lower basilica of Assisi, next to a Virgin with Child. This famous work, realized in a context that we know nothing about, marks a qualitative leap, considerable in relation to previous works, and probably constitutes one of the most eloquent testimonies that the art of the Middle Ages has handed on to us of the Poor Man of Assisi.

The influence of the biographies of France soon made themselves felt on the great retables of a single panel which were then being painted for the convents of the Friars Minor in Tuscany as well as in Umbria. Here, various episodes of his life and some of his miracles figured on either side of the central image and on the *prédelle*. Among those that have come down to us—according to the specialists, they represent barely one percent of those that existed at the time—a certain number of them were painted during the years 1244–1257, during the generalates of Crescentius of Jesi and John of Parma. But these years were marked, as we have seen with respect to the written sources, by the search for new testimonies relative to Francis and by the composition of various texts by the first companions, with the aim of exalting his role as "new evangelist" and the exceptional character of his sanctity at a time when the place of the Friars Minor within the Church was beginning to become problematic.

Such is the intent that one finds in a tableau of Byzantine style that is called the *Bardi Tavola*, so named because of its location, since the sixteenth century, in the chapel of the Bardi family in the Franciscan church of Santa Croce in Florence. Art historians have not been able to pinpoint its dating, which varies, according to author, from 1243 to 1263. It is in any case before the *Legenda maior* of Bonaventure and even, according to Chiara Frugoni, before the *Memorial* of Thomas of Celano, from which it does not borrow any scenes. This would suggest a realization in the years 1243–1245.[35] This work has value less for the fairly conventional image that it presents of Francis than for the twenty painted panels which appear under an inscription, held by two angels, inviting the onlooker to contemplate these *dogmata vitae*—that is, the precepts and specific teachings that one could draw from the different episodes of his life. The author of the tableau drew his inspiration from the first *Life of Saint Francis* by Thomas of Celano. But the principal interest of the work stems from scenes that appear here, some of which were never depicted afterward: Francis freed by his mother from the place where his father had imprisoned him; his taking off his shoes out of devotion, like Moses before the Burning Bush, at the moment when the priest begins to read the Gospel that will be the start of his conversion—an episode that finds no attestation in the written sources; his snatching some lambs from a herd of goats or from the slaughter, after he was given an alms by a passerby; his choosing for himself and his brothers a habit in the form of a cross; his stripping naked, attached to a column, in front of his astonished fellow citizens; or even his carrying a leper seated on his knees, much like a mother her child and washing the feet of several others. We would be wrong to attribute this work, anachronistically, to a milieu of Spirituals or zealot-friars, hostile to the interventions of the papacy in the life of the order, since other aspects of Franciscanism are highlighted there: several "classic" and expected scenes (the renunciation by Francis of his goods and the abandoning of his clothing to his father; the approval of his rule by Innocent III; Christmas Mass in Greccio; the appearance of the saint at the chapter in Arles; the stigmatization and death of the Poverello; his canonization by Gregory IX) are all found there, and the ensemble is marked by a strong presence of the clergy and hierarchy. On the other hand, three scenes depict Francis in the process of preaching: to the birds, to the Saracens (pictured as peaceful and attentive listeners), and to shepherds. The image that emerges from the whole seems in conformity with the spirit of the Poverello, and the accent is on the concrete and even provocative aspects of the Franciscan message: the poverty, humility, and nakedness of Francis, penitent and friend of lepers, whose example the onlooker is urged to follow. At the same time, the friars, faced with the controversies that their order was beginning to be the object of, exalt the exceptional character of this stigmatized saint, who had accomplished so many wonders while alive and who remained after his death an efficacious intercessor (we find here no fewer than four miracle scenes), as well as the importance of preaching in his apostolate. In sum, the *Bardi Tavola* reflects a Franciscanism that is both faithful to its origins and sure of its mission, ever in contact with the testimony of the first companions of the Poor Man of Assisi, several of whom were still living at the time when it was painted.

During the second half of the thirteenth century, especially in Assisi, at the basilica of Saint Francis, a whole iconography of the founder of the Minors began to develop within the great compositions which constitute veritable ideological syntheses inspired by the hierarchy of the order, under the control of the papacy, whose Sacro Convento had become one of its preferred residences. During the 1250s and 1260s, an unknown painter who is called the Master of Saint Francis covered the lower basilica with frescoes.[36] This cycle, which unfolds along the length of the northern side of the principal nave, was damaged in the fourteenth century during the construction of the side chapels. We thus get only a fragmentary idea of it from the paintings which remain. Enough of it remains, however, to confirm that this was an ambitious program, since a certain number of episodes from the life of Christ are depicted parallel to those from Francis' life. Thus, in the first scene, Francis is depicted at the moment when he had just taken off his clothes in front of his father, while, on the other side of the nave, we see Christ stripped of his clothing before the crucifixion. The message is clear: it is an affirmation of the conformity of Francis to Jesus, suffering and crucified, which makes of him a new or second Christ. The exceptional holiness of the stigmatic of La Verna has repercussions for his order, which carries out a mission of major importance within the Church and the world, as the following scenes illustrate, depicting, respectively, the dream of Innocent III in which Francis holds up a church threatening to collapse, and the preaching to the birds. Then follow the stigmatization and the death of Francis, opposite which are to be found the descent of Christ from the cross and the meal at Emmaus.

But it is in the upper basilica of Assisi that the Franciscan epic is presented in its most elevated form in the cycle of twenty-eight great scenes realized by Giotto and his collaborators, probably between 1295 and 1304—that is, during the pontificate of Boniface VIII, the great adversary of the Spirituals.[37] It is far beyond our scope here to treat the exceptional artistic quality of this pictorial ensemble, which marks a decisive turning point in the history of Italian and Western art; even less can we enter into questions of attribution and stylistic influences which have in recent decades inspired divergent interpretations by art historians. But this vast iconographical program reflects the image that the ruling authorities of the Church and Franciscan order were creating of Francis and intending to diffuse in the 1300s. This is what interests us here.

The sponsors of these frescoes—among whom were the Franciscan cardinal Matthew of Acquasparta, minister general in 1287–1288—drew their inspiration from the *Legenda maior* of Bonaventure, which is not at all surprising for that was, since 1266, the only official and authorized Life of the Poor Man of Assisi. But far from simply transposing that account into images, they made deliberate choices here, which, in some cases, have been heightened by the work of the artists. Thus the figure of the saint, who is depicted for the first time without a beard in the period prior to his conversion, is modeled on that of an ancient hero, with the bearing robust and somewhat emphatic, and he appears as if detached from the context in which he is depicted. This does not simply constitute a background, splendid nonetheless, with a landscape of urban architecture inspired by Rome and depictions of the Umbrian countryside, flowering or uncultivated according to the case. Francis now lives in the legend and appears here "more admirable than imitable," according to the expression employed about him by Bonaventure (*LMaj* 6:2). This illustration of his life constitutes the exaltation of a magnificent adventure, detached as it were from time, as it seems to drift in a dreamworld. Indeed, we cannot fail to be struck by the considerable place made for dreams and visions in this cycle. One after the other they appear: the palace full of arms that Francis saw the morning after his failed departure for war; the crucifix which spoke to him at San Damiano; the dream of Innocent III; the vision of Rivo Torto, where the friars present saw the Poverello go up into the heavens on a chariot of fire; the vision of Brother Pacificus of a throne and the seats of the fallen angels in heaven reserved for Francis and his companions; an ecstasy of Francis lifted up from the earth into a kind of cloud; his vision of Christ in the crèche in Greccio, placed in a marble structure resembling a kind of basilica, with neither animals nor hay; the apparition of the saint at the chapter in Arles, where Anthony of Padua was preaching, illustrating the approval by the Poor Man of Assisi of Anthony's preaching, founded on a knowledgeable exegesis; and, finally, two visions of Francis which an anonymous Friar Minor and Bishop Guido II of Assisi were blessed with at the moment of his death. In addition are depictions of six miracles (three while he was alive and three others posthumously, one of which concerning a heretic) and three episodes tied to the stigmatization of Francis (the contemplation by the Poverello of the crucified Seraphim at La Verna; verification of the reality of the stigmata on his corpse by Jerome, a notable of Assisi, in the architectural framework of the basilica of San Francesco—which obviously did not exist in 1226—whereas the legend of Bonaventure clearly situates the scene at the Portiuncula; and the vision of Gregory IX wracked by doubt about the reality of the side wound that Francis received at the time of his stigmatization and to whom Francis appeared by showing it to him, gaping and bloody). In sum, we can say that almost two-thirds of the scenes (eighteen out of twenty-eight) are consecrated to supernatural phenomena or presented as such.[38] Those which refer to well-attested episodes from the biography of the Poor Man of Assisi—twelve to be exact—are faithful representations from the beginning of his life, up to his conversion and the approval of the rule by Innocent III, as well as the end of his life, his death, his burial, and his canonization.

But of the sixteen years of Francis' apostolic ministry, Giotto and his sponsors have retained only three episodes, all concerning preaching: before the sultan of Egypt, to the birds, and in the presence of Pope Honorius III and the curia, in such a way as to underscore that the fundamental vocation of the Franciscan order was to preach to all creatures with the approval of the Roman Church. Throughout the cycle, Francis is compared, in an explicit or implicit manner, to the great figures of the Old and New Testaments (Jacob when he blessed his brothers; Moses when he made the water spring up from the rock to give a thirsty peasant to drink; Elijah in the scene of the chariot of fire; Mary, to whom he is substituted as intercessor; Peter and Paul when he broke the chains of the heretic detained in prison), and to the greatest Christian saints (Martin, whom he excels in holiness when he gives his entire cloak to a poor man). He is identified even with Christ, certainly in the stigmatization but also from the first episode where one sees a simple man unfurling a cloak under his feet in the streets of Assisi, as the inhabitants of Jerusalem had done for the Messiah on Palm Sunday; or again when he shows to an incredulous pope, as did Jesus to Saint Thomas, the reality of his wound in his side and of the blood which was flowing from it. On the other hand, there are also odd absences: no poor person, other than the needy but noble knight, to whom Francis had given his cloak; and no reference to poverty, other than the scene depicting the renunciation of Francis of a share in his inheritance; no leper either (we are worlds away from the *Bardi Tavola!*); not the least allusion to the life of penance or to the horror of money that characterized the Poverello; no woman either, other than the homage to his remains by Clare and her companions the day after his death. The cycle of frescoes dedicated to Francis thus accentuates the mystical and allegorical tendencies already present in the *Legenda maior.* The Poor Man of

Assisi appears there as an eminently respectable spiritual figure, a great thau-
maturge and an exceptional saint whose essential merit has been to found a
religious order called to play a leading role by collaborating in the mission of
the Church, represented by the papacy.[39]

This distance from the life of the Poor Man of Assisi reaches its culmination
in the paintings in the vaults of the transept of the lower basilica, dated to
around 1320, where his message is reduced to the cold allegories of Franciscan
virtues, corresponding to the three vows sworn by the friars: obedience, chastity, and poverty. One could imagine, in seeing the depiction—truly beautiful
all the same—of the mystical marriage of Francis and Poverty, with the traits of
a woman in rags, scarcely attractive and surrounded by thorns, that at least
something of the original Franciscan message has ended up in the decoration
of this edifice in the first decades of the fourteenth century. Enough! The interpretation which the artists and their sponsors gave to this theme constitutes a
contradiction, for, as the *Sacrum commercium* shows well, Francis considered
poverty never as his "lady" or fiancée, but as the spouse of Christ, and he was
seeking not to marry her but to follow her. With respect to the complex and man-
nered images consecrated to the glorification and the apotheosis of Francis (*Glo-
riosus Franciscus*) on the adjoining vaults, they could reinforce in the onlooker
of today only the feeling of a lack of understanding that borders on betrayal.
Since that time, just as it occurred during the same period in the realm of hagiography, contact having been broken with the living tradition, the images of
Francis, which will continue to appear in great number in the churches and
convents of Christianity, will no longer bring anything new to the understanding of his person, except for the depiction of the story of the wolf of Gubbio,
probably due to the diffusion of the *Actus,* which one finds for the first time in
San Francesco de Pienza in Tuscany in the second half of the fourteenth century. And in the last great medieval cycle which was devoted to him, that of
Benozzo Gozzoli in the church of San Francesco di Montefalco in Umbria
around 1450, the legend of the Poor Man of Assisi is recounted as a kind of fable that is inserted into the history of the order presented as a foyer of perfection, illustrated by a line of saints and blessed sprung from its ranks, of which
Francis constitutes merely the point of departure. We will have to wait for the
Renaissance and in particular the *Saint Francis of Assisi in the Desert* of
Giovanni Bellini (around 1490), where we see him in front of his hermitage
before his stigmatization, in order to discover in art a depiction that might give
back to the Poverello the breath of life and enable us to appreciate his true
greatness.[40]

BETWEEN TEXTS AND IMAGES:
THE EXALTATION OF THE STIGMATA

Among the new characteristics of the holiness of Francis which have retained the attention of hagiographers and artists are obviously the stigmata,
which, in Western iconography, became his identifying attribute after his
death. Before going any farther, let's try to detail what this phenomenon is. The
Latin term *stigmata*, a simple transposition from the Greek, was used by Saint
Paul in a passage from the Letter to the Galatians (6:17), where he cried out:
"I bear within my body the marks of Jesus." Strictly speaking, the word "stigmata" means "marks"; and Paul, who says nothing more on this subject, may
simply have been alluding to his having been struck and beaten by his adversaries during his ministry, and still bearing the physical traces of the blows which
he had received. But later tradition has often attributed to the apostle to the
Gentiles the privilege of bearing on his body the wounds that had been visible,
according to the Gospel accounts, on the dead body of Christ after his descent
from the cross: those which the nails had opened on his hands and feet, and the
side wound made by the blow of the lance given to the Crucified by a soldier in
order to confirm that he was in fact dead. Afterward, the term was scarcely used
except by Peter Damian in his Life of the ascetic Dominic the Shielded in the
middle of the eleventh century, until Brother Elias applied it to Francis in the
Encyclical Letter which he sent to all the Friars Minor the day after the death
of their founder on October 4, 1226:

> I announce to you a great joy, a miracle of a new kind. One has never heard
> tell of a similar wonder in the whole world except in the person of the Son of
> God, Christ our Lord. Indeed, a little before his death, our brother and father
> (Francis) appeared as if crucified, bearing in his body the five wounds which
> are truly the stigmata of Christ. In fact, his hands and feet had had some-
> thing like perforations made by the nails, front and back, that retained scars
> and showed the blackness of the nails. As to his side, he seemed to be pierced
> and blood often flowed out.[41]

This text has prompted many commentaries since the end of the nineteenth
century. Elias describes here quite well the phenomenon of the stigmata, but
he gives no account of how this could have happened, remains vague on the
dating ("a little before his death"), and does not talk about its origin. Moreover,
if he gives testimony about the body of his master and friend at the moment of
his death, he says nothing about what happened afterward. Did the stigmata

remain visible on the body until its burial, as Franciscan tradition would have
it; or would they have rapidly disappeared without leaving a trace, as a contemporary English chronicler, Roger of Wendover, claims, in testimony prior to
1236? In his letter, Elias passes on to another wonder, well known to specialists of
hagiography, for we find it in numerous Lives of the saints: the body of Francis,
which had shrunken under the effect of the pain during his agony and where
"there was no part of his body which had not been marked by terrible suffering,"
became beautiful, radiant and supple like the flesh of a child from the moment
he had given up his soul. This showed to the eyes of witnesses that he had passed
from mortality to the state of a glorified body, one of the principal attributes of
holiness.

In 1229 Thomas of Celano offered, in his first *Life of Saint Francis*, a much
more elaborate description of his stigmatization.[42] First, he specified that the
phenomenon happened on La Verna—that austere mountain where the saint
wanted to retire into solitude to pray and to give himself over to contemplation—
and he dated the phenomenon "two years before his death." According to
Thomas' account, Francis, at a moment when he was in doubt about his vocation, having consulted three times a Gospel book which each time opened
onto an account of the passion of Christ, saw above him a man having the appearance of a seraph fixed to a cross, the arms outstretched and the feet joined,
and endowed with six wings: two above his head, two ready for flight, and two
covering his body. Unsettled by this apparition, he remained for a little while
without understanding what had happened to him, tossed as he was between
joy and sadness, until the signs of the four nails and the side wound appeared
on his own body. Thomas of Celano does not hesitate to contradict the previous version of Brother Elias concerning the form of the stigmata: "The wonder
was that, in the middle of his hands and feet, not nail holes, but the nails themselves, formed out of the fibers of his flesh, of the brownish color of iron, and
the right side made purple with blood."[43] In Thomas' account Francis bore not
scars or holes but fleshy and bloody protuberances. The difference can appear
minor; it is in fact fundamental. The version of Elias indeed suggests an identification, which could then appear quite daring, of the life of Francis with the
tragic ending of Christ. By underlining that the points of the nails were turned
outward and that their heads were found within the hands and feet, Thomas
maintains, between the image and the model, a respectful distance. For him,
Francis had known painful moments at La Verna. To understand their meaning, he had pondered the life of Christ, while having already surrendered
himself to God's will. God now gave him a mark of favor through which he
fulfilled, by surpassing it, the hope of martyrdom to which the Poor Man of

Assisi had aspired since his journey to Egypt; but this sign was in itself a trial. Indeed, from this point forward, he lived until his death in great suffering, while endeavoring to hide, for better or for worse, his bloody wounds, which did not prevent some of his closest companions from catching a glimpse of them and even sometimes from touching them. In this perspective, the stigmatization appears as the last step of the climb to Calvary, which was to allow Francis to actively participate in the passion of Christ, before acceding with him to the glory of the Cross and becoming, in his turn, an intercessor for all those who suffer in the world.

The task of Thomas of Celano was not an easy one, for he had to account for a mysterious phenomenon which had hardly any precedent in the hagiographical tradition. It also presented risks on the theological level, as shown by the negative reactions in certain ecclesiastical circles. Thus did he show great prudence by limiting himself to evoking the stigmata which he places immediately *after* the end of the vision, while avoiding all spiritual or allegorical interpretation of the phenomenon that he was describing. In his account, the man-seraph does not address any words or message to Francis and simply plays the role of mediator between the body of Christ and that of Francis, for it is not possible for a human being to see God or directly touch him. The biographer guarantees the historical reality of the reported facts by relying on the testimony of Elias and Rufino, but he respects the mysterious character of the event of La Verna and of the divine design that remains impenetrable. As such, the account of Celano truly struck the hearts of contemporaries and it is at the origin of the common image of the stigmatized Francis that one finds in the iconography and literary texts of the period. Thus the author of the *German Legend of Saint Francis* (between 1230 and 1235) closely follows the account of Celano:

> It really seemed
> that a piece of darkened flesh
> pierced there and filled the place,
> as if it was a nail . . .
> Above was seen the top of the nails which below
> were pulled back.[44]

In northern France, meanwhile, Philippe Mouskès (around 1245) in his *Rhymed Chronicle*, in spite of a serious error about the location of the tomb of Francis, does not fail to mention the presence of the stigmata when he talks about him:

> In Perugia [!] lies the holy body
> Whose hands and feet were not whole . . . [45]

In addition to Elias and Thomas of Celano, we must consider another tradition regarding the stigmata of Francis: that which comes from Brother Leo, his secretary and faithful companion. Beginning in the second half of the thirteenth century, Leo is depicted on some images as the only witness of the stigmatization, even if, absorbed in the reading of a book, he does not seem to have paid much attention to what was happening around him. Leo has left two testimonies on the event of La Verna. The first one, direct and in his own hand, has been added by him, probably after 1260, onto the piece of parchment (*chartula*), on which Francis had written the *Praises of the Most High God* as well as the blessing formula which he had addressed to him:

> Two years before his death, Saint Francis made a Lent at the place of La Verna, in honor of the blessed Mary, mother of God, and of the holy angel, Michael, from the feast of the Assumption of the Virgin up to the feast of Saint Michael in September. After the vision and the words of the seraph and the impression of the stigmata on his body, he composed these praises which are written on the other side of this piece of parchment; he wrote them with his own hand in thanksgiving to God for the grace which had been granted to him.[46]

The second testimony, indirect, which appears in the chronicle of Thomas of Eccleston, rests on the testimony of an English Franciscan who had met Leo and gathered in his version of the facts.[47] Here the accent is put on the revelations and promises that the seraph addressed to the saint, especially concerning the future of his order. The account of the episode, quite different from the one that we find in Thomas of Celano, evokes certain angelic apparitions to prophets like Isaiah, whose lips were purified by a seraph before the beginning of his ministry, as described in the Bible. The seraph is an angel—not a man having the appearance of an angel—and this encounter constituted for Francis a very difficult physical trial. According to the English chronicler, Francis said that "when he had seen the angel from afar, he had been absolutely terrified and that this angel had touched him." On the chartula, Leo simply declares: "And the hand of the Lord was upon him," while referring to the words of Ezekiel ("*Facta est super me manus Domini*": Ezek 3:22–23). The celestial envoy was not flying in the air but seems to have physically touched Francis, who afterward had had Brother Rufino wash and anoint with oil the rock upon which the angel had stood. In the "Leonine" tradition, Francis thus appears as a prophet whom God came to purify through the intercession of the seraph, the angel closest to God, who inflicted on him a burning that was both painful and consoling, while the *Legend of Perugia* mentions a "vision of the seraph that filled his soul with consolation and united him closely to God for the rest of his life."[48] The differences that exist between the accounts of the event of La Verna must not nevertheless be exaggerated; they only reflect different approaches to the same supernatural phenomenon. In the Western liturgy, at least since the twelfth century, the angel is a figure of Christ, as is shown really well by the example of Saint Michael, toward whom Francis had a strong devotion; it is in his honor that he had withdrawn into solitude at this moment. Whether it might be described as an angelophany or as an anthropomorphic or christic vision, whether we use the term "stigmatization" to describe an event that seems to have been infinitely more complex, the mysterious spiritual experience that he had in this place was perceived by the first witnesses as a theophany—that is, as a divine revelation from which the Poor Man of Assisi emerged transformed on the physical and spiritual plane.

In the *Legenda maior*, Bonaventure tried to move beyond the contradictions that could exist between the versions by conferring on the stigmatization of Francis an importance which it had not had in the previous texts. Indeed, he devotes to it the whole thirteenth chapter of his biography, which ends with a veritable hymn to the stigmatic of La Verna, with military and triumphal accents:

> Bear now, valiant knight of Christ, the arms of the invincible Leader who will confer them upon you. They will give you victory over all your adversaries. Lift up the standard of the Great King, his gaze holds firm all those who fight in the army of God. Show forth the seal of Christ, the Supreme Pontiff![49]

Such a passion contrasts with the insistent reminder by Thomas of Celano of the necessity to respect the discretion that Francis showed up to the end of his life vis-à-vis his stigmata and on the mystery that surrounded this spiritual experience. Bonaventure did not have the same scruples and sought to integrate the stigmatization into a coherent theological vision. For him, Francis was animated by a strong desire for God and by a lively compassion for the one who, in an "excess of love," had wanted to be crucified for the salvation of humanity. In the hermitage of La Verna, in the company of Brother Leo, around the feast of the Exaltation of the Holy Cross, while he was plunged into intense contemplation and was struggling with his spiritual destiny, he saw come down from the height of heaven a seraph or rather—the nuance is important—Christ under the appearance of a seraph. At first disconcerted by this vision and oscillating between sadness and joy, he ended up understanding that "it was not the martyrdom of his body but the love burning in his soul that was going to transform him into the likeness of Christ crucified."[50] Then the vision disappeared and the wounds which he had seen on the one whom he was just contemplating appeared on his body. With Bonaventure, we pass from an angelophany to a resolutely christological interpretation of the event of La Verna and from the mystery to the mystic. Indeed, the *Legenda maior* emphasizes that the stigmata appeared on the body of Francis only at the conclusion of the vision. This made of them a response of divine love to human love through the intermediary of the Christ-seraph, who transformed the friend of Christ that was Francis into the likeness of the one whom he loved. Coming back later to the question of the stigmata in another one of his works, the *Itinerarium mentis in Deum*, the minister general of the Friars Minor compares Francis to Saint Paul transformed into Christ after being caught up to the third heaven, and to convey this he uses a significant formula: "The spirit revealed himself in my flesh."[51] As a result, the flesh of the stigmatized was presented as the exterior manifestation of a mystical relationship between the human person and God and gave it an intelligibility in the order of the visible: the wounds of the hands, feet, and side being the proof of the transformative and assimilating power of love.

From this, Bonaventure draws completely new conclusions by giving to the event of La Verna both a centrality in the life of Francis that none of his previous biographers had given it and a major eschatological significance. Indeed, he compares the impression of the wounds of Christ in the flesh of the saint to the effect produced by "a seal on wax that the heat of fire had first melted," similar to that which the pontifical chancery utilized for authenticating the bulls that popes were sending at that time throughout Christianity. The stigmata constitute the royal seal (*sigillum*) by which God has authenticated the teaching and rule of the Friars Minor, which are identified with the Gospel itself. For him, Francis is really the Angel of the sixth seal of the Apocalypse, "who arises from the East while bearing the sign of the living God" (Rev 7:2)—that is, the stigmata—and who will help the Church and humanity enter into a new phase of history. From that moment, the wounds became the cornerstone of the argument that the order of Friars Minor was going to oppose its detractors in the difficult circumstances which it was passing through by allowing it to sanctify its rule and its way of life, objects of strong criticism on the part of the doctors of the university of Paris, a good part of the secular clergy, and even the Dominican order with whom the Franciscans had found themselves in a situation of rivalry.[52]

In the eyes of Bonaventure and of the whole Franciscan tradition after him, the stigmata effectively constituted a unique and inimitable privilege granted by God to Francis alone. But from the second half of the thirteenth century, certain Dominican hagiographers—and others after them—contested this priv-ilege by stating that some members of their order, like the Blessed Walter of Strasbourg or various female saints who circulated in their orbit had benefited from the same favor.[53] The papacy, which in the beginning, had abstained from taking a position on this burning subject, came to the rescue of the Minors. Indeed, in 1237, Gregory IX declared that it was because of the stigmata that he had canonized Francis: an astonishing affirmation since it had not been men-tioned in the bull of canonization in 1228. Afterward, the popes promulgated no less than nine bulls up until 1291 in order to vouch for the reality of the stig-mata of the Poor Man of Assisi, to hunt down their detractors, and to oblige the faithful to believe in them. One pope, Alexander IV (r. 1254–1261), even declared that at the time when he was a young cardinal, he had had occasion to see the holy wounds. In his *Treatise on the Miracles*, which constitutes the second part of his *Memorial*, Thomas of Celano introduces for the first time miracles tied to the stigmata of Saint Francis (3Cel 6–13). In 1250 a church was built on the site of La Verna, and pilgrimage to the "holy mountain" was soon graced with indul-gences by the papacy. In 1282 the Franciscan order organized an inquiry into the specific circumstances of the stigmatization, whose date was definitively fixed on September 14, 1224, the date of the feast of the Exaltation of the Holy Cross. The official act that was established on this occasion mentions "certain secret words" that Christ had addressed to Francis at that time, while adding that they would soon be revealed. In 1337 the feast of the Holy Stigmata made its entrance into the liturgy of the order and was, from that time forward, celebrated every year in all Franciscan convents.

Even the Spiritual Franciscans, who were not kindly disposed in their writ-ings to Bonaventure, whom they accused of having distorted Franciscan life and poverty, adhered unreservedly to the idea that the stigmata attested to the identification of the rule and the Gospel. But they especially emphasized the words which the seraph had addressed to Francis and the promises that he made concerning the future of Francis' order: words which gave assurance to them that the trials they were passing through at that time would soon be fol-lowed by a renewal of evangelical fervor within the order. The convent of La Verna was one of their bastions. In the *Actus beati Francisci* of the 1330s there appears an important chapter titled "On the Discovery of Mount La Verna," where this place is compared to Horeb and Francis to Moses before the burn-ing bush, while the *Fioretti* ends with the long and fastidious "Considerations on the Stigmata."[54] The process of the sacralization of the "Mount of Angels" reached its culmination at the end of the fourteenth century with the treatise "On the Conformity of Francis to Christ," whose author, Bartholomew of Pisa, explained that the splintered rocks, so characteristic of the site of La Verna, had broken apart on Good Friday, at the moment of the passion of Christ; and he also located here the episode—numbered early on among the miracles of Francis and illustrated by Giotto in the upper basilica of Assisi—in which the saint made a source spring up in this place in order to allow a thirsty peasant to slake his thirst.[55] This prolonged and systematic effort on the part of the Franciscan order to exalt the figure of the stigmatic of La Verna has a monk of Foligno say—he was judged and condemned in 1361 for these imprudent words—that "one is making of this Saint Francis a new God."[56] Whatever might have been his motivation, he joined with all those, clerics as well as laity, who, since the end of the 1230s had been shocked to see the stigmatization of the Poor Man of Assisi exploited by his spiritual sons to their advantage and who could not in conscience accept this extraordinary claim.

These medieval debates can seem complicated and excessively subtle to interest the modern reader. I have found it necessary to mention them, however, because they have played an essential role in the construction of the image of Francis. Today, what can the historian say about these stigmata without abandoning his or her role? To start, let's leave aside the hypothesis of hysteria, which has predominated in the scientific critique in the late nineteenth and early twentieth centuries. Francis is not a faker, less still an impostor; and a medical and psychiatric approach to the phenomenon of the stigmatization leads nowhere in his case. One cannot, on the contrary, remain insensitive to the contradictions that exist between the different contemporary testimonies. The first among them—the *Encyclical Letter* of Brother Elias, in October 1226—mentions no place and situates the event a little before the death of Francis, whereas Thomas of Celano, in his first *Life*, places it at the hermitage of La Verna in 1224—that is, two years before Francis' death. According to the versions, the wonder had occurred while the saint was alone (in the first *Life* of Thomas of Celano and in Bonaventure) or in the presence of a companion (unnamed in the *Memorial* of the same Thomas of Celano, identified as Brother Leo by later tradition). According to the testimony written by Leo himself, Francis was in ecstasy at the moment of the apparition (the English monk and chronicler Matthew Paris has even depicted him asleep in a beautiful sketch which appears in the margins of his chronicle), whereas Bonaventure affirms that he was awake. The mysterious being that appeared to him was an angel for Brother Leo, a handsome man having the appearance of a crucified seraph for Thomas of Celano and the author of the *Legend of the Three Companions*, Christ under the appearance of a seraph for Bonaventure, and Christ in person for Giotto and his sponsors on the frescoes of the upper basilica of Assisi. This personage remained silent according to Thomas of Celano, but Leo, Bonaventure, and the whole later Franciscan tradition mention, on the contrary, a conversation in the course of which the divine messenger revealed to the saint important secrets relative to his fate and to the future of his order.

All of this can "make things messy," as we say today, and prompt us to dismiss the idea as some kind of a trick. Two recent historians have done just that, and it is fitting to mention their positions and examine their arguments before going further. Richard Trexler contests the reality of the stigmata based on the contradictions which we have enumerated between the various testimonies, but he does not stop there. For him—and we can only agree with him on this one point—Francis lived within a wider current of devotion within which, in the late twelfth century and the thirteenth, a growing role was given to the humanity of Christ and to the desire to imitate him, sometimes to the point of a real identification with him.[57] In fact, we know of several laypersons, between 1200 and 1230, who inflicted wounds on themselves in order to imitate Christ in his suffering. Among such was the Beguine Marie d'Oignies († 1213), whose Life was written by Jacques de Vitry and who was going to meet Francis and Clare during his sojourn in Perugia in 1216. From her biographer we learn that this holy woman,

> intoxicated with spiritual fervor, mistreated her flesh in order to taste the tenderness of the Paschal Lamb. With a knife, she cut sizable portions of her skin, which by modesty she hid in the ground. And as she had supported the pain of the flesh under the appearance of the love with which she was enflamed, she perceived in the course of rapture which had seized her spirit a seraph standing next to her. When, at the moment of her death, they were washing her body, the women discovered the places of her wounds and were astonished. Those who had knowledge of these deeds as a result of her confessions understood what this was all about.[58]

If it is difficult to imagine that Francis might have inflicted on himself with his own hand the stigmata, we should not forget that at this time religious—and Francis is not the exception to the rule—often gave themselves over to the discipline or had themselves flagellated by their companions in order to expiate their sins. We can thus suppose that when the Poor Man of Assisi gave up his spirit and when his entourage was able to observe his body, it was covered with bleeding wounds associated perhaps with his illnesses but also with the mortifications and corporal penances he had inflicted on himself. Elias, with the practical and concrete spirit that characterized him, would have chosen to see there the mark of the wounds of Christ, while highlighting in an arbitrary fashion certain wounds more spectacular than others, and would have hurried to announce to the Friars Minor that the body of their founder, at the moment of his death, was similar to that of the Savior at the time of his descent from the cross in order to reassure them about his holiness and the future of the order.

Let's say right up front that this interpretation seems debatable. Unless we consider all the companions of Francis as phonies, we can hardly believe that personalities as different as Elias, Rufino, Leo, and "Brother Jacoba" might have passed on the message to invent this story out of whole cloth. It is, on the other hand, undeniable that the stigmata were seen while Francis was still alive by several witnesses, some of whom were outside the Franciscan order, like Cardinal Raynaldo of Jenne, and, after his death, by notable laity of Assisi, including the lawyer Jerome. Besides, when he was stripped of his clothing as death was nearing, the brothers who witnessed the scene were too numerous to have a collective fabrication foisted on them. All contemporary witnesses of the event agree with each other in stating that the wounds were visible on the body of Francis the day after his death and that they corresponded well to those of Christ crucified. Moreover, Brother Leo, in the few lines that he wrote on the chartula at the end of his life, mentions "the impression of the stigmata" among the phenomena to which he was a witness on La Verna. This text is relatively late, but it is difficult to imagine that the affection which he bore for his master would have led him to introduce this notification, devoid of any ambiguity, if it had not had a foundation in his own personal experience. Even if we do not accept the conclusions of Richard Trexler, his study has, however, the great merit of reminding us that Francis was probably not the only stigmatic of the thirteenth century. In addition, the very success of this image helped to accelerate the spontaneous evolution of piety by highlighting the new concept of "deification," an important theme in Byzantine spirituality but about which the West hardly knew anything at all. In the theological doctrine elaborated by the Greek Fathers, the deification of the human person was conceived as the end of a progressive ascent toward Christ in glory in the light of the Resurrection. At the beginning of the thirteenth century, another avenue opened which was going to become preponderant in Western Christianity: that of the identification of the human person to the suffering Christ of the Passion, whose marks, reproduced in the body of Francis, were the tangible sign as well as the proof of his assimilation to his divine master. And this extraordinary novelty was welcomed with joy by the faithful because it allowed them to become the protagonists of their own salvation by giving themselves, in their turn, to the following of the humble and crucified Christ.

Another historian, Chiara Frugoni, has also recently challenged the physical reality of the stigmata by beginning with the contradiction between the testimony of Elias, in his *Encyclical Letter* of 1226, and that of Brother Leo, who remains discreet on the phenomenon of the stigmatization and who especially emphasizes the "struggle with the angel" and the revelations that he had made to the saint.[59] Without rejecting the possibility of a stigmatization of Francis, Frugoni proposes a metaphorical interpretation of it, and, like Richard Trexler, she accuses Elias of having "invented" the stigmata in October 1226 for the greater glory of his master and his order. According to her, the vision of La Verna was rather a manifestation of the Triune God, thus a theophany and not a christophany. Her proof is that Francis wrote immediately afterward the *Praises of the Most High God*, which is addressed to the Deity—of which the seraph burning with love is the perfect image—and not to the Son of God.

But why would such an overwhelming shock not have left physical traces and remain purely spiritual? "This place is fearsome" (*Terribilis est locus iste*), says Jacob, who, upon waking from his dream, emerges limping due to his struggle with the angel; and Jesus himself sweated drops of blood in the Garden of Olives before suffering his Passion (Luke 22:44). Some medieval painters, in depicting the scene of the stigmatization, did not hesitate to place the seraph next to an altar, which takes us back to the sacrificial virtues of the redeeming blood, but also, ultimately, to the idea of a "real presence" of the apparition marking the body of the one who had contemplated it with burning and wounding. For, beyond the differences that exist between the various "early" accounts relative to the stigmata, the essential message that they transmit is fundamentally the same: the wounds present on the body of Francis corresponded to those of Christ crucified. On the other hand, I am wholly in agreement with Chiara Frugoni when she speaks of the deviation that occurred during the thirteenth century and which has continually made of the stigmatization the principal message of La Verna. Thomas of Celano said it well: "The sign may hide but the thing signified is eloquent."[60] The stigmata are the physical manifestation of an interior upheaval, rooted in the passionate devotion of Francis to the cross and in his heartfelt desire to personally participate in the sufferings of Christ.

The reality of the stigmata of Francis cannot be proven on the historical plane; but it is even more difficult, at this level, to reject their possibility, so much do they fit into the spiritual journey of the Poor Man of Assisi. The significance of this episode has been overemphasized by his later biographers, beginning in the second half of the thirteenth century. From the idea of a Francis imitator and follower of Christ, accounts have passed to the unnuanced affir-mation of a literal identification of the former to the latter, while voiding the mysterious aspects of the event of La Verna. By painting the scene of the stig-matization on the walls of the upper basilica of Assisi at the start of the 1300s, Giotto put the finishing touches on this evolution by replacing the seraph with Christ, and in depicting golden rays coming out of his wounds that strike Fran-cis in the corresponding places on his body, thus making of the founder of the Friars Minor a kind of *Christus redivivus* in this world.

6

FRANCIS BETWEEN HISTORY AND MYTH: SIXTEENTH TO TWENTIETH CENTURIES

FROM LUTHER TO VOLTAIRE: *DAMNATIO MEMORIAE* AND TRANSFORMATIONS OF THE IMAGE

Beginning in the sixteenth century, a period of crisis opened for the way in which Francis was remembered which was to be both challenged by certain religious and philosophical currents and championed by his spiritual sons, though in a perspective rather removed from the life he had actually lived. Even before the Reformation, the image of the Poor Man of Assisi conjured up by the excessive language of certain Friars Minor had proved costly. Thus, in the 1500s, did secular clergy in the diocese of Meaux, denouncing some Franciscans who were identifying their founder in sermons as "a second Christ," initiate proceedings against them, which ended up before the Parlement of Paris. And in 1695 the archbishop of Reims ordered public retractions by a Friar Minor and a Capuchin who, in the pulpit, had presented Francis as the new redeemer of the human race.

But the polemic doubled in intensity beginning in 1542, when, in Frankfurt, the Protestant pastor Erasmus Albert published his *Alcoranus Franciscanorum*, with a preface by Martin Luther, who approved of its spirit. In this work, whose French translation appeared in 1560 under the title *Alcoran des Cordeliers* and which was frequently republished up to the middle of the eighteenth century, the author especially attacked "this stigmatized idol who is called Saint Francis," as well as *The Book of Conformities*. According to Erasmus Albert, the friars had become so foolish and idolatrous that they would have preferred this latter book to the Gospel; it had become for them the equivalent of the Qur'an for Muslims. Holding back no insult, he even suggests that Francis received the stigmata during a dispute with Saint Dominic, who pierced Francis several times with a roasting spit! Luther was more moderate. He testified to a certain admiration for a Francis "moved by the Holy Spirit," while at the same time deploring the error which he had committed in reducing the Gospel, intended for all, to a rule which concerned only the Friars Minor and in forbidding them what God had permitted all Christians: marriage and the use of money. But Luther, too, was particularly virulent regarding the Franciscans who, he believed, had so exalted their founder that they ended up adoring him in the place of Christ. For his part, the Protestant historiographer Matthias Flacius Illyricus (1520–1575), in his *Magdeburg Centuries*, presented Saints Francis and Dominic as the precursors of the Antichrist and the henchmen of papism, while at the same time lauding Vaudès, the founder of the Waldensians, who had been condemned by the Church as a heretic, as a fully evangelical man and a precursor of the Reformation.

Faced with these venomous attacks, the defenders of Francis were hardly defenseless, especially within the order, where Henry Sedulius published a refutation of the *Alcoran des Cordeliers*. Afterward, the Catholic reaction developed along two lines. First, in terms of history, we witness a brilliant expansion of Franciscan erudition, which began with Francesco Gonzaga and Petrus Ridolfi and culminated in a great history of the Order, the *Annales Minorum*, whose first eight volumes were published by the Irish Franciscan Luke Wadding between 1625 and 1634. This remarkable work, for which numerous archival documents were edited for the first time in chronological order, begins with a study of almost six hundred pages devoted to the life and holiness of Francis. The same author also had the distinction of having published in 1623 the first edition of the writings of the Poor Man of Assisi, referred to as the *Opuscules*.

On the other hand, in terms of art, the figure of Francis acquired a considerable importance for El Greco and Zurbaran, as well as with almost all the great Italian painters of the sixteenth and seventeenth centuries. During this period, the iconography of Francis highlighted withdrawal, solitude, interiority, examination of conscience, and knowledge of the self. He was frequently depicted as a hermit meditating, at the threshold of a grotto, on the vanity of the things of this world, his hand placed on a skull and his gaze fixed upon a crucifix, in a perspective that was both ascetic and mystical. These images, which took their inspiration from the *Legenda maior* of Bonaventure, were influenced by the eremitical and contemplative orientation which the Capuchins were giving at that time to Franciscan spirituality. These friars, who saw themselves as the refounders of Franciscanism and who advocated a pure and simple observance of the rule, were in fact determined to underscore the central place of spiritual experience in the Gospel life as it had been conceived and practiced by the Poor Man of Assisi. Later, the stigmatization became the favored subject of painters, in conformity with the ideals and heroic virtue promoted by the Catholic Counterreformation. In general, these works of art had been executed at the request of the friars for the decoration of their churches and convents, at that time very numerous, since the number of male and female religious who were claiming the patronage of Saint Francis was about 130,000 throughout the world at the start of the seventeenth century. The image of the Poor Man of Assisi was diffused as far away as Latin America and India; but at the same time it was becoming rather banal, as that of one founder of an order among others. Thus does his statue appear in the nave of the basilica of Saint Peter's in Rome next to that of Saint Norbert, Saint Dominic, and Saint Ignatius of Loyola.

In the eighteenth century, the criticisms of the *philosophes* and the adherents of the Enlightenment took up the baton of the Protestants, the transition being assured in France by the *Dictionnaire historique et critique*, published in the Netherlands in 1702. Francis is treated poorly there by Pierre Bayle, who sees in his life only ridiculous quirks and manifestations of excess contrary to all propriety. In his *Essai sur les moeurs*, Voltaire makes of the Poor Man of Assisi the antithesis of the sultan Saladin, who in his eyes incarnated justice and tolerance, and presents Francis as a fanatic, more ridiculous than dangerous. Other authors of the same period, in particular those in the *Encyclopédie*, go even farther, reproaching him for fanaticism, laziness, and lack of learning; or deriding him for the love which Francis had conceived for the women whom, one day, he had built out of snow, according to an episode from his legend. In refusing to work and marry, Francis had been the originator of a religious order composed of lazy men and sterile celibates, rebels against the laws of nature, and strangers to those in their own country, whose begging constituted a heavy burden for the same society. A libertine novel like *Thérèse philosophe*, by Boyer d'Argens (1748), went so far as to describe the lewd usage that a bawdy Cordelier had made of a piece of the "cord of Saint Francis, . . . relic which, through its use, was supposed to chase away what had remained impure and carnal in his penitent and to lead her to ecstasy," as well as the "false stigmata" that he inflicted on her.[1] In this climate, the president of Brosses, when he traveled through Umbria on the occasion of his voyage to Italy, judged it not worth his while to make a detour through Assisi, being content to admire its famous landscape from afar: "I am keeping myself from going there," he wrote, "fearing the stigmata like all demons."[2] And when Goethe visited Assisi in 1786, he remarked only about the Temple of Minerva on the main piazza; he did not even go to see the basilica and convent of the Friars Minor.

But even when interest for Francis was at its lowest in Europe, we neverthe-less witness a renewal of erudition tied to the diffusion of texts and documents about him. In October 1768 the Bollandists—a group of Jesuit scholars special-izing in the study of hagiographic texts—consecrated, in the second tome of the *Acta Sanctorum*, an important article about the founder of the Minors, where they presented the first published edition of the *Life of Saint Francis* by Thomas of Celano, followed by the *Legend of the Three Companions.* In 1806 the Italian Rinaldi published the *Memorial,* or *Second Life of Saint Francis* by Thomas of Celano, which had also disappeared from circulation for a long time. Thus were laid the bases from which the historians of the nineteenth century were going to be able to rediscover the sources essential for the under-standing of the spirituality of the Poor Man of Assisi and of the Franciscan phenomenon.

THE REDISCOVERY OF FRANCIS (NINETEENTH CENTURY–BEGINNING OF THE TWENTIETH CENTURY)

However, it was not only at the time of the Restoration and, in France, of the July Monarchy that the disastrous image which the modern era had given to Francis began to be modified. In 1818, on the occasion of archaeological digs that were being done in the basilica of Assisi, his tomb and his relics, lost since the fifteenth century, were rediscovered, and in 1850 those of Saint Clare, which had also been hidden in the great church dedicated to her, were also found. This helped relaunch pilgrimages to the two saints, whose cult had become purely local since the end of the Middle Ages.

A ROMANTIC HERO . . . AT THE ORIGINS OF THE RENAISSANCE!

With the fashion of romanticism, being a reaction against the sterile ratio-nalism of the Enlightenment, we witness a total reevaluation of the figure of the Poor Man of Assisi. In 1826 the Catholic publicist Joseph Görres devoted an important book to him: *Franziskus, ein Troubadour* (Francis, a troubadour). The book marked a decisive turning point in the interpretation of the Pover-ello, whom the author presents as an inspired jongleur and a great poet, the Orpheus of the Middle Ages. Different schools of art in the period, in particu-lar the so-called Nazareens and some Pre-Raphaelites, became interested in Francis by reason of his evangelical tenderness and the mysticism which he incarnated in their eyes: for was he not the first to have understood that God is both beautiful and good? The German painter Overbeck covered with shim-mering paintings the outside of the ancient church of the Portiuncula, encased since the seventeenth century within the immense and cold basilica of Saint Mary of the Angels.

In fact, it is through art that many people of the period discovered Franciscanism. In the Parisian painting salons, the number of tableaux devoted to Franciscan subjects, insignificant at the beginning of the nineteenth century, became sizable between 1830 and 1850; and the visit of Assisi was soon integrated into the framework of "The Great Tour" of Italy undertaken by artists and cultured people.[3] Indeed, the city of Saint Francis, where the Middle Ages is very present and where time seems suspended, struck travelers and pilgrims by allowing them to see it as it was at the time of the Poverello. At any rate, was this not how people saw it, for there was, of course, in this impression of absolute authenticity a part played by the imagination. In any case, the belief in a perfect consistency between the monuments of the Umbrian city and the beginnings of the Franciscan movement was often at the heart of the enthusiasm attested to in the letters or journals of those who, in ever increasing numbers, had come to visit. Thus does Frédéric Ozanam, who had gone there in 1847, say with emotion:

> Assisi and its cloister which formerly had enclosed six thousand monks [!] and its two churches, symbols of the two lives of the saint, the one earthly and the other immortal and resplendent, where the best painting of the Middle Ages developed from its cradle to its maturity, from Cimabue and Giotto up to the time of Perugino and his disciple [Raphael].

And he adds a little farther on: "I begin to understand how this popular saint who had only lived for the poor, who preached in their language, was truly the father of painting, as well as of all eloquence, and all Italian poetry."[4] It is this last aspect which, a few years later, the same Ozanam emphasized in his thesis on *Les Poètes franciscains en Italie au treizième siècle, avec un choix des petites fleurs de saint François traduites en Italien* (Paris, 1852), which included the first French translation of the *Fioretti*. The author credits Francis with having made it possible for the medieval person to enjoy freedom and personal autonomy. And he makes of Francis the inspiration of a new art which, through Dante and Giotto, had led to the civilization of the Renaissance. In a book published in Berlin in 1885 and translated into French in 1909 titled *Saint Francis and the Origins of the Art of the Renaissance*, the German art historian Heinrich Thode took up again, in a more developed way, similar ideas. Through his suggestive conception of a harmony between nature and religion, Francis, the new Adam having rediscovered this dimension of Eden lost since the Fall, had recovered the notion of the "man of God"; but he had also revealed the human person to himself, thereby altering his view of the world. In this sense, he was preparing

Giotto: the one was the prophet of the new art, the other its interpreter. Thus begins to take shape and assert itself an approach both aesthetic and spiritual of the Franciscan phenomenon, which attracted to Assisi numerous artists and literary authors. Some of them converted to Catholicism there at the beginning of the twentieth century and became afterward biographers of the Poor Man of Assisi, like the Englishman G. K. Chesterton († 1936) and the Dane Jan Jørgensen († 1956). Jørgensen, who in 1894–1895 had discovered Assisi and the little convents of Umbria and there rediscovered his faith, published in 1907 a *Life of Saint Francis* in which he presents Franciscanism as one of the most authentic expressions of the essence of Christianity. Translated into all the European languages, this work, characterized by an approach more poetic and literary than historical, spread widely and greatly influenced the image of the Poverello between 1920 and 1950.

ERNEST RENAN, PAUL SABATIER, AND THE "FRANCISCAN QUESTION"

Parallel to this aesthetic and spiritualized interpretation of Franciscanism, the first studies having a scientific aim begin to appear. In this line is the work of Karl Hase, *Franz von Assisi: Ein Heiligenbild* (Francis of Assisi: The image of a saint). Published in Leipzig in 1856 and translated into French beginning in 1864, it marks a significant turning point in the sense that it constitutes the first nonconfessional and critical biography of the Poor Man of Assisi. Its author challenges the historicity and credibility of the stigmata, attributed to a ruse of Brother Elias, thus initiating a debate that endures to our own day. Simultaneously, a whole historiography of Protestant or liberal inspiration presented Francis as a precursor of the Reformation, insofar as he had tried to encourage an authentic evangelical Christianity in reaction to the betrayals of the Roman Church, which had gone astray through a thirst for power and wealth. Michelet, who in his *Histoire de France* considered Francis the father of the Reformation, writes: "He cried out, as later would Luther: 'Down with the law, long live grace!'" and underlines Francis' dramatic genius, while at the same time deploring his excessive zeal and naïveté.[5] Renan, author in 1865 of a *Life of Jesus* which caused a scandal and cost him dismissal by Napoléon III from his chair at the Collège de France, likewise became enamored with the Poor Man of Assisi, to whom he devoted some wonderful pages.[6] He highlighted the simplicity of Francis and the popular character of the Franciscan legends, which he contrasted to the stiffness and rigor of the writings coming from ecclesiastical milieus: "After Christianity, the Franciscan movement is the greatest popular work that history records. One senses there the naïveté of human beings who know only nature and what they have seen and heard from the Church, which then combines all that in the freest possible manner."[7] In a way inherently surprising, Renan makes his own the theme, so contested in the modern era, of the conformity of Francis to Christ, while at the same time stripping it of its supernatural dimension: "Francis of Assisi has a larger-than-life interest for religious criticism. After Christ he is the person who has had the most limpid conscience, the most absolute naïveté, the keenest appreciation of his relationship with the Heavenly Father. God was truly his beginning and his end. In him, Adam seems to have never sinned."[8]

Francis was truly the image of Christ; but let's not forget that for Renan, Christ was only an "admirable human being," according to the expression which he used about him in his *Vie de Jesus*. In fact, the conclusion that he drew from the legacy of the Poor Man of Assisi clearly situates itself in the perspective of the "de-catholicizing" of his subject, whom modern science ought to snatch away from the Church in order to give him back to humanity: "Two things appear as thus coming from Francis: first, a religious order which has done more bad than good; second, a ferment of freedom and popular initiative that has produced the majority of reformers of the second half of the Middle Ages."[9] But Renan did not have the chance to deepen his intuitions, and his knowledge of the Franciscan dossier—the complexity of which it is not certain that he was fully aware—remained superficial. Thus did he entrust its study to one of his disciples, the liberal Protestant pastor Paul Sabatier. The latter put himself to work in the 1880s and published in 1893–1894 a *Life of Saint Francis*, a fundamental work which had an enormous success and rocketed the Poor Man of Assisi to the first level of contemporary concerns. In this book, which spurred violent reactions from the Catholic Church and was put on the Index of Prohibited Books as soon as it appeared, Sabatier presents Francis as a deeply human person who lived a profound spiritual experience but outside of any theological reference point: a totally free spirit, a friend of animals, enthusiastic poet, precursor by his radical poverty of later social revolutions, and, even though he never broke with the Roman Church, of the Protestant Reformation. Sabatier synthesizes here two "readings" of Francis which had predominated since the beginning of the nineteenth century. In one he was above all a troubadour of genius who, by ushering in a new relationship between the human person and nature, had opened the way to the Renaissance; the other—the Protestant and anticlerical interpretation—was particularly keen on the oppositional aspect of his radical evangelicalism. For Sabatier, the Poor Man of Assisi, because of the resistance that he quickly ran into from the papacy, had not been able to pursue his intentions all the way; but he saved Christianity by the strength of his own personal witness: "Without Francis of Assisi," he writes, "the Church would perhaps have gone under and the Cathars would have won."[10] In saying this, Sabatier joins the opinion of Machiavelli († 1527), for whom the holiness of Francis and the action of his order had given the papacy breathing space for about three centuries, which it did not know how to take advantage of and which ended with the Reformation and Luther.

The profound shock created by Paul Sabatier's *Life of Saint Francis*—a veritable thunderclap in a serene sky—comes from its substitution for the peaceful image and mystique of Francis, driven since Bonaventure by the tradition of the Franciscan order and the Catholic Church, with a dissonant view of the life of the Poor Man of Assisi. The work, written in a poetic and enthusiastic style much appreciated in its day, was the fruit of erudite research and reflection which continued up to the death of the author in 1928. The book marked a fundamental turning point in studies devoted to Franciscanism, as Sabatier placed all the testimonies then known on Francis within a critical perspective and for the first time made a place for the writings of the Poverello to which no one had given much attention up till then. Taking as his starting point the idea that the Gospel-centered Christianity ushered in by Francis had been overturned by the papacy while he was yet living and distorted after his death by the order which he had founded, Sabatier laid down the foundations of a "historiography of suspicion," which has predominated to the present day in Franciscan studies. Indeed, in his book, the life of Francis and the transmission of his message bask in a dramatic atmosphere: Cardinal Hugolino, afterward to become Pope Gregory IX, while multiplying protestations of esteem and friendship regarding the Poor Man of Assisi, at the same time sought to put the energies and enthusiasm aroused by his preaching at the service of the Roman Church and its policy of power. After Francis' death, Thomas of Celano, through his *Life of Saint Francis* of 1228–1229, was the unwitting executor of these bad deeds of the cardinal and of Brother Elias, who used Francis and his writings to counter the intransigent purity of the first companions, the only authentic interpreters of the thought and project of their master and friend. On this foundation, Sabatier establishes a distinction between the official sources of the life of Francis (the two *Lives* of Thomas of Celano and the *Legenda maior* of Bonaventure) and the nonofficial sources (from the *Legend of the Three Companions* to the various *Mirrors* composed by the Spirituals from the end of the thirteenth century through the first third of the fourteenth), which reflect the thinking of the friars that remained faithful to the original message of the founder of the Minors.

In 1898 Sabatier believed that he had found the missing link which his investigation had been lacking: he discovered, in a manuscript of the Bibliothèque

Mazarine in Paris dated 1227, the *Speculum perfectionis*, which he published under the title of *Legenda antiquissima* ("The Earliest Legend").[11] This text, which corresponded, according to him, to the chapters on the life of Francis which had been purposely eliminated from the *Legend of the Three Companions*, had, he proposed, been written right after Francis' death by Brother Leo; and it was to oppose this disturbing interpretation of the facts and deeds of the Poverello that Hugolino and Elias had Thomas of Celano draw up an official Life, which was quickly imposed and which cast into the shadows the one written by Leo. Thus was the fundamental thesis of the work confirmed: there existed from the beginning two different interpretations of Franciscanism, whose trace was found in a very unequal manner in the historiographical production regarding Francis. The one which had the support of the papacy and the hierarchy of the order of Minors predominated over and obscured the other tradition, which was, however, the only one in conformity with the authentic spirit of the Poverello.

As might be imagined, Sabatier's thesis provoked violent reactions on the Catholic side, notwithstanding the author's repeated affirmations of respect toward the Roman Church, and the support his work found among certain clerics and Christian intellectuals, who came to be suspected of modernism after the condemnation of this current of thought by Pius X in 1907. Learned polemics of great virulence followed one after the other, marking the beginning of what came to be called the "Franciscan Question," an expression that describes all the research and critical reflections relative to the different medieval sources concerning Francis and their respective value. But it soon became clear that Sabatier had approached the dating of the biographies of the Poor Man of Assisi in an excessively schematic and largely erroneous manner. In fact, the *Speculum perfectionis*, on which he based the main point of his argument, dated not from 1227 but from 1317. Once this error was corrected, it could no longer be seen as an early legend indicative of the opposition he believed that he had established between Thomas of Celano and Brother Leo. But whatever might have been his errors of interpretation, Sabatier's great achievement was in moving Franciscanism out of the framework of sclerotic ecclesiastical historiography and making of it an object of research in the broadest sense of the term: an innovation that would make possible, in the twentieth century, the gradual rediscovery of the historical and human dimension of the Poor Man of Assisi. Moreover, thanks to this book, which had forty-four editions in its French version between 1893 and 1931 and was translated into twenty languages—in Russian by Tolstoy—Francis became a fashionable figure in intellectual circles and among the literate bourgeoisie: almost too much so in the eyes of Paul Sabatier, who in 1908 said to a friend: "When I see the theories of English aesthetics and American snobs whom I led to Assisi, I repent but for a moment to have written a *Life of Saint Francis!* . . ."

FRANCIS OF ASSISI BETWEEN NATIONALISTIC RECUPERATION AND HISTORICAL RESEARCH

Italy was obviously at the heart of this resurrection. Assisi had been restored between 1925 and 1940, as a purely medieval town, under the direction of its "podestà," Arnaldo Fortini, who obtained financial help from Mussolini in order to do this. This erudite mayor, author of a book, *Assisi in the Middle Ages*, and a *New Life of Saint Francis* in five volumes, reestablished celebrations fallen into oblivion. For example, his administration revived the vow connected to the memory of the intercession of Saint Clare on behalf of the city besieged by the Saracens in the hire of Frederick II. The feast of Calendi maggio, at the beginning of May, was also restored to welcome the return of spring: every year since, the two neighborhoods of the city, the upper (*parte de sopra*) and lower (*parte de sotto*), confront each other in medieval dress for playful jousts and chorales.[12] In 1926 the celebration of the seven hundredth anniversary of the death of Saint Francis was the occasion for solemn ceremonies presided over by the Cardinal Merry del Val, a ceremony that contributed to a rapprochement between the Church and the Italian state in a new climate that helped bring about the Lateran Accords in 1929. From this moment on, every year the various regions of Italy offered a votive lamp to the sanctuary of Assisi intended to burn night and day before the tomb of Saint Francis; even today all the regions take turns providing the lamp with oil.

The city was, moreover, graced with a bell tower, the *campana delle laudi*, installed in the campanile of the Palazzo of the Captain of the People, on the piazza del Comune, which is rung on great occasions. King Victor-Emmanuel III went to Assisi in great pomp: for the first time since 1870, a sovereign of the House of Savoy visited the basilica and the tomb of Saint Francis. Il Duce, for his part, extolled the memory of this great historical person, in whom he saw "the most Italian of saints and the most saintly of all Italians"; and Pope Pius XI made Francis the patron saint of Italy in 1939. The nationalist poet, Gabriele d'Annunzio, celebrated him as the spirited hero, engaged with the Crusades on the roads of the East, while Father Agostino Gemelli, a Franciscan university man, ideologically close to fascism, provided Franciscanism with a clear interpretation in a work titled *Il Francescanismo*, well-received in Catholic circles.[13] Paul Sabatier was invited to the festivities of 1926, which, in a sense, constituted the crowning of his ongoing efforts over more than thirty years to bring the

Poor Man of Assisi out of oblivion and to give him back to history. But the combination of crowds recruited by the regime, the clerical triumphalism, and the flow of patriotic rhetoric that marked these demonstrations quickly became too much for the man who, in 1902, had founded in Assisi the *Società internazionale di studi francescani* to gather men and women of all nations, opinions, and religions, drawn together by the figure of the Poverello. Thus did Sabatier leave the official ceremonies the moment he could, in order to go and pray alone and to cry at the hermitage of the Carceri. He was to die two years later.[14]

The movement which Sabatier had launched continued after him. And the interpretations or hypotheses, sometimes dubious, even erroneous in some cases, that he had advanced helped to spur new research and works of scholarship which have allowed us to get beyond some of the polemics of the beginning of the twentieth century. Thus the Friars Minor, who in 1885 had begun to publish ancient documents relative to the history of their order in their *Analecta francescana*, released in 1941 a critical edition of the ensemble of medieval hagiographical texts relative to their founder which is still authoritative today. Finally, in 1976, a German Franciscan of great learning, Father Kajetan Esser, published the first critical edition of the *Writings* of Saint Francis, which serves as the basis for the translations in use today in all Western countries.[15] Following the work of German and French scholars who played an important role in the rebirth of Franciscan studies in Europe in the early decades of the twentieth century came numerous university professors and religious—Italian, English, and, since the 1960s, American—so that today this historiography has become completely international and is the work of clerics as well as laity. But for the past half-century, it has been the Italian historians and philologists who have played the most important role in the realm of the history of Franciscanism: the works of scholars like Raoul Manselli, Edith Pasztor, Ovidio Capitani, Giovanni Miccoli, Claudio Leonardi, Grado Merlo, Luigi Pellegrini, Roberto Rusconi, Chiara Frugoni, Giulia Barone, Pietro Messa, and many others have profoundly renewed the problematic of Franciscan studies, as well as our understanding of the sources regarding Francis.[16]

A PLURIFORM MYTH FOR OUR TIME

Francis is currently so well known—for better or for worse—that he has become an element of Western culture. And for several decades, he has been invoked as witness or warning in many areas where we would not necessarily expect to find him. As Raimondo Michetti has seen it, the Poor Man of Assisi has today become a "weak myth": a figure both omnipresent and fuzzy that oscillates among several images according to the aspirations and disturbances of our time.[17] But to avoid all misunderstanding, let's be precise from the start about what we mean by "myth." In contemporary language, this term has become more or less synonymous with fiction, if not a lie or something fake. Obviously that is not what we mean. By myth, we mean a widely diffused idea that takes on in some cases a perceptual certitude, even though it might contain elements of exaggeration or error. Thus we talk about the myth of Rome or that of Napoléon, which means, of course, not that the history of this city or of this emperor might be made up but rather that an interpretation of them has long come to predominate in the popular imagination that does not necessarily coincide with historical reality. Similarly, the myth of Francis necessarily is anchored in his story and his personality, but for certain elements of that myth, this link can be tenuous or even artificial.

Thus, since the nineteenth century, Francis—who had been at the origin of a lay movement of popular inspiration and of confraternities gathering together men and women living in the world—has often been presented as the symbol of fraternity among the social classes and as the instrument of a regeneration of Christian society worn down by individualism and money. Frédéric Ozanam, who, as we have seen, around 1850 contributed to help the French rediscover the figure of the Poverello, was also the founder of the Conferences of Saint Vincent de Paul, which sought to make the Catholic bourgeoisie aware of the misery of the working world. In his book of 1852 on Franciscan poetry, he was one of the first to present the Poor Man of Assisi as an important, ever-relevant figure of social Catholicism:

> By making himself poor, by founding a new order of poor like him, he honored poverty, which is the most disdained and most common of human conditions. He showed that one can find peace, charity, and happiness therein. He thereby brought calm to the resentments of the indigent classes; he reconciled them with the rich, whom they learned to envy no longer. He eased that old conflict between those who do not own against those who do own and strengthened the bonds already loose within Christian society.[18]

In this same perspective, to combat the influence of the unions of socialist inspiration and that of the Freemasons, Pope Leo XIII sought, beginning in 1882, to reinvigorate and develop the Franciscan Third Order, in which he saw "a real school of freedom, fraternity, and equality . . . such as Jesus Christ wanted to enrich human kind with and which Saint Francis practiced."[19] The pope's attempt did not have much success, but the idea was taken up again at the beginning of the twentieth century by the founders of Italian Christian Democracy, who placed their movement under the patronage of Saint Francis, promoter of civil peace and of a harmonious collaboration between the different classes of society. It is precisely this peaceful conception of relations between social groups that Catholic milieus then attributed to him that earned for the Poor Man of Assisi the criticisms of Antonio Gramsci, one of the founders of the Italian Communist Party. Indeed Gramsci reproached Francis for having contributed, through his pacifism, to condemning to powerlessness the popular masses of his day, contrary to the heretics who had dared to defy the Church and feudal power.[20]

More recently, a whole current of influential thought from the 1970s to 1990s in South America, referred to as the "theology of liberation," has seen in Francis the defender of the oppressed and, in some way, the founder of a "Church of the poor," which struggles alongside the mass of exploited for their human advancement. Indeed, the Poor Man of Assisi, as Leonardo Boff, one of the leaders of this movement, has recalled, converted to the Poor Christ. He did not limit himself to charity toward the disadvantaged of his own day; rather, he wanted to share their condition and become the brother of the poor by living with them and for them.[21] His rule is marked by an unconditional rejection of the desire for power and enrichment and, through the movement that he launched, he sought to lead the Church back to the ideals of the poverty and simplicity of its apostolic origins. This choice had had social implications: was not the first public act of Francis to break with the "pre-capitalistic" society of his time and with the avarice—in the medieval sense of the term, the cupidity—of his father? We find an echo of this in his diatribes against money, which he blamed for being the source of injustice and exclusion, to the degree that it contributes to the marginalization of those who do not possess it. But for all that, he did not exalt misery but sought to bring forward a remedy for it through fraternity and solidarity with those who were immersed in it. The radical poverty desired and lived by Francis is a means of realizing perfect fraternal justice. In the eyes of Boff, the Franciscan order did not understand this central intuition of its founder. It remained faithful to it only superficially, for if the order never stopped talking about poverty, it quickly became an abstract notion and the object of endless discussions about what one could possess or use without violating the rule. It could not have been otherwise, once poverty was no longer lived by the friars as a concrete sharing of the life of the forgotten of society. For Boff, to rediscover the authentic spirit of Francis today, his spiritual sons and the Church must make common cause with the poor against their poverty and to participate in their struggles. Various authors have taken up the same ideas in a secularized perspective, like Albert Jacquart, who describes himself as a "rationalist and atheistic" intellectual and, nevertheless, a great admirer of the Poor Man of Assisi.[22]

Francis also has become in our time a leading figure of ecology; and this role has been made official by Pope John Paul II, who declared him, in 1980, the patron saint of ecologists. The key texts which are referred to in this perspective are obviously the *Canticle of Brother Sun*, where Francis' admiration for the beauty of creation and gratitude toward the Creator are expressed in a cosmic vision extolling the wonders of the universe, and the hagiographical accounts about the close relationships which the saint maintained with animals. Through the figure of the Poor Man of Assisi, the contemporary world is offered a model of potential harmony between human beings and nature and a global vision transcending the tensions between the North and South of our planet, which have become so marked in our day.[23] At the moment when we are discovering the limits of an unregulated economic exploitation of natural resources and the risks of exhausting or polluting elements as essential to us as air and water, Francis is being called to the rescue in order to help humanity establish a new, less destructive relationship with its milieu.

Finally, during the last decades, Francis is above all celebrated as an emblematic figure of the harmony which ought to reign between human beings and religions. In fact, the invitation to make peace, addressed to individuals but also to parties and collectivities, is really found at the heart of his message, as it is at the heart of the Gospel message that inspired him. This aspect of Franciscanism has been brought back into the light, in the postwar period and especially since the 1970s, in a politico-religious perspective by militants and Christian movements desiring to attenuate the tension between the two antagonistic blocs that were dividing the world at the time of the Cold War. At the initiative of nonviolent organizations arising from diverse ideologies but ultimately dominated by the left and the extreme left, "peace marches" were organized in Italy which drew considerable crowds to Assisi, once a year, on a specific date. The basilica of Saint Francis and the attendant Sacro Convento became key places of militant pacifism; numerous political personalities were invited and came. Thus, on the eve of the second war against Iraq, Tariq Aziz, Saddam Hussein's minister of foreign affairs and the only Christian member of his government, came to pray for peace with the Friars Minor at the tomb of Francis, a gesture denounced in the press and by Italian and American public opinion, as a show of propaganda. Pope John Paul II, for his part, had earlier, in a different context, proposed Assisi as the place par excellence for collaboration among the various religions of the world, Christians as well as non-Christians, on behalf of peace. Thus did he organize in October 1986, with the Sant'Egidio community, a first gathering for peace, followed by a second in January 1993, making the city of Saint Francis the symbol of interreligious dialogue on the scale of the universe, under the sign of what has been called "the spirit of Assisi."[24] It is significant that almost all of the great denominations and the religious dignitaries who led them accepted the invitation and came together in order to pray for peace around the tomb of Francis. But Cardinal Ratzinger, who disapproved of these gatherings and who feared that they might engender relativism, put an end to them as soon as he became Pope Benedict XVI; he placed the Conventual Franciscans of the Sacro Convento, who had organized the convocations, under the supervision of the Bishop of Assisi. If representatives of Islam, Judaism, and Buddhism—which probably would have refused to gather in Rome—agreed to come to Assisi, it was because the city of the Poverello appears today as a world spiritual center, something of an "Anti-Rome," free of the power and pomp which many object to in the Eternal City, seat of the papacy. Assisi, on the contrary, appears in the collective imagination as a town, simple and pure, a reflection and visible metaphor of this Francis, to whom has been wrongly attributed a beautiful peace prayer—which in fact dates from the end of the nineteenth century—but who was effectively an artisan of concord between human beings while he was alive.[25]

Finally, for several decades, as witnessed by the recent multiplication of books on the subject, the Poor Man of Assisi is presented as the protagonist of the dialogue between Christians and Muslims and even, more broadly, of the dialogue between civilizations which, since September 11, 2001, has become one of the major issues of our time. The idea, however, is not new. It had haunted the great French Arabist, Louis Massignon, who, in 1922, established a parallel between Francis and Hallaj, a mystic filled with the desire of martyrdom who was burned at the stake in Baghdad in 992 after offering his life for the salvation of Muslims. Massignon, a professor at the Collège de France and a Franciscan tertiary, founded a confraternity in 1947 whose aim was to work toward the manifestation of Christ in Islam, "not simply as a prophet recognized by the Qur'an but as true God and true Man."[26] Massignon refers in this approach to all those who have accepted to be the victims of "substitution" to obtain from God the conversion of Islam, among whom he places in the first rank Francis of Assisi. Even if the real content of the exchange between Francis and the sultan of Egypt in large measure escapes us, it is certain that he approached Islam with an exceptional commitment and attentiveness for his day. In fact, we know that the encounter between Francis and the sultan had virtually no follow-up within his own order. Yet it is precisely because of this failure, and the critical obligation to reestablish a relationship today between the West and the Islamic world founded on mutual esteem and a spirit of peace, that the figure of the Poor Man of Assisi can recover exemplary value once again. This does not, however, allow us to present Francis as an adversary of the Crusade, as various authors have made of him in recent years; and we have shown earlier that this affirmation hardly had any meaning in the cultural and religious context in which he moved.[27]

All these more or less justified references to Francis go back in the last analysis to a fundamental question: why is he invoked even today in order to legitimize all kinds of ideologies and aspirations, some of which have little to do with what we know of his personality and life? The answer is simple: if the Poor Man of Assisi has become, since the twentieth century, such an important figure in so many essential domains, it is because he incarnates in the eyes of many of our contemporaries the essence of Christianity in all its purity, to the extent that he might be considered the first authentic Christian since Jesus Christ. Dante had already expressed this idea in poetic terms in *The Divine Comedy*, at the beginning of the fourteenth century:

> Widow of his first spouse, Poverty,
> A thousand one hundred years and more disdained and obscure,
> Remained until him [Francis] without claimant.[28]

And Julien Green echoes this in our own time when he writes that in Francis "God has offered us his Gospel a second time at twelve hundred years' distance."[29] These authors, however, merely return to the medieval theme of "Francis, a second Christ," already implicitly present in some Franciscan hagiographical texts of the thirteenth century and explicitly among the Spirituals in the fourteenth century, without drawing from it new consequences. In fact, it is Ernest Renan, once again, who gave to this conviction a modern and incisive formulation that was going to influence people up to our own day: "One can say that, since Jesus, Francis of Assisi was the only perfect Christian. What makes his uniqueness, is to have undertaken, with a faith and love without limit, the fulfillment of the program of the Galilean."[30] For Renan, the example of Francis thus constitutes proof that Christianity, at least once, has been lived by a human being in all its radicality within the context of a historical life: this allows us to sustain the hope that this great movement, taken and distorted by the Church, might be able one day to resume its influence. Till then, the Poor Man of Assisi will be considered as the paragon of Christian authenticity and the incarnation of the Gospel message. For Paul Sabatier, disciple of Renan, Francis was not only the greatest saint of the Middle Ages and the history of Catholicism, as the Franciscan tradition affirms, but a figure of universal holiness who, beyond its particular religious rooting, belongs to the common patrimony of humanity. In our own days, we often place him, alongside Gandhi and Martin Luther King, Jr., among those rare personalities who transcend confessional and ideological divisions. The figure of the Poor Man of Assisi retains even more attention in that his life illustrates the contradictions which inevitably exist between the demands of the Gospel, which he had fully integrated into his life, and the historical realizations of this ideal, often quite far from this perfection. Thus did Sabatier reproach the papacy for having marginalized his message of poverty and humility, and the order of Friars Minor for not having understood what its founder was expecting of it and for having rapidly deviated from his original project. Gramsci, for his part, wondered "why Franciscanism had not become the whole religion, as was the intention of Francis, but was reduced to being only one of the numerous existing religious orders"—the only legitimate response to the question for Gramsci being the seizure by the Roman Church of the Franciscan message, whose subversive elements it carefully eliminated in order to use it for its own objectives.[31]

But by conferring on the Poor Man of Assisi this stature of "super saint" and the incarnation of evangelical perfection against whom all other religious and human experiences ought to be measured, have we not gilded the experience lived by the Poor Man of Assisi with timeless categories that hardly help us understand its reality and significance? Even the great historian of Franciscanism Giovanni Miccoli has not entirely escaped this shortcoming. In a brilliant synthesis of the religious history of Italy that appeared in 1974, he asserted that the failure of the proposal of evangelical marginality which was at the heart of the experience of the Poverello illustrated "the tragic inability of the Church of Rome to translate into practices of governance and life the holiness of the message which it is the depository of."[32]

Must the problem which the life of Francis of Assisi poses be defined in these terms? Speaking for myself, I do not think so. For the idea of a betrayal of the naïve Francis by the wily Cardinal Hugolino and by Brother Elias, which was at the root of Sabatier's interpretation, Miccoli has substituted the affirmation of a structural incompatibility between the Gospel and the Church, which constitutes an unproved postulate. Moreover, the relationship of Francis with the Church does not allow itself to be defined in such a simple fashion, as we will later try to show, and cannot in any case be reduced to a schematic opposition between charism and institution. To go no farther than that would be to come around to a vision of the history of Christianity that is both inexact and depressing, founded on the constant of a recurring failure of the Gospel spirit, smothered in every era by the weight of structures and the clergy's lack of understanding.

But Miccoli came back to the question in his masterpiece of 1991, titled *Francis of Assisi*, which profoundly renewed the methodological and historical approach of Franciscan sources.[33] The subtitle of his work, *Reality and Remembrance of a Christian Experience*, if one takes it literally, seems to really imply the possibility of other authentically Christian experiences. This is important since the affirmation of the centrality of Francis in the religious history of the human race and of its absolute exemplarity as the perfect realization of the Christian message creates a problem for the historian. Certainly, the Poor Man of Assisi greatly advanced—probably more than all of his predecessors—the incarnation of evangelical values in a human life. But we do not see why this experience would have a singular character and would not take or might have taken other forms in different historical and cultural contexts. In short, if one wants to understand who Francis really was, it is necessary to begin by "deconstructing" the previous schemas, anthropological as well as mythological, which tend to assign him a quasi-messianic role or to make of him a model having a universal and permanent validity. To try to put an end to the enterprise of dehumanizing the figure of the Poor Man of Assisi which began the day after his death is not to undermine his grandeur or to attenuate the sometimes dramatic character of his life but simply to restore him to history, which has known great men but also supermen.[34]

THE ORIGINALITY OF FRANCIS AND HIS CHARISM

Since Francis is known to us especially through the *legendae*, and since he has been the object of various fabrications throughout the centuries, can we have only a deformed picture of him, partial or anachronistic? Must we give up ever coming to know him as he really was? I do not believe so because, different from many of the great religious figures of his time—Saint Dominic, for example—he has left behind a certain number of writings. This does not, of course, mean that we must reject as defective or suspect the testimonies of medieval hagiographers who have grasped, each in his own way and degree, part of the truth of Francis' person and have handed down to us some of his words. Without their contribution, many aspects of the personality and life of the Poor Man of Assisi would completely elude us. But his writings have the great advantage of allowing us to enter into his inner self, without having to pass through the filter of a "reading" done by another, which, however honest or intelligent, implies an interpretation and thus choices that have been made.

THE WRITINGS OF FRANCIS

The writings of Francis comprise a collection of disparate texts, of destination and date often uncertain and of varied import. Today we recognize as authentic about thirty of them, which range from a note of a few lines addressed to Anthony of Padua, permitting him to teach theology to the Friars Minor, to a relatively long and complex composition like the "Psalms of the Mystery of Christ" (*Officium Passionis Domini*). This collection is not a work that boasts a cohesive design. Moreover, the survival of these texts is largely due to chance. Most of the correspondence of Francis, in particular those letters he exchanged with Cardinal Hugolino, has left behind no trace; and many of these *opuscula* (little works), as they have been referred to for some time now, have come down to us only in a small number of manuscripts. We cannot but be astonished at this lack of appreciation for the writings of the founder except for the fact that, while he was still living, due to the itinerant way of life which was his, there was, as a rule, little concern about preserving them—something which he probably would have been opposed to anyway. After his death, most were quickly forgotten, except, of course, the rule of 1223. We had to wait until Paul Sabatier, at the end of the nineteenth century, to bring the importance of these writings back into the light. But as the authenticity and the dating of a number of them became the object of erudite debates and sometimes long polemical fights, it is only since 1976 that we have had at our disposal a complete and viable edition of these writings and that historians have been able to use them for their work.[1]

The writings of Francis, if one leaves aside his very personal *Testament*, comprise an ensemble of moral exhortations and spiritual counsels referred to as *Admonitions*, twelve letters or notes addressed to Brother Leo, Anthony of Padua, unknown friars, the whole order or lay believers, various prayers, *laude* or blessings, a religious office, and a few legislative texts: the rules of 1221 and 1223, which are the result of work certainly influenced by Francis, but in which he did not figure as its redactor, and the *Rule for Hermitages*, probably after 1223. To all these are to be added different words or *logia* (sayings or discourses reported outside of their context), which can be attributed to him but which have been transmitted by other authors, like Clare of Assisi for the *Form of Life* of the Poor Ladies and the *Last Will* of the Poverello; or reported through collective memory—like the parable of the woman made pregnant by the king, cited already in 1219 by the English cleric Eudes de Cheriton in a sermon collection drawn up in Paris.

But it does not suffice that words which Francis may have said have been preserved by his biographers in a direct style in order that we might be certain of their authenticity. Even those which have been introduced with the phrase "We who were with him" (*Nos qui cum eo fuimus*) are not necessarily attributable to him, because this mention has been added after the fact by some of his former companions in support of one or another of their positions. Some of these writings are autographs, like the two notes addressed to Brother Leo conserved today, one in Assisi and one in Spoleto, or had been dictated directly to a secretary in the Latin of the Poor Man of Assisi that was full of italianisms. Others—such as the letters addressed by him to broad categories of people (the "custodes" of the Minors; the "rulers of the peoples") or to groups (the Franciscan order; all the faithful)—have been rewritten and put into good Latin by friar-clerics, for it was the language that was used at that time in social and institutional relations. And finally, some texts have been directly redacted by Francis himself in Italian, or more exactly in the Umbrian dialect which was his native language. Such is the case for the famous *Canticle of Brother Sun* or *Canticle of the Creatures*, and perhaps even the *Exhortation to the Poor Ladies*, which begins with the words "Audite poverelle."

Because of their very diversity, these writings are of paramount importance for the understanding of his personality and the meaning of his mission. Other than the *Testament*, they tell us nothing or almost nothing about his life. The Poor Man of Assisi, who was lacking in literary skill, did not behave like an author, nor did he give himself over to it with any confidence. He was writing only to deliver a message, but he attached to it the highest importance, inspired as he was by the certitude that the words he was writing or dictating were not from him, or not only from him, to the extent that it was God himself who had inspired them in him. Indeed, the semi-illiterate person that he was attributed a sacred character to the writing. Thus we know from his biographers that he did not like anyone to edit his letters, even if a few spelling or grammatical mistakes had slipped in here and there, and that he showed the greatest veneration for texts where the name of God appeared or was referred to, even if they had been written by pagans. Francis wrote to transmit to others "the fragrant words of the Lord" (*EpFid* [Long Version], v. 2) and to witness to the way that he was living from them. A man of word and gesture, he resorted to writing only when circumstances required it. Thus did his letters become relatively numerous at the end of his life, when it had become difficult for him to move around and preach due to his illnesses. It appears that he sought to give them the widest possible diffusion, as if he had been haunted by the urgency that he had to deliver his message and make it known to all before leaving this world. For their part, the friars, seeing his health rapidly declining, were more careful to preserve his works, as the presence of a collection of writings of Francis in manuscript 338 of the Sacro Convento in Assisi around the middle of the thirteenth century seems to indicate.

7

THE EXPERIENCE OF GOD

The writings of Francis allow us to especially gather a rather clear idea of his relationship with God. God is not an idea for him, even less so a concept. Francis never gave a theological formulation to his spiritual intuitions or experiences, nor did he ever feel the need to give any explanations for them. Not having been educated in the schools, he did not have the intellectual tools to do this. And he always seemed to dread what could become, in the abstract language of theologians, a barrier between Sacred Scripture and the faithful. God was, above all, for him a presence tied to expressions of physicality and to an experience that begins in the senses, passes into the body, and leads to the soul. To hear and to see were especially to be desired. It was while he was gazing upon the crucifix of San Damiano and meditating on the sufferings of the Crucified that he heard the words of Christ addressed to him. For this invisible God has a face turned toward the human person, as indicated in the famous form of blessing which he gave to Brother Leo, a biblical citation, in fact, that comes from the book of Numbers (Num 6:24–26): "May the Lord bless and keep you; may he show his face to you and be merciful to you. May he turn his countenance to you and give you peace! May the Lord bless you, Brother Leo."[1] To speak about God, Francis used the same terms as a troubadour speaking to the lady of his dreams. And the words that sprang to his pen when he mentioned the highlights of his spiritual journey are expressed in terms of sweetness and pleasure. Each time that God intervenes in his life—for example, after the visit to the lepers that was at the origin of his conversion—an influx of pleasant and tender sensations overcomes him: "You are all our sweetness!" he exclaims in the *Praises of the Most High God*.[2] The encounter with God likewise prompted in him a sensation of warmth and light: God is a fire that burns, that illuminates the angels and saints, and whose reflection in our universe is the sun. He is perceptible only through his concrete, palpable manifestations: nature, parchment leaves on which his name is written, churches of stone where the Eucharist is celebrated, the bread and wine that are the tangible signs of his Incarnation and infinite love for the human race.

This same embodied approach to the divine is the result of an extremely sensitive nature. In Francis, that which we call religious feeling is of the order of the emotions and is expressed outwardly. His God was first of all perceptible not to the heart, as Pascal and the mystics of the seventeenth century would say, but to the body. Thus, when he heard someone use the expression "For the love of God!" he was immediately overcome, gripped, and stirred. His prayer was interlaced with tears, groans, and supplications. His relationship with God did not follow a regular progression whose steps coincided with the seven degrees of the "heavenly ladder," such as the monastic authors of the twelfth century had defined them. It was, rather, an eruption of sounds, smells, and sights which led him into a state of spiritual inebriation. Sigmund Freud, studying "the transformations of sublimation" among which he included friendship with and love of creation, wrote that Francis "is perhaps the one who went the furthest in this direction leading to the complete channeling of love towards inner happiness," and that, in him, "the principles of pleasure and religion could actually be joined in those deeply-recessed places where the ego is no longer differentiated from other objects or one object from another." Whence "this tender manner, stable and freed from feeling, beyond every influence," which characterized, in his eyes, the Poor Man of Assisi.[3]

What then was this exalted truth which made the Poor Man of Assisi so joyful? In a few words, it comes from the certitude of being loved by a God who had extended the meaning of love all the way to saving the human race through the Incarnation and Passion of Christ. The spiritual message of Francis has often been rendered insipid when he is presented as the artisan of a kind of desacralizing of Christianity and the initiator of a gentle transition toward humanism and the Renaissance. After centuries of religious formalism and utter transcendence, God, thanks to Francis, took on a human face. Formulated in this way, such a thesis is debatable; and it is enough to simply read his writings to be convinced of it. Thus in the *Praises of the Most High God*, which appears on the parchment that he entrusted to Brother Leo, he addresses the Creator in terms that call to mind the Greek liturgical hymn *Agios kai ischuros o theos* (God holy and strong):

> You are holy, Lord, the only God,
> You who do wonders.
> You are strong, you are great, you are the Most High,
> You are an almighty king
> You, holy Father, king of heaven and earth.[4]

God is thus for Francis plenitude and perfection itself, the sovereign good, supreme beauty, whose grandeur is unimaginable. Few people in the West have had as much of a sense of transcendence as did Francis, as is evident from the attributes that he lists after the name of God in the rule of 1221.[5] For him, as he says with a Johannine tonality in his *Admonitions*, "the Father dwells in inaccessible light; and God is spirit and no one has ever seen God."[6] His God is really the God of the Bible, surrounded by angels and archangels, who is beyond all understanding: "And no one is worthy to pronounce his name!" he exclaims at the beginning of the *Canticle of Brother Sun*.[7] But this all-powerful God, who remains for us a mystery, is at the same time a merciful and "most good Lord," who willed that his Son become human so that the human person might become God. Indeed, he has given us the grace of revealing himself in his Son, Jesus of Nazareth, who alone is the "bridge" between heaven and earth, in whom God has manifested himself as "the lowliest."[8] Following Saint Paul and perhaps under his influence, the Poor Man of Assisi has a keen sense of the descent or *kenosis*, that is, of the mystery of love by virtue of which the invisible God, Creator and master of the universe, humbled himself and made himself poor in Christ, taking on flesh and the human condition, without involving for him any loss or diminishment of his divine character:

> This word of the Father, so worthy, so holy and so glorious: the Most High Father sent him from heaven by the holy Gabriel, his angel, in the womb of the holy and glorious Virgin Mary. It is from her womb that the Word received the true flesh of our humanity and our fragility. The one who was rich above all others wanted, along with the most holy Virgin Mary his mother, to choose poverty in this world.[9]

Throughout his life, Francis was overcome each time that an event or something he saw evoked for him the willing humiliation of God who became flesh for the salvation of all. For him, the Incarnation was a re-creation of humanity, since it gave back to men and women, in Christ Jesus, their dignity as sons and daughters of which the sin of Adam had deprived them. Such an extraordinary act of love could only incite an act of gratitude and praise which was for him the first and natural form of prayer. This is the whole meaning of the famous episode of the crèche at Greccio, when Francis asked the lord of the village to prepare, for Christmas night in 1223, a manger filled with hay and to lead an ox and ass to the foot of the altar where the Mass of the Nativity was to be celebrated. When the day arrived, he himself read the Gospel and preached to the faithful gathered in great numbers, indispensable partners in this ceremony which was no mere ritual for him, while speaking of the One "whom he called with great tenderness 'the child of Bethlehem,' and he exclaimed this [word] Bethlehem which he drew out like the bleating of a lamb. . . . One could even believe, when he was saying 'Jesus' or 'child of Bethlehem,' that he was passing his tongue over his lips so as to savor the sweetness of these words."[10] Then, a "man of great virtue"—probably the lord John who had organized the ceremony—"noticed a small motionless baby in the manger who appeared to wake from sleep at the approach of the saint." Indeed, this folksy paraliturgy of the crèche, which would soon afterward become widely diffused thanks to the Friars Minor, and which holds an important place today in the religious life of the Christian world, indeed constituted a veritable "sacred representation," a narrative of living images destined to draw attention to the mystery of the Incarnation and the birth of Christ which brought to human beings the certainty of salvation and associated impoverishment with joy. It was thus necessary to give thanks to God for this gift, and the whole world was urged to participate in this feast. If the Nativity fell on a Friday, the brothers were dispensed from the fast. Even better, on this day the rich had to feed beggars and birds and to offer to oxen and asses an extra ration of oats and hay: "If I saw the emperor, he said, I would ask him to issue a decree ordering all those who are able to scatter grain upon the roads on this feast day for the feeding of the little birds and especially our sisters the larks."[11]

It is in this perspective that we need to place the devotion of Francis to the suffering Christ and his own stigmatization, if we want to understand their exact meaning. He is not the apostle of a "more human Christianity"—this is a little soppy or, conversely, moralizing. Grief and suffering are secondary for him compared with the joy of being saved by the sacrifice of Christ on the cross and by his glorious wounds, which allow the human person to have access to life through the flowing of blood and water. His faith is less christocentric than Trinitarian; more exactly, the Father is at the center of his Trinitarian consciousness of God. Nor does this prevent him from having a keen sense of the distinctions among the divine persons. In his last writings, like the *Canticle of Brother Sun*, he addresses only God, as if the awareness that he had of sharing in the suffering and soon-to-be resurrected body of Christ allowed him to speak to him as to a Father: to his Father, like Jesus in Gethsemane. His aim was not to find a perfect theological or spiritual balance between transcendence and immanence, between the Pantocrator and the Child Jesus, but to reconcile human beings with this God by showing them that he could become just as much their Father, on the condition that they accept to open themselves to the action of the Spirit.

To do this, the Christian had need, in Francis' eyes, of two points of support here below: the word of God present in the Bible and the Eucharist, which are the two principal signs of his presence in this world. If the importance of the Gospel in the life and action of the Poor Man of Assisi is obvious and does not need to be demonstrated, the Eucharist was not less essential for him, as it was for the Beguines and the Church of his time, who were emphasizing the real presence of Christ in the sacrament of the altar. The offering of the bread and wine by the priest during the Mass constitutes the moment and the place where the Son makes himself known through the Spirit to human beings. When men and women worthily receive the body and blood of Christ, they become capable of seeing the Father because the Son is in him. Indeed, only God can see God, and the human person is able to only by becoming like Christ. Thus, in his writings, Francis never ceases calling and urging his contemporaries to embrace this sacrament with the greatest respect and to accord it the highest honors. For: "no one can be saved except the one who receives the most holy body and blood of the Lord."[12]

At first glance, the experience which Francis had had of God can seem banal to us, to the degree that it became an integral part of the history of religious feeling in Western Christianity. However, if we put it into historical perspective, its novelty is striking. Late Antiquity and the Early Middle Ages had been dominated by the problem of the divinity of the Word and his equality with the Father. Beginning in the eleventh century, questions arise about the reasons and modalities of the Incarnation: "Why did God become human?" (*Cur Deus homo?*) was the question asked at the time by Saint Anselm, abbot of Bec and then archbishop of Canterbury, situated at the beginning of a renaissance of theological reflection in the West. He was exploring the manner in which the divine had come down into the human and how the human had become associated with the divine. This fundamental question is tied to that of the Eucharist, that is, to the problem of the nature—"real" or symbolic—of the presence of God in the consecrated bread and wine, about which it was just beginning to be said that they were "transsubstantiated" into the flesh and blood of Christ. In the twelfth century, Saint Bernard invented a language to express the relationships between the soul and God while at the same time emphasizing the role of the Holy Spirit, whereas William of Saint Thierry and Richard of Saint-Victor were elaborating a veritable mystical journey at whose conclusion the human being became by grace that which God is by nature. But this path was accessible only to a minority of men or women, no longer living in the world, by meditating on the sacred texts and by giving themselves over to contemplation.

Francis, who had not received any clerical education or studied any theology, did not know these authors and scarcely seems to have been influenced by these spiritual currents. His vision of God was built on the basis of the Bible and the liturgy, with a sense of the concrete and tangible, which instinctively led him to grant a central place to the Eucharist in the relationship between the human person and its Creator and Savior. Francis speaks about the "altar of the cross" where Christ chose to offer his sacrifice, as one sees on the large Italian crucifixes from the beginning of the twelfth century where Christ is often represented, in the background, with a table covered with a colored cloth, usually red, that once again accentuates the Eucharistic symbolism of the scene. For Francis, Christ is neither the Eternal Word, master of wisdom, nor loving Spouse of the soul; he is the crucified Redeemer. Indeed, in his eyes, the passion of Christ marks the summit of the Incarnation and of divine love: "We adore you, Lord Jesus, and we bless you because by your holy cross you have redeemed the world." This text, borrowed from the liturgical office of the feast of the "finding" of the Cross, was to become the Franciscan prayer par excellence. And Francis himself was to compose an "Office of the Passion of the Lord," a veritable mosaic of scriptural texts taken from the Old and New Testaments, which he placed in the mouth of the suffering Christ. God has suffered for us: impossible to remain indifferent or passive in front of this overwhelming reality! The Passion of Christ concerns all Christians because it is for them the source of salvation and life. Faced with this gesture of love, the only worthy response consists in putting oneself in the place of Christ and carrying one's own cross, "for we must love much the love of the one who has so loved us."[13]

But how can one become like the Crucified? The Son of Man, rejected from the moment of his birth and who, according to his own words, "had nowhere to lay his head" (Matt 8:20), has assumed not only the fleshy condition but the entire misery of the human race. To enter into the truth and life of Christ, it was thus necessary to become one, as much as possible, with the indigent and marginalized—all those who, like him, were rejected and disdained by the society of the secure. For Francis, the poor and humble not only constitute the necessary instruments for the salvation of the rich and powerful, as the traditional understanding of the Psalms would have it. They are images of Christ and acquired by this fact their own human and spiritual dignity. Here again, it is a matter not of a theological *a priori* but of a concrete experience. Not until he encountered the lepers and, under the impulse of the grace of God, accepted, according to his own words, to "do mercy" to them and thereby to enter into marginality, did he finally discover the crucified Christ. Following this overwhelming experience, Francis received the central revelation of his life: all men and women are brothers and sisters, the ones to the others, and everything that breaks the bonds of this fraternity desired by God is sin. "To live according to the Holy Gospel" thus meant for him and for those who would follow him to change their relationship with the Other and to live in contact with the excluded—without necessarily becoming blood brothers or sisters—in such a way as to abolish the distance that separates word from life and to give to the word all its effectiveness.

Others before Francis, beginning with Saint Bernard in the previous century, had already spoken of a relationship between the human person and God founded upon love, and had evoked the passionate search for and encounter between Christ and the espoused soul. But for the Poor Man of Assisi, the relationship between God and the human person concerned not just the soul but the totality of one's vital forces. Breaking with the traditional distinction between the soul and the body that monastic spirituality had borrowed from ancient philosophy, he placed the emphasis more on the body and on concrete things. Thus, up to the very end, did he want to work with his hands and commanded his brothers, in his *Testament,* to do the same.[14] Moreover, for Francis, the "conjugal" relationship between the human person and God left nothing out. As he wrote in his *Letter to the Faithful,* those who followed this path of conversion all the way

> will be sons of the heavenly Father whose works they do, and they will be spouses, brothers, and mothers of our Lord Jesus Christ. We are spouses when by the Holy Spirit the faithful soul is united to Jesus Christ; we are truly brothers when we do the will of his Father who is in heaven; mothers when we carry him in our heart and in our body, through love and through a pure and sincere conscience, and when we give birth to him through holy works which must shine out as an example for others.[15]

Thus is it that the one who accepts to die to oneself and to lead a life in conformity with the Gospel becomes the brother or sister and even the mother of Christ, since one can, through one's witness, produce sons and daughters for him.

But must we, for all that, consider Francis a mystic? Everything depends on the meaning that one gives to this term. If by "mystic" we mean that he had an experiential knowledge of God, we can apply the term to him without hesitation. But if we define the term according to particular interior states and supernatural phenomena like ecstasy or levitation, Francis does not belong in this category even if Bonaventure, in the *Legenda maior*, mentions certain forms of supernatural rapture (*raptus*). At most, we might say that Francis was a mystic of the Gospel. Indeed, for him, spiritual experience consisted in leading the very life of God in becoming human. This means allowing to be born and grow within oneself the person of Christ to the point of making of one's whole life a commitment that is ready for total surrender and martyrdom. The one who, in the midst of suffering and humiliation, preserves perfect joy, rejoices in being persecuted, and gives proof of the love of one's enemies can only give thanks to God for the divine life—the eternal life—which God has graced that person with here below.

8

A New Relationship to Scripture: The Spirit of the Letter

One of the characteristics that strikes us most often about the Poor Man of Assisi is his special approach to Sacred Scripture. The desire to return to the Gospel is certainly not unique to him; it had played an important role in various religious movements of the twelfth century. But in some cases, this will to rediscover and be faithful to the sacred text had led to erroneous interpretations or had been marked by a narrow literalism. This had allowed clerics to deride those unlettered laity who claimed the right to criticize their parish priests while being incapable of correctly understanding the Latin text. Thus the monastic chronicler Guilbert of Nogent had mocked some peasants of Picardy who had translated the phrase *Beati eritis* ("Blessed will you be . . ."), proclaimed by Jesus at the beginning of each of the Beatitudes, as "Blessed are the heretics!" Again, around 1180, the curial official Walter Map drew the same lesson from certain naïve interpretations of the Gospel by the Waldensians. Recalling that "it is not permitted to cast one's pearls before swine," he noted that, in the Church, authority does not derive from the public squares and that "the word must not be given to the simple who we know to be incapable of receiving it and, even more, to give what they have received."[1]

The relationship of Francis to the word of God follows along the lines of these movements, but he knew how to avoid their exaggerations and deviations. As a simple layman unfamiliar with the worlds of learned culture, he had no idea of the hermeneutical principles which governed biblical exegesis at the time; he employed, rather, a direct reading of the sacred text, without resorting to glosses or erudite commentary. For him, the understanding of the word of God came not from an outside master or from subtle analysis but from an awakening that each person can receive, on the condition of being engaged with one's whole heart in its reading. The Gospel was not in his eyes a narrative or a holy story but a call addressed by one person to another; it is the very life of Christ which is communicated in order that it might be taken up and continued. By this token, the word constitutes, along with the Eucharist, a sign left by God to assure his presence in a permanent way in the midst of human beings, as he writes in the *Letter to the Faithful*: "No one can be saved except by the holy words of our Lord Jesus Christ, which clerics speak about, proclaim, and administer."[2]

This immediacy with respect to the sacred text can appear surprising to us. But let's not forget that simple believers, at the beginning of the thirteenth century, did not own a Bible. If they knew how to read, they had at the very most a psalter. Only monks and clerics—especially the "great clerics" who had gone to the schools—had a direct access to the text of Sacred Scripture, of which a full translation in the vernacular still did not exist. Thus the majority of laity knew only those passages that were used in the liturgy, provided of course that they understood Latin at least in a rudimentary fashion. And the direct and committed approach to Scripture that Francis practiced and advocated—"to live according to the form of the Holy Gospel"—could take the most diverse forms: reading for those who, like him, knew Latin at least approximately, or simple rumination over a few verses memorized by heart, or the stringing together of various passages of the Bible in such a way as to constitute something like scriptural "chains," as he did in the *Psalms of the Mystery of the Lord Jesus* (or Office of the Passion).[3] The Bible of Saint Francis—a virtual Bible, we are quick to say, since he never possessed a complete copy—was a collection of chosen morsels which he found in the breviary or in an evangeliary rather than a whole text of which he might make a continuous reading, as in monasteries, throughout the liturgical year. Using the very words of Scripture, he addressed God in his own language. In the most concrete sense of the term, one can say that he "speaks Bible" to the extent that his writings consist for the most part of words and phrases drawn from the sacred text which he appropriates and recomposes in a kind of "patchwork." Whence the rather unoriginal, sometimes even disappointing character of his writings, at least at first glance—except for the *Canticle of Brother Sun* and the *Testament*, which have a more personal character—for they have their full meaning only in reference to his experience of God and of lived poverty. But we would be wrong to see here only simple repetitions or compilations, because these texts comprise something more like his personal reflections on the Bible than quotations properly speaking, with the exception of the rule of 1221, which he had asked Caesar of Speyer to adorn with scriptural references once he had finished its redaction. When he was writing alone, Francis made up prayers or meditations based on passages of Scripture which had attracted his attention and which had been etched into his memory. A phrase heard by chance during a sermon or read on a piece of parchment was enough to prompt in him an interior illumination or burst of enthusiasm and sometimes furnished a response to something he was wondering about. Thus, when in 1209 the Poor Man of Assisi, who had yet been joined only by Bernard of Quintavalle, was still seeking his way, "as they were without learning, they did not know where to find the passages of the Gospel on the renunciation of the world, they devoutly prayed that the Lord would deign to manifest his will on the first page that they would see upon opening the holy book."[4]

After this Francis and Bernard opened the New Testament three successive times and landed each time on verses where Christ urged those who wished to follow him to strip themselves of their goods, to carry nothing for the journey, and to deny themselves. They immediately decided to follow his advice—which allows Francis to write, when he mentioned this event in his *Testament* of 1226: "The Lord himself revealed to me that I must live according to the form of the Holy Gospel."[5] Even later, when clerics had entered the order and Francis had acquired a more advanced knowledge of the Bible through reading and meditation on the texts of the liturgical office of the Hours, his relationship to Scripture never became academic. Moreover, according to Thomas of Celano and the author of the *Assisi Compilation*, the only copy of the New Testament that the friars possessed at the time, from which they read the lessons at Matins, Francis had sold in order to take care of the needs of a poor woman whose two sons had just entered the fraternity.[6] Francis was thus not a writing man, even if he probably turned to it more often than we might think, given the small number of texts that have come down to us from him. It suffices to think about the role that dreams and visions had in his life, without even mentioning his deeds and spoken words, in order to gauge to what extent it would be anachronistic and inexact to see in him one religious author among so many others and to reduce his spiritual experience to what we can gather from his writings. According to the *Anonymous of Perugia* and Bonaventure, although Francis may have received the tonsure in 1209, making him a cleric, the Poor Man of Assisi behaved his whole life like a layman when it came to learning; and it is in this perspective that we must place the prohibitions that the rule of the Friars Minor contains on this matter: "Let those who do not know how to read not go seeking to learn how; but let them remember that they must above all else desire to have the Spirit of the Lord and his holy operation."[7]

This rejection of every intellectual advancement within the order is somewhat shocking to modern sensibilities. But it constituted an indispensable precaution—ineffective, as succeeding events will show—for maintaining the original characteristics of the Franciscan movement. The praise of simplicity by Francis was not to be equated with ignorance. If he left to intellectuals, whom he mistrusted, "the verbal jumble, the embellishments, the displays of knowledge and subtleties," it is because he dreaded above all else the search for wisdom and knowledge that had led his spiritual sons to cut themselves off from the poor by enclosing themselves in a "wooden language" that was allegorical or academic.[8] In his eyes, the relationship to Scripture had to remain above all operational (the "holy operation"), and the profound meaning of the sacred text resided in an action designed to make it effective in the world. In every divine word, Francis first saw an invitation to begin to do something so that the words might become life through the personal commitment of the speaker or reader. Nothing was more painful for him than to see his brothers be moved at the reading of certain hagiographical texts, like the passion of the Franciscans martyred in Morocco in 1220, and to draw glory from their exploits. Thus did he prohibit them from reading it by saying: "Let each one glory in his own martyrdom and not in that of others!"[9]

This direct and personal implication in and through Scripture is likewise demonstrated through his selective reading of the Bible. Francis did not go searching for obscure passages requiring learned commentaries; his preferences were for the Psalms and the New Testament. In the texts of the Gospels, he especially valued the words that we might call radical because they forced the human being to correct and reorient himself at the very core of his being and behaviors.[10] Nourished by the sacred text, he privileged a few passages or themes which we find, for example, in the two rules that have come down to us. Sometimes he even changed the text ever so slightly in order to adapt it to his purpose. Thus, in the *Officium Passionis Domini*, he says, with respect to the Nativity, that "the most holy beloved Child has been given to us and was born for us on the road and was placed in the crèche because there was no place for him in the inn."[11] Francis' text draws both on the antiphon *Puer natus est nobis*, taken from the liturgy of the feast of Christmas, and on the passage from the Gospel of Luke (Luke 2:7) that is read at Mass the same day. But he adds that Jesus had been born "on the road" (*in via*), which does not appear in any of these two texts and puts the emphasis on the condition of pilgrim and wanderer which was his from the moment of Jesus' birth. Francis has, however, not invented this, for we find the mention of Christ "who was born on the way" already in a homily of Gregory the Great.[12] Francis certainly had not had direct access to this writing, but he had come to know of it through the breviary of the Roman Curia which he, as well as his friars, were using; there the passage in question is the second of four readings for Christmas night borrowed from the patristic literature. Beginning with these texts, Francis made a montage of texts that corresponded to his vision of Christ. Indeed, for him the Son of God is a child without a country who was refused lodging. Likewise, he wrote in the rule of 1221 that Jesus "lived on alms, he and the Virgin Mary and his disciples," which corresponded to his intimate conviction but not to any explicit mention of it in the Gospels.[13] Indeed, in the life of Christ, Francis had a predilection for the figure of the newly born Jesus and for the dying Jesus: that is, the moments of the greatest weakness of the God-made-man. But he did not remain outside the biblical text: in recomposing it, he placed himself in a parallel, if not identical, situation to that of Christ in order to discover from the inside that which could have been the concrete life and feelings of the Son of Man, who was born in a stable, suffered the suffering of the world, and identified himself with it in his Passion. In this approach, Francis ushered in a veritable spiritual revolution, because this was tantamount to saying that humility and pain were the real face of God.

The passages of the Gospels most frequently cited by the Poverello are first of all those from the synoptic Gospels.[14] We have seen the decisive importance for his vocation of the discourse of the sending of the disciples on mission (Matt 10; Luke 9:10). It is necessary to add to this the verses from Luke where Christ says that God alone is good (Luke 18:19) and where he urges those who want to follow him to put themselves in the most unassuming place (Luke 22:26), as well as, of course, the Sermon on the Mount (Matt 5:3–11) and the Infancy and Passion narratives. The borrowings from John, though more rare, are no less important. Francis often cites the passages which exalt Christ glorified and those which underline the bond existing between the Spirit and life. The whole first chapter of the *Admonitions* is but a paraphrase of the last Gospel, centered on the revelation of the Triune God in Jesus Christ, only mediator and sole "channel" between heaven and earth. Among the epistles, the most employed are those of Paul to the Corinthians and Romans, as well as that of James concerning the concrete demands of charity, and the First Letter of Peter. From this last text the Poor Man of Assisi has especially retained the call to follow the footprints of Christ (2:13), the definition of the Christian as "pilgrim and stranger" in this world" (2:11), and the ideal of mutual love advocated by the prince of the apostles (1:22). In contrast, we might be surprised to find in all of Francis' writings only two quotations from the Acts of the Apostles, which had had an important role in most of the popular religious movements of the twelfth century. Moreover, Jacques de Vitry, witness of the beginnings of the Franciscan fraternity in 1216, had cited, in reference to them, the famous passage from this text about the first Christian community of Jerusalem, where it is said that the "group of believers was of one heart and one soul" (Acts 4:32).[15] Jacques' allusion is not surprising, since the prelate, as open as he was to the new spiritual currents of the day, had not yet understood the real novelty of the message of Francis. After visiting him during the siege of Damietta in 1219, Jacques showed a greater understanding of him when (in Palestine, it seems) he wrote: "This order is that of the true poor men of the Crucified."[16]

When we try to summarize the religious experience of Francis in "a few words" (to use an expression that was familiar to him), it appears as a concerted effort to conform himself to the Gospel and to make of it an absolute norm of behavior. Defining in the first paragraph of the rule of 1221 the specificity of the life of the friars, he simply writes: "This is the life of the Gospel of Jesus Christ"; it is an affirmation that will be taken up again in a more developed manner at the beginning of the rule of 1223: "The rule of the Friars Minor consists in observing the Holy Gospel of our Lord Jesus Christ."[17] Thus for him, Christian perfection is identified with the faithful and complete observance of a text of divine inspiration.

At first glance, this looks like an approach that comes from what we would today call fundamentalism, defined as the desire to go back to the fundamental texts of a religion, to put them fully into practice, and to look there for a response to all the problems of private and public life. Indeed, the behavior of Francis often seems to come from a literal approach to the word of God, which can indeed seem naïve. Thus when Christ asked Francis to "rebuild my house," he began to rebuild with his own hands the little church of San Damiano that was falling into ruin. Moreover, his desire to apply in a direct and immediate fashion certain precepts or evangelical examples relative to rejection and "folly" was reminiscent of other "fools for Christ," so numerous in the eastern tradition, who led an existence both marginal and scandalous in the eyes of the contemporaries they hoped to shock.[18]

Even if it is not likely that Francis would have read the Lives of these personages, he is nevertheless similar to them in his manner of behaving: crazy in the eyes of the world, as when he had had himself dragged naked, a cord around his neck, by one of his brothers through the streets of Assisi, or had himself attached to a column on the town's public square. Indeed, did he not define himself, in his Latin-Italian jargon, as "unus novellus pazzus"—not, as it is sometimes mistranslated, a "young crazy person" but "a new kind of fool"—obsessed by the holy folly of the Cross and of divine love?[19] Such attitudes attest to a desire in him of a fidelity to the very letter of the New Testament and a rejection of every reading distanced from the word of God. Francis, however, never employs the expressions "literally" (*litteraliter*) or "to the letter" (*ad litteram*), except in a passage of the *Admonitions* where, along the lines of Saint Paul, he speaks in severe terms of "religious who are killed by the letter who do not want to follow the spirit of the divine Scriptures but desire only to know the words and interpret them for others."[20]

But was it possible to adhere to the texts of the Bible while avoiding every gloss or interpretation without falling into a deadening or laughable literalism? To resolve this contradiction, we have to go back to the conviction which inspired the Poor Man of Assisi, according to which the spiritual meaning resides in the very letter of the sacred text. In his eyes, the relationship between the letter and the spirit is similar to what intellectuals of the period had established between matter and form: the letter serves to give flesh to the spirit and gets its value to the degree that it contains it and expresses it. This explains the emphasis that Francis puts, tenaciously and passionately, on the necessity of a concrete and immediate observance of the Gospel. But the literal respect of the sacred text was not for him an end in itself, because, in order to become operative, it had to be put into practice "in a spiritual and pure way." We might be tempted to say that he was a champion of a "spiritually literal" reading of the Scriptures, centered not on the detailed accomplishment of its prescriptions but on a necessity of a thorough and personal consistency. The important thing was not to remain fixated on the words themselves (however sublime they might be) but to allow oneself to be implicated by them and to commit oneself to the path that they opened, the purpose being to make the inner and outer person the same, behavior identical with word, in order to come to a perfect conformity to Christ. For Francis, the true word of God is Christ himself; the Scriptures are but the witness given by men and women to the Incarnate Word. Three centuries before Luther, Francis believed, like the later reformer, that the Bible is not to be confused with Christ: the one is the servant, the other is the Lord. The authority of the Bible is not that of a Scripture holy in itself; it derives from the one of whom this Scripture speaks and who must guide its reading and comprehension.

Lexical analysis proves fruitful for penetrating into the mental and spiritual world of the Poor Man of Assisi.[21] Indeed, we can see that in the texts where he evokes the relationship between the human person and Christ, Francis uses not the term "imitate" (*imitari, imitatio*) but the verb "to follow" (*sequi*). The model, for him, is "Our Lord Jesus Christ whose footsteps we must follow."[22] Between the two words there is more than a nuance, for what he advocates is not a literal imitation but rather a creative endeavor: every Christian who wants to be seriously engaged on the path to salvation will have to accept, in a context unique for each, to endure trials similar to those which Jesus suffered during his earthly life (poverty, solitude, suffering, and rejection) while striving to discover his fundamental attitudes, especially his spirit of prayer and love. Only at such cost will one be able in turn to escape the "second death," after the Last Judgment, as Francis writes in the *Canticle of Brother Sun:* "Blessed are those that she [death] will find in your most holy will / for the second death will do them no harm."[23]

To become like Christ is thus, for Francis, nothing other than to live in fidelity to the Spirit that was animating him. Thus does he urge the Friars Minor to read the rule and to act "in a spiritual manner," that is, in all simplicity. This "spirit of the letter"—if we can express it in this way—is, for Francis, in opposition to what we might call the "spirit of the flesh": the "flesh," in this context, signifies not the physical body but the natural tendency of human beings, by reason of their sinful nature, to appropriate the gift of God to themselves and to glory in their own talent or wisdom as if it belongs to them. This false holiness is incarnated for Francis in the preacher who is content to announce the word of God without putting it into practice: "Woe to the religious who delights in lazy and vain words! . . . Woe to the religious who does not keep in his heart— and does not show to others in deeds—the goods that the Lord has shown to him but, under pretext of some recompense, desires rather to show them to people in words!"[24] To talk about the truth without acting on it is, for Francis, the very essence of its perversion—the sin against the Spirit that destroys the word of life. In Francis' eyes, hypocrisy is the letter that kills, according to the expression used by Saint Paul, in contrast to the letter that saves, which is a readiness to follow the Word and, for the Friars Minor, the rule which actualizes it in this world. The authentic spirit is recognized by its fruits, which are the embrace of poverty, purity of heart, humility, patience in persecutions and illnesses, the love of enemies, and the forgiveness of offenses: spiritual attitudes that are at the very heart of the notion of "minority" (*minoritas*).

When all is said and done, one can thus firmly state that Francis is not a fundamentalist, to the extent that he values the letter of the sacred text less than the attitude of the one referred to therein. In this sense, the distinction between a "carnal" approach and a "spiritual" approach to Scripture plays a central and decisive role. For the Poor Man of Assisi, religious life is defined as a struggle not against others or against the world but rather against oneself. The human person must not impose his truth or his law or do violence to anyone. One must hold only oneself and one's evil inclinations accountable. The desire to live in a spiritual manner or, what amounts to the same, "according to the form of the

Holy Gospel," is expressed above all in an effort to purify the heart and in the search for an increasing intimacy with God in prayer. The "form of life" of the Minors is nothing other than a spiritual fidelity to the letter of the evangelical text, considered as the touchstone of Christian behavior and the standard against which all religious observances of the friars had to be measured. Thus we know that in 1220 Francis annulled the statutes regarding fasting and eating which his "vicars" had promulgated during his sojourn in Egypt. The dispositions contained in the rules of 1221 and 1223 about this subject confirm this: "And let them be permitted to eat all foods set before them, according to the Gospel."[25] It is by fidelity to the letter—but simultaneously to the spirit—of the Gospel that he rejects the prohibitions regarding eating which surely belonged to the monastic tradition and Christian asceticism but which contradicted the fundamental demands of the word of God, namely charity and evangelical freedom. Francis is aware that there is no one single way to follow Christ and that it is incumbent upon each one to find his or her way, even within the fraternity and within the framework of the rule. This is what led him to write to Brother Leo, seized by doubt, on the best manner to live out his vocation: "In whatever manner it seems best for you to please the Lord God and to follow his footsteps and his poverty, do it with the blessing of the Lord God and my obedience."[26] Thus it is right to consider authentic, as much as it was in conformity with his spirit, the words of Francis to the friars on his deathbed: "I have done what was mine to do; may Christ teach you what is yours!"[27] Never wanting to consider himself a founder of an order, he admonishes his spiritual sons not to imitate him but to follow the footsteps of Christ, in a creative fidelity which ought not be a mere repetition.

From the life and writings of Francis we get a new definition of what it means to be religious: it ceases being a separate category, distinct from the profane, and becomes a commitment embracing all aspects of one's personality and life. For him, salvation is not to be won through the begging of alms or through rituals: it is a way of living in a relationship of intimacy with Jesus, the incarnate God, while at the same time seeking to gain the world for Christ through the example of a dynamic and joyful asceticism. In this perspective, poverty is not something negative—to lack something, to be deprived of this or that thing—but rather something positive. It is, first of all, to recognize God as the one from whom every good comes and as a means of attaining perfect joy. This is not a blessed optimism but the refusal to let oneself be distracted by the failures and humiliations of the fundamental certainty of being a sinner, both saved and reconciled. At the same time, this kind of religiosity opens itself up to the affective depths of the human person, since it is founded on compassion toward Christ, human beings, and the animate creatures with whom one must seek to establish a relationship of friendliness and tenderness. The beauty of the marvels of nature, the taste of things as they are and for what they mean, goes back, for him, to the exuberant sweetness of the Creator God, and to the universal love that embraces the world and the human race—the fundamental reason for joy and exaltation in courtly poetry as well as in Franciscan spirituality.

9

FRANCIS, NATURE, AND THE WORLD

One of the most distinctive characteristics of Francis' personality is undoubt-edly his closeness to nature and animals. Who has not heard of his preaching to the birds, so often depicted in medieval painting, or of the wolf of Gubbio? And is not one of his most famous writings, quite rightly, the *Canticle of Brother Sun*, where a vision both spiritual and lyrical of creation is expressed? It is, in fact, one of the masterpieces of Italian poetry in the Middle Ages. When Francis of Assisi was rediscovered in the nineteenth century, his effusive enthrallment before beauty struck the poets and artists who wanted to see in him a forerunner of the Renaissance; some even presented him as a new Orpheus. Indeed, as we will see, this aesthetic vision of a Francis in love with nature and his finding in it his own flowering is open to scrutiny. This does not mean that his relationship to creation was not revolutionary in many regards.

When we read the medieval Lives of the Poor Man of Assisi, we are struck by the place that animals have there, whether it be the falcon who woke him up at dawn every morning during his stay on La Verna, the pheasant who never wanted to leave his cell, the swan whose noise pleased him, or even the larks whose modesty and always joyous song he praised.[1] But he could also harshly scold animals whose behavior appeared monstrous to him, as happened when, passing through the abbey of San Verecundo, he discovered one morning that a sow had killed a newborn lamb:

Moved with pity for this little lamb, he said in the presence of the monks and people of the monastery: "Little lamb, my brother, innocent animal and very useful to human beings, you who were always calling out and announcing good!" Then he said: "Cursed be the sow who killed you: let no one, beast or bird, eat your flesh!" . . . Immediately the sow fell ill; it died three days later, and its carcass was thrown out beyond the wall of the monastery at the place where charcoal is made. And what the holy father had predicted happened: in fact, it remained there for a very long time without decomposing.[2]

This episode, which has come down to us through Brother Leo and which Thomas of Celano used in his *Memorial* to illustrate the efficacy of Francis' prayer, depicts well his attitude toward the animal world.[3] At first glance, it looks like a spectacular demonstration of power over creation traditionally recognized in the saints in the hagiographical literature; we could cite other examples, in the East as well as the West. In this sense, there is nothing extraordinary about this miracle, except the use of the word "brother" for this lamb "who was announcing good"—that is, whose bleating was pleasant to hear and a good omen. Indeed, this description goes back to the onomatopoetic "bah-bah-bah" typical of this animal, mentioned in the context of the celebration of Christmas night at Greccio, where the sound evoked for Francis the sweetness of the word "Bethlehem," which, in his mouth, was drawn out like the bleating of a lamb. By the simple fact that it had suffered an unjustified violence, the innocent lamb of Saint Verecundo became for Francis a figure of Christ: a brother whose tragic end one had to mourn. And the offending sow became the incarnation of the evil deserving of punishment. The curse that struck the sow caused its death; but by rendering its flesh impervious to putrefaction, Francis also caused it to lose its social usefulness—to serve as food for others—which was its reason for being in creation. We understand better, in the light of this episode and its brutal ending, certain hostile reactions that Francis inspired in the rural world, if we can believe an account of unidentifiable origin in a Franciscan compilation of the fifteenth century: "As Saint Francis was going outside the cloister to pray, some shepherds were saying about him: 'That's the one who casts spells over oxen and who causes them to die!' for there had once been an epidemic of bovine plague. And for this reason, those rascals threw stones at him and called him Bacchus."[4]

We see through these examples that the attitude of the Poverello toward animate creatures did not flow from a sentimental compassion or from any pantheistic fervor that would have caused him to swoon when he was in nature. We need to let go of, once and for all, these soppy images—alas, all too widespread!—which tout his idyllic relationship with animals. There were beasts that he loved a great deal and others that he loved less, like mice and flies, which made him suffer when he was sick and bedridden near the end of his life. He did not hate them—even if he did call those religious who were inclined to laziness "brother flies" (certainly no compliment). But he could not help considering such flies instruments of the devil.

Indeed, his sensitivity to nature, like that of his contemporaries, was influenced by a mindset that stemmed from a long cultural and religious tradition, enriched by his own sensibility. Francis saw in water the symbol of the repentance that cleanses the soul of sin; in the sun, the image of the God who shines on all human beings; and trees remind him of the wood of the cross. The animals mentioned in the Bible, especially those that evoked Christ, especially drew his attention, and he was moved to compassion, indeed sadness, at the sight of their lost liberty or the cruel destiny that awaited them. Thus he was careful not to step on worms on the ground, figures of humility if such ever existed, recalling a passage that was recited in the liturgical prayer: "I am a worm and not a man!" (Ps 21:7). Several times he rescued sheep from shepherds who were leading them to the slaughter, because they reminded him of the slaughter of the Lamb of God. Another time, he acquired custody of a lamb lost in the middle of a herd of goats and sheep, for it made him think about Jesus in the midst of the Pharisees and priests intent on his ruin; he later gave it to some female religious so that they might watch over it.

In other cases, his attitude toward certain animals could be determined by the social status which they symbolized. Thus the horse was, for him, associated with wealth and power. Even when he was seriously ill at the end of his life, he refused to ride any animal other than the donkey, remembering Christ on Palm Sunday, surely, but also because in the society of his time the poor used donkeys for their travels. By contrast, he had a particular predilection for fish and birds: species that had been created at the same time by God on the fifth day, according to the account in Genesis and which God had spared during the Flood. Were not fish, as an image of the active life, always in movement but capable of attentiveness and sensitive to his bounty when he threw back into the water those that had been offered to him? Birds, meanwhile, made him think of those religious who devoted themselves to contemplation, especially the larks: humble birds who suffer from hunger but who sing nonetheless, giving an example of perfect joy. Christ had, moreover, used them as an example to his disciples (Matt 6:26) for their surrender to Providence on whom they were totally dependent for their survival. On the other hand, the migratory birds, which depart in autumn for faraway places and return in springtime, were for him figures of the human soul, which is capable of returning to God as the bird returns to its nest.

In other instances, Francis' symbolic reading of the animal kingdom could be ambivalent, if not frankly negative. According to the English chronicler

Roger of Wendover, who wrote in the years 1230–1236, Francis, having come to Rome, where he had preached without success and had been poorly received by the pope, left town in order to announce the word of God to the birds, who listened to him attentively for half a day. Finally, the Roman clergy and citizens, apprised of the wonder, went in search of Francis and brought him back to Rome, where they now listened to his sermons.[5] This scene is situated in a very different context from the joyous preaching to the little birds which took place later at Alviano, near Lugano in Teverina, and which the frescoes of the basilica of Saint Francis have immortalized. Rome, which initially had been closed to the message of the Poverello, is here likened to Babylon, and the wild birds that listen to him are not joyful larks but ravens, crows, and magpies, "impure and disgusting birds" which, in the Apocalypse, an angel calls to "swarm for the great feast of God" and to devour the flesh of the powerful and kings who do not obey his Word (Rev 18:1–2 and 19:17–20).[6] In addressing himself to these birds of destruction, Francis sought less to exalt the animal kingdom than to shame human beings in absentia for their indifference to the word of God, and to threaten them with divine punishment if they did not repent.

This symbolic interpretation, no doubt heightened by Thomas of Celano and Bonaventure, who sought to "normalize" the behaviors of the Poor Man of Assisi in order to inscribe them into a hagiographical perspective, is not, however, sufficient to account for his attitude vis-à-vis creation in general, the specificity of which struck his contemporaries. Indeed, among the authors and artists of the Middle Ages, the allegorical or moral meaning attributed to animals is superimposed onto their actual reality, erasing it, as we see in the sculptures, often inspired by Aesop's fables, on the porches and capitals of churches or in the Romanesque bestiaries peopled with monstrous figures incarnating the forces of evil. It is not the same for Francis. He was touched by sensible reality and the beauty of creatures which had, in his eyes, particular value, independent of their symbolic significance or social usefulness. He certainly believed, as reported in the Bible, that creation had been made for the human race; but, in his eyes, the human person was not radically distinguishable from animals. They, too, could behave poorly, like the sow of San Verecundo or the robin redbreast which, having stuffed itself full of food, prevented other birds from taking part in the feast and ended up drowning in front of Francis by falling into a jug filled with water.[7] Even better, the wonders of nature inspired in him a lesson in humility: "All creatures in the sky, each in its own way, serve their creator, know him, and obey him better than you," he says in his *Admonitions*.[8] All creatures are worthy of respect because they reflect the All-Powerful: foundation of a universal fraternity in which the human being participates at his or her own level. To each of them, God has assigned a place in the world, which was, for Francis, "an ordered collection of creatures," according to the definition of William of Conches (around 1150), implying both a perfect continuity between the human person and the environment and a hierarchical relationship between beings according to their degree of consciousness and responsibility.

Once again, it is probably Ernest Renan who has best expressed this critical aspect of the message of the Poor Man of Assisi when he wrote:

> The great sign by which one recognizes souls preserved from typical narrowness—namely, the love and understanding of animals—was greater in him than in any other human being. He recognized only one form of life; he saw degrees in the scale of beings but not sharp divisions. He did not acknowledge, any more than did India, the classification that puts the human person on one side and, on the other, the thousand forms of life of which we see only the outside, where the inattentive eye sees only uniformity and which perhaps hides different infinities. Francis himself heard only one voice in nature.[9]

In this perspective, the human person must seek to establish with creatures a nonviolent relationship which implies on one's part a refusal of domination and a nonresistance to aggression to the point of being subject "not only to human beings alone but also to all beasts and all wild animals, so that they might be able to do with him what they want, as much as it will be given to them by the Lord." And if God has truly created nature and animals in order that they might be useful to human beings—"for every creature proclaims: God has made me for you, O Man!"—it is really incumbent upon the human person to reestablish within the world the harmony that has been ruptured by sin and to restore between nature and the human race a relationship which ought to be not destructive but fraternal.[10]

Such is the meaning of the famous story of the wolf of Gubbio. This story appears in Franciscan historiography as a structured narrative only in the fourteenth century, but it must have circulated in written form for several decades since it figures already as an exemplum in a sermon preached in Paris by an unknown Franciscan on October 8, 1273.[11] In fact, there are already accounts of the relationship of Francis to wolves—incarnation of the forces of evil but also animals dreaded by peasants for the damage they were inflicting on their flocks—in the legends of the thirteenth century. Thus, in the *Legenda maior*, Bonaventure mentions bands of wolves that were snatching the livestock and inhabitants of Greccio; the human victims were saved through the intervention of the saint, after which they did penance.[12] Moreover, an addition to the *Versified Life of*

Francis by Henry of Avranches, which probably dates from the end of the thirteenth century, specifies that during this episode "a wolf, thanks to the intervention of Francis, became gentle and was reconciled with the village."[13] Finally, the author of the *Passion of Saint Verecundo*, who wrote during the second half of the thirteenth century, while invoking eyewitnesses, gives the following account:

> One evening, very late, Francis was making his way along on his donkey, accompanied by one of his brothers. He had thrown around his shoulders a course sack as a kind of mantle. They were passing by way of San Verecundo when peasants called out to him: "Brother Francis, remain here with us; don't go any farther! Ferocious wolves are prowling around here. You risk seeing your mule devoured and getting yourself attacked and hurt." "I have done no harm to Brother Wolf," the blessed Francis responded. "He will not dare to devour our brother donkey. Good evening, my children, and fear God!" And Brother Francis continued his journey without incident.[14]

We do not know when or how these different accounts were amalgamated and transposed into a different context: that of the relationship between the town of Gubbio and a ferocious wolf that was attacking its inhabitants. According to certain historians, the wolf was in fact an outlaw lord of the contado who was terrorizing the Umbrian town. Francis resolved the conflict by negotiating the wolf's right to reside in the town and, probably, to receive financial reimbursement, since according to the legend, the wolf was maintained to the end of his life at the expense of the commune. But whichever reading we give to this account, its lesson is the same: between the human person and the animal, as in relationships between human beings, exclusion is at the origin of violence, whereas a fraternal and welcoming attitude makes its object aware of the joy of being included and prompts that individual to make peace. In this sense, this "miracle"—whether it reflects an ecological reality or not—is typically Franciscan in spirit. In numerous medieval legends, saints appear as protectors of populations against wolves. The faithful expected them to move the animals away from their lands or to place the wolves in their service as guard dogs or companions for the blind. Nothing similar at Gubbio: here the wolf is simply invited to be integrated into the civic world to lead a tranquil life there, by virtue of a pact that places the human person and the animal on a footing of equality by the servant of God.

As exceptional as the relationship between Francis and the animals might have been, we would be wrong to give them too important a place to the detriment of the rest of creation. Animals are not mentioned in his writings, and he does not hesitate to eat them, especially fish (which he particularly liked), or to offer some to others. Moreover, he is never depicted by artists with an animal—except in the very particular case of the preaching to the birds; rather, he is seen with a book, whether it be the Gospel or the text of the rule. His attitude with respect to animate creatures can perhaps be distinguished from his vision of the cosmos, that is, of the universe in its totality. To truly understand it, we can happily rely upon a major text, the *Canticle of Brother Sun* or *Canticle of the Creatures*, which reveals more than any other writing or legend Francis' feelings about nature. Rather than extract numerous quotations from it, it is preferable to reproduce the whole text, so central is it to our purpose:

(1) Most High, All-Powerful, good Lord,
to you are the praises, the glory and the honor,
and every blessing.
(2) To you, Most High, they belong,
and no one is worthy to pronounce your name.
(3) Praised be to you, my Lord, with all your creatures,
especially sir Brother Sun,
who is the day, and by him you give us light.
(4) And he is beautiful and shining with great splendor,
of you, Most High, he bears the sign.
(5) Praised be to you, my Lord,
through Sister Moon and Stars,
in the heavens you have formed them
clear, precious, and beautiful.
(6) Praised be to you, my Lord, for Brother Wind,
and for Air and Cloud and the serene Sky
and all weather.
(7) Praised be to you, my Lord, for Sister Water,
who is very useful and humble,
and precious and chaste.
(8) Praised be to you, my Lord, for Brother Fire,
through whom you light up the night,
and you are beautiful, joyous, robust, and strong.
(9) Praised be to you, my Lord, for Sister Our-Mother-Earth,
who sustains us and governs us,
and produces diverse fruits,
with colored flowers and grass.
(10) Praised be to you, my Lord,
for those who grant pardon for love of you

and support illnesses and tribulations.
(11) Happy those who support them in peace
for by you, Most High, they will be crowned.
(12) Praised be to you, my Lord,
through our Sister Bodily Death,
from whom no living person can escape.
(13) Woe to those who will die
in mortal sin,
  happy those whom she will find in your very holy will,
for the second death will do them no harm.
(14) Praise and bless my Lord
and give him thanks
and serve him with great humility.[15]

Before undertaking the analysis of this exceptional work, let's pause for a moment on the circumstances and reasons for its composition. According to the testimony of contemporary sources, for once unanimous, Francis composed the *Canticle* in several stages. In April or May 1225, worn out by illness, he had himself transferred to San Damiano, where he spent almost two months in the grip of terrible physical and emotional pain, incapable as he was of even supporting the light because of an ocular infection which no treatment had been able to cure. He was constantly disturbed by mice that were scurrying around in the little cell that had been made up for him. Feeling a great spiritual abandonment, he called out to God for help and received from him, one night, the surety of his salvation. The following morning, he recounted to his companions what had happened to him and then drew up the first nine strophes of the *Canticle*. A few weeks later, in June or July, while he was bedridden in the episcopal palace of Assisi, he added strophes 10 and 11 to it regarding forgiveness, which he had a couple of friars sing in front of the house of the bishop and the podestà, currently in open conflict with each other, to urge them to be reconciled. Lastly, he dictated to Brother Pacifico the final two strophes (13 and 14) that mention death, a little bit before entering into agony, at the end of September or at the very beginning of October 1226.

This text was intended to be sung; and so Francis sang it, accompanied by his companions, during his last moments. The *Canticle* is a *laude*, that is, a prayer of thanksgiving to the Creator; it constitutes a praise not of creatures for themselves but of the One who had made them so beautiful and useful. After so many ascetic endeavors and suffering due to illness and the trials of life, Francis sees the world in a soft light, pure as on the first day, and as reconciled with him through the universal fraternity of all creatures which are "under heaven." At the same time, he is aware of the ingratitude of the human person toward this God who has showered this being with goods and graces; he himself rediscovers them as a marvelous and free gift in which he perceives the reflection of the Most High, who is for him, as for every being, "my Lord."

This poem in assonated prose has inspired many commentaries and glosses; but in spite of its apparent simplicity, it raises numerous questions. If Francis draws from different biblical texts—in particular Psalm 148, the Canticle of the three young men in the furnace (Dan 3:51–89), and various passages from the book of the Apocalypse, which Francis knew through the reading of the breviary—it is striking that his vocabulary has nothing strictly Christian about it, beyond a reference to "mortal sins" (strophe 13), and that there is no explicit reference to Christ. Everything happens as if Francis, at the end of his life, had become sensitive more to the grandeur of God, transcendent and ineffable, invoked twenty-one times in fewer than fifty verses, than to distinctions among the persons of the Trinity, and that he had sought to go beyond christocentricism in order to reclaim the very heart of divinity. Just as astonishing, at first sight, is the absence of the human being—evoked only at the beginning of the poem as a being unworthy to name God (strophe 2)—and the animals within creation such as it is presented in the first nine strophes. There God is praised for inanimate nature alone: the heavenly objects—sun, moon, stars—and the four primordial elements—air, water, fire, and earth—in the order handed down from Classical Antiquity, where they appear on the frescoes of the crypt of the cathedral of Anagni, more or less contemporary to the *Canticle*. Francis had already said in his *Admonitions* that the silent creatures, as simple as they might be, merited more than human beings to be exalted, for, unlike men, they had never rebelled against their Creator and they sang his glory.[16]

But the human person is not absent from this part of the poem. Indeed, the human being is the speaker who, like Adam in the Garden of Eden (Gen 2:19), gazes with wonder upon the world and contemplates God with his creatures. It is for the human person that creation has been made, as emphasized by the presence of an epithet in the four strophes devoted to the elements (strophes 6 to 9), noting the usefulness of things which God has put at its service ("Sister Water who is very useful and chaste," for example). That animals are not mentioned in this prayer probably derives from the fact that, similar to human beings through their suffering (that is, animals' concrete needs like hunger, thirst, and so on) but also through their beauty, the witness that they bear is not essentially different from that of humans. Francis gives thanks to the Creator for the world—the causal meaning of the Italian word *per*, which is primary, not excluding the modal meaning: by, through, with—and more precisely for the creative act that made the human person go from nonbeing to being by assigning to each creature a predestined place within the whole.[17]

The *Canticle*, however, is not just a cosmic liturgy because the last five strophes are centered on human beings. The exegetes of the twelfth century, especially the commentaries of the book of Genesis, had emphasized the central place of the human person, created by God "in his image and likeness," within the universe. Honorius Augustodunensis, in particular, had emphasized that the human being constitutes a veritable microcosm in the sense that it participates in all the creatures: having discernment like the angels, sensation like the animals, growth like the plants, being like the rocks, and a body composed of the four elements.[18] Even if it is really doubtful that he would have known these texts, such a perspective was not foreign to Francis who, in his *Canticle*, mentions the four elements just before introducing the human being. But what he gives thanks to God for, above all else, is having given him a new birth through a new creation, evoked through the words "pardon," "love," and "peace" (strophes 10 and 11). Behind the Poor Man of Assisi, we ultimately perceive the voice of Christ, instrument of this redemption—particularly in the phrase "Happy those who support them [illness, trials] in peace" (*Beati*, strophe 11), where we find the echo of the Beatitudes—and the one who alone is capable of "naming" God, that is, to give us mastery over him and to help us to know him. It is as son (that is, as a human person saved by Christ and divinized by his Spirit) that Francis addresses the Father and can join his voice to the silent praise of creatures. For the greatest glory of the Creator is not to have created the world but to have liberated humanity from sin and the "second death," an expression borrowed from the Apocalypse (Rev 2:11 and 20:6) that refers to eternal death, distinct from bodily death, which is only a passage.

One of the most unsettling formulations that one finds in the *Canticle*, especially for a modern mentality, is that concerning "our Sister Bodily Death from whom no living person can escape" (strophe 12). Before Francis, no one had ever had the idea of speaking about death as a "sister" for human beings. What exactly does that mean? The most profound aspiration of the Poor Man of Assisi, we know, is the birth of a fraternal world: to live as brothers and sisters, without appropriating anything as one's own, in a world where the human person would act as son or daughter respectful of the earth, which constitutes for Francis both an element of nature ("sister") and a nourishing environment ("our mother"). Death itself finds a place in this harmonious vision. Assured of his salvation, Francis is delivered from the fear of dying, natural in the human being who perceives himself as ephemeral and who seeks to master time in order to postpone as much as possible the fatal moment. For Francis, by contrast, time is not our enemy. The existence which God has given us is not a substance which could disappear; it is a current that draws us toward a luminous beyond, provided that we know how to acquire the true wisdom that consists in enjoying life without possessing it.[19]

When all is said and done, we can say that the *Canticle of Brother Sun* constitutes a kind of "mass for the world" spoken by Francis while joining himself to the cosmic office sung by nature in honor of God. The role of the human person is not essential in this celebration, for the world has such coherence in his eyes that it is able to sing the glory of God all by itself. Born of the earth and enveloped by the cosmos, the human being, however, is neither its center nor its master, even if such things have all been made for it. These realities thus remain distinct—which excludes all pantheism—but they can be joined in a common prayer of praise addressed to the Father, whose love has brought them all into existence. Henceforth, as Teilhard de Chardin will say in the twentieth century, "a Christian can say to God that he or she loves him, not only with one's whole body and whole soul but with the whole universe."[20] Thus from the simple fact that he felt himself to be an integral part of creation and not outside it, Francis has contributed to the evolution of Western sensitivity vis-à-vis nature, rehabilitating and ennobling it by rediscovering therein the image of God. To be drawn from the knowledge of the created up to the knowledge and love of the Creator (*cognoscere Deum per creaturam*) was a familiar path in medieval thought, from Suger to Bonaventure, who applies it to Francis in the *Legenda maior.* According to this speculative mysticism inspired by neoplatonism through the work of Pseudo-Dionysius the Areopagite and translated into Latin in the ninth century at Saint-Denis, creatures constituted stepping stones or trampolines by means of which the human mind—by nature lacking in acuity (*mens hebes,* writes Suger)—could detach itself from materiality and be lifted up by following the ladder of the "celestial hierarchy" toward "the things above." The Victorines, for their part, from Hugh to Richard of Saint-Victor, had privileged the allegorical interpretations of Scripture which enabled the human soul to have access to the contemplation of the mystery of Creation and Redemption based on biblical symbols like the ark of Noah. Francis' attitude is different in the sense that he seeks to recognize the presence of God in all the effects of his actions, be they natural or supernatural, and to love him in his creatures, which he perceives as associated with him in a universal concert of praise and glory. For him, things are not mere instruments of an elevation of the spirit toward God; each one contains within it a part of the divine. And it is by decrypting the "book of the world" that one can enter into relationship with the Creator. This singular approach caught the attention of Henri Rey-Flaud, who devoted a very fine page to the love of creation in Saint Francis of Assisi:

> There is no longer a love of the individual object. Each object refers back to the ensemble of objects, to the totality of signifiers of the world. Saint Francis brought to bear upon all objects the attitude which all lovers bring to bear upon the object chosen. . . . The abolishing of difference prompts a great relief to the extent that the amorous impulse dissolves *ad infinitum* into the great ocean of the world. In the final analysis, this love purely and simply abolishes the principle of the limits of language. In preaching to the birds, Francis rediscovers the Adamic language which is the universal language of nature before the Fall, sin, division, and death.[21]

In this sense, the message of the Poor Man of Assisi constitutes the most effective response to all forms of Gnosticism or dualism that had infiltrated certain dissident currents, especially the one that the Church of his day called the heresy of the Cathars. Indeed, in their eyes, the world, corrupted for some and radically evil for others, was the domain of the devil, who ensured the presence of evil there, whereas God, a purely spiritual being, had withdrawn from it. On the contrary, Francis understood and saw creation as a positive reality, without absorbing the selfish motivations and often disappointing actions of creatures. Different from the monastic spirituality, especially Cistercian, which was then prevailing in the West, he calls not for the rejection of or withdrawal from the world but for the abstention from ownership. He does not flee the world; he plunges himself into it without prejudice or ulterior motive because, if it is necessary to renounce the possession of goods and creatures, it is legitimate for one to enjoy them on the condition that their enjoyment be referred to the One who has given such things to us for our good. But whereas in the biblical or apocalyptic accounts of visions, the man or woman of God was raised up above the earth— and sometimes up to the seventh heaven!—in order to receive a divine illumination, for Francis, heaven descends to earth, both in the creation where he encountered God, but also through the figure of the seraph, who manifested to him the union of the divine and human in the person of Christ crucified, whose living image he was going to become, in his turn, by his stigmatization.

10

FRANCIS AND THE CHURCH:
THE CHARISM WITHIN THE INSTITUTION

Since the publication in 1893–1894 of Paul Sabatier's *Vie de saint François*, the majority of biographies of the Poor Man of Assisi have presented the relationship between Francis and the Church of his time as a tension between the evangelical freedom he incarnated and the fearful closed-mindedness of the ecclesiastical hierarchy, personified by Cardinal Hugolino, who strove to tamp down the originality of the Franciscan movement and corral its potential energies. Thus the biographers find, in a medieval context, the classic opposition between prophecy and priesthood, charism and institution, which represents a fundamental element of the history of Judeo-Christianity. This reading of the life and work of Francis is out of step with that expressed in the first *Life* of Thomas of Celano and in the *Legend of the Three Companions*, which, on the contrary, highlight the role played by the cardinal in the birth and development of the order of Friars Minor and emphasize the relationship of esteem and friendship which united the saint to the future Pope Gregory IX (r. 1227–1241). In fact, the question is more complex than these simplistic affirmations would have us believe. An attentive examination of the writings and actions of the protagonists leads us to situate the rapport between the two men in another perspective.

Francis always refused to set a Church of the pure and perfect in opposition to an institutional Church that was "carnal" and corrupt. For him, the visible Church was not the more or less diminished reflection of a spiritual Church which was the only authentic Church. Indeed, he never rejected the former based on the idea that he could create the latter. Like Joan of Arc two centuries later, he would have said that "concerning Christ and the Church, they are one"; his ecclesiology does not allow it to be disconnected from his Christology. Christ is living in the Church, both in its priesthood and in its people, to whom he has entrusted the responsibility of mission among all men and women. The attitude of Francis on this point separates him from the Patarines and other dissident or heterodox sects of his day who made the validity of the sacraments contingent on the worthiness of their ministers and who considered invalid, indeed diabolical, those sacraments offered by clerics whose lives were not in conformity with the precepts of the Gospel. Indeed, Francis fully adhered to the concept which the Roman Church had made its own since the end of the eleventh century, according to which the two aspects had to be separated: the personal faults of the celebrant had no effect on the validity of his liturgical acts as long as he had been canonically ordained and was in communion with his bishop. In the priest, whatever might be his moral state, Francis wanted to see only the instrument and mediator of divine grace. Far from publicly denouncing the insufficiencies or vices of clerics, he always endeavored to avoid dwelling on the scandal and, if he could not, to lead the clergy back onto the right path while reminding them of the eminent dignity of their state. Thus when he arrived in a village, after preaching to the people, "He gathered together the priests who were there and led them apart so as not to be overheard by the laity. He talked to them of the salvation of their souls and especially reminded them of the care that they needed to take to keep their churches, altars and everything that is at the service of the celebration of the divine mysteries clean."[1] An anecdote reported by a Dominican preacher, Stephen of Bourbon († 1261), in a treatise for preachers, illustrates particularly well—even if the episode cannot be dated and if its reality is attested by only one other source—the concrete problems which Francis had to encounter in his relations with the clergy and laity in the places he was passing through:

> Francis was travelling in Lombardy. He entered into a church to pray. A Patarine or Manichean [heretic], who knew of Francis' reputation of holiness among the people, wanted to exploit this influence in order to draw people to his own sect, to demolish their faith, and to expose the priesthood to disdain. Now the pastor of this parish was causing scandal by living with a woman. The man, therefore, ran and said to the saint: "If a priest maintains a concubine and stains his hands, must one put faith in his teaching and respect the sacraments which he administers?" The saint was not unaware of the trap being laid by the heretic. In front of all the parishioners, he went to this priest, knelt down before him and said: "I do not know if these hands are really stained as the other claims. What I do know, in any case, even if they were, that that would not in any way diminish the power and efficacy of the sacraments of God. These hands remain the channel through which the grace and benefits of God stream toward the people. That is why I kiss them

out of respect for the one who has delegated his authority to them." And he prostrated before the priest, kissing his hands, to the greatest confusion of the heretics and their sympathizers who were present at the scene.[2]

Even if the authenticity of this "exemplary" account—that is, one used as an exemplum to teach—is not verifiable, it perfectly illustrates the attitude which was the Poor Man of Assisi's from the very beginning toward people in the Church. Another version of the same text adds the following phrase which clearly underscores its meaning: "These hands have touched the Lord. Whatever it is that they may want, they cannot render my Lord impure nor diminish his power. Out of respect for the Lord, I honor his minister. He can be bad for himself, but for me he is good."[3]

No clericalism in him, but a respect for God's plan who has chosen to rely upon human mediations, with all the risks that that might entail, in order to convey salvation. Francis thus believes in the Church such as it is and shows obedience to the clergy, but he calls the priesthood back to the reason for its existence: its sacramental function and its transmission of the Word, since the Eucharist and the Bible are the only concrete links between the faithful and the grace of God. No moralizing claims either: he always refrained from pointing the finger at others, whether it might be unworthy priests or heretics. To act otherwise would be, in his eyes, to place himself in a position of superiority, whereas he had chosen the path of *minoritas* and humility.

The attitude of Francis with respect to the ecclesiastical hierarchy drew its inspiration from the same principles. For him, without a doubt, the pope was truly the "bishop of the whole universe," as he once wrote to Cardinal Hugolino, in whom he probably was already discerning the sovereign pontiff he was to become. Once Francis had gathered a few companions around him, he went to Rome, where he met Innocent III (r. 1198–1216), less to have the rule approved by the pope, as is often said, then to obtain from him the authorization to preach everywhere. Indeed, Francis had his own reasons for getting close to the Roman Church. In direct line with the "Gregorian Reform," which had elevated the role of the pope in the Church, he was all the more prone to see in this figure a kind of "super-bishop" whose jurisdiction extended over the whole world. His own project of calling all to conversion knew no boundaries and was in sync with the universalistic claims of the Roman Church. After the contacts between the Poverello and the Roman Curia in 1209, Innocent III established, through his own person, a direct link of obedience between the modest fraternity of penitents of Assisi and the bishop of Rome, without reference to intermediate authorities, thereby creating for it a kind of personal, nonterritorial prelature. Moreover, to the very extent that he asked for the Friars Minor the extraordinary privilege—since totally in contradiction with the canonical norms in force—to be able to lead a religious life in common without possessing any goods or fixed revenues (which the pope alone could grant him), Francis was led from the very beginning to tie his destiny and that of his companions to the Roman Church.

This was, at first, something positive, since the recognition of the orthodoxy of their movement by the Curia opened many doors for them. But this constitutive agreement was afterward going to become the Achilles' heel of the Franciscan order, which could protect its privileged status within the Church only by relying upon the support of the papacy and by placing it, with respect to the Church, in a relationship of dependence that quickly became a constitutive element of its identity. Thus did the rules of 1221 and 1223 remind the friars of the necessity to faithfully obey the pope and priests, while in many of his writings Francis encouraged them to pray "according to the form of the Roman Church," even adding in regard to this: "Those who do not wish to observe this, I consider them to be neither Catholic or my brothers."[4] In fact, the Minors adopted from the beginning the liturgical usages of the papal chapel in what concerns the texts of the missal and breviary and later propagated them throughout all of Christendom, to the point of appearing in the eyes of external observers as the agents of Roman centralization.

If the profound fidelity of Francis toward the Church is not to be doubted, that does not imply, however, any renunciation of his own vocation. He sought till the end of his life to maintain a balanced relationship—respectful, but neither servile nor always on call—with respect to the ecclesiastical hierarchy. Indeed, his action in this regard was never identified with the triumphal vision of Christianity which the papacy was then seeking to propound or with the political strategies which the realization of this ambitious project might have implied. The Poor Man of Assisi seems to have understood very early on that, as soon as ecclesiastical authority was used as a coercive power, God risked being likened to an instrument of domination: the domination of clerics over the laity in the name of their cultural superiority and the sacred character of their functions; but also the hegemony of the papacy over Christian society within the context of the theocratic program of a Church which, conscious of its eschatological status, was seeking to establish the kingdom of God here below. For Innocent III, Honorius III, and Cardinal Hugolino, the simultaneous appearance of Francis and the Minors and Dominic and his Preachers was a providential opportunity to reform the Church. Taking advantage of the disintegration of the structures of the local Church, of feudal construction, and of the relative eclipsing of episcopal power, the papacy sought to set in place hierarchical ecclesiastical structures conducive to making its pastoral priorities known among the faithful. With the mendicant orders, the papacy was going to finally be able to rely upon religious who were educated and full of apostolic zeal and who were going to help it recapture the towns which had become real centers of power and to snatch back their inhabitants from the false seductions of heresy.

Francis did not place himself in this line of thought. His intention was not to reform the Church or society but to prompt a second conversion of the world to the Gospel message, through which men and women would be able once again to recognize the infinite love which God had shown them and consequently to behave in like manner in their relations with each other and creation. In Francis' eyes, the only important thing here below was not to make or remake Christianity but to propose to men and women models of action and behavior offered by the life of Christ as it is described in the Gospels, because a society cannot claim itself to be Christian unless its people begin to live the very life of God. Francis' public "performances"—which we hesitate to call preaching since they combined gestures and music with word—were meant to inspire everywhere he went a movement of "revival," as in the expression used in the Anglo-Saxon world to describe those manifestations of collective enthusiasm and joy at the end of which worshipers would be invited by a fired-up preacher to become personally engaged in a spiritual experience and to adhere to the religious values illustrated by the example of Christ. Francis was looking not to change institutions (to which, in any case, he attached only a secondary importance) but to inspire people to a necessary and continual conversion by showing them "the new signs in the heavens and the earth that are great and excellent in the eyes of God and which many religious and other people count for nothing at all."[5] In saying this, he was probably referring to the new forms of Christian presence in the world that were at the heart of his ideal of "minority": to go among the poor and the infidels, where there were no guarantees or protection that one could expect from anyone, and to show oneself "subject to all," including the forces of evil, in order to manifest the power of love and to live in its unmerited lavishness.

This different orientation with respect to the ambitions of the papacy was based by Francis on the keen awareness of having been called by God to accomplish a specific mission, as he clearly says in his *Testament*: "The Lord gave me, Brother Francis, to begin to do penance . . . and, after the Lord gave me brothers, no one showed me what I ought to do, but the Most High himself revealed to me that I had to live according to the form of the Holy Gospel."[6] At first glance, this certainty of having been the beneficiary of a particular revelation can appear shocking. Would this not be, as someone has recently suggested, an expression of great pride or of an oversized ego?[7] But if we define revelation as a moment when God seeks to reach out to the human person, and if we see in the one who receives it a witness to the way God bends down toward the human person, then we can without hesitation apply the term "revelation" to Francis' experience. We find in this affirmation of Francis an echo of the passage from the Letter to the Galatians where Paul, challenged by certain of his disciples, justifies his claim to the title of apostle in this way:

> Know this, my brothers and sisters, that the Gospel that I have announced is not something of human making. It is not from a human person that I received or learned it, but through a revelation from Jesus Christ. . . . The one who from my mother's womb has set me apart and called me by his grace has deigned to reveal in me his Son so that I might announce him among the pagans.[8]

The Poor Man of Assisi never mentioned in his writings any particular mystical graces of which he would have been the beneficiary. But he did not hesitate to claim a charism—a notion that appears in Saint Paul (1 Cor 12:4–11) to describe the spiritual gifts given by God to the community of the baptized and the different manifestations of his grace in the life of human beings. Among these gifts figures the prophetic charism that allows a believer to discern hidden thoughts and the secrets of hearts, and to read the "signs of the times" by virtue of a divine revelation. It is to one such intervention of God in his life that Francis attributed the foundational intuition of which he was the bearer; and it is to this same revelation that we must attribute the surety with which he defended it, in spite of everything, after his conversion. Already in 1209, during his encounter with Innocent III, Francis manifested real boldness when he compared himself to the woman whom a king had made pregnant in a desert or the woods—a different place according to various versions—and who later came in search of the king to ask him to feed her offspring. He explained this parable "by saying that he was this woman whom the Lord had made fruitful by his Word and through which he had given birth to so many spiritual sons." One could not urge any more clearly the ecclesiastical hierarchy to recognize in the Minors its true sons and to consecrate less effort and fewer resources "to nourish so many unjust."[9] Later, he showed at different times a great authority, not hesitating to harangue prelates and priests in order to remind them of their duties and loudly claiming the right to command his brothers what they had to do and to demand obedience from them.

The notion of charism has likewise been used in another context by the sociologist Max Weber to define the informal power recognized in a leader exercising a real fascination over the masses by reason of his or her extraordinary bearing, poor or strange clothing, and especially his or her fiery eloquence that prompted the enthusiastic attention of hearers. After that, such people were then led to attribute to this leader extraordinary capacities and gifts which made of that person someone both feared and revered to whom the crowds accorded, at least for a time, a certain power. Without any doubt, Francis was a charismatic personage very much in this sense. And, as we have already seen, the success achieved by his preaching owed much to the prestige that he had among those who were listening to him.

But it is not this aspect that will hold our attention, since he willingly restrained himself from using this power except when he was convinced that it could produce positive effects, as in the case of the dispute between the podestà and the bishop of Assisi, when his intervention led the two adversaries to be reconciled and to make peace. His refusal to use his immense prestige against the Church or even within the Church to force it to reform itself flowed from his fundamental attitude of nonviolence. Like Waldo (Vaudès), the founder of the Waldensians, a few decades earlier, the Poor Man of Assisi could have brandished the standard of revolt while stating, following Saint Peter, that "it is better to obey God than men" (Acts 5:29). But even if he knew moments of despair and disgust because of the demands of the Curia and the incomprehension of his brothers, he never took this path. To a minister who had written to him to complain about the insubordination of some members of his community, Francis recalled that he was not their jailer, that he ought not try to make of them better Christians, and that, even if they covered him with blows, he had to consider that a grace.[10] This recommendation allows us to understand his attitude toward the Church of his day, which he had not sought to advance at his own pace. To attack her or cover her with reproaches would only have led her to harden her positions or to react in a violent manner. Such restraint by Francis was probably founded not on simple prudence but on an intimate conviction which he never talked about, but which Yves Congar (who had himself come up against hostility and persecutions from the "guardians of the Temple") expressed in these terms: "In a quarrel between a father and son, the functions are never equal. Authority can be wrong; but it is never fundamentally wrong. One can have good reasons against it; but one is never right against it."[11] Francis, for his part, spoke of the Church as a mother, not a father, even if she sometimes behaved like a stepmother toward him in the last years of his life. But in Francis as in Congar, the great Dominican theologian unjustly accused of "progressivism" during the 1950s, this submission to authority was not accompanied by the least surrender. Till the end of his life, Francis stated his right to

interpret his own charism himself, a synthesis of which comprised the rule of
the Friars Minor, as illustrated by the fact that he presented his own *Testament*
as the sole authorized commentary on this text. The papacy, for its part, recognized and authenticated the charism of Francis to the degree that it granted
him the right to preach and to have the members of his fraternity preach penance on his authority. In this sense, one can say that the papacy at that time
showed prophetic discernment. But Innocent III, in 1209, had refrained—if only
by way of prudence and a desire to wait to see how the order would develop—
from confirming in writing the draft based on Gospel citations which Francis
had submitted for his examination. Over the next years, the Friars Minor expanded rapidly and evolved apparently in the right direction, as evidenced in
the testimony of Jacques de Vitry, by the success of their preaching and their
fidelity toward the Roman Church. This author had had the occasion to encounter them in Umbria in 1216 and noted that "they are held in great esteem
by the Lord Pope and by the Cardinals."[12] As we have seen, the difficulties began around 1220, when the papacy undertook to standardize the Franciscan
movement and to make it into a masculine religious order.

The unique relationship which Francis had tried to establish between charism
and institution was solidified, between 1220 and 1226, within the context of the
ties between himself and Hugolino. Because the stakes were so high, the inter-
action of this emblematic duo has been the object, since the thirteenth century, of differing opinions. According to Thomas of Celano in his first *Life*, the
Anonymous of Perugia, and the *Legend of the Three Companions*, the cardinal
not only was the principal spokesperson for Francis within the hierarchy but
"the great benefactor and defender of the Friars Minor." This leads one to believe that after his death he had merited "to belong to the assembly of the
saints."[13] This point of view is again stressed by the author of the *Life of Gregory
IX*—a notary of the Roman Curia writing around 1240—when he states that the
future pope

> established and organized the new orders of the Brothers of Penitence and
> the Cloistered Ladies. With respect to the order of Friars Minor, who at the
> beginning were wandering around without any precise boundaries, he took it
> in hand by devising for it a new rule, thus giving form to this unformed
> movement at the head of which he placed Francis as minister and leader.[14]

If this source is credible, Cardinal Hugolino established Francis as superior
of the new order; this was thus the fruit of a collaborative effort between the
Poor Man of Assisi and the future pope, with the latter playing an essential role.
On the other hand, the whole later Franciscan hagiographical tradition, in-

cluding the testimony of Bonaventure (who died a cardinal and could not be suspected of hostility toward the Roman Church), emphasizes that the order of Minors proceeds from the will of Francis and that it is really his work. Hugolino is presented in these texts as a well-meaning personage and very understanding toward the Friars Minor, but in no way their founder. Moreover, these Franciscan authors recall that if he had often been edified by Francis, the cardinal had never been, for all that, his official counselor. The sources after 1246, including those of the Spirituals, even stress that Hugolino understood only the external manifestations of the Franciscan experience and not its veritable originality, which was the search for an ever deeper identification with the Christ of the Gospels.

What does this in fact mean? The hagiographical sources which tend to collapse the flow of time and blend together, into a single narrative, events from different periods, are scarcely useful to us in this regard. But Francis himself mentioned the figure of the cardinal protector in the rule of 1223 and in his *Testament*, by presenting him in both cases as the "governor, corrector, and protector of this fraternity."[15] It is difficult to say how far back this institutional innovation proper to the order of Minors and Poor Ladies goes. One does not find it among the Friars Preacher, who certainly posed fewer problems to the Holy See. As we have seen, beginning in 1217 and especially after 1220, Francis had maintained frequent and close but informal relations with Cardinal Hugolino. With the tensions and drifting that became evident within the order between the founder's resignation and the promulgation of the *regula bullata* of 1223, the papacy, at the request of Francis, gave an official and statutory form to the function of guide and adviser which the cardinal-bishop of Ostia had already been performing for several years. At first glance, the reference to the cardinal protector which appears at the end of the rule seems to be in contradiction with the passage of the *Testament* where Francis firmly forbids his friars from seeking after letters of protection from the Roman Curia.[16] How could he both place the destiny of the Minors into the hands of an eminent representative of the Curia and ask them to not have recourse to the same Curia?

In fact, it seems there had been a divergence of views between the Poor Man of Assisi and Hugolino concerning the very content of the protection which the cardinal was supposed to be exercising with respect to the order. For Francis, this notion had a moral and spiritual meaning, the role of prelate consisting in helping the friars remain faithful to their vocation and mission. Thus does he put the accent in his *Testament* on the disciplinary procedure at the conclusion of which the wayward or seriously disobedient religious would be referred to the cardinal protector in such a way as to preserve the spiritual unity of the fraternity founded on respect of the rule. Indeed, for Francis, the gravest danger was located inside the fraternity and stemmed from the divisions of the Friars Minor. No longer feeling himself capable of leading and protecting his sons with his own strength, he entrusted them to the Roman Church, as indicated in the story of the mother hen and her chicks inspired by a passage from the Gospel of Saint Matthew where Christ exclaims: "Jerusalem, Jerusalem, . . . long have I wanted to gather in your children as a mother hen gathers her chicks under her wings . . . but you did not want it!" (Matt 23:37).[17] For the cardinal, by contrast, the protection that he owed the Minors is to be found on the institutional level and was being exercised especially with respect to those who, outside the order, were impeding the friars from settling in this or that town or region, or were opposing their pastoral activity. By heaping privileges and dispensations upon them, he was surely favoring the growth of the order. But in the eyes of the founder, interventions of this kind were not what the friars needed; he was of the opinion, on the contrary, that such privileges risked increasing the tendencies toward relaxation and deviation that he was already noticing among them.[18]

When all is said and done, we can say that the Church welcomed Francis and his brothers without really understanding the whole import and meaning of his message. This resulted in numerous misunderstandings, which led the Poor Man of Assisi to voluntarily abandon the direction of the order in 1220 and to be on the defensive with respect to the pontifical initiatives until the end of his life, in an effort to safeguard the original characteristics of his movement. In the same period, other religious personalities found themselves in a situation comparable to his own—that of "dissident founder," to use the apt phrase of Maria Pia Alberzoni.[19] This was the case, for example, with Saint Dominic, who, in 1220, during the general chapter of the Preachers of which he was the master general, wanted to submit his resignation—it was immediately refused by his brothers—because he was in disagreement with certain directions that the papacy wanted to impose on his order. One finds the same case in the life of blessed Giovanni Bono: this jongleur from the Romagna, who underwent a conversion in 1209, lived first as a solitary, then, having attracted disciples in 1217, he founded a religious congregation of eremitical orientation which had a certain success in northern and central Italy. But when the Roman Curia demanded that the congregation adopt the rule of Saint Augustine, he gave up its direction in 1238 and withdrew to a hermitage. He died in Mantua in 1249, with a reputation of holiness. As is evident from these examples, the pressure exerted by the Holy See to standardize and centralize the new religious experiences was so strong at the beginning of the thirteenth century that the founders, in seeing them evolve in a rather different direction from the one that they wanted, were sometimes led to take some distance from their orders. It is not far off the mark to see in this reaction one of the culminating points of the process of the ascent of the individual and individual rights that had been under way since the twelfth century in medieval society.

Francis, for his part, while abandoning the direction of the movement which he had launched, chose at the same time to remain present to it but in another manner. From this moment until his death, the order of Friars Minor was directed by a double hierarchy: the one, normative and disciplinary, incarnated by Hugolino and, at the level of ordinary administration, by a "vicar," Peter Cattani and then, after his death in March 1221, Elias; the other, a hierarchy of charism and holiness, founded on his own person, for which he endeavored to be the example of fidelity to the rule. The conflict between the two poles ought be avoided—and it actually was—thanks to the primacy of obedience, called to mind by Francis in his *Testament*, where he presents himself as a prisoner submitted, ahead of time, to every decision that his superiors would want to make in his regard, including the one to get rid of him.[20]

Charism and institution, cardinal protector and founder, rule and *Testament*: up to the end, Francis played all the notes to guarantee the permanence of his ideal of "minority" in the life of the order which he had founded. He had probably understood that his experience of God, placed under the sign of poverty and humility, had a renewing dimension capable of challenging the Church of his day, and that a conflict with the hierarchy could only compromise the achievements and advances that had been possible for him to realize. Thus he preferred, whatever it might cost him, to act within the ecclesial institution, in the hope that the seeds which he had sown there would later bear fruit. But we would be mistaken to define the behavior of the Poor Man of Assisi in tactical or strategic terms, for it was rather for him a question of an existential attitude, which Bernanos perfectly defined in a famous text comparing and contrasting Francis with Martin Luther:

One reforms the Church only by suffering for her; one reforms the visible Church only by suffering for the invisible Church. One reforms the vices of the Church only by multiplying the example of its most heroic virtues. It is possible that Francis of Assisi may not have been less disgusted than Luther by the lasciviousness and simony of the prelates. It is even certain that he cruelly suffered from them, for his nature was really different from that of the monk of Weimar. But he did not challenge iniquity; he did not try to confront it. He threw himself into poverty; he devoted himself to it to the deepest extent possible, as into the source of all remission, of all purity. Instead of stripping away from the Church unjustly acquired goods, he showered it with invisible treasures and, under the gentle hand of this beggar, the mound of gold and wealth began to flower like a bush in springtime.[21]

In the last years of the life of Francis, the Minors evolved in a direction which was surely not the one that he wanted. This distancing from the person and message of the founder has been interpreted by the hagiographers as the sign of a relaxation among the Friars Minor; but this hardly seems convincing. Indeed, it resulted rather from the inability of Francis to clearly present the missions and functions that he wanted to give to his order, whereas the pontifical project of a pastoral engagement in the structures of the Church militant was much easier to understand and put into action. In any case, from the moment when he no longer was there to put the brakes on this development, the process of the standardization of the Minors accelerated; and in 1230, the will of the Poor Man of Assisi was even openly scorned when Hugolino, having in the meantime become Gregory IX, decided that his *Testament* had no juridical value and that the brothers were bound to observe only the prescriptions expressly contained in the rule. To justify such a decision, the pope claimed that he was fully competent to interpret his charism in that he had been very close to Francis while he was yet alive.

At first glance, the story of Francis thus ended in failure, marking the end of a great illusion. The institution had been right on the charism, and the papacy was going to be able to use the Minors as a mighty corps at the service of its aims by transforming them into Crusade preachers and, even later, into inquisitors. In fact, this negative balance must be nuanced and the role of Hugolino/ Gregory IX objectively assessed. If he really emptied the order of some of the most original aspects of the message of the Poverello, the cardinal also saved the movement from shipwreck and the coming apart that was threatening it in 1220–1223 by forcing it to become structured. For if nothing is done without human action, nothing endures without institutions. Francis himself then accepted engagement in this process, conscious as he was that, as a spiritual movement, if it was to survive and perdure in time, it had either to be integrated into an existing framework or to create a new one. And what can appear to us as a defeat of the charism or a rejection of the ideal, in fact, constituted the only way to safeguard the intuition of the founder and to assure its transmission.

It would, moreover, be unfair and inexact to define the relationship between Hugolino and Francis as one simply of force, or as a somewhat sadistic game of cat and mouse. Francis was probably less naïve than Paul Sabatier believed him to be. And the cardinal was not the crafty or cynical operator that Sabatier wanted to see in him. In fact, Hugolino represented the energetic forces of the Curia that were striving to implement the pastoral program of Lateran IV in a context made difficult by the conflict with emperor Frederick II and the growth of the heretical challenge. Under pressure, it was tempting to turn everything to good effect. This is precisely what the papacy believed itself authorized to do with the Friars Minor, at the risk of abandoning along the way what, in the heritage left by the founder, no longer appeared useful in the historical context of the moment.

In the end, in spite of all the things eliminated or reduced that it had to endure at the hands of the papacy, the intuition of the Poor Man of Assisi has not been entirely smothered. Even if impoverished or deformed, it has been for many men and women, over the course of the thirteenth century and well beyond, a source of inspiration. Through the preaching of the Friars Minor, the hagiographical texts, and the iconography, the figure of Francis has been widely diffused throughout Christendom, influencing the behavior of such saints as Elizabeth of Thuringia/Hungary († 1231), Louis IX († 1270), and Margaret of Cortona († 1297), to cite only the best known, who have taken over and put into action, each in his or her own way, certain aspects of Francis' evangelical spirituality. Even better, the Franciscan fervor, for a time dormant within the order in the second half of the thirteenth century, later underwent numerous reawakenings, some of which ended in open dissidence (with the Spirituals and Fraticelli in the fourteenth century), and some in vigorous movements of reform and a return to the sources (like the Franciscan Observance in the fifteenth century and the Capuchins in the sixteenth, again to cite only the best-known cases). Source of permanent challenge within the ecclesial institution, the message of Francis has profoundly renewed the face of Christianity, and it surely has not yet exhausted all its vitality. We would thus be on the wrong track to believe that Gregory IX, having confiscated Francis' heritage for the benefit of the Roman Church, has destroyed it by emptying it of its substance. We could even reverse the statement, inasmuch as the grafting of the Franciscan charism onto and into the ecclesial institution has been painful and betrayed by an impressive number of crises. We might consider to what extent the Church has been profoundly shaken up, in the thirteenth and fourteenth centuries, during the conflicts that pitted the Friars Minor against the secular clergy, then the Spirituals against the papacy under Boniface VIII (r. 1294–1303), and finally John XXII

(r. 1316–1334) against the hierarchy of the order of Minors beginning in 1328! We can imagine that, faced with such a power of destabilization, certain high ecclesiastical dignitaries of the period could sometimes have been tempted to say, along with the pastor of Torcy from the *Journal d'un curé de campagne:* "God save us from the saints! . . . These admirable people resemble those wines which are precious but slow to mature, which require too much trouble and care by the grower just to enjoy the palace of his great-nephews. . . . All too often they were a travail for the Church before becoming their glory![22] Simple quip or paradoxical formula, we might say. But that does not mean that it might not be applied particularly well to Saint Francis, who, while remaining faithful to the Church and in the very measure that he remained faithful to her, instilled a seed of evangelical "folly" which has shaken it up, put it into crisis, and renewed it at different times in the course of the centuries which followed his death.

11

THE GOSPEL IN THE WORLD: A TRANSFORMATION OF RELIGIOUS ANTHROPOLOGY

From the moment that the community founded by Francis was recognized by the papacy and acquired a certain importance, contemporaries were struck by its originality with respect to other forms of consecrated religious life that existed at the time. One of them, Jacques de Vitry, observed in 1220:

> Three groups of religious have existed up to now: hermits, monks, and canons. The Lord wished to thoroughly assure the stability of the foundation; and so during these last days, he has added a fourth religious institution, the beauty of a new order, and the holiness of a new rule. . . . This order is that of the truly poor of the Crucified and it is also an order of preachers: they are called Friars Minor.[1]

Another witness of the expansion of the Franciscan movement, the German Premonstratensian Burchard of Ursperg, said about them, not without a kind of grandiloquence: "At this time [before 1230] when the world was growing old, two orders rose up within the Church whose youth they have renewed like the eagle and the Apostolic See approved them: the Friars Minor and Friars Preacher."[2] However interesting they might be, these witnesses nevertheless give a somewhat simplistic view of things by reducing the Minors and Preachers to a supporting role coming to complete the system of existing religious orders and to reinforce the structure of the Church at a moment when it was in a perilous situation. It does not seem that Francis would have seen himself in this perspective: he who in his writings only one time uses the word "order" (*ordo*) to describe his foundation, preferring the terms *religio*—which was applied to any religious movement—and especially "fraternity" (*fraternitas*) or "life" (*vita*). These differences in vocabulary, which are not by chance, oblige us to ask

about the deeper meaning of the Franciscan movement in the eyes of its creator. Even today, in some books, the sons of Saint Francis are occasionally referred to as "mendicant monks," a term which it would be better to avoid even
though it has been used by several fine authors. Of course, entrance into the
Franciscan fraternity really involved a break with the world ("I left the world," as
Francis wrote in his *Testament* after mentioning his conversion), and, with the
companions who had joined him, the founder did not wait long before adopting
an ascetic way of life, centered on prayer and work, which involved the vows of
chastity, obedience, and poverty. At first glance, this common life can thus appear rather close to that of cenobites and, in particular, to that of the Benedictine monks. The similarity, however, is only apparent; once we look more closely,
we find that the resemblances are only superficial.

To understand the uniqueness of Franciscanism, we must not forget that Francis was and remained a layman. This statement might seem surprising, since we
have already mentioned that he probably received the tonsure after his encounter with the pope in 1209—which incorporated him into the clerical state—as
well as the diaconate, probably in 1220, when Honorius III and Hugolino forced
him to transform his movement into a religious order. But the "grades" which
he thus acquired, contrary to his desire (*volens nolens*), in the clerical state did
not prevent him from remaining fundamentally a layman in his behavior and
in his conception of religious life. If he sometimes received advice from certain
ecclesiastics like Bishop Guido I of Assisi and Cardinal Hugolino, no clerical or
monastic mediation seems to have had a decisive influence on him in the
choice of his way of life. Did he not declare in his *Testament* to have followed
the voice of God who was speaking in his heart? If we have doubts about this,
the best proof of the fundamentally lay character of the Poor Man of Assisi resides in the praise accorded him by the French Cardinal Eudes of Châteauroux, chancellor of the University of Paris from 1228 to 1244 and one of the chief
figures in the Roman Curia between 1246 and 1273. During a sermon which he
delivered at the Portiuncula, before an audience composed of Friars Minor, on
the theme of the Good Samaritan, the cardinal said:

> When I was a child, I was seeking to understand a stained-glass window one
> day in which the parable of the Samaritan was depicted. Given my igno-
> rance, a young layman, unknown to me, explained it to me. This window, he
> said, exposes the clerics and religious in the eyes of the laity for they have no
> compassion for the poor and indigent, whereas lay people share their pain
> and serve them in their need. . . . It seems to me that this parable has been
> fulfilled in the time of Saint Francis. . . . He was that Samaritan: he was lay;

he never became part of the men of the Church. He was a merchant living in a world of merchants whose appetite for profit and the love of an easy life he shared.

In another sermon, the same prelate, demonstrating keen human and spiritual discernment, marveled at the ease with which Francis later overcame all the handicaps associated with his state:

> It seemed bizarre to witness such a man—who had known absolutely nothing about religious life and had had no experience of it—creating new orders. It was insane for a man—who knew nothing about the Scriptures and was not accustomed to listening to sermons—to preach to the Saracens and even to Christians. It was crazy and even dangerous to preach in areas suffused with heretics. And, was it not also presumptuous on the part of a recently converted sinner to come and boldly teach a thing or two to sinners?[3]

The claim of independence which characterizes the action of Francis in the spiritual realm and which goes with a sincere submission to the Church and the clergy makes him a typical representative of a new kind of Christian that appeared at the end of the twelfth century in the West: the "religious layman" (*laicus religiosus*). Certainly, for a long time, believers of both sexes had been placing themselves at the service of monastic or canonical communities as "oblates" or conversi, while offering to contribute both their goods and their ability to work. But religious life remained mostly the domain of clerics, and the laity could have access to it only through their mediation, especially since the Gregorian Reform, which had elevated the role of the clergy and emphasized the submission of the faithful to their legitimate pastors. Around 1200, in Italy as in the regions extending from northern France to the Netherlands, new forms of lay religiosity had been affirmed, in spite of all obstacles—they are sometimes described with the awkward and ambiguous expression "semireligious"—whether they be penitents, beguines, or those "brothers" and "sisters" who placed themselves voluntarily at the service of the poor and lepers in the hospices and other hospitals ("*maisons-Dieu*").

Francis, from the very beginning, belonged to this same current. His experience, however, was soon distinguishable from existing forms of religious life. Different from the Humiliati of Lombardy, who intended to give an evangelical value to their working activities, he did not seek, after his conversion, to become holy through the exercise of his own profession; indeed, hagiographers later emphasized that his best business success during his lifetime had been the acquisition of treasure in heaven when he renounced his mercantile activities and goods in order to go and "sell" the kingdom of God among men and women. Thus it was actually wrongheaded—and unsuccessful to boot—of the Archbishop of Pisa, Federico Visconti, to propose to businessmen of this great commercial city in 1260 to take as their patron saint this "heavenly merchant."[4] On the contrary, if the Poverello showed his concern toward lepers and often visited "poor Christians," as he called them, he refused to transform the Minors into a Hospitaller order, devoted to their service; and in 1220 he made the Curia strike down measures that had been taken in this regard by John "of the Hat" (or *de Campello*) while he had been in the East. For in the meantime, the confraternity of the penitents of Assisi, which he had created with his first companions before going to Rome, had evolved and broadened his intentions. Through the movement that he had launched, Francis strove to put into action an ideal of full adhesion to the Gospel. The friars lived in chastity and recited the liturgical prayer of the Hours together, as did the Benedictines; but they devoted themselves especially to the proclamation of the word of God: an urgent task in the face of which the traditional distinctions between clerics, monks, and laity were losing their relevance, though without completely disappearing.

Did such a new form of religious life constitute an absolute novelty, as the thirteenth-century biographers of Francis have attested? In fact, one cannot but be struck by the real continuity that ties it to the eremitical movement of the eleventh to thirteenth centuries. When we consider hermits, we immediately think of persons living apart from the world, in deserts or grottoes, eschewing relations with the surrounding society and ecclesiastical hierarchy. But for Western Christianity after the year 1000, this vision hardly corresponds to reality: most anchorites had found their place without much difficulty in the religious world of the faithful and within the structures of the Church. Whether they were stationary or itinerant, many of them preached readily in public, taking John the Baptist as their model and denouncing the abuses of the powerful of this world or the immorality of simoniacal or married clergy. Certain reforming bishops appreciated that hermits had taken responsibility, on the moral and religious level, for marginal populations and encouraged them in this. The most famous of these *Wanderprediger* (itinerant preachers) had, at the start of the twelfth century, traveled around the forests and farmlands of western France (Robert of Arbrissel, Bernard of Tiron, Vital of Savigny) and those of the Limousin (Stephen of Muret). But they were also found in the Alpine regions and, from the start of the eleventh century, in Italy, where a monk and hermit named Dominic of Sora († 1031) had as his goal to convert, through the word of God and example, the laity and especially the priests whose unworthiness was imperiling the salvation of the faithful. He addressed all in the vernacular and, contrary to custom, he used no Latin biblical text in his sermons. The prestige which their ascetic behavior and moral rigor earned for these preaching hermits often allowed them to intervene successfully in the arbitration of conflicts and to reestablish peace—the preliminary condition of all evangelization.[5]

Francis of Assisi probably had never heard about these French hermit-preachers who had lived almost a century before him and had not been officially recognized as saints by the papacy—the lone exception being Stephen of Muret, founder of the order of Grandmont, who, like Francis but a century earlier, wanted only to have the Gospel as his rule. In Italy the most noteworthy figures of the eremitism of the eleventh century—Romuald, Peter Damian, and John Gualbert—had certainly given birth to religious congregations—the Camaldolese and the Vallombrosians—well established in Umbria, Tuscany, and the Marches. But it did not take long for these groups to evolve toward rather classic forms of cenobitical life, so that the heritage of these pioneers had fallen into oblivion. That does not necessarily mean that the Poverello and his companions had taken over from them the model of the hermit-preacher, probably because they had discovered in the Gospels the foundational texts of this way of life. Indeed, their life was shaped at the start by three essential traits, foreign to the monastic and canonical rules: life in the "desert" (which in the West simply meant deep within the forests or, more frequently, at the edge of towns and cities); wandering for God and itinerant preaching on the pathways; and gatherings at which they recruited disciples who abandoned everything to follow them. At the beginning, the friars refused to settle down in a specific place, except at the church of the Portiuncula, to which they returned during their annual general chapters and where they alternated times of meditation and prayer in the hermitages—places for the spiritual life and contemplation par excellence—with preaching tours in the cities and villages. They lived, moreover, in little cells devoid of all comfort, on the model of the Fathers of the Desert, who constituted, along with the Baptist, the obligatory reference for this style of austere life. Finally, their poverty had to be as stringent as possible, while their work with their hands enabled them to cover their needs without putting them in competition with the real poor. Contrary to a common misperception, the city had no particular fascination for them. They went there for reasons both economic—begging was better there than in the countryside—and ministerial. Were not the cities the quintessential place of sin under its most varied forms: dishonest gain, civil unrest, prostitution, heresies, and so on? Everything happened there as if the devil, who since the Early Middle Ages had made his home in the countryside and the woods, had moved to an urban environment, and it was there, or so it seemed, that one had to go in order to confront him. This is what

Francis had done both in Perugia and in Arezzo, where the exorcism done at his command in 1217 by Brother Sylvester, a priest, caused demons to flee the town: that is to say, he put an end to the struggle between the factions that had been fighting each other for power since the beginning of the century.[6]

Another major aspect differentiates the form of life of the Minors from that of monks: their rejection of the cloistered life. Jacques de Vitry, an informed observer and full of sympathy for the friars since their beginnings, talks about a "cloister with the dimensions of the world," and the same expression is found, more or less, in the *Sacrum commercium*, where, "Lady Poverty" having asked the friars to show her their cloister, "they led her up the hill and showed her a splendid panorama while saying to her: 'This, Lady, is our cloister!'"[7] This is not an edifying apologue or simple lyrical expression. At the beginning, the friars asked hospitality from those clerics or laity who could welcome them for the night, and then they left again the next day. Everywhere they went, they conducted themselves "as pilgrims and strangers" in the footsteps of Christ, who had also been itinerant on the roads of Galilee and Judea and who was often depicted in the clothes of a hermit, either alone or surrounded by the "pilgrims of Emmaus." Indeed, they wanted neither convent nor even a chapel, and they were happy to recite the Hours and attend Mass in those which they found open.

After 1220 and especially outside Italy, the Minors gradually abandoned this style of life. Transitory guests that they were, they eventually took on the status of residents; churches were offered or constructed for them, and buildings as well to shelter them which were not yet convents but simple houses or spaces for living (*domus, loca*). Francis acknowledged this evolution, as we notice in his *Testament*; but he asked his spiritual sons not to accept churches or dwellings which were not in conformity with "holy poverty" and absolutely to refuse to become their owners.[8] Even later, after they had adopted a conventual manner of life, the Minors would not reside in a permanent fashion in their convents. Ever on the move, whether for begging or for preaching, they often changed places and even demonstrated a real detachment with respect to their own churches to the extent that they would not hesitate to preach in the public squares.

Finally, what most distinguishes the form of life advocated by Francis from that of existing religious orders was the rejection of certain forms of separation which characterized the religious state, which had been clearly segregated from life in the world and judged incompatible with it. Indeed, in Western Christianity until then, the quintessential religious person was the monk who lived apart from the people in the shelter of the cloister. Even if their monasteries had a social function founded especially on prayer for the living and the dead, the Cistercians or Carthusians were first of all penitents who had renounced the world in order to seek their own salvation. The fundamental intuition of Francis turned its back on this nearly-thousand-year tradition. Indeed, for him, the world was not the place of external appearances or vanity from which it was necessary to flee in order to find God but the area where charity is deployed, a place to go through—without settling down—in a living *peregrinatio* on which one waged spiritual battle against evil and against oneself. Francis and the Minors innovated by trying to get beyond the opposition, elaborated in Late Antiquity and having become classic, between contemplation (*theoria*), reserved to an elite of specialists separated from the world, and the active life, worldly, in which the mass of believers was confined. To make of activity itself an act of contemplation in a spirit of service and submission; to incorporate the experience of God into human experience: such was going to be the aim of this "new and humble people" about whom Christ himself would have asked his Father that it "be distinguished by its humility and poverty from all those who had preceded it and who, for all its wealth, would be content to possess me alone."[9]

Along this same line, the initial renunciation of every fixed settlement by the Minors likewise demonstrated their desire to enter into contact with the greatest number of people possible, whether through the practice of manual work in the fields and workshops or through begging or preaching, in order to urge them to do penance. Given this, one might want to speak of an apostolic aim, but this would be an exaggeration, for it was a matter not of indoctrinating or recruiting anyone but of bearing witness and addressing a call to each one. Through their joyful demeanor and the mutual affection which united them, the brothers demonstrated that a new type of relationship between human beings was possible, for their message of peace and conversion had no chance of being received unless they themselves presented the image of a reconciled humanity and one without borders. The call that they presented was indeed addressed to all human beings without exception. As Saint Paul had sought to go beyond the opposition between Jews and Gentiles in a universalizing vision, Francis desired to go beyond the differences or oppositions between genders, age, and various juridical and social categories in a living spiritual communion. Thus in the rule of 1221 does he lay out all the "states of the world" of his day, while respecting the framework of universal prayer recited during the Mass, as if he had been haunted by the idea that the members of one of them could feel themselves excluded:

And all those in the holy Catholic and Apostolic Church
who want to serve God, and all the following orders: priests, deacons,
sub-deacons, acolytes, exorcists, lectors, porters, and all clerics,
all religious, male and female,
all *conversi* and all children,
the poor and the indigent,
kings and princes,
workers and farmers,
servants and lords,
all virgins, both those who remain celibate and those who are married,
laymen and laywomen,
all little children and adolescents,
the young and the old,
the healthy and the sick,
the small and the great,
and all peoples, races, tribes, and tongues,
all nations and all people everywhere on the earth who are and who will be:
we humbly beg them,
Friars Minor all of us, useless servants,
to all persevere in the true faith and in penance,
for no one can be saved in any other way.[10]

In the letters which he sent between 1222 and 1226 to "all the faithful," to "clerics," and to "the leaders of the people," Francis emphasized the universal character of this call to holiness and the exact nature of his purpose is shown here with particular clarity. Presenting himself as "your smallest and most despised servant," he does not claim to lecture his readers but stresses that his role is to tell those who "do not follow the true light, our Lord Jesus Christ," that they are on the wrong path and are living in illusion and falsehood. If they persist in their desire of ownership and power, they will find themselves deprived of everything at the decisive moment:

Consider and see that the day of death is coming. I thus beg you with reverence not to forget the Lord and not to separate yourselves from his commandments because of the cares and concerns of this world which you have; for all those who completely forget him and separate themselves from his commandments will be cursed and forgotten by him. And when death comes, everything will be taken away from them. And the wiser and more powerful they will have been in this world, the greater will be the torments that they will endure in hell.[11]

In this perspective, the proclamation of the word to Christians and to unbelievers comprised an essential element of the activity of Francis and his companions. Their project was part of a broader movement, noticeable since the last
decades of the twelfth century, through which the Church had been seeking to
promote preaching in order to reconnect with lay audiences, especially in the
towns, contaminated by movements and ideas that were deemed heretical. In
the very heart of Christianity, a new front line was being opened: the spiritual
conquest to which had consecrated themselves, since the 1210s, Saint Dominic
with the order of Friars Preacher approved by the papacy in 1216, Francis and
his Minors, and many others. The change in pastoral focus at the beginning of
the thirteenth century marks a decisive step in the history of medieval Christianity. Indeed, this new dynamic was not limited to a heightened effort at gathering in the faithful and a program of reorganizing ecclesiastical structures. It
was a matter, more profoundly, of a transformation of religious anthropology,
henceforth centered on the valuing of the word as an instrument of social communication and pastoral action.[12]

What did this newness consist of? Christian Antiquity had known a brilliant
flowering of sacred eloquence, as the sermons of Saint Augustine testify to. But
in the course of the Early Middle Ages, outside the monasteries and cathedrals,
the religion lived and practiced by the faithful had been reduced to a collection
of gestures and formulas, especially since the liturgical language—Latin in the
West—had become unintelligible to them, and the priest was, above all, the man
who knew and performed the efficacious rites. Beginning in the last decades of
the twelfth century, the desire to announce the word of God arose in certain
lay milieus. In 1179 Pope Alexander III had given a rather favorable welcome to
the request of Waldo (Valdès) and his disciples, who were asking to be able to
preach the Gospel; but he had first required the agreement of the local clergy.
This rendered the concession inoperative at the time of the archbishop of Lyons, Jean de Bellesmains, who in 1180 revoked the authorization given to the
Waldensians by his predecessor, the Cistercian Guichard. As this episode shows,
the opinion of the clerics was not unanimous on this point. In the same years,
the *scholasticus* of Notre Dame of Paris, Peter the Chanter († 1197), wrote: "In
our days, we gag the mouths of the simple who preach the truth and thus make
the prelates indignant,"[13] whereas the Premonstratensian Bertrand of Font-
caude and Joachim of Fiore accused the Waldensians of having usurped the
ministry of preaching and having twisted Christian doctrine. In 1215 the Fourth
Lateran Council was pleased to mandate prelates to designate preachers from
within their clergy, especially in large dioceses where the population was

scattered, for "the hearing of confessions, the levying of penances, and all activities pertaining to the salvation of souls."[14] In fact, the principal problem
facing the Church was that of mission: the papacy and bishops wanted to get rid
of, once and for all, "self-proclaimed" preachers who rose up one fine day and
started haranguing the crowds without having received any mandate from the
hierarchy, as had just been seen with the Children's Crusade, a branch of
which arrived in Rome in September 1212 under the direction of its charismatic
leader, Nicholas of Cologne, to the great displeasure of the Roman Curia.

This is the context necessary for understanding the hesitations of the papacy
when Francis and his companions came to ask Innocent III for authorization to
preach penance everywhere—and which was granted in 1209. In doing this, the
pope was in line with some of his predecessors who had granted the *licentia
ubique praedicandi* to various hermit-preachers throughout the twelfth century. But perhaps he also remembered the lessons of his masters, Peter the
Chanter and the canonist Huguccio, both favorable to the preaching of the
laity. Huguccio, in particular, while stressing that preaching within the framework of the liturgy was reserved to priests, had defended the idea that simple
believers could legitimately admonish their brothers and sisters in the faith
and to urge them to do the good in virtue of their baptism—a distinction which
Innocent III seems to have adopted in responding to the request of the Poor
Man of Assisi.

The specific task which the pope assigned to Francis and his companions, at
the time of their first meeting in 1209, was indeed to preach penance. In the
context of the period, this apparently vague term had a specific meaning. It re-
lied on a distinction, within biblical texts, between, on the one hand, the narrative or moralistic episodes easily accessible to everyone, called the *aperta* ("open"
texts, those whose meaning is obvious), and, on the other hand, expositions having a dogmatic character, or *profunda* (profound, hidden truths), as in a good part
of the Gospel of John or the Apocalypse, whose comprehension demanded the
interpretation of someone learned in the exegetical and theological fields. To
these two levels of revelation corresponded two distinct forms of speech: on the
one hand, penitential exhortation, accessible to "religious laity" if authorized
by the local bishop or the pope, and, on the other hand, preaching in the strict
sense, which explained the mysteries of the Christian faith and was reserved to
learned clerics having the care of souls. Innocent III had granted to the Humiliati of Lombardy and the Poor Catholics the authority to preach penance; he
extended this authorization to Francis and his brothers, who used it widely, addressing everywhere they went, in churches or in public places, calls to conversion. Did the pope go farther and authorize them, as the *Legend of the Three*

Companions suggests, to pass from simple exhortation to actual preaching "according to the doctrine of truth and the power of the Holy Spirit"?[15] This seems doubtful. But in any event, the distinction between these two forms of speaking was in practice difficult to realize, and the Minors soon ran up against difficulties in this respect.

Indeed, the evolution of the Church, circumscribed by the rapidly growing weight of canonical codifications and the fear of heresy, was not moving in the direction of openness to the preaching of laity. A decree of Lateran IV prescribed excommunication for "those who, under the trappings of piety but without possessing the reality behind it, arrogate to themselves the power to preach." This sanction was surely aimed at wayward preachers, but it could also be applied to laymen and laywomen within religious life.[16] The authorization given by Innocent III to Francis and the Minors to preach penance among the faithful made them indispensable instruments for a Christian renewal within the towns, first in Italy and afterward well beyond. Thus did the field of their preaching tend to widen, especially when a number of clerics later entered the fraternity. Without having wanted it, Francis had opened the way to a clericalization of his movement that was to occur, over the next decades, through the admission of a growing number of priests and theologians. These last, thanks to their cultural and social superiority, soon took over the leadership of the order and, within the space of less than twenty years, eliminated the lay component of the order on the level of recruitment and in terms of the values of poverty and simplicity which the unlearned brothers, in particular, gave testimony to.

This evolution, which became apparent especially after the death of Francis, did not prevent his message from touching many men and women who were living in the world. A tenacious legend in Franciscan hagiography and historiography attributed to the Poverello the merit of having founded for these laypeople the Third Order (the First Order consisting of the Friars Minor and the Second Order of the "Poor Cloistered Ladies," later called the "Clares"). The idea of a "triple militia of elect" coming forth from the Poor Man of Assisi, which we find already in 1229 in Thomas of Celano, is incontestable. Moreover, around 1240, the biographer of Gregory IX attributed to this pope (and not to Francis) the creation of the orders of the Damianites and of the penitents.[17] It is nonetheless undeniable that the apostolic work of Francis and his companions throughout the towns and countryside of Italy found a broad echo among the faithful, who, engaged in the bonds of marriage and family life, could not leave everything to join them—like that couple of estranged nobles of Limisiano who, under Francis' influence, had come to a better understanding between themselves and who then adopted the status of penitents while continuing to live together.[18] Certain young single women also seem to have been responsive to the call of the Poverello and, under his influence, to have adopted a way of life that was similar to that of the Beguines of northern Europe, if one can believe the author of the *Assisi Compilation:*

> Many women made a vow of virginity and adopted a religious habit. Each had her own cell but they led a common life. They practiced virtues, mortification, fasting, and prayer. One had the impression that they were living apart from the world and their own kin. In spite of their young age and great simplicity, they appeared to have been formed by other holy women in the service of the Lord for a long time.[19]

Nothing proves that, during Francis' lifetime, the friars had been concerned with establishing, in the course of their travels, devout groups bringing together men and women who had been moved by their preaching and who wanted to set forth on a path toward conversion. In fact, it seems that the confraternities of lay penitents which had been multiplying in central Italy during the years 1215–1220 had organized themselves and that they had remained for a rather long time autonomous on the institutional level. Their first known rule, the *Memoriale propositi*—a program of religious life adapted to their situation— makes no mention of any attachment to the order of Friars Minor. And the confraternities which it did institute were placed under a lay authority, submissive to the supervision of the local bishop. In fact, it was not until the years 1240–1250 that "penitents of Saint Francis" appeared, and it was only in 1289 that the Franciscan pope, Nicholas IV, promulgated the rule of the Third Order through the bull *Supra montem*.[20] That being said, this does not mean that the diffusion of the penitential ideal within civic lay milieus had not been in large measure the work of the Friars Minor. It was. This is attested by the letter known today as the *Letter to the Faithful*, which Francis addressed around 1223 to "religious Christians," in which he gave such people advice on how to live in a holy manner in the world:

> Let us, therefore, have charity and humility and give alms because it washes from our souls the stains of our sins. . . . We must also fast and abstain from vices and sins and from an excess of food and drink and be Catholics. . . . In the love that is God, we pray that all those to whom this letter comes truly receive with divine love these aforesaid and fragrant words of our Lord Jesus Christ. And let those who do not know how to read have these words read to them frequently and let them hold them within themselves through holy works, for they are spirit and life.[21]

Thomas of Celano summarizes Francis' intention when he wrote that the latter "gave to all a rule of life and indicated the true means for being saved, each according to one's condition," for, even if he was not the founder, the Poor Man of Assisi gave a decisive impetus to the emergence of the figure of the "religious layperson," which came to be diffused under different forms throughout Christianity during the thirteenth century.[22]

Whether they were lay or religious, women were the principal beneficiaries of this evolution. Not that Francis might have had a particular tenderness for them, or that he considered Clare as his alter ego or his mystical spouse, as Paul Sabatier and many others after him have said. Jacques Dalarun has shown that it is necessary to set aside, once and for all, these well-worn clichés and to question the idea that a relationship of equals existed between these two persons.[23] Like all religious of his time, the Poor Man of Assisi, in fact, believed that women needed to be directed, because they could not achieve perfection by themselves, and that visiting them often risked being, for men, the occasion for sexual temptation or sin. Thus does he strictly forbid his brothers from taking penitents under their care—at the very most they could direct them toward an appropriate place for the purpose of their conversion—and he forbade women from entering the church of the Portiuncula.[24] Accordingly, there is no reason to make him a precursor or to see in him a paragon of the liberation of women. But nor was Francis misogynistic—far from it. When he speaks about original sin, he mentions the sin of Adam, never that of Eve; and the simple fact that his was always an all-inclusive discourse addressed to the whole human race is already in itself an important fact. To define his position in contemporary terms, let's say that he was not particularly sensitive to the question of gender and that, as in many other areas, he strove to muddy the waters by going beyond the traditional divisions and oppositions between the sexes. Moreover, if he carefully made sure to keep a respectful distance from women whom he had the occasion to have close contact with, that does not prevent him from being conscious of the spiritual figure of the Madeleine, the first of the female penitents who was at that time considered like an apostle, and especially of the Virgin Mary, who had shared poverty and humility with her son. The essential role that he gave to these two virtues made him more open than a good number of his contemporaries to the feminine condition, which was commonly believed to be inferior. To the extent that they were excluded from power and knew only, as a general rule, the vernacular tongue, women were situated on the side of weakness and lack of learning. To be interested in them thus constituted a form of voluntary humbling and charity.

But his attitude with respect to Clare and the community of San Damiano can also be read from the perspective of the courtly culture which he had made his own. Indeed, Francis wanted his friars to call them not "sisters" but "ladies," implying a relationship of service vis-à-vis these "spouses of the Holy Spirit," as he called them in the "form of life" that he gave them. For in feudal society, as Georges Duby has shown, love is due to one's lord and service to one's spouse. Sensitive to certain dimensions of the feminine condition, like clemency, softness, and generosity, Francis did not hesitate to compare himself before Innocent III to a beautiful and poor woman who had given sons to a king who had made her pregnant. Francis "played the woman" as he "played the holy man." Within his order, he intended to treat his brothers "as a mother" (*sicut mater*) who nourishes, raises, and governs her household. This defines a kind of very different—but not less demanding— relationship from the patriarchal one that existed in monastic or canonical orders, between the superior and ordinary religious. For Francis, other than the Father of heaven, there were only mothers and sons; and the vocation of each Christian was to give birth to God in the world. Thus can one accept without any qualms the affirmation of Jacques Dalarun, according to whom, Francis, "without having had a feminist program, . . . contributed to the femininizing of Christianity." This constitutes a fundamental turning point in the history of Western spirituality.[25]

We now understand better, in this context, the fascination that Francis' message had upon women during his lifetime and throughout the century after his death. Other than Clare, of course, one immediately thinks of his contemporary Elizabeth of Thuringia/Hungary († 1231), probably the most faithful imitator of the Poor Man of Assisi; Rose of Viterbo († 1251), who went through the streets of her city carrying a diptych on which was painted the face of the Savior, urging her fellow citizens to be converted; and, around 1330, the three holy lay penitents and great mystical figures Margaret of Cortona († 1297), Clare of Montefalco († 1308), and Angela of Foligno († 1309). Two of them—Margaret and Angela—belonged to the Franciscan Third Order, while Clare of Montefalco, a recluse who had to take the rule of Saint Augustine, died while saying: "Here comes eternal life, my Saint Francis!"[26] These women have been called veritable continuators and heirs of the Poor Man of Assisi and his message, which his men had betrayed by intellectualizing and rationalizing it. But precisely which Francis were these women the imitators of—worn down by meditation on the sufferings endured by Christ during his Passion and blessed with numerous visions and "spiritual consolations"—if not the only one whom they could have known: that of the *Legenda maior* of Bonaventure and of the Spirituals, who put great emphasis on the ecstasies, revelations, and prophetic warnings in the life of the Poverello? Without entering into this complex debate, we owe it to ourselves to note that Francis of Assisi—through the image that his disciples had given to him—has played an important role in the process of the spiritualizing of religious phenomena that characterizes the last centuries of the Middle Ages: a process in which women were both the protagonists and its principal beneficiaries. And it is probably not by chance that the only other person whose stigmata were recognized by the Church as authentic was a laywoman, virgin, and mystic: Saint Catherine of Siena († 1379).

It would be an exaggeration to attribute to the person and influence of Francis all the changes that were produced in the thirteenth century in the realm of religious life and spirituality. Some things had begun well before him, like the Beguine movement or the engagement of laymen and -women in works of mercy; and others owe nothing to him, like Joachimism or the mystical currents that were condemned by the Church, beginning around 1300, under the name of the Heresy of the Free Spirit. But without the Poor Man of Assisi, the religious history of the West would have been very different; and certain key figures of the medieval period, like Saint Louis and Dante, would be incomprehensible and, at most, unthinkable. Thus it is not an exaggeration to say that, with Francis, a profound mutation of religious anthropology occurred in the West, which Ovidio Capitani has defined in terms which we can only reiterate here:

> To become the poor and to remain men, to not be content to imitate the marginality which flight from the world implies by fleeing the company of men and women into the hermitage or the monastery; to not see society, nature, history, as a "necessary evil"; to bring enthusiasm . . . into a humanity inflicted with all kinds of debasements though made sacred as humanity by Christ; to extend to all the involuntary poor the title "poor of Christ" which was, up to then, reserved to the voluntary poor, to monks; to rediscover the value of the world while rejecting the negative image of it that was current; to not condemn the rich as rich but only to the extent that one was blinded by one's wealth, or the powerful as powerful but because one was not just. In a word: to not make of poverty either an occasion for the rich to "justify themselves" or for the poor an excuse to always remain poor.[27]

12

A Cultural Mediator of a New Religious Sensibility

The immediate success of the message of Francis of Assisi in Italy is also due to the unique relationship that it had with the culture, or rather the cultures, of his day. Because of his social origins and formation, the Poor Man of Assisi had nothing clerical about him; and if he had attended the cathedral school of San Rufino, he had done so only in order to learn to read and write while also absorbing a few basics of Latin, as the children of proper society in the towns did. His education was that of a merchant who had to be able to keep his accounts and write up a receipt. As the two handwritten texts which we have from him show—the blessing to Brother Leo and the few lines that he sent to him after a conversation together—his ability to write was mediocre. These notes, which date from the last years of his life, are drafted in the minuscule letters used in the area of the central Apennines, with the large letters separated from each other and often including heavy downward strokes. At the beginning of the thirteenth century, apart from notaries, lawyers, and some businessmen, few laypersons knew how to write; the practice was largely reserved to clerics.

We should not forget how slow and laborious was the triumph of writing, how late it prevailed in western Europe, where, for a long time, it was used only for setting down for posterity decisions and precepts so as to confer upon them the force of an official norm. As a general rule, one wrote in Latin, which was the language of the liturgy and of abstract knowledge: law, theology, exegesis, philosophy, the sciences. The only texts which were starting to be drawn up in the vernacular, as early as the twelfth century, were acts connected to professional life, especially certain commercial contracts and literary works—*chansons de geste*, Arthurian "novels," and the lyrical poetry of the troubadours—as well as a few paraliturgical or apotropaic formulas used by laymen and -women to do penance or to ward off a bad end.

Francis mastered writing, but it did not constitute his natural form of expression; and his relationship to the written word was different from what we think would be typical today. In his eyes, every text had a sacred character, as attested by his concern to have his brothers gather up the parchment leaves that they found along their way, since the name of God could sometimes appear there. At important moments, in order to find his way forward, he resorted to "opening the Bible" or "the Gospel"—that is, consulting the Sacred Scriptures with three successive random openings—and he was persuaded that these sacred words or signs, like the Tau which he drew below the blessing to Brother Leo, had the capacity to have an effect on the minds of those to whom they were addressed. When he wrote in Latin, as was the case in the two autographs mentioned earlier, he showed his knowledge of this language was rather elementary. The farther he moved from the biblical citations or references and the more he sought to express his own personal feelings, the more did "barbarisms" multiply under the effect of a strong impulsion toward the vernacular tongue, which contaminated the orthography. The style lacks refinement, the phrasing is hasty and awkward, the material is not neatly divided, and almost all the phrases begin with the word *et*. Francis judged himself well when he described himself as "unlettered" (*illiteratus et idiota*); this meant that he did not know Latin, the language of literature, and that he lived outside the world of formal education.

This hybrid status of a layman knowing how to read and yet "unlettered," in the medieval sense of the term, revealed itself to be a strength to the extent that it allowed Francis, after his conversion, to realize spectacular advances in the cultural and religious realm. For him, writing was not confined to institutional and legal usages prevalent in the Church—we need only think of the numerous bulls that the papal chancery was churning out!—and the commune, where only the acts of those notaries who enjoyed the "public trust" (*publica fides*) had any authority. The Poor Man of Assisi innovated by making writing a personal practice, detached from any limiting context, juridical or liturgical. Indeed, he did not hesitate to write down spiritual texts, whether they be blessings, letters of direction or consolation (like the note addressed to Brother Leo preserved at Spoleto and the *Letter to a Minister*), or even the poems written to be sung like the *Canticle of Brother Sun*. In his writings, Francis used a virtual bilingualism. Latin was a noble, prestigious language; its forms were stable, and it was the only language that had a fixed grammar and orthography. The vernacular languages were still developing and evolving: Italian did not yet exist as a separate and cohesive language. There were at that time only regional dialects, like the vernacular Umbrian which Francis spoke. In addition, he knew French, the language of the novels of knighthood, which "travels the world and is the more delightful to read and hear than any other," as the Venetian chronicler Martino da Canal wrote around 1275. But it seems that Francis used it only for singing and begging alms.

The historical role played by Francis in the cultural domain can be understood only by situating him in an evolving perspective. At the beginning of his life, the Poverello knew only Latin texts like the Pater Noster, the Ave Maria, perhaps the Credo, and a few Psalm responses which would have been taught to him at the cathedral school. After his conversion, he became more interested in Sacred Scripture, seeking to read the Gospels in order to find there the confirmation of his intuitions. Finally, after the approval of his fraternity by Innocent III and the reception of the tonsure which made religious of them, his companions and he had to recite the office of the Hours every day and to read, at least those who were capable of it, the breviary—a copy of which Francis himself possessed that has come down to us. This book of prayers contained a large number of liturgical texts from various sources—mostly biblical but also patristic and hagiographical—that considerably enriched his knowledge and understanding of Scripture. Without ever becoming a learned cleric, Francis deepened his religious culture during the last fifteen years of his life with the aid of a few priests who had entered into the fraternity, like Brother Sylvester—the first cleric to have joined him—and Brother Leo, his faithful secretary.

The familiarity with the Bible that he then acquired allowed him to go beyond the barriers which separated the clerical world from that of the laity and to play a role of mediator, or rather of courier, between these two distant cultural universes. In the majority of his writings, Francis used Latin like a living language, even if it meant mangling its grammar in the process. In doing this, he softened that rigidity and solemnity which the sacred language could have in order to make of it an instrument of communication. Similarly, he ennobled the vernacular by using it in domains which had been foreign to it up till then, like poetry and religious song. The *Canticle of Brother Sun*, in this regard, constitutes a radical innovation: Francis must have had real boldness to dare to address God, orally and especially in writing, in this rough patois; and he was probably one of the first, if not *the* first, to have this audacity in the Italy of his day. It is a simple canticle, or more exactly a *laud* of paraliturgical character, but its transcription was the starting point of Italian religious literature and its first great achievement. Regarding the poem that begins *Audite, poverelle*, which he addressed to the Poor Ladies of San Damiano, he demonstrates his concern to maintain contact with women who knew only their mother tongue. By making the vernacular an instrument of the celebration of the Creator on the same level as Latin, Francis "redeemed" the oral and popular element of lay culture. He freed it of its structural inferiority and reshaped it through his own way of thinking and expressing himself, thus opening the way to a personalization of religious experience. Through his writings and preaching, he enabled numerous laity of both sexes to have access to a religious culture which had remained foreign to them and transmitted the most meaningful fragments of it to them in a striking form.

This osmosis between profane culture and that of clerics had important consequences. Henceforth, the piety of the Italian people could be expressed in a language which was that of everyday life, with its joys and pains, through poetry and song. For with Francis, the praise of God did not go without the song he often associated with preaching, by accompanying himself or having himself accompanied by the zither, a kind of lyre; this *psalterium decem cordarum* (psaltery of ten strings) was, according to tradition, what King David played when he sang the Psalms which he had composed in praise of the God of Israel and danced before the Ark of the Covenant. Over the next decades, however, a split occurred between singing and preaching among the Minors, who feared to be taken for street entertainers or to be accused of lacking seriousness in the accomplishment of their pastoral tasks if their preaching took on the allure of a spectacle. But the baton was, so to speak, handed on to laymen and laywomen wanting to actively participate in liturgical prayer, especially within the confraternities of devotion which were then proliferating in urban areas in tandem with the apostolate of the Mendicants. From monastic prayer, the *laude* became, over the course of the thirteenth century, the expression of the intimate bond between the laity and their God, the exterior sign of an affective and sometimes mystical relationship. The joyful songs which accompanied the popular religious movements of the Alleluia in 1233; the growth of confraternities of *laudesi*—singers of the *laudi*—in the praise of Christ, the Virgin Mary, and the saints; the processions of Flagellants who traveled around the north and center of the country in 1260 by associating song with theatrical expression: all extended and amplified that breakthrough achieved by Francis into the cultural and linguistic domain.[1] This meeting of religious sentiment and secular emotion gave birth to a poetic and lyrical repertoire which, in certain Mediterranean countries, remained the fundamental element of popular devotion up to the middle of the twentieth century. Such a phenomenon of successful acculturation is equaled in the history of Western Christianity only by the synthesis that Luther and the Protestant Reformation brought about in the sixteenth century between evangelical Christianity and the Germanic genius, by favoring the growth of choral singing in the German language in which a whole people rediscovered its soul.

The role of Francis in the realm of culture cannot, however, be reduced to a simple linguistic transference or to an adaptation of Christian teaching to new audiences. With him, the use of the vernacular and of more simplified speech was not a mere pedagogical or didactic technique. It was a choice that corresponded to his own level of learning and to his ideal of "minority," which led him to recognize the presence of hidden but very real values within the world of the excluded. Rejecting the great genres of sacred eloquence, he preferred to proceed by way of brief speeches or harangues from vernacular eloquence (*concio*) as was then used by political figures in the public squares. By making the figures of Christ and Mary come alive once again in his words and gestures, the Poverello conferred relevance and potential meaning on them which they had not had for simple believers up till then. At the same time, he added to the wealth of images in Christian culture—the habit of the Minors in the form of a cross, the crèche of Greccio, the tree of life—and forms of expression some of which were borrowed from the sphere of daily life and others from biblical culture.

The most significant example of this type of transposition is that of the Tau: the mark that Francis placed as a signature at the end of certain letters and which he painted on the walls of his cells. This was related to the last letter of the Hebrew alphabet (*tav*), which is in some way the equivalent of the Greek Omega in casting God as the end of all things, but which was assimilated by Christian tradition to the Greek Tau (T) because of its crosslike shape. The prophet Ezekiel had described the Hebrew letter in the form of an **X** as "the sign marked on the forehead of the people of Jerusalem who groan over the abominations which they are committing therein" (Ez 9:4). We find it again in the Book of Revelation (Rev 3:12 and 7:2–3), where angels mark it on the foreheads of the servants of God—that is, upon the elect who will be saved at the time of the Last Judgment. This biblical theme belonged to high ecclesiastical culture, as shown by the opening sermon at the Fourth Lateran Council in 1215, where Innocent III, having made a connection between the Tau and the cross of Christ and insisted on their redemptive power, stated that "those who grieve and deplore the abominations that are being committed within the Church will appear marked on their forehead by the sign of the Tau."[2]

Francis took the ecclesiastical discourse literally and transposed it according to his own cultural formation. Thomas of Celano, in his *Treatise on the Miracles*, describes a miracle which Francis worked by touching the end of a small stick in the shape of a Tau to the paralyzed leg of an inhabitant of Cori in the Latium.[3] At root, this sign had an apotropaic value and was supposed to ward off ills of the spirit from those to whom Thomas was writing. At the same time, the hagiographer put Francis' activities into an eschatological perspective by placing his mission of preaching under this sign, in order to make hearers understand the urgency of conversion "in these days which are the last." Thus we are not surprised to learn that Brother Pacificus, during a vision which he had had after his entrance into the order, "noticed on the forehead of Saint Francis a large multicolored and magnificent Tau, spread out like the feathers of a peacock."[4]

We would, however, be on the wrong track if we considered this choice of evocative symbols as an expression of Francis' ever-vigilant mistrust toward the "knowledge that puffs up" and that leads to self-importance. In fact, his primary aim was to connect with "simple people" in their own cultural world, where gestures, images, and song were more important than speeches or writing. The more the public whom he addressed was of a modest social level, the more his interventions resembled religious spectacle or, to use an Italian expression that has passed into contemporary usage, a *sacra rappresentazione* (sacred drama). Thus, for the peasants of Greccio, did he improvise one Christmas night an original dramatization, bringing together in a scenic play—the "play of the crèche," which received its fame on that day—the celebration of the Eucharist and that of the child of Bethlehem, during which Francis spoke of the "birth of the poor king."[5] Indeed, Francis loved to preach to creatures with created things, for he was seeking less to transmit a message or to extol moral behavior than to urge his listeners to establish a new relationship with God and neighbor by revealing to them the divine character which lay buried deep within themselves. Starting from the cultural and social condition of those whom he was addressing, he used that as a fulcrum to open up their spirits and hearts to spiritual realities: the rusticity of the peasant and the cleverness of those of modest condition—objects of mockery for aristocratic or bourgeois authors of the period—were transformed by him into evangelical simplicity. The real poverty that he shared with the majority of his listeners thus became for him "the queen of virtues," whereas it was commonly disdained and dreaded in the world. It is not a paradox or a "preacher's trick," meant to play to the audience by using its language or by flattering its image of itself. The Poverello often spoke to people and groups situated at the margins of well-to-do and cultured society: the poor, the humble, the unlearned who had neither the opportunity nor the means to express themselves. He offered them a way of redemption in a style accessible to all through what was called, in medieval Latin, the *sermo humilis*:

a way of speaking, full of common and concrete words drawn from the real world and yet aimed toward the sublime through the truth that it reveals—a discourse which draws closest to the audience but which involves it, instructs it, and elevates it above itself. Thanks to his witness of holiness which in some way gave him credibility, the religious culture of Italian laity could develop its possibilities and become in its turn generative of new expressions.[6]

Is it therefore legitimate to see in Francis of Assisi a spokesperson for folkloric culture or of the "populist soul," as was being said in the nineteenth century? This is the idea which inspired Frédéric Ozanam, one of the first French writers to have rediscovered Francis—initially in his pioneering book *Les Poètes franciscains en Italie au treizième siècle*. There he evokes that "instructive and charming moment when art begins to comprehend popular inspiration . . . because poetry is within the people as bread is within the furrow: one needs an inspired harvester who by his work is able to gather up its fruit."[7] After thirty years of research and debate over "popular religion," contemporary historians have become more circumspect in the use of this adjective. In fact, Francis, this "inspired harvester," to use the apt expression of Ozanam, did not belong to the neglected levels of the society of his day, even if he primarily addressed his word to them. His personal formation had nothing to do with that of rustics and "woodsmen," even if he and his companions sometimes seemed to be from among them, at the start of their experience together. It was situated rather at the convergence of all the literary currents that ran through the upper levels of lay and urban society at the beginning of the thirteenth century: the *fin-amor* of the troubadours of the Occitan tongue, the taste for prowess greatly esteemed by the epic ever since the *Chanson de Roland*, and the knightly adventure that lies at the heart of the Arthurian legend.

It is hardly likely that the excitable young man that Francis was, impelled more to action than to reading, would have had a direct knowledge of all these texts, even though we cannot completely rule that out. These were in the air at that time, and the heroes of the *Song of Roland*—Charlemagne, Roland, Oliver, and other "paladins" whom the Pseudo-Turpin had made into martyrs of the Christian faith in a crusading context at the beginning of the twelfth century—or the Knights of the Round Table: all were familiar figures for whom Francis had had such enthusiasm in his youth. Afterward, the Franciscan tradition favored the thrusts of these epics and the knightly expressions within secular culture. Francis and his companions—among whom were former courtly poets like Brother Pacifico—managed the fusion of these cultural traditions, up to then quite distinct, by reformulating them in words and texts whose tonality was both lay and religious. It seems pointless to wonder whether Francis, during his lifetime, had been particularly marked by courtly influences or knightly values. His own writings are devoid of courtly observations, except the *Salutation of the Virtues*, where he refers to the virtues as noble ladies. Among the hagiographers, the accent varies from text to text. In his first *Life*, Thomas of Celano presents Francis as a merchant; in the second, less than twenty years later, he makes him a paragon of courtliness. The *Sacrum commercium*, probably drawn up around 1237–1239, is imbued with a thoroughgoing courtly tonality—Francis is presented here as a man who has left on a quest for Lady Poverty, the spouse of Christ for whom he longs with love—while the *Legend of the Three Companions*, written ten years later, gives a preponderant place to knightly values. In fact, when it comes to Francis' cultural formation, it is better to speak of a knightly ideal lived within the framework of the commune and expressed in a courtly language.

The Poor Man of Assisi certainly emphasized the courtliness of God "who gives the sun and the rain to the good and the bad alike" (*Fioretti*, 37), thus opening the way to a new interpretation of the Almighty which would allow Dante to define God as "the one who is the lord of clemency."[8] But knightly literature had changed since its beginnings, and, in this respect, the culture of Francis fits well into the evolution of Western culture marked, between the end of the twelfth century and the beginning of the thirteenth, by the transitions from knightly values to courtly values and from courtly values to religious values. Simultaneously, his audience had widened to the upper levels of the urban bourgeoisie, desirous to imitate the tastes and values of the aristocracy, whose models had undergone a shift. The ideal that the literature was propagating was no longer only the bravery of a valiant warrior, who was praised at every opportunity, because prowess, generosity, and wisdom were henceforth to be found all interconnected. As Raoul de Houdenc wrote at the time:

> *Chevalerie* is the fountain
> of a clemency that cannot run dry
> as long as one knows how to draw from it.
> From God does it come, and knights who have it . . .[9]

In the same period, in northern France, the secular adventure of courtly novels was being transformed into spiritual knighthood. This is what the *Queste del Saint Graal* really illustrates, definitively fine-tuned in a Cistercian or Cistercian-influenced milieu during the 1220s–1230s, exalting the figure of Galahad, the valiant and pure. But in this work, which had an enormous influence north of the Alps, the poetic form of the novel is only a means of conveying a message of monastic inspiration, wholly traditional in its content. It is not the same in

Francis, who strove to transpose into the religious realm the knightly and courtly ideal, while at the same time making it accessible to urban circles and to all laity. For him, every Christian, not just the monks and members of the military orders (Templars, Hospitallers, or Teutonic Knights), was called to become a knight of Christ and to do battle against the vices—that is, in the last analysis, against oneself. His message was oriented toward action and initiative, as illustrated by the frequency in his writings of the words "begin" and "do" ("do penance!" *Poenitentiam agite!*). His preaching and writings urge the friars, whom he called his Knights of the Round Table, to make of their lives an adventure placed under the sign of the "following of Christ" (*sequela Christi*). These are not just images or simple metaphors but an integration of the modalities and content of the epic into a religious experience which had the whole world as its theater and all those who joined him as its actors.

Even the poverty that was so close to his heart is placed in a direct line with the knightly culture of which he had become, since his youth, an enthusiastic disciple. In the *chansons de geste* and courtly novels, the most despicable person is the one who is avaricious; and the one who is praised is the one who is generous. That which is condemned and serves as a foil to the idealized knight who distributes his riches with prodigality is the bourgeois or merchant who hoards, that is, who keeps for himself that which he has gained and makes his fortune an end in itself, thus dissociating his being from his having. The attitude of Francis toward goods and money fits into this logic, but he gives it a new significance by extending to all—beginning with the most disadvantaged—this ideal of generosity and liberality which, within aristocratic society, was recognized only among equals and people who shared the same world. When, at the beginning of his life, he gave a cloak to a down-on-his-luck and penniless knight whom he had encountered by chance, he was only acting in accord with a knightly code. But from the day when he "did mercy" to the lepers, he widened to all humanity "for the love of God," in whom all are sons and daughters, the relational circle inside of which this code of "good conduct" had to apply. Overcoming the disgust which their physical appearance generated in him and acting in a manner foolish in the eyes of the world, Francis subjected himself to a veritable rite of initiation, comparable to that which Guinevere had imposed on Lancelot by making him mount the cart of shame; and it is this spiritual ennobling that was going to permit him to become a true knight of Christ. We could say as much of the spirit of liberty and mischievous gaiety that marks his whole witness, where we discover a tone typical of the poetry of the troubadours. But there is a small difference: in Francis, the reason for his happiness was not the love of his lady or the prospect of a joyful war but the certitude of being loved and saved by God in Jesus Christ, as well as the ability to arrive at "true joy" by being subject to all and by accepting suffering and humiliation without protest.

These themes and this language place Francis, without any doubt, in the camp of the culture of the urban ruling classes. But another aspect of his behavior allows him to be in the thrall of the mindset of the popular classes. This is shown by his way of making the public laugh at his expense by presenting himself as a "jongleur of God." At that time, this title was used to depict people who were both actors and narrators of legends and farces, but also mimes, acrobats, and clowns, capable of improvising comic skits to amuse their listeners. Different from troubadours who moved around in lordly courts and benefited from a certain consideration, these entertainers were marginal folks, generally poor and doomed to vagrancy, living from day to day from whatever the public wished to give them. The great ones of this world despised them but could scarcely do without them because their presence livened up their gatherings and feasts. It even happened sometimes that jongleurs could say to the powerful, with a farcical tone of derision, what people at court or their subjects really thought of them, but which no one in their immediate entourage dared to say to their face. And for the clergy who castigated their blasphemies and their "sins of the tongue"—vulgarity, obscenity, crudeness—the jongleurs were truly "the devil's minions," according to the expression of the monk and chronicler Rigord of Saint-Denis († 1209), who took to task the princes for the generosity they showed the jongleurs.

To associate, as did Francis, jongleurs and God thus constituted a real provocation that consciously challenged the traditional boundaries between the sacred and the profane. The technique proved generally effective. When Francis arrived in a village in his raggedy clothes and presented himself before his astonished listeners as the knight of Lady Poverty or the herald of the Great King—that is, the spokesman for God—he was certain to make them laugh at his expense and to hold the attention of his audience. Certain ecclesiastics looked with suspicion on this form of cultural mediation, which was not respectful of the hierarchical relationship between clerics, who alone were empowered to produce and disseminate religious culture, and the laity, who normally were its recipients and beneficiaries. By the end of the twelfth century, a French churchman, Peter of Blois († 1212), archdeacon of London, had sharply criticized the celebration of the heroes of the *chansons de geste* and knightly novels—King Arthur, Gawain, Tristan—whom their creators had dressed up with all kinds of qualities and whose misfortunes comic actors recounted in public, "tugging at the hearts of listeners for compassion and moving them to tears": should they not rather weep over the life and sufferings of Christ![10] When Francis and his brothers called the faithful to conversion while depicting themselves as "jongleurs of God," they were not only committing an infraction against the institutional model then in force; they were also risking debasing the status of preaching by placing the sacred Word on the same level as fables, songs, and other "novels"—in short, profaning in every sense of the term. Thus did the papacy endeavor, even during the lifetime of Francis and especially after his death, to restrict the right to preach only to the learned brothers and, after his death, to prohibit it to those who were not clerics, in both meanings of the term, canonical and cultural. But in the eyes of the Poor Man of Assisi, these distinctions hardly made any sense because the vocation of the Friars Minor was not, like solemn preachers, to sprinkle their sermons with sixty or eighty Latin citations but to seek after the "utility" and edification of the people by sharing with them, on an equal footing, their experiences and beliefs. Francis struck and convinced his listeners because he traced out for them a path forward by paring down the words. He etched on the surface of this language, devoid of standing or syntax, the power that the public word can have when it is clearly announced and backed up by the life of the one who is offering it. His exhortations, like those of the biblical prophets, were not presented as well structured discourses; rather, by finding words that acted directly upon his listeners, he enabled such people to pass from mistrustful closed-mindedness to enthusiastic adherence. Both in form and in content, it really was "a new word."[11] We can say without exaggeration that by refusing the amalgam that had been created in the medieval Church between the transmission of the word of God and cultural superiority, Francis has virtually created in the West—for the first time since the *Dialogues* of Gregory the Great—a religious culture of poverty.

It is difficult to measure the impact of the message of Francis on the hearts and minds of his contemporaries and, maybe even more, to distinguish what was attributable to him from what was due to the efforts deployed by his disciples or other religious orders during the decades after his death. To try to establish a good accounting in this area would be an enterprise doomed to failure in advance. But we must clearly affirm that, during the thirteenth century, a decisive revival and a fundamental renewal of the spiritual life in the West occurred. Materializing in the space of a few decades, especially in Mediterranean regions, was a new religious sensibility that it is tempting to attribute to the person and message of the Poor Man of Assisi, and which one can characterize as popular to the extent that it affected the most varied social circles. Whereas Christianity had especially, until then, stimulated rational reflection and artistic activity, in the wake of Francis, emotional forces emerged to modify its look and enrich its content. This decisive turning point was translated into an opening to the affective depths of the human person, tied to an intimate familiarity with the birth and sufferings of the Redeemer and characterized by the appearance of new dimensions of religious sensibility like mercy, compassion for the weak, and tenderness toward creatures. It is, of course, in Italy that the message and way of life of the Poor Man of Assisi awakened the most echoes and exercised its most lasting influence. Through his witness, he freed the dramatic dimension of the Italian language, its absence of restraint in the expression of feelings—from love to indignation—and this fervent enthusiasm for justice and humility which would find their strongest expression at the beginning of the fourteenth century in the Franciscan poet Jacopone da Todi.

Conclusion: Francis, Prophet
for His Time . . . or for Ours?

By way of conclusion, it is important to try to define the fundamental newness of Francis in the eyes of his contemporaries, as well as what he might still
mean for our own time. All who knew him were convinced that he was a saint;
the exceptionally large number of Lives and works devoted to him in the Middle Ages leaves no doubt about this. But, as many saints, male and female, were
venerated in the Christianity of their day, the authors of these works emphasized the exceptional characteristics of the Poor Man of Assisi: his stigmata, of
course, but also a way of living and an original message that they had difficulty
defining with any precision. This explains the various qualifiers that were applied to it; and its frequent repetition risks looking, to a modern reader, like a
simple rhetorical device or a kind of superficial emphasis. Indeed, in his first
Life, Thomas of Celano characterized Francis as "a man truly new and of another time."[1] But Thomas also speaks of him as a "new evangelist" or a "new
apostle," while the *Actus*, echoed by the *Fioretti*, presents him unabashedly as a
"second Christ" (*alter Christus*).

Rather than wonder about the exact meaning of each of these terms, let's
recall what place "novelty" had in the ecclesiastical culture of the period. In
contrast to modern and postmodern societies, where what is new automatically
receives a favorable welcome, medieval thought honored tradition and custom.
Like the authors of Antiquity, the clerics of the thirteenth century, with only a
few exceptions, mistrusted innovations, seeing in them only dangerous attempts
to question, if not subvert, the established order. In their eyes, *novitas* was invested with a positive content only to the extent that it was based on the past
and gave contemporary relevance to it. One could make the new out of the old
only by breathing life into what had already existed and by making reappear

what had become dead or enfeebled. In order for medieval hagiographers to legitimately qualify their hero as "new," it was still essential that his life and deeds could be referred back to a precedent having authority. In their eyes, Francis merited praise to the degree that he had reconnected with the perfection of the beginning: for had he not given a new impulsion across the centuries to the movement begun by Christ and his apostles, as it was described in the Gospels, and had he not reproduced its profound dynamism in his own life? Rupture with the family at an adult age, vagabond existence, rejection of every political and social revolt, particular interest for the "lost sheep of Israel" and those on the margins, radicalization of the moral requirements flowing from faith in God to the detriment of ritual prescriptions, and eschatological emphasis of preaching: all these specifically "christic" traits were found in the life of the Poor Man of Assisi. And we understand that his biographers, starting with Bonaventure, did not hesitate to emphasize his conformity to the Son of God.

But the theme of "Francis as a second Christ" or "another Christ" rested, as we have seen, on a fundamental ambiguity: as authors outside the order since the Middle Ages have been reminding Franciscans who were not all envious or adversaries, the mediation of Christ the Savior, in orthodox theology, has a singular and definitive character. A saint can be visited by God to the highest degree, but he or she does not for all that become God. Francis himself, moreover, never claimed this identification with the person of Christ, whose footprints he simply attempted to follow in this world. In this discourse, the conformity of Francis to Christ is expressed not as the self-consciousness of the Poor Man of Assisi but as an ideology tied to the historical vicissitudes of the Franciscan order and its desire to affirm its own uniqueness through the exaltation of the figure of its founder.

Even after we have deconstructed the discourse and rejected certain clichés attached more or less artificially to the life of the Poor Man of Assisi, we must recognize that his contemporaries were struck by the profound originality of his religious experience. The problem, for the historian, is to try to take account of this newness without becoming trapped in the categories of that time which are not necessarily compatible with those of our own. Thus various medieval hagiographers have characterized Francis as a prophet. Thomas of Celano depicts him in his *Memoriale* as "the prophet of our age."[2] Julian of Speyer, in his *Life of Saint Francis*, says that "filled with the spirit of prophecy (Is 52:7), he announced peace and preached salvation." Around 1240, the Franciscan theologian and preacher John of La Rochelle speaks of him as a "new Adam" and underscores that, like the first human being before sin, he offered prophetic words, while Bonaventure states that he was "endowed with the spirit that animated the prophets."[3] To understand the exact meaning of these statements, we must evaluate them according to the idea that the clerics of this time had of prophecy, which differs considerably from what we understand by this term.

In the thirteenth century, this notion still had a rather imprecise content. It sometimes described the gift of spiritual clairvoyance—that is, the ability that the saints had to read the hidden thoughts of their listeners or to discern the realities which deceptive appearances concealed. In other cases, it was an ability to predict the future, especially the future destiny of certain persons with whom the man of God found himself in contact. Thus did Francis announce to Cardinal Hugolino that he would become pope—something which did not take long to happen—and "prophesy" the approaching death of the knight of Celano, in whose home he had been welcomed and who died not long afterward. With the *Legend of the Three Companions*, we see introduced into the life of the Poverello premonitory dreams and visions absent from earlier texts. Thomas of Celano, in his *Memoriale*, accentuated this tendency by attributing to him sober predictions about the future of his order, which allowed him to deplore a certain relaxation of the primitive fervor and attachment to simplicity of the Friars Minor.

With Bonaventure, the prophetic dimension of the Poor Man of Assisi took on a more ambitious dimension. For him, Francis really was the "new Elijah," thus a figure of great importance who has been assigned a providential role. At the end of a progressive ascension toward perfection, Francis, having become fully conformed to Christ, had put humanity back on the path of salvation at the coming of the Last Days by preaching, like John the Baptist, penance and peace. For the author of the *Legenda maior*, as for most university personnel of his day, the prophetic function consisted above all in revealing the hidden meaning of the word of God through preaching and constituted, by this fact, the privilege of clerics and doctors. By defining Francis as a prophet, Bonaventure legitimated the ever more pronounced orientation of the Friars Minor toward pastoral activities, with all that that implied in terms of the value of studies and theology. But if the minister general of the Friars Minor and the principal Franciscan preachers during the course of the second half of the thirteenth century really present Francis in this perspective, as the first prophet of his order, we must acknowledge that Saint Anthony of Padua might have had a better claim to this title, in that he fulfilled better than did the Poor Man of Assisi such a definition of prophetic ability.[4] Later, the Spiritual Franciscans, on the contrary, emphasized the prophecies relating to the future of their order that were attributed in growing number to Francis beginning in the 1270s. Thus, according to the *Verba fratri Conradi*—the words of Conrad of Offida († 1306), a collection of thirteen stories that he heard from Brother Leo and other similar texts—the Poor Man of Assisi, having announced the tribulations that would come to shake the order's foundation after his death, promised to personally come to the aid of those brothers who remained faithful to absolute poverty.[5] Like Thomas of Celano—but in a much more systematic and aggressive manner— these authors attributed to Francis pronouncements and warnings that, in fact, reflected the negative judgment they themselves had about the recent developments in the order of Friars Minor, in such a way as to try to turn the course of events in a direction more favorable to their ideas.

When all is said and done, we can say that the medieval authors, while intuiting a prophetic role for Francis, never managed to clearly define it; instead, each interpreted it according to his own attitude toward the transformations of the Franciscan order. However, the Poor Man of Assisi had clearly claimed divine inspiration when he stated in his *Testament:* "The Most High himself revealed to me that I must live according to the form of the Holy Gospel."[6] To our eyes, his message can especially be characterized as prophetic to the extent that it had a collective dimension and a considerable historical impact. According to the apt phrase of Régis Debray, "The prophet is one who opens up a perspective by bringing others toward a vanishing point over the horizon."[7] In Christian terms, we can say that the prophet's word opens up a new or neglected path toward the kingdom of God. Such has really been the role of Francis, who is situated "at that hidden juncture where eternal reality breaks into the visibility of things and into the march of history," and from which "an understanding of the divine plan can become actualized in the movement of the world."[8] At the beginning of the thirteenth century, the Church found itself, within the society of its day, an owner of its own goods, with that assurance and satisfaction which the Gospel denounces for the rich. With the ruling classes it had made compromising alliances, thereby becoming the support and guarantor of an order of which it was the first beneficiary. Moreover, every time that a transformation of economic and social structures occurred, the Church, finding itself out of step with the times, ended up being rocked back on its heels because it was poorly prepared for change and reacted to it by hardening its positions.

Faced with this "established disorder" and the rise of the power of money within the society of his day, Francis affirmed the fundamental value of poverty and humility, understood not as forms of asceticism but as symbols of a rejection of feudal arrogance and the greed of a new world, urban and bourgeois, which was being born right in front of him. Poverty and prophetic gift: the ancient biblical connection reappeared in him with a determined character and an absolute confidence in the humble means which impelled him to act outside of the ways of power and opportunism. In this sense, the message of the Poverello was profoundly subversive, for, by emphasizing the impossible establishment of the kingdom of God on earth, it exposed as relative the very notion of a Christian society—Christianity—which the papacy was seeking to establish here and now. That is why the Roman Church—while at the same time welcoming Francis because of the truly evangelical character of his witness and the obedient fidelity that he showed toward her—judged it appropriate, shortly after his death, to redefine his prophetic charism in terms acceptable to the institution and eliminated its most radical aspects.

However, we cannot understand the prophetic project of the Poor Man of Assisi without placing it within an eschatological perspective. This word need not induce fear; it describes every form of belief relative to history that interprets its unfolding, in a theological perspective, in the light of those events that will characterize the end of time (*ta escata* in Greek) and their fulfillment. Certainly Francis, in his writings, appears quite removed from the grand apocalyptic perspectives that marked, for example, the work of Joachim of Fiore; nor does he manifest any particular interest in the modalities and chronology of the Last Days. But like all Christians of his time, he was convinced that he was living in the last age of humanity, at that time associated with the sixth period of the millennium, which, in the unfolding of the history of salvation as Saint Augustine had described it, was going to end with the opening of the seventh seal and the glorious return of Christ. Thus did he seem convinced of the urgency of a universal mission; and thus was he animated by the desire for the martyrdom which should make the conversion of the pagans possible at the approach of the end of time. The role that he gave to his fraternity was to teach men and women by word and example to prepare themselves for the Last Judgment, from which no one could escape. Moreover, his own visionary experiences—especially the one on La Verna at the conclusion of which he received the stigmata—place him in the line of the great prophetic figures of the Old Testament, in particular Isaiah and Ezekiel, whose missions had been confirmed by heavenly signs. For all these reasons, it seems to me legitimate to say that Francis of Assisi was a prophet. His spiritual sons were not mistaken in recognizing in him the Angel of the sixth seal from the Book of Revelation (Rev 7:2). Whereas Joachim of Fiore assigned this role to Christ or to a pope of the Last Days, the Franciscans effectively assimilated their founder, beginning in the 1250s, to this mysterious personage who was going to "arise from the East bearing the sign of the living God and to mark the foreheads of the elect," thus making him a special messenger sent by Providence to call men and women to repentance and to lead them to salvation.

To what degree was the prophetic message of the Poor Man of Assisi welcomed by his contemporaries? It is undeniable that he left an indelible mark on society, especially in Mediterranean countries but also, to a lesser extent, in areas far distant from where he had lived his life. In Italy cities have kept the memory of his presence, and chroniclers gladly attribute to the friars the merit of having renewed religious life, as evidenced, for example, by the *Anonymous Chronicle of Siena*, composed at the beginning of the fourteenth century, whose author wrote concerning the year 1228:

> This year Saint Francis was canonized and a great feast was celebrated on this occasion at the Roman Curia for the great mystery of the stigmata which he had received from Jesus Christ and for the great miracles which he showed forth in his life and in his death. And it was said that Saint Francis, along with Saint Dominic, had such great merit that they renewed the Christian faith which had been weakened by the great and abominable sins which were being done at this time when almost the whole world was full of tyrants and brigands and when heresies were multiplying throughout Christianity in great number. And the holy Christian faith was renewed by Saint Francis and Saint Dominic.[9]

We cannot fail to be struck by the fact that the memory of the Poor Man of Assisi is identified in this text with the moralizing action and antiheretical struggle of the mendicant orders, as confirmed by the parallel that the author sets up between Saint Dominic and Saint Francis. But what remained of his evangelical project, and what influence did it actually have upon the society of his time? Historians have often presented Francis as the founder of a "new age" and stated that his success was due to the attention that he had drawn to what theology in the twentieth century has called the "signs of the time."[10] Along the same lines but in a more precise manner, Jacques Le Goff states that Francis' success was tied to the fact that he responded to the hopes of a significant percentage of his contemporaries, both in what they welcomed in his message and in what they refused.[11]

These converging assessments correspond to a part of the reality. Francis and his companions realized to a high degree the aspiration to voluntary poverty which had inspired the majority of religious movements of the thirteenth century. Their way of life corresponded to the hopes of the men and women of their day to the extent that it demonstrated that it was possible to live the Gospel while remaining faithful to the Church. Unlike the secular or regular clergy, the Friars Minor claimed for themselves no privilege or position of power, and they remained outside the feudal and signorial system—which explains why the communal authorities looked approvingly upon their apostolate and often helped them settle within the towns. Finally, by emphasizing that temporal and cultural goods had value only in their use and that the worst error that a man could commit was to desire to appropriate them to himself in order to enjoy them only for himself, Francis favored a new approach to economic realities centered on the rejection of hoarding and on the necessity of enabling wealth to circulate. His condemnation of the sterile accumulation of unproductive riches was, in fact, going to lead the Friars Minor to elaborate, beginning near the end of the thirteenth century, a doctrine of exchange and credit helping to surmount the opposition between ecclesiastical culture and mercantile culture about loaning with interest and a just price, and to create the Monte di Pietà in the fifteenth century in order to save the poor from the power of usurers.[12]

But there are other areas—and not the least important—where the failure of Francis has been obvious and where his message was quickly obliterated. A witness of the evangelical impulse of the twelfth century at the time of the papal theocracy and a simple layman lacking scholastic and university training, the Poor Man of Assisi often found himself out of step and sometimes even at odds with the dominant tendencies of the evolution under way. Thus did his lay mentality clash with the particularly strong evolution of the Church of his day toward a clericalization and increasing juridicization of religious life, which forced him to transform his fraternity into a religious order subject to the same rules as others. By imposing on Francis the tonsure and, later, the diaconate, the papacy initiated a process which, with the complicity of the friar-clerics quickly becoming predominant within the order, led, beginning in the 1240s, to the elimination of its lay component and to an alignment of its structures and aims with those of the Dominican order. Similarly, one cannot but be struck by the rapidity with which the majority of the Friars Minor were in a hurry to forget "Brother Francis" so as to embrace only "Saint Francis," whose historical role the bulls of canonization and most of the hagiographical texts had defined in terms quite distant from the concrete demands that characterized his message, especially in the matter of poverty and the renunciation of power. Living in convents, devoting lots of time to studies and pastoral activity—leaving them no time now to work with their hands—the Minors drifted away from the poor. Soon they were accepting donations and testaments in compensation for the celebration of numerous anniversary masses for the dead. This influx of resources allowed them to construct churches of vast proportions, richly decorated by the best artists, contrary to the recommendations of the Poor Man of Assisi in his *Testament*. They probably could not have done otherwise, and we should not be unduly scandalized by this evolution. But it constitutes a failure for Francis—whether as a result of contradictions inherent in his message or of the inability of his spiritual sons to grasp its demands.

The evolution of the attitude of the Franciscan order toward studies and intellectual culture likewise testifies to a rapid estrangement regarding the values of its founder. We have seen that Francis was not hostile to theology and praised theologians in his writings. But he did not want his brothers to become savants, fearing that they might separate themselves from the simplicity which had to be their first virtue, and from poverty by the purchasing of expensive books. Even more, his personal formation was similar to that of the troubadours of his day who, like Peire Cardenal, cursed a world in which magistrates and jurists threatened relationships between individuals founded on the integrity of one's word by favoring notarial acts and legal statements. A stranger to the subtleties of Parisian scholasticism and the decretists of Bologna, the Poor Man of Assisi saw in the gloss a means for getting around the prohibitions in the Gospel and for voiding the obligations that appeared in the rule of his order. He was not wrong to be mistrustful of jurists, as is shown by the way that the *Decretum* of Gratian—the first compilation of canon law, drawn up around 1140 and the definitive authority by the beginning of the thirteenth century—treats the matter of oaths. The author begins well by evoking the two passages from the Gospel, where we see Jesus forbidding his disciples from swearing, after which Gratian asks about the reasons behind this prohibition. He demonstrates that the proscription was motivated above all by the fear of perjury. This allows him to conclude that the oath was licit in dubious affairs (as is almost always the case in the judicial realm!), since we have no proof that Jesus ever condemned the verbal assertion of any truth having God as one's witness. We thus can understand better, in this context, the heartfelt exhortations which Francis, near death, addressed to his brothers in his *Testament:*

> Let the minister general and all other ministers and custodes be bound by obedience to neither add nor subtract anything from these words. . . . And I strictly forbid all these brothers, clerics as well as lay, by obedience, to ever gloss the rule or these words by saying: "This is how we are to understand them." But as the Lord has given me to say and write the rule and these words simply and purely, understand them simply and without gloss, and observe them and put them into practice up to the end.[13]

Francis wanted his message to be kept as a whole and without interpretation. To analyze the rule was for him to risk altering its meaning by fitting it into a system of rational argumentation and to transform it into a series of abstract principles. The tragedy of Francis is that no rule was made *more* the object of glosses than that of the Friars Minor throughout the Middle Ages and even beyond. There was probably some naïveté and even a certain pride on Francis' part in prohibiting any interpretation of a text which he considered inspired by God but which was, like everything written by human beings, tied to a historical context, subject to evolve over the course of time. To attempt to fix his own reading of the rule as he had given it in his *Testament*—was this not, in fact, to delegitimize in advance his successors at the head of the order and to seek to impose his own law, beyond death, upon his spiritual sons? Indeed, from the moment that Gregory IX, in the bull *Quo elongati* of 1230, declared that the *Testament* of the Poverello had no juridical value, these friars began to wonder about the meaning of certain passages of the rule; and beginning in the 1240s, treatises began to appear by Franciscans aimed at defining what had been the *intentio regulae*—the real meaning of the rule. On this point, the defeat of Francis was definitive and without appeal, because he was at odds with the evolution that was leading the Church to make an ever-increasing place for law and the rational exegesis of texts, be they scriptural or juridical.

Finally, the emphasis placed by Francis on the renunciation of power and the fundamental role of poverty in the religious life were quickly defeated by the historical evolution of the order—and then lost from sight. The thirteenth century in the West was marked by the development of public institutions, communal as well as monarchical, and the Church itself became a structure of government whose functioning was increasingly slow and complex. The popes of this period, from Gregory IX to Boniface VIII, drafted and then diffused throughout the whole of Christianity imposing collections of canonical texts in which the papal decretals held an authoritative position and which were supposed to govern all areas of the social and religious life of clergy and laity. At the same time, these popes stated their claim to actually direct Christian society, including the temporal realm; and, beginning in 1227, they engaged in a fierce struggle against the emperor and king of Sicily, Frederick II († 1250), which ended only with the death of his last descendants at the end of the 1260s and the conquest of southern Italy by Charles of Anjou, brother of Saint Louis. Emboldened by this success, the Roman Church sought to subject to its authority the national monarchies which had continued to grow. Boniface VIII (r. 1294–1303) did not hesitate to enter into conflict with the king of France, Philip IV (the Fair), reminding him in the bull *Clericos laicos* that the laity ought to be subject to the clergy and in particular to the first among them, the pope, supreme judge of all Christians.

In these politico-religious battles, the Friars Minor played an important role by fully aligning themselves on the side of the papacy, whose indispensable collaborators they had become. Certain friars had rapidly acceded to the episcopacy, then to the cardinalate (Bonaventure, Matthew of Aquasparta, Jerome of Ascoli). In 1288 Jerome of Ascoli became pope as Nicholas IV. Such promotions, as well as disagreements among the friars over the issue of poverty, exacerbated tensions, provoking a rupture between the Spirituals and the majority of the order, who began to be called the Friars of the Community. After the futile attempts at reconciliation between the two parties during the Council of Vienne (1311–1312), John XXII (r. 1316–1334) decided to have done with the recalcitrant friars. In 1317 he unleashed a violent persecution against the Spiritual Franciscans and laity, referred to as male and female Beguines, who were their sympathizers. In 1323 he went even farther by promulgating the constitution *Cum inter nonnullos*, which sparked a violent crisis between the papacy and the hierarchy of the order. Indeed, in this bull, the pope declared heretical the affirmation that Christ and the apostles had lived in absolute poverty, basing his position—among other arguments—on the passage of the Gospel where Judas is said to have held the purse of their little community, which implied that they at least possessed money. Thus, nearly a century after the death of Francis, one of his fundamental intuitions was officially condemned by the Roman Church, which led many Friars Minor who wanted to remain faithful to his message to enter into conflict with the Avignon papacy. Some set themselves up as defenders of Christian freedom; William of Ockham († 1349), for example, in his works after 1328 never ceased passionately disputing the power of the pope and declaring that "the law of the Gospel is a law of freedom." Others, more radical, slipped into clandestinity; and a number of these ended up on the pyre, after having been persecuted by the Inquisition under the name of Fraticelli or "Little Brothers of the Poor Life." To those who, like Brother John of Roquetaillade (or John of Rupicessa, † c. 1366), refused to break with the institution while remaining faithful to the message of Francis, all that remained was to maintain the hope of an imminent coming of a "Restorer" who would, thanks to a major eschatological crisis, lead the order of Minors back to the perfection of its beginnings.

At the end of this journey, readers will perhaps be surprised not to have found in this volume an unequivocal picture of Francis that would reinforce what they knew or thought they knew about this person. But as an exegete, the author of a book about Jesus, has recently written, "Today the historian is not so much the one who declares a historical truth with fresh new facts, but one who slowly learns what one cannot say about the object of one's desire."[14] After more than a century of historical criticism, it has become difficult, if not impossible, to reduce the Poor Man of Assisi to a simple idea. From the day after his death, as we have seen, different "readings" of Francis began to appear, and the diversity of these interpretations complicates the task of his biographer, unless one is content to mix together without nuance all the sources in order to draw out of them a composite picture. These divergent approaches to the same person are all the more understandable as the Poor Man of Assisi, during his own lifetime, held positions that can sometimes appear contradictory. Thus, in spite of his strong consciousness of having been called by God to accomplish a particular mission, he always gave witness of a flawless submission—if not without some murmuring and suffering—to a Church whose weaknesses he knew better than anyone else. We can likewise wonder how to reconcile his fundamentally nonviolent attitude toward persons and institutions with the extreme harshness he showed in his *Testament* toward disobedient or wayward brothers.[15] Similarly, the attitude that he showed toward prohibitions of every kind, especially regarding food, seems to us hardly compatible with his own asceticism, which was sometimes carried to extremes.

But by what right should we reduce Francis to a simple idea? And why would he not have been, like every other human being, shaped by contradictions that he alone was capable of overcoming? His heirs have not satisfactorily resolved the "difficult heritage" that he has left them.[16] Instead, they have favored certain aspects of his message at the expense of others, based on their own sensibilities and needs of the moment. We would be ill-tempered to reproach them for this, for in our own day the life and work of this or that complex or controversial contemporary personality is often subject to divergent judgments. In the case of the Poor Man of Assisi, a tension was quickly established between a hagiography inspired by the papal bulls and liturgical offices drawn up at the time of his canonization, on the one hand, and, on the other, the traditions founded on the memories of some of his closest companions who sought to keep alive "another Francis," whom they judged to be more authentic. We have no right to choose between these interpretations: the truth of a historical person is inseparable from his or her transmission to history. But the historian embraces his or her role by favoring those accounts which have a greater degree of probability and coherence with what we can know of a person through that subject's thought or writings. This is really what I have tried to do in this book.

The difficulty that we have in understanding the figure of Francis in his historical reality results in large measure from the fact that his religious experience has often been presented as the pure and simple reproduction of that of

Jesus, as indicated by the title *alter Christus* (a "second Christ") applied to him by different authors since the end of the thirteenth century. But the figure of Christ, such as can be lifted up from the Gospels, is not unequivocal, and it varies considerably according to whether we place ourselves in the perspective of Matthew or John. Francis of Assisi surely sought to "follow the footsteps" of Jesus of Nazareth, such as he had discovered them in the Scriptures (the Gospels but also the Psalms!), and among human beings whom he had met. But he made choices between the different images of this Christ whom he had placed at the center of his life. To be brief, let us say that Francis, as a layman whose mind was not weighed down by doctrinal formulations or by the influence of philosophical currents, gave to the life of Christ an especially radical interpretation. Rereading the Gospel in the light of his own personal experience and that of civic and knightly culture, Francis chose to follow a poor and begging Christ, always on the road and sharing with the marginalized the precariousness of their conditions of life, and to worship a God full of mercy who made the sun shine and the rain fall on the good and the bad alike. In doing this, he was not replicating a model: he was creating one by virtue of his own personal sensibility, which was keen and which made for its originality. In the course of the decades after his death, the Minors clouded the message left by their founder by asserting that their way of life was equivalent to evangelical perfection to the degree that they possessed nothing individually or in common. This definition, which was going to constitute a distinctive trait of their identity, provoked violent conflicts with the secular masters of the University of Paris and the secular clergy, and it soon became a sign of contradiction among the friars themselves. But it now had little to do with the idea that the Poverello had of poverty, and even less with the way that he had lived it.[17]

These last reflections evidence the necessity, not always clearly perceived even in recent times, to distinguish between Francis of Assisi and Franciscanism. Such a statement does not mean that the Friars Minor have, in their collectivity and since the beginning, abandoned or betrayed his message. To say this would be an absurdity. No religious order has maintained such a strong affective bond with its founder or tried as often to call itself back by listening to him through the centuries. But we must recognize that the spiritual families that have claimed him have sometimes been content to repeat formulas that have lost all concrete meaning, whereas authentic fidelity consists in creating a now. The Poor Man of Assisi was the protagonist of another story, different from that of his disciples, which could probably not have succeeded to take shape and be perpetuated in the context of the Church and society of its own time. This relative failure takes nothing away from the pertinence of his message. On the contrary, it is in the measure that it contains within it numerous possibilities which could not be realized in the past that it conserves a real "force of contemporaneousness" and that it still interests us today.[18] Francis has not been the only true Christian that history has ever known, or even perhaps the most perfect. But he has not ceased, since the thirteenth century, to exercise a real fascination on people. And he constitutes even today a figure to whom individuals and societies look to compare themselves in order to find in him, to use the Gospel term, *nova et vetera:* old truths and new ideas.

APPENDIX:
THE *TESTAMENT* OF
FRANCIS OF ASSISI, SEPTEMBER
1226

The introductory paragraph and the following translation are reproduced from FA:ED I, 124–127. It is reprinted here, with a few modifications, by permission of Franciscan Institute Publications.—Trans.

Those "who were with him," the brothers who write in *The Assisi Compilation*, tell of a number of documents or "testaments" which Francis dictated as his health deteriorated and death drew near: that of Siena, in which he outlined the basic principles of his Gospel vision; that concerning the Portiuncula, in which he asked his brothers to care for this special symbol of their life; and another in which he provided guidelines for building new dwellings. The document, which has come to be known as "The Testament," reprinted here below, has remained a primary expression of Francis' profound wisdom and vision. While popular tradition maintains that it was written at the Portiuncula while he was dying, the document's different styles of writing suggest that it was written at different moments during those final days and was prompted by different questions swirling around his simple Gospel vision.

1 The Lord gave me, Brother Francis, thus to begin doing penance in this way: for when I was in sin, it seemed too bitter for me to see lepers. 2 And the Lord Himself led me among them and *I showed mercy* (Sir 35:4) to them. 3 And when I left them, what had seemed bitter to me was turned into sweetness of soul and body. And afterward I delayed a little and left the world.

4 And the Lord gave me such faith in churches that I would pray with simplicity in this way and say: 5 "We adore You, Lord Jesus Christ, in all your churches throughout the whole world and we bless You because by Your holy cross You have redeemed the world."

6 Afterward the Lord gave me, and gives me still, such faith in priests who live according to the rite of the holy Roman Church because of their orders that, were they to persecute me, I would still want to have recourse to them. 7 And if I had as much *wisdom* as *Solomon* (3 Kgs 4:30) and found impoverished priests of this world, I would not preach in

their parishes against their will. 8 And I desire to respect, love, and honor them and all others as my lords. 9 And I do not want to consider any sin in them because I discern the Son of God in them and they are my lords. 10 And I act in this way because, in this world, I see nothing corporally of the most high Son of God except His most holy Body and Blood which they receive and they alone administer to others.

11 I want to have these most holy mysteries honored and venerated above all things and I want to reserve them in precious places. 12 Wherever I find our Lord's most holy names and written words in unbecoming places, I want to gather them up and I beg that they be gathered up and placed in a becoming place. 13 And we must honor all theologians and those who minister the most holy divine words and respect them as those who minister to us *spirit and life* (Jn 6:63).

14 And after the Lord gave me some brothers, no one showed me what I had to do, but the Most High Himself revealed to me that I should live according to the pattern of the Holy Gospel. 15 And I had this written down simply and in a few words and the Lord Pope confirmed it for me. 16 And those who came to receive life gave *whatever they had* (Tb 1:3) to the poor and were content with one tunic, patched inside and out, with a cord and short trousers. 17 We desired nothing more. 18 We clerical [brothers] said the Office as other clerics did; the lay brothers said the *Our Father* (Mt 6:9); and we quite willingly remained in churches. 19 And we were simple and subject to all.

20 And *I worked with* my *hands* (Acts 20:34), and I still desire to work; and I earnestly desire all brothers to give themselves to honest work. 21 Let those who do not know how to work learn, not from desire to receive wages, but for example and to avoid idleness. 22 And when we are not paid for our work, let us have recourse to the table of the Lord, begging alms from door to door. 23 The Lord revealed a greeting to me that we should say: "May *the Lord give* you *peace*" (2 Thess 3:16).

24 Let the brothers be careful not to receive in any way churches or poor dwellings or anything else built for them unless they are according to the holy poverty we have promised in the Rule. As *pilgrims and strangers* (1 Pt 2:11), let them always be guests there.

25 I strictly command all the brothers through obedience, wherever they may be, not to dare to ask any letter from the Roman Curia, either personally or through an intermediary, whether for a church or another place or under the pretext of preaching or the persecution of their bodies. 26 But wherever they have not been received, *let them flee into another* (Mt 10:23) country to do penance with the blessing of God.

27 And I firmly wish to obey the general minister of this fraternity and the other guardian whom it pleases him to give me. 28 And I so wish to be a captive in his hands that I cannot go anywhere or do anything beyond obedience and his will, for he is my master.

29 And although I may be simple and infirm, I nevertheless want to have a cleric always with me who will celebrate the Office for me as it is prescribed in the *Rule*.

30 And let all the brothers be bound to obey their guardians and to recite the Office according to the Rule. 31 And if some might have been found who are not reciting the Office according to the Rule and want to change it in some way, or who are not Catholics, let all the brothers, wherever they may have found one of them, be bound through obedience to bring him before the custos of that place nearest to where they found him. 32 And let

the custos be strictly bound through obedience to keep him securely day and night as a man in chains, so that he cannot be taken from his hands until he can personally deliver him into the hands of his minister. 33 And let the minister be bound through obedience to send him with such brothers who would guard him as a prisoner until they deliver him to the Lord of Ostia, who is the Lord, the Protector and the Corrector of this fraternity.

34 And the brothers may not say: "This is another rule." Because this is a remembrance, admonition, exhortation, and my testament, which I, little brother Francis, make for you, my blessed brothers, that we might observe the Rule we have promised in a more Catholic way.

35 And let the minister general and all the other ministers and custodes be bound through obedience not *to add to* or *take away* (Dt 4:2; 12:32) from these words.

36 And let them always have this writing with them together with the Rule. 37 And in all the chapters which they hold, when they read the Rule, let them also read these words. 38 And I strictly command all my cleric and lay brothers, through obedience, not to place any gloss upon the Rule or upon these words saying: "They should be understood in this way." 39 But as the Lord has given me to speak and write the Rule and these words simply and purely, may you understand them simply and without gloss and observe them with a holy activity until the end.

40 And whoever observes these things, let him be blessed *in heaven with the blessing* of the Most High Father, and *on earth* (cf. Gen 27:27–28) with the blessing of His Beloved Son with the Most Holy Spirit, the Paraclete, and all the powers of heaven and with all the saints. 41 And, as far as I can, I, little brother Francis, your servant, confirm for you, both within and without, this most holy blessing.

Chronology

1182 (or 1183):	birth of a son to Pietro di Bernardone, cloth merchant in Assisi, and his wife, Giovanna. At first named John in the absence of his father, he receives the name of Francis upon his return.
1184:	Peter Waldo (Vaudès) and the Waldensians and the Humiliati of Lombardy are condemned as heretics in Verona by Pope Lucius III.
1198:	insurrection of Assisi against the imperial troops and destruction of the citadel.
1198–July 16, 1216:	pontificate of Innocent III.
1200:	revolt of the popolo of Assisi against the government of noble families, who take refuge in Perugia.
1202:	after the battle at the San Giovanni Bridge at Collestrada where he had fought, Francis is made a prisoner in Perugia for a year.
1203:	peace accord between the popolo of Assisi and the noble families, who return to the city. Francis is freed from prison.
1204:	the long illness of Francis after his imprisonment.
1205:	Francis leaves to join a military expedition in Apulia, but he has to stop at Spoleto and returns to Assisi. Beginning of the process of his conversion.
1206:	in conflict with his father, Francis renounces his goods and his inheritance in the presence of Guido I, bishop of Assisi, and chooses the state of voluntary penitent. He restores several small churches outside the city and devotes himself

to the aid of lepers. A little while later, two bourgeois of Assisi, Bernard of Quintavalle and Peter Cattani, join him.

1208:   Francis decides to live "according to the form of the Holy Gospel." Beginning of the itinerant preaching of the little group of penitents of Assisi, which then numbered twelve members.

1209 (or 1210): Francis and his "fraternity" go to Rome. Wary welcome by the Roman Curia. Finally, Innocent III orally approves the "form of life" which Francis submits to him and gives them authorization to preach penance everywhere.

1210–1211:   stay at Rivo Torto, alternating with preaching tours in central Italy, and transfer of the community to the Portiuncula (the church of Our Lady of Angels).

1212:   during the night of May 18 or 19, Clare, daughter of a nobleman of Assisi, comes to join Francis, who cuts her hair, marking her entrance into the penitential state. After a violent reaction by her family, a community of "Sisters Minor" led by Clare settles in the little church of San Damiano. Francis writes a "form of life" for her.

1212:   the Children's Crusade takes place in Italy. Victory of the Christian kings of Spain over the Muslims at Las Navas de Tolosa. Francis tries to leave for the Muslim east but has to abandon his effort due to a storm.

1215:   Fourth Lateran Council.

1216:   death of Innocent III on July 16. Testimony of Jacques de Vitry, who meets the Friars Minor and Sisters Minor during his time in Perugia. First mention of an annual general chapter.

1216–1217:   pontificate of Honorius III.

1217:   the general chapter of Pentecost decides to send friars beyond Italy. Francis leaves for France, but Cardinal Hugolino, whom he meets in Florence, urges him to return to Italy to protect his fraternity, whose status is fragile.

1219:   after the failure of the first missions, a new sending of friars outside of Italy. On June 11, the first papal bull addressed to the Friars Minor in which the pope attests to their orthodoxy. Francis leaves for the East (in June) and goes to Damietta in Egypt, where he joins the troops of the Fifth Crusade.

At the beginning of September, he meets the sultan, al-Malik al-Kamil. After the capture of the town by the Crusaders, Francis goes back to the Holy Land.

1220:   martyrdom of five Friars Minor in Morocco. Francis returns to Italy. He goes to Viterbo to meet the pope and Cardinal Hugolino, who force him to incorporate the Friars Minor into the institutional framework of religious orders. A novitiate of one year is required before admission. Francis gives up the governance of the order, which is entrusted to Peter Cattani, then to Brother Elias, after Peter's death.

1221:   Francis writes the first rule of the Friars Minor (*regula non bullata*) but meets opposition within the order and from the papacy, which refuses to promulgate it. Sending of an important mission to Germany.

1222 (or 1219):   Chapter of Mats, where Francis refuses to adopt a monastic rule or that of the canons regular for his order. Francis preaches in Bologna on August 15 trying to reestablish peace within the town. Preaching to the birds in Alviano, between Orte and Orvieto.

1223:   Francis draws up a second rule (*regula bullata*) which is finally approved and promulgated by Pope Honorius III in the bull *Solet annuere* (November 29). Hugolino is the first cardinal protector of the order. Christmas at Greccio: the first "crèche."

1224:   *Rule for Hermitages*. Francis, increasingly seriously ill, writes a number of letters. Lent of Saint Michael in solitude upon La Verna (August 15–September 29) and the stigmatization. *Blessing to Brother Leo*. At the end of the year, last preaching tour in Umbria and the Marches.

1225:   Francis receives medical treatment at Fonte Colombo near Rieti, which only aggravates his condition. Beginning of the writing of the *Canticle of Brother Sun* or *The Praises of the Creatures* at San Damiano. The Holy See authorizes the Friars Minor to pray the Office and to celebrate Mass in their churches or on portable altars.

1226:   In the spring, Francis, extremely weakened, dictates a first testament at Siena; taken back to Assisi at the end of the summer, he writes his definitive *Testament* and dictates the final verses of the *Canticle*. Upon his request, he is brought back to the Portiuncula, where he dies during the night of October 3–4. His body is taken inside the city, after stopping in front of the monastery of San Damiano, where Clare and her sisters say their final farewell.

1227:   on March 19, Cardinal Hugolino becomes pope as Gregory IX (r. 1227–1241).

1228 (July 16):   canonization of Francis in Assisi by Gregory IX.

1230 (May 25):   translation of the relics of Francis into the new basilica built in his honor.

MAPS

Central Italy

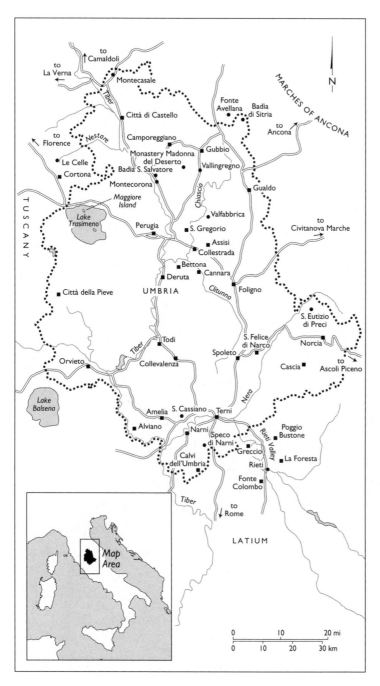

Major Franciscan Sites and Centers of Religious Life in Umbria

ABBREVIATIONS

COMPILATIONS OF EARLY SOURCES RELATING TO FRANCIS,
CLARE, AND THE ORIGINS OF THE ORDER OF FRIARS MINOR

FrDoc   *Saint Francis of Assisi: Documents, Writings, and Early Biographies.* Ed. T. Desbonnets and D. Vorreux. Paris, 1968; 2nd ed., 1981.

ClDoc   *Saint Clare of Assisi: Documents, Biographies, and Writings.* Ed. D. Vorreux. Paris, 1983.

FrÉcrits   *Francis of Assisi: Écrits.* Ed. and trans. T. Desbonnets, T. Matura, J.-F. Godet, and D. Vorreux. Latin and Italian texts translated into French. Paris, 1981.

FF   *Fontes Franciscani.* Ed. E. Menestò and S. Brufani. Contains the Latin texts of the writings of Francis and Clare, and major hagiographical texts of the thirteenth and early fourteenth centuries concerning the two saints. Assisi, 1995.

FFr   *Fonti Francescane.* Ed. E. Caroli. New edition, a translation into Italian of the Franciscan sources from the thirteenth and fourteenth centuries relating to Francis. Padua, 2004.

FA:ED   *Francis of Assisi: Early Documents.* Ed. Regis Armstrong, J. A. Wayne Hellmann, and William Short. English translation from the Latin texts of the writings of Francis of Assisi, major biographies and thirteenth- and early-fourteenth-century hagiographical sources. 3 vols. New York, 1999–2001.

CA:ED   *Clare of Assisi: Early Documents, The Lady.* Ed. Regis Armstrong. English translation from the Latin texts of the writings of Clare of Assisi, major biographies, and documents relating to her canonization. New York, 2006.

PL   Migne, *Patrologia latina.* 222 vols. Paris, 1844–1855.

AF   Analecta franciscana. 10 vols. Quaracchi, 1885–1941.

BF   Bullarium franciscanum. Vols. I–IV. Rome, 1759–1768.

Testimonia minora   Ed. L. Lemmens. Quaracchi, 1926.

NOTES

PREFACE

1. Christian Bobin, *Le Très Bas* (Paris, 1996); Jacques Le Goff, *Saint François d'Assise* (Paris, 1999) (Engl. trans.: *Saint Francis of Assisi* [London, 2004]).

2. Paul Ricoeur, *La Mémoire, l'histoire, l'oubli* (Paris, 2000), 364 (Engl. trans.: *Memory, History, Forgetting* [Chicago, 2004]).

3. Jacques Le Goff, *Saint Louis* (Paris, 1996) (Engl. trans.: *Saint Louis* [Notre Dame, IN, 2009]).

4. Peter Brown, *La Vie de saint Augustin* (Paris, 2001), 655, cited by François Dosse, *Le Pari biographique. Écrire une vie* (Paris, 2005), 314 (Engl trans.: *Augustine of Hippo: A Biography* [Berkeley, CA, 1967]).

5. Raoul Manselli, *Saint François d'Assise* (Rome, 1981) (Engl. trans.: *Saint Francis of Assisi* [Chicago, 1988]); Théophile Desbonnets, *De l'intuition à l'institution: les Franciscains* (Paris, 1983) (Engl. trans.: *From Intuition to Institution: The Franciscans* [Chicago, 1988]); Giovanni Miccoli, *Francesco d'Assisi: Realtà e memoria di un'esperienza cristiana* (Turin, 1991); Grado Giovanni Merlo, *Au nom de saint François. Histoire des Frères mineurs jusqu'au début du XVIe siècle* (Paris, 2006) (Engl. trans.: *In the Name of Saint Francis: History of the Friars Minor and Franciscanism until the Early Sixteenth Century* [Saint Bonaventure, NY, 2009]).

1. FRANCESCO DI BERNARDONE

1. *Paradiso*, XI, 43–48, in *The Divine Comedy of Dante Alighieri: Paradiso: A Verse Translation*, trans. Allen Mandelbaum (Toronto, 1984), 95, slightly adapted. The Tupino (or Topino)—the river that once flowed into the plain that extends to the foot of Assisi—has dried up in modern times and no longer exists. "The water that flows down the hill" is the stream of Chiascio.

2. Thomas of Celano, *The Life of Saint Francis*, in *Francis of Assisi: Early Documents*, I, ed. Regis Armstrong, Jay Hammond and J. A. Wayne Hellmann (New York, 1999), 180–308 (hereafter cited as 1Cel).

3. *Testament*, in *FA:ED* I, 123. I will be referring to this edition and translation every time I cite the writings of Francis, unless otherwise noted.

4. 3Soc 23, in *FA:ED* II, 82–83.

5. Ibid., 4, pp. 69–70.

6. Otto of Freising, *Gesta Friderici I. imperatoris*, II, 13, ed. Bernhard von Simson (Hanover-Leipzig, 1912).

7. Carlo Ginzburg, "Folklore, magia, religione," in *Storia d'Italia*, I: *I Caratteri originali* (Turin, 1972), 614–616.

8. 3Soc 2, in *FA:ED* II, 68–69.

9. Ibid., 4, pp. 69–70.

10. Ibid., 5, p. 70.

11. Thomas of Celano, *The Second Life of Saint Francis* or *The Memorial of the Desire of a Soul* 6, in *FA:ED* II, 245 (hereafter cited as 2Cel). [Translator's note: the author refers to this text, in abbreviated form, as the *Memorial*. We have retained his designation throughout the text].

12. 3Soc 6, in *FA:ED* II, 71.

13. The full English translation of 2Cel is found in *FA:ED* II, 239–393.

14. Cf. Francis De Beer, *La Conversion de saint François selon Thomas de Celano* (Paris, 1963).

15. 3Soc 12, in *FA:ED* II, 75.

16. *Test* 1–3, in *FA:ED* I, 124.

17. Ibid., 3.

18. On the attitudes of thirteenth-century society toward lepers, cf. Girolamo Arnaldi, "San Francesco oggi," *La Cultura* 15 (1977), 102–121, esp. 108, and François-Olivier Touati, "François d'Assise et la diffusion d'un modèle thérapeutique," *Histoire des sciences médicales* 16 (1982), 175–185.

19. *Et feci misericordiam cum illi* (*Test* 3, in *FA:ED* I, 124).

20. Pietro Maranesi, *Facere misericordiam. La conversione di Francesco d'Assisi: confronto critico tra il Testamento e le biografie* (Assisi, 2007).

21. 3Soc 13, in *FA:ED* II, 76.

22. Jacques de Vitry, "Sermo II ad virgines," edited by Joseph Greven in his article "Der Ursprung des Beginenwesens," *Historisches Jahrbuch* 35 (1914), 47.

23. 1Cel 21, in *FA:ED* I, 201.

24. *Test* 3, in *FA:ED* I, 124.

25. 3Soc 13, in *FA:ED* II, 76.

26. 1Cel 22, in *FA:ED* I, 201–202.

27. 1Cel 16, in *FA:ED* I, 194.

28. *Fioretti* [*The Little Flowers of Saint Francis*] 37, in *FA:ED* III, 627–629.

29. *Test* 3, in *FA:ED* I, 124.

30. 3Soc 7, in *FA:ED* II, 82.

2. BROTHER FRANCIS

1. *Test* 1–3, in *FA:ED* I, 124. It is only in 1246–1247, in the *Memorial* of Thomas of Celano, that the "miraculous" version of the account appears, according to which, once Francis had gotten himself back on track after embracing the leper and giving him money, the leper disappeared before his very eyes (2Cel 9, in *FA:ED* II, 248–249).
2. Innocent III, *Letters to the Bishop of Metz* (July–December 1199), in *PL* 214, cols. 695–699.
3. Michel Mollat, *Les Pauvres au Moyen Âge. Étude sociale* (Paris, 1978), esp. 147–191 (Engl. trans.: *The Poor in the Middle Ages: An Essay in Social History*, trans. Arthur Goldhammer [New Haven, 1986], 119–157).
4. Marie-Dominique Chenu, *La Théologie au XIIe siècle* (Paris, 1957), 248–251, as well as the chapter "Le réveil évangélique" (Engl. trans.: *Nature, Man, and Society in the Twelfth Century*, ed. and trans. Jerome Taylor and Lester K. Little [Chicago, 1968], 234–238, esp. chapter 7: "The Evangelical Awakening," 239–269).
5. Cf. *Actus* [*The Deeds of Blessed Francis and His Companions*], in *FA:ED* III, 435 and 511 (hereafter cited as *Deeds*).
6. *Test* 14, in *FA:ED* I, 125.
7. 3Soc 29, in *FA:ED* II, 86.
8. Desbonnets, *From Intuition to Institution*, 5.
9. 3Soc 36, in *FA:ED* II, 88–89.
10. Ibid., 34, p. 88.
11. Cf. G. G. Meersseman, *Dossier de l'ordre de la Pénitence au XIIIe siècle*, 2nd ed. Spicilegium Friburgense 7 (Fribourg, 1982).
12. Jacques de Vitry, *Writings of Jacques de Vitry, Letter I*, in *FA:ED* I, 578–579.
13. Meersseman, *Dossier*, 8–11, 91–112 (the text of the *Memoriale propositi* of 1221–1228).
14. 3Soc 37, in *FA:ED* II, 90.
15. Ibid., 40, p. 92.
16. *Anonymous of Perugia*, 20–22 (hereafter cited as *AP*), in *FA:ED* II, 55–59. The AP, composed in 1240–1241, was for a long time considered anonymous; its real title is *On the beginning or foundation of the order and the acts of the Friars Minor who were the first companions of Saint Francis*. On this text, see Pierre Béguin, *L'Anonyme de Pérouse: Un témoin de la fraternité primitive confronté aux autres sources contemporaines* (Paris, 1978).
17. 1Cel 24, in *FA:ED* I, 203–204.
18. AP 17, in *FA:ED* II, 41.
19. *The Earlier Rule* 9:1, in *FA:ED* I, 70 (hereafter cited as *ER*).
20. Jacques Paul, "La signification sociale du franciscanisme," in *Mouvements franciscains et société française (XIIIe–XIXe siècles)*, ed. André Vauchez (Paris, 1984), 9–25, esp. 19–21.
21. Cf. André Vauchez, "Un modèle hagiographique et culturel en Italie avant saint Roch: Le pèlerin mort en chemin," in *San Rocco: Genesi e prima espansione di un culto*, ed. Antonio Rigon and André Vauchez (Brussels, 2006), 57–70.

22. 3Soc 35, in *FA:ED* II, 88–89.

23. *ER* Prologue and ch. 1, in *FA:ED* I, 63–64.

24. Cf. Jean Becquet, "La première crise de l'ordre de Grandmont," *Études grandmontaines* (Ussel, 1998), 119–160.

25. Cf. André Vauchez, *La Spiritualité du Moyen Âge occidental (VIIIe–XIIIe siècle)* (Paris, 1994), 191–192 (Engl. trans.: *The Spirituality of the Medieval West: The Eighth to the Twelfth Century*, trans. Colette Friedlander [Kalamazoo, MI, 1993], 110–112).

26. On Homobono, see: André Vauchez, "Innocent III, Sicard de Crémone et la canonisation de saint Homebon," in *Innocenzo III: Urbs et orbis*, Vol. I, ed. Andrea Sommerlechner (Rome, 2003), 435–455.

27. Jacques de Vitry, *Letter I*, in *FA:ED* I, 578; and *Histoire occidentale*, ed. Gaston Duchet-Suchaux and Jean Longère (Paris, 1997), 170–173.

28. Burchard of Ursperg, *Chronicon*, in *FA:ED* I, 593–594.

29. On this theme, see: André Vauchez, "Les songes d'Innocent III," in *Francesco d'Assisi e gli ordini mendicanti* (Assisi, 2005), 81–98.

30. Roger of Wendover, *Flores Historiarum*, in Matthew Paris, *Chronica maiora*, ed. H. L. Luard, Rerum Britanicarum Medii Aevi Scriptores 57, no. 3 (London, 1896), 132–133.

31. 1Cel 33, in *FA:ED* I, 212.

32. *AP* 35 and 3Soc 50, in *FA:ED* II, 50 and 97, respectively.

33. Burchard of Ursperg, *Chronicon*, in *FA:ED* I, 593.

34. *Test* 8–10 and 13, in *FA:ED* I, 125.

35. 3Soc 52, in *FA:ED* II, 98.

36. Ibid.: "Blessed Francis and the other eleven brothers were given the tonsure, as the lord cardinal had arranged, wanting all twelve of them to be clerics."

37. Bonaventure of Bagnoregio, *Legenda maior*, III: 10, in *FA:ED* II, 548–549 (hereafter cited as *LMaj*).

38. 2Cel 193, in *FA:ED* II, 371.

39. 1Cel 52, in *FA:ED* I, 228.

40. Cf. Jean-Marie Moeglin, "*Harmiscara, Harmschar, Hachée:* Le dossier des rituels d'humiliation et de soumission au Moyen Âge," *ALMA: Bulletin du Cange* 64 (1996), 11–65. A few decades later, a Parisian preacher, Gilles du Val-des-Écoliers, mentioned from the pulpit that "Christ permitted the *hachée* in order to reconcile us with his Father" (*Christus ut nos Deo patri reconcilaret hacheiam—la haceie— sustinuit pro nobis*): cf. Nicole Bériou, "Latin and the Vernacular: Some Remarks about Sermons delivered on Good Friday during the Thirteenth Century," in *Die deutsche Predigt im Mittelalter*, ed. Volker Mertens and Hans Jochen Schiewer (Tübingen, 1992), 282.

41. Thomas of Celano, *The Legend of Saint Clare*, 8, in *Clare of Assisi: Early Documents*, 286–287 ("*manu fratrum crines deponens*") (hereafter cited as *CA:ED*). Cf. Marco Bartoli, *Clare of Assisi* (Quincy, IL, 1993), 39–46: this was not a monastic tonsure but one given during the ritual for a penitent.

42. Jacques de Vitry, *Letter I* (early October 1216), in *FA:ED* I, 579–580.

43. Text cited by Clare in her rule of 1253: cf. *CA:ED* 6:2, 118.

44. *Acts of the Process of Canonization of Clare of Assisi*, 6:15, in CA:ED, 170.
45. Michele Faloci Pulignani, ed., "San Francesco a Gualdo Tadino," *Miscellanea francescana* 9 (1902), 189–193.
46. Cf. André Vauchez, "Frères mineurs, érémitisme et sainteté laïque: Les *Vies* des saints Maio († c. 1270) et Marzio († 1301) de Gualdo Tadino," *Studi Medievali*, 3rd ser., 27 (1986), 274–305.
47. On the validity of the notion of "revival" applied to medieval history, see Gary Dickson, "Medieval Revivalism," in *Medieval Christianity*, ed. Daniel Bornstein (Minneapolis, 2009), 147–176.
48. Jacques Le Goff, "Le vocabulaire des catégories sociales chez saint François d'Assise et ses biographes du XIIIe siècle," in *Héros du Moyen Âge: Le saint et le roi* (Paris, 1999), 89–128.
49. "Passio sancti Verecundi," in *Testimonia minora saeculi XIII de S. Francisco*, ed. Leonhard Lemmens (Quaracchi, 1926), 10–11.
50. Jordan of Giano, *Chronicle*, chapter 16, in *XIIIth Century Testimonies*, trans. Placid Hermann (Chicago, 1961), 31–32.
51. *Test* 10, in *FA:ED* I, 125.
52. *Letter to the Entire Order*, 30–32, in *FA:ED* I, 119.
53. 3Soc 26, in *FA:ED* II, 84; *Test* 23, in *FA:ED* I, 126.
54. Cf. André Vauchez, "La paix dans les mouvements religieux populaires," in *Pace e guerra nel Basso Medio Evo* (Spoleto, 2004), 313–333; and Nicolas Offenstadt, *Faire la paix au Moyen Âge* (Paris, 2007), esp. 31–48.
55. *Canticle of the Creatures* (hereafter cited as CTC), in *FA:ED* I, 114.
56. Thomas of Spalato, *Historia Salonitanorum atque Spalatinorum pontificum* (Engl. trans. in: *St. Francis of Assisi: Omnibus of Sources*, ed. Marion Habig [Chicago, 1973], 1601–1602) (hereafter cited as *Omnibus of Sources*).
57. *Assisi Compilation* 75, in *FA:ED* II, 178–179 (hereafter cited as AC).
58. Ibid., 74, pp. 177–178.
59. Salimbene de Adam, *Cronica*, Vol. I, ed. Giuseppe Scalia, Scrittori d'Italia (Bari, 1966), 99 (Engl. trans.: *The Chronicle of Salimbene de Adam*, ed. and trans. Joseph L. Baird et al. Medieval and Renaissance Texts and Studies 40 [Binghamton, NY, 1986], 47–48).
60. Alexander of Bremen, *Expositio in Apocalypsim*, ed. A. Wachtel (Weimar, 1959), 469.
61. *Fioretti* 10, in *FA:ED* III, 583.
62. Cf. Thomas of Spalato, *Historia Salonitanorum* (Engl. trans. in *Omnibus of Sources*, 1601).
63. 1Cel 83, in *FA:ED* I, 252–253.
64. Ibid., 62, p. 238.
65. AC 80, *FA:ED* II, 181–182.
66. On the depictions of holiness in the Middle Ages, see André Vauchez, *La Sainteté en Occident aux derniers siècles du Moyen Âge*, 2nd ed. (1988; Rome, 1994), 241.
67. 1Cel 65–66, in *FA:ED* I, 239–240.

68. Cf. Edith Pasztor, "Fonti francescane e storia del francescanesimo nel Duecento: San Francesco, l'agnellino e la scrofa," in *Francesco d'Assisi e la "Questione Francescana"* (Assisi, 2000), 279–280.

69. *AC* 69 and 70, in *FA:ED* II, 172–173.

70. Ibid., 116, pp. 222–223.

71. 2Cel 142, in *FA:ED* II, 339.

72. 3Soc 25, in *FA:ED* II, 84.

73. Thomas of Spalato, *Historia Salonitanorum* (Engl. trans. in *Omnibus of Sources*, 1601).

74. *Later Rule* 9:3, in *FA:ED* I, 105 (hereafter cited as *LR*).

75. "Tanto è il bene che aspecto / ch'ogne pena m'è delecto," *Deeds* 9, in *FA:ED* III, 453.

76. *Letter to the Faithful* (= Long Version), 72–81, in *FA:ED* I, 50–51 (hereafter cited as *EpFid* (Long).

77. *ER* 21, in *FA:ED* I, 78.

78. *EpFid* (Long), 2, in *FA:ED* I, 45.

79. 2Cel 107, in *FA:ED* II, 318.

80. Ibid., pp. 314–315.

81. Ibid., pp. 380–381.

82. Cf. Carlo Delcorno, "Origini della predicazione francescana," in *Francesco d'Assisi e francescanesimo dal 1216 al 1226* (Assisi, 1977), 125–160; and Jean-Claude Schmitt, *La Raison des gestes* (Paris, 1990).

83. *AC* 83, in *FA:ED* II, 185–186.

84. 2Cel 201, in *FA:ED* II, 375–376.

85. Lateran IV, canon 13, in *Decrees of the Ecumenical Councils*, Vol. I, ed. Norman Tanner (London, 1990), 242.

86. *AC* 108, in *FA:ED* II, 216.

87. On the Pastoreaux movement of 1212 and its arrival in Italy, see Gary Dickson, *The Children's Crusade* (London, 2008), 17–35 and 112–115.

88. 1Cel 54–55, in *FA:ED* I, 228–230.

89. Jordan of Giano, *Chronicle*, chaps. 7–9, 24–25.

90. Cited by John V. Tolan, *Saracens: Islam in the Medieval European Imagination* (New York, 2003), 194.

91. Cf. John V. Tolan, *Saint Francis and the Sultan: The Curious History of a Christian-Muslim Encounter* (Oxford, 2009).

92. Jacques de Vitry, *Letter VI*, in *FA:ED* I, 581.

93. Tolan, *The Saint and the Sultan*, 181: "dont dit li cardenals que bien i pooient aller s'ils vouloient, mais ce n'estoit mie par son congiet" (cf. *Chronique d'Ernoul et de Bernard Le Trésorier*, in *FA:ED* I, 605 [hereafter cited as *Chronique d'Ernoul*]).

94. Jordan of Giano, *Chronicle*, chap. 10, 25–26.

95. Jacques de Vitry, *Letter VI*, in *FA:ED* I, 580–581.

96. Jacques de Vitry, *Historia occidentalis*, in *FA:ED* I, 584.

97. 1Cel 57, in *FA:ED* I, 231.

98. *LMaj* IX: 8, in *FA:ED* II, 671.

99. Dante, *The Divine Comedy: Paradiso*, XI, vv. 100–105.

100. Tolan, *Saracens*, 201–202.

101. Louis Massignon, "Mystique musulmane et mystique chrétienne," in *Opera minora*, Vol. II (Beirut, 1972), 482–484; and Tolan, *Saint Francis and the Sultan*, 295.

102. Jordan of Giano, *Chronicle*, chaps. 17–18, 33–36.

103. Cf. *The Acts of the Process of Canonization of Clare of Assisi*, 6, 18–19, in CA:ED, 168–169; and Marco Guida, *Legenda sanctae Clarae virginis* (Rome, 2007), 252.

104. On these martyrs, see Paolo Rossi, *Francescani e islam: I Primi cinque martiri* (Anghiari, 2001); and Tolan, *Saint Francis and the Sultan*, 6. The account of these travails is told in the *Passio sanctorum Martyrum fratrum Beraldi, Petri, Adiuti, Accursii, Othonis in Marochio martyrizatorum*, in *Analecta Franciscana*, III (Quaracchi, 1897), 579–596 (hereafter cited as AF).

105. It is regrettable that John Tolan, in his otherwise excellent book devoted to the encounter of Francis and the sultan, was concerned only with the historiographical issues and did not ask about the specifics and meaning of this event, which, for more than eight centuries, has continuously fascinated people in the West.

106. Jacques de Vitry, *Letter VI*, in *FA:ED* I, 580–581.

107. *Chronique d'Ernoul*, in *FA:ED* I, 606.

108. LMaj IX: 8–9, in *FA:ED* II, 602–604.

109. "Se por grant bien non, se i pooient exploitier" (*Chronique d'Ernoul*, 37) which John Tolan questionably translates in the French original of his volume (*Le Saint chez le sultan*, 75) as "si ce n'était pour le bien de Dieu."

110. *Verba Fratris Illuminati*, in *Omnibus of Sources*, 1614–1615.

111. 2Cel 30, in *FA:ED* II, 265–266.

112. AC 103, in *FA:ED* II, 209.

113. Cf. Henri Bresc, "Les historiens de la croisade: Guerre sainte, justice et paix," *Mélanges de l'École française de Rome. Moyen Âge* 115 (2003), 727–753.

114. Jean Flori, *L'Islam et la fin des temps* (Paris, 2007), 348–350.

115. G. K. Chesterton, *Saint Francis* (New York, 1937), 180.

116. *L'Histoire de Eracles empereur et la conqueste de la Terre d'Outre mer*, ed. Girolamo Golubovich, vol. 1, *Biblioteca bio-bibliografica della Terra Santa* (Quaracchi, 1906), 14.

117. Jordan of Giano, *Chronicle*, chap. 13, 28.

118. 3Soc 63, in *FA:ED* II, 105; 2Cel 23, ibid., pp. 260–261.

119. Thomas of Eccleston, *The Coming of the Friars to England*, chap. 6, in *XIIIth Century Chronicles*, 121.

120. Jacques de Vitry, *Letter VI*, in *FA:ED* I, 580–581.

121. Boncampagno of Signa, *Rhetorica nova*, cited in *Testimonia minora*, 92 (English trans. in: *FA:ED* I, 590).

122. Gabriel Le Bras, *Institutions ecclésiastiques de la chrétienté médiévale*, Vol. I [=A. Fliche and V. Martin, gen. ed., Histoire de l'église 12] (Paris, 1959), 181–182.

123. 2Cel 61, in *FA:ED* II, 287–288.

124. Jordan of Giano, *Chronicle*, chap. 16, 32.

125. AC 81, in *FA:ED* II, 183.

126. 2Cel 133, in *FA:ED* II, 333.

127. *Bullarium Franciscanum*, I, 2 (hereafter cited as BF).

128. *Vita Gregorii papae IX*, in *Testimonia minora*, 12–13 (Engl. trans. in *FA:ED* I, 603).

129. Cf. Werner Maleczek, *Chiara d'Assisi. La questione dell'autenticità del* Privilegium paupertatis *e del* Testamento (Milan, 1995), and, with a contrary point of view, Attilio Bartoli Langeli, *Gli Autografi di Frate Francesco e di Frate Leone*. Corpus Christianorum. Autographa Medii Aevi 5 (Turnhout, 2000), esp. 104–110.

130. *ER* 12:4, in *FA:ED* I, 72–73.

131. Cf. Jacques Dalarun, *Francis and the Feminine* (Saint Bonaventure, NY: 2006).

132. *AC* 18, in *FA:ED* II, 132–133.

133. The text of the *Earlier Rule* is edited and translated in *FA:ED* I, 63–86. Recently a new edition of the Latin text, more reliable than previous versions, has been established by Carlo Paolazzi, *La Regula non bullata dei Frati Minori* (Grottaferrata, 2007), 125–148.

134. The full text of the *Later Rule* is edited and translated in *FA:ED* I, 99–106.

135. Cf. David Flood and Thaddée Matura, *The Birth of a Movement: A Study of the First Rule of St. Francis* (Chicago, 1975); and David Flood, *Francis of Assisi and the Franciscan Movement* (Quezon City, 1989).

136. *ER* 1:1–2, in *FA:ED* I, 63–64.

137. *Admonition* 2, 2–4, in *FA:ED* I, 129.

138. *ER* 9:7–9, in *FA:ED* I, 70.

139. Ibid., 8:6.

140. *AC* 96, in *FA:ED* II, 198–199.

141. *ER* 9:6–8, in *FA:ED* I, 71.

142. *ER* 7:1–9, in *FA:ED* I, 68–69.

143. *AC* 114, in *FA:ED* II, 220–221.

144. Ibid., 64, 93 and 113, pp. 167, 196, 220, respectively.

145. *ER* 7:13, in *FA:ED* I, 69.

146. *AC* 52 and 57, in *FA:ED* II, 151–152, 158–159.

147. *ER* 10 and 15, in *FA:ED* I, 71, 73.

148. Ibid., 17:6–7, p. 75.

149. Cf. Georges Duby, *The Three Orders: Feudal Society Imagined* (Chicago, 1982).

150. *ER* 17:3–4, in *FA:ED* I, 75.

151. *A Rule for Hermitages*, 10, in *FA:ED* I, 62.

152. *ER* 6:3–4, in *FA:ED* I, 68.

153. Ibid., 5:4, p. 67.

154. Carolyn Walker Bynum, *Jesus as a Mother: Studies in the Spirituality of the High Middle Ages* (Berkeley, 1982).

155. *ER* 5:14, in *FA:ED* I, 67–68.

156. *Admonition* 3, 5, in *FA:ED* I, 130.

157. *ER* 9:10–11, in *FA:ED* I, 71.

158. Ibid., 9:12.

159. Jacques de Vitry, *Letter I*, in *FA:ED* I, 579.

160. *ER* 3:4, in *FA:ED* I, 65.
161. 2Cel 31, in *FA:ED* II, 266–267, and AC 72, ibid., 174.
162. *Admonition* 1, 16, in *FA:ED* I, 129.
163. *ER* 9:1, in *FA:ED* I, 70.
164. *Letter to a Minister*, 1–2 and 5–9, in *FA:ED* I, 97. On this text, see Erich Auerbach, *Mimesis: The Representation of Reality in Western Literature* (Princeton, 1953), 165–168, who stresses that "parataxis becomes a weapon of eloquence."
165. *Letter to a Minister*, 14–17, in *FA:ED* I, 98.
166. *ER* 12 and 13, in *FA:ED* I, 72–73.
167. Ibid., 16:1–2, p. 74.
168. Ibid., 16:5–7.
169. *LR* 12, in ibid, p. 106.
170. Thomas of Chobham, *Summa de arte praedicandi*, ed. Franco Morenzoni (Turnhout, 1988), 85–86, cited by Flori, *L'Islam et la fin des temps*, 349.
171. Jacques de Vitry, *Historia occidentalis*, in *FA:ED* I, 584–585.
172. *ER* 16:12–13, in *FA:ED* I, 74.
173. *Letter to the Rulers of the Peoples*, 7–8, in *FA:ED* I, 58–59.
174. *First Letter to the Custodes*, 8, in *FA:ED* I, 56.
175. 1Cel 82, in *FA:ED* I, 251.
176. *Test* 12, in *FA:ED* I, 125.
177. English translation of the bull *Solet annuere* (containing the text of the *Later Rule*) is found in *FA:ED* I, 99–106.
178. *Letter to Brother Anthony of Padua*, in *FA:ED* I, 107.
179. AC 101, in *FAED* II, 204.
180. Ibid., 104, p. 209.
181. *True and Perfect Joy*, in *FA:ED* I, 166.
182. AC 109, in *FA:ED* II, 217.
183. *True and Perfect Joy*, in *FA:ED* I, 167.
184. 2Cel 188, in *FA:ED* II, 366–367.
185. AC 106, in *FA:ED* II, 211.
186. 2Cel 197, in *FA:ED* II, 373–374.
187. *Epistola encyclica de transitu sancti Francisci*, in *Annales Minorum*, II, ed. Luke Wadding (1732; Quaracchi, 1931), 167–169 [and also in *AF*, X, 525–528]; in a recent English translation, the encyclical appears as *A Letter on the Passing of Saint Francis attributed to Elias of Assisi*, in *FA:ED* II, 489–491. This text, certainly authentic in its substance, has come down to us only in a late version, bristling with textual difficulties.
188. 1Cel 94, in *FA:ED* I, 263–264.
189. AC 118, in *FA:ED* II, 226–227.
190. *The Praises of God*, 5, in *FA:ED* I, 109.
191. *A Blessing for Brother Leo*, in *FA:ED* I, 112.
192. 2Cel 115 and 116, in *FA:ED* II, 324–325.
193. *Testament of Siena* (cf. AC 59), in *FA:ED* II, 161–162.
194. *Test* 34, in *FA:ED* I, 123–127.

195. Ibid., 1 and 14, pp. 124, 125.
196. Ibid., 31, p. 127.
197. Oretta Muzzi, "Il comune di Colle Valdelsa e gli insediamenti mendicanti," in *Gli ordini mendicanti in Val d'Elsa. Convegno di studio*, Miscellanea storica della Val d'Elsa 15 (Castelfiorentino, 1999), 261–278.
198. Grado Giovanni Merlo, *In the Name of Saint Francis*, 68.
199. *Test* 39, in *FA:ED* I, 127.

3. BECOMING SAINT FRANCIS

1. *AP* 99, in *FA:ED* II, 202–203.
2. Ibid., 6–7, pp. 120–121.
3. Ibid., pp. 121–123.
4. 1Cel 124–126, in *FA:ED* I, 293–297.
5. Ernst Kantorowicz, *Frederick the Second, 1194–1250* (New York, 1957). This thesis has been taken up again and clarified by Wolfgang Schenkluhn, *San Francesco in Assisi: Ecclesia specialis* (Milan, 1994; 1st ed. in German: Darmstadt, 1991).
6. Cf. André Vauchez, *La Sainteté en Occident*, 71–98.
7. On this question, as on so many others, we benefit by consulting the dissertation of Michael F. Cusato (Sorbonne, 1991), which unfortunately remains unpublished: "La Renonciation au pouvoir chez les Frères mineurs au XIIIe siècle," Vol. I, 195–197.
8. 1Cel 54, in *FA:ED* I, 229.
9. Jordan of Giano, *Chronicle*, chap. 59, 62–64.
10. 3Soc 2 and 4, in *FA:ED* II, 68, 70; and 2Cel 4, ibid., p. 243.
11. Jacques Dalarun has proposed also attributing to Celano the redaction of the *Umbrian Legend*, which was composed between 1237 and 1244: cf. Jacques Dalarun, *Vers une résolution de la question franciscaine: La* Légende ombrienne *de Thomas de Celano* (Paris, 2007).
12. *FA:ED* I, 180–308.
13. See, in particular, the important study of Raimondo Michetti, *Francesco d'Assisi e il paradosso della* minoritas: La Vita beati Francisci *di Tommaso da Celano* (Rome, 2004), which has profoundly renewed our approach to and understanding of this text.
14. 1Cel 18 and 116, in *FA:ED* I, 197, 285.
15. On the role given to the basilica of Assisi by the papacy and on the stages of its construction, see Guy Lobrichon, *Les Fresques de la basilique inférieure d'Assise* (Paris, 1985), and Serena Romano, *La Basilica di San Francesco in Assisi: Pittori, botteghe, strategie narrative* (Rome, 2001).
16. Thomas of Eccleston, *The Coming of the Friars Minor to England*, in *XIIIth Century Chronicles*, chap. 13, 153.
17. *Speravimus hactenus* (June 30, 1230), in *Annales Minorum*, II, 261.
18. Richard Trexler, "The Stigmatized Body of Francis of Assisi conceived, processed, disappeared," in *Frömmigkeit im Mittelalter*, ed. Klaus Schreiner (Berlin, 2001),

463–497; Roger of Wendover, "Flores historiarum," in Matthew Paris, *Chronica maiora*, 134–135 (in Engl. trans.: *FA:ED* I, 601).

19. 1Cel 118, in *FA:ED* I, 286–287.

20. 1Cel 106, in *FA:ED* I, 274–275.

4. THE "SECOND DEATH" OF FRANCIS

1. The bull *Quo elongati* (September 28, 1230), in *BF*, I, 68–70.

2. The bull *Nimis iniqua* (August 21, 1231), trans. into French in Gratien de Paris, *Histoire de la fondation et de l'évolution de l'ordre des Frères mineurs au XIIIe siècle* (Paris, 1928), 123–124.

3. Salimbene, *Cronica*, Vol. I, 144–147 (in Engl. trans. in *The Chronicle of Salimbene of Adam*, 81–83).

4. "Mal vedemo Parisi/che àne destrutt' Assisi," in Jacopone da Todi, *Laude* XXXI (91), ed. Franco Mancini (Bari, 1974), 293.

5. Elias of Cortona, *Epistola encyclica*, in *Annales Minorum*, II, 168.

6. 1Cel 90, in *FA:ED* I, 260–261.

7. 3Cel 8–9, in *FA:ED* II, 405–406.

8. The bull of Gregory IX, *Usque ad terminos* (April 11, 1237), cited by André Vauchez, *Religion et société dans l'Occident médiéval* (Turin, 1980), 145.

9. The texts of these hymns are found in *AF*, X, 372–388 (and, in Engl. trans. in *FA:ED* I, 327–45). On their meaning, see Michael F. Cusato, *La renonciation au pouvoir*, Vol. I, 218–228.

10. Thomas of Pavia, *Liber exemplorum Fratrum minorum* (Engl. trans. in *FA:ED* III, 793–796).

11. *Fioretti*, 24, in *FAED* III, 605–607.

12. See Damien Ruiz, "Le chapitre d'Arles (1224–1226) ou la rencontre de François et d'Antoine: Un échange de charismes," *Il Santo* 43 (2003), 445–459.

13. *Sacrum commercium beati Francisci cum domina Paupertate* (Engl. trans. in *FA:ED* I, 529–554).

14. Ibid., 13, in *FA:ED* I, 533.

15. Ibid., 37–51, in *FA:ED* I, 542–548.

16. Ibid., 63, in *FA:ED* I, 552.

17. On this process and, more broadly, on the relationship between Clare of Assisi and the papacy, see Maria Pia Alberzoni, *Chiara e il papato* (Milan, 1995).

18. *The Last Will*, in *Omnibus of Sources*, 76 and *CA:ED*, 118, vv. 7–9.

19. LR 11, in *FA:ED* I, 106.

20. *The Legend of Saint Clare*, 37, in *CA:ED*, 311–312.

21. *The Second Letter of Clare to Agnes of Prague* (1235), in *CA:ED*, 48–49.

22. Thomas of Eccleston, *The Coming of the Friars Minor to England*, chap. 13, 156.

23. *BF*, I, 290, 541, 560.

24. Cf. Giuseppina De Sandre Gasparini, Introduzione to *Le carte dei lebbrosi veronesi fra XII–XIII secolo*, ed. Annamaria Rossi Saccomani (Padua, 1989), 1–20.

25. Matthew Paris, *Chronica maiora*, 98.
26. Giuseppe Abate, ed., "Vita prima," *Miscellanea francescana* 52 (1952), 227–231.
27. *The Acts of the Process of Canonization*, 3, 29, in CA:ED, 161.
28. *Fioretti*, 15, in FA:ED III, 590–591.
29. *The Acts of the Process of Canonization*, 13, 3, in CA:ED, 186.
30. One can find the text in English translation in CA:ED, 108–126. On the significance of this rule, see Marco Bartoli, *Clare of Assisi*, 94–97.
31. *The Form of Life of Saint Clare*, in CA:ED, 109.
32. 1Cel 18 and 116, in FA:ED I, 196–197 and 284–285.
33. 3Cel 37, in FA:ED II, 417–418.
34. The bull *Quia pietas* (January 2, 1199), in *Das Register Innocenz III*, ed. Othmar Hageneder and Anton Haidacher (Graz, 1964), 761–764. On this individual, see André Vauchez, "Le trafiquant céleste: Saint Homebon de Crémone († 1197), marchand et père des pauvres," in *Horizons maritimes, itinéraires spirituels (Mélanges Michel Mollat)*, Vol. I, ed. Henri Dubois, Jean-Claude Hocquet, and André Vauchez (Paris, 1987), 115–122.
35. On this movement, see Augustine Thompson, *Revival Preachers and Politics in Thirteenth-Century Italy: The Great Devotion of 1233* (Oxford, 1992); and André Vauchez, "Une campagne de pacification en Lombardie autour de 1233," in Vauchez, *Religion et société dans l'Occident médiéval*, 71–118. See also *La pace fra realtà e utopia* (Verona, 2005) [*Quaderni di storia religiosa* 12 (2005)].
36. *Letter to the Rulers of the Peoples*, 7, in FA:ED I, 58–59.
37. Thomas of Eccleston, *The Coming of the Friars Minor to England*, chap. 5, 117.
38. Henri d'Avranches, *The Versified Life of Saint Francis*, in FA:ED I, 480, vv. 173–176.
39. "Frater mi simplizone." Cf. AC 97, in FA:ED II, 200.
40. Salimbene, *Cronica*, Vol. I, 86; Vol. II, 595–596, 605–606, 609 (Engl. trans., *The Chronicle of Salimbene de Adam*, 37–38, 415, 423–424, 426). On Salimbene's attitude toward Francis, see Edith Pasztor, "L'esperienza religiosa nella *Cronica* di Salimbene," in *Salimbene da Parma: Curiosità umana ed esperienza politica in un francescano di sette secoli fa. Studi in occasione delle celebrazioni nel VII centenario della morte di Fra Salimbene da Parma (1221–1277)* (Bologna, 1987), 13–21 (*Zenit Quaderni: Supplemento*).
41. Thomas of Eccleston, *The Coming of the Friars Minor to England*, chap. 10, 140; chap. 13, 158.

5. MEDIEVAL INTERPRETATIONS OF FRANCIS

1. Cf. A. Vauchez, "Les réactions face aux ordres mendiants dans les chroniques rédigées en France au XIIIe siècle," in *Finances, pouvoir et mémoire: Hommage à Jean Favier* (Paris, 1999), 539–548.
2. Hippolyte Delehaye, *Cinq leçons sur la méthode hagiographique* (Brussels, 1934), 146.
3. Cf. Christian Ducoq, "A propos Francis: The Theological Value of the Legend," in *Francis of Assisi Today*, 81–85.

4. "*Plus suis nutritoribus/se gessit insolenter*," replaced by "*Divinis charismatibus/preventus est clementer*." Cf. André Vauchez, *La Sainteté en Occident*, 601–602.

5. But this mention of Perugia simply refers to the fact that one of its manuscripts—no longer extant—was found in this city. It is better to refer to this text by the first words of its title: *On the Beginning or Foundation of the Order and Deeds of the Friars Minor who first entered and were the Companions of Saint Francis*] (*De inceptione*, in Latin). On this text, cf. Pierre Béguin, *L'Anonyme de Pérouse* (Paris, 1979), and Jacques Dalarun, *The Misadventure of Francis of Assisi* (Saint Bonaventure, NY, 2002), 176–189.

6. Cf. FA:ED II, 66–67.

7. *Scripta Leonis, Rufini et Angeli, sociorum S. Francisci*, ed. and trans. Rosalind B. Brooke (Oxford, 1970); Jacques Cambell, *I Fiori dei tre compagni* (Milan, 1967); Raoul Manselli, *Nos qui cum eo fuimus, Contributo alla Questione Francescana* (Rome, 1980).

8. Thomas of Celano, *Vita secunda* [2Cel], in FA:ED II, 239–393.

9. *Compilatio Assisiensis* [AC], in *Fontes Franciscani*, ed. Enrico Menestò and Stefano Brufani (Assisi, 1995), 1471–1690. We will usually refer to this text rather than to that of the *Legend of Perugia*, which constitutes the original core of this compilation. On the exact relationship between these two texts, see Dalarun, *The Misadventure of Francis*, 204–219.

10. Cf. Dalarun, *The Misadventure of Francis*, 207–215.

11. As Giovanni Miccoli has shown in his wonderful book *Francesco d'Assisi: Realtà e memoria di un'esperienza cristiana* (Turin, 1991). On this great historian who has profoundly renewed the knowledge and understanding that we are able to have of the Franciscan phenomenon, see André Vauchez, "François d'Assise rendu à l'histoire: l'oeuvre de Giovanni Miccoli," *Études franciscaines*, n.s. 1 (2008), 7–19.

12. Cf. Jacques Dalarun, "Comment détruire les légendes franciscaines?" in *Miscellanea Bibliothecae Apostolicae Vaticanae*, Vol. XIV (Vatican City, 2007), 215–229.

13. Bonaventure of Bagnoregio, *Legenda maior* [LMaj], in FA:ED II, 525–649. On this text, cf. Dalarun, *The Misadventure of Francis*, 234–245.

14. As Joseph Ratzinger has shown in his thesis *The Theology of History in St. Bonaventure*, trans. Zachary Hayes (Chicago, 1971), 1–55; see also Miccoli, *Francesco d'Assisi*, 281–302.

15. *LMaj* Prologue, 1, in FA:ED II, 526–527.

16. *Epistola de tribus quaestionibus*, in Bonaventure, *Opera omnia*, Vol. VIII, 336. Cf. Miccoli, *Francesco d'Assisi*, 264–280.

17. *LMaj* I: 5, in FA:ED II, 533–534. But Thomas of Celano had already said the same thing in his *Vita secunda*.

18. *Test* 26, in FA:ED I, 125.

19. Cf. Angelo Clareno, *Historia septem tribulationum ordinis minorum*, ed. Orietta Rossini and Hanno Helbling (Rome, 1999), 179–184 (for the vision of James of Massa).

20. A *Mirror of Perfection* [SP], in FA:ED III, 253–372; on the origin of this work, cf. Jacques Dalarun, "À propos de quelques sources franciscaines: Plaidoyer pour l'histoire des textes," *Journal des savants* (2007), 319–358.

21. "Ma non fia da Casal ne d'Acquasparta/Laonde vegnon tali a la scrittura/ch'l'uno la fugge e altro la coarta" (*Paradiso*, XII, vv. 124–126). The English translation is slightly adapted from *The Divine Comedy of Dante Alighieri: A Verse Translation*, trans. Allen Mandelbaum (Berkeley, 1984), 108.

22. *Deeds*, in *FA:ED* III, 435–565.

23. *Fioretti*, in *FA:ED* III, 566–658; *Considerations on the Holy Stigmata*, in *Omnibus of Sources*, 1429–1474.

24. Frédéric Ozanam, *Les poètes franciscains, avec un choix des petites fleurs de saint François* (Paris, 1852), 282.

25. *Fioretti* 24, in *FA:ED* III, 606.

26. Ibid., 34, pp. 625–626.

27. Ibid., 21, pp. 601–604.

28. Ibid., 15, pp. 590–591.

29. *"Franciscus quasi alter Christus datus in mundo,"* in *Deeds* 6, 1, in *FA:ED* III, 448.

30. *De conformitate*, in *AF*, IV and V (Quaracchi, 1907–1912).

31. Chiara Frugoni, *Francesco, un'altra storia* (Genoa, 1988); Chiara Frugoni, *Francesco e l'invenzione delle stimmate* (Turin, 1993).

32. Cf. 1Cel 83, in *FA:ED* I, 253.

33. Cf. Francesco Mores, *Alle origini dell'immagine di Francesco d'Assisi* (Padua, 2004).

34. As has been nicely demonstrated by Pietro Scarpellini, "Iconografia francescana nei secoli XIII e XIV," in *Francesco d'Assisi: Storia e Arte* (Milan, 1982), 91–126. See also Eamon Duffy, "Finding St. Francis: Early Images, Early Lives," in *Medieval Theology and the Natural Body*, ed. Peter Biller and Alastair J. Minnis (New York, 1997), 193–236; William R. Cook, *Images of St Francis of Assisi* [. . .] *from the Earliest Images to 1320 in Italy: A Catalogue* (Florence, 1999).

35. Frugoni, *Francesco, un'altra storia*; Chiara Frugoni, "Francesco, un vescovo e due pontifici," in *Francesco a Roma dal signor Papa*, ed. Alvaro Cacciotti and Maria Melli (Rome, 2008), 247–342.

36. The detailed plan of this cycle can be found in Guy Lobrichon, *Les Fresques de la basilique inférieure d'Assise* (Paris, 1985), 66–77, with numerous photographic reproductions of the surviving frescoes.

37. On this cycle of frescoes, whose artistic importance is fundamental, cf. Giuseppe Basile, *Giotto: Le storie francescane ad Assisi* (Milan, 2001); Joanna Cannon, "Giotto and Art for the Friars," in *The Cambridge Companion to Giotto*, ed. Anne Derbes and Mark Sandona (Cambridge, 2003), 255–266.

38. As Rosalind Brooke has shown in *The Image of Saint Francis: Responses to Sainthood in the Thirteenth Century* (Cambridge, 2006), 382–415.

39. Cf. William R. Cook, "Giotto and the Figure of Saint Francis," in *The Cambridge Companion to Giotto*, 135 ff. and 268 ff.

40. On this painting of Bellini, today in the Frick Collection in New York, cf. John V. Fleming, *From Bonaventure to Bellini: An Essay in Franciscan Exegesis* (Princeton, 1982).

41. Elias of Cortona, *A Letter on the Passing of Saint Francis*, in *FA:ED* II, 489–491.

42. 1Cel 94–95, in *FA:ED* I, 263–265.

43. Ibid., 113, pp. 280–281.
44. *Passional allemand*, vv. 1576–1581, cited by Élie Berger, "La forme des stigmates de saint François," *Revue d'histoire ecclésiastique* 35 (1939), 60–70.
45. Philippe Mouskès, *Chronique rimée*, vv. 30347–30360, rpt. in *Saint François d'Assise: Documents, écrits et premières biographies*, 2nd rev. ed., ed. and trans. Théophile Desbonnets and Damien Vorreux (Paris, 1981), 1454: "A Perrouse gist li cors sains / Ki n'ot mie mains ni pies sains."
46. Cf. Attilio Bartoli Langeli, *Gli autografi di Frate Francesco e di Frate Leone* (Turnhout, 2000), 31–32.
47. Thomas of Eccleston, *The Coming of the Friars Minor to England*, chap. 13, 161.
48. AC 118, in *FA:ED* II, 227.
49. *LMaj* 13: 9, in *FA:ED* II, 637.
50. Ibid., 13: 3, pp. 632–633.
51. "*Mens in carne patuit*" (Bonaventure, *Itinerarium mentis in Deum*, VII, 3).
52. Note that the sanctoral of the office of the Dominican order, drawn up under the direction of Humbert of Romans between 1254 and 1256, when it comes to the feast of Saint Francis on the date of October 4, does not refer, in mentioning the stigmatization, to the Life of Thomas of Celano or to any other biography of Franciscan origin but to the Life *Quasi stella*, the work of a curial official in the entourage of Gregory IX. Moreover, it limits itself to the modest characterization, "In a hermitage [*in heremitorio quodam*], a man [*vir quidam*] who had the appearance of a Seraph who was as if hanging [*quasi patibulo crucis affixus*] on the gibbet of the cross appeared to him and impressed into his hands and feet scars that were like nail marks [*quasi stigmata clavorum*], while on his right side there appeared the scar of a wound produced by the lance which had pierced it." Cf. Anne-Élisabeth Urfels-Capot, *Le Sanctoral de l'office dominicain (1254–1256)* (Paris, 2007), 386.
53. Cf. André Vauchez, "Les stigmates de saint François et leurs détracteurs," in Vauchez, *Religion et société*, 152–156.
54. "De inventione montis Alvernie," in *Deeds* 9, in *FA:ED* III, 452–458; *Considerations on the Holy Stigmata*, in *Omnibus of Sources*, 1429–1436.
55. *De conformitate*, in *AF*, IV, 38, and V, 387–388.
56. Cited by André Vauchez, "Les stigmates de saint François," in Vauchez, *Religion et société*, 163.
57. Trexler, "The Stigmatized Body of Francis of Assisi," 463–497.
58. Jacques de Vitry, *The Life of Saint Mary of Oignies (Vita B. Mariae Oignacensis)*, in *Acta Sanctorum (Iun., V)*, (Paris, 1867), 552.
59. Frugoni, *Francesco e l'invenzione delle stimmate*.
60. 2Cel 203, in *FA:ED* II, 377.

6. FRANCIS BETWEEN HISTORY AND MYTH

1. Cf. Raymond Trousson, *Romans libertins du XVIIIe siècle* (Paris, 1993), 587–594.
2. *Le Voyage en Italie du président de Brosses, 1739–1740*, ed. Hubert Juin (Paris, 1964), 263.

3. Bruno Foucart, "Saint François d'Assise et l'art français du XIXe siècle," *Revue d'histoire de l'Église de France* 70 (1984), 157–166.

4. Texts cited by Matthieu Brejon de Lavergnée in his "Ozanam et Assise: Genèse du regard romantique sur le Moyen Âge," *Études franciscaines*, n.s. 1 (2008), 89–111.

5. Jules Michelet, *Histoire de France* (Paris, 1981), 360–363.

6. Cf. Ernest Renan, *Nouvelles études d'histoire religieuse*, rev. 2nd ed. (Paris, 1884), 323–351 (though the texts themselves go back to 1866).

7. Ibid., 341.

8. Ibid., 325.

9. Ibid., 350.

10. Paul Sabatier, *Vie de saint François* (Paris, 1894), 32 (Engl. trans.: *Life of Saint Francis of Assisi* [New York, 1894]). A first printing, with a very small run, had appeared in 1893. Its favorable reception inspired a new edition soon after; this 1894 edition is the one usually cited.

11. *Speculum perfectionis*, ed. Paul Sabatier (Paris, 1898).

12. Arnaldo Fortini, *Assisi nel Medioevo* (Assisi, 1940); Arnaldo Fortini, *Nuova Vita di San Francesco*, 5 vols. (1926; Assisi, 1959). Two parts of Volume 1 were published in a translation by Helen Moak, as *Francis of Assisi* (New York, 1981).

13. Agostino Gemelli, *Il Francescanesimo*, 2nd ed. (Milan, 1933) (Engl. trans.: *The Message of St. Francis*, trans. Paul J. Oligny [Chicago, 1964]). About this author, see Maria Bocci, *Agostino Gemelli rettore e francescano: Chiesa, regime e democrazia* (Brescia, 2007).

14. Cf. the volume *Paul Sabatier e gli studi francescani: Atti del XXX Convegno della Società internazionale di studi francescani* (Assisi, 2003), esp. 483–490.

15. *Analecta franciscana*, 10 vols. (Grottaferrata, 1895–1941), in particular Volume X, which contains the critical edition of the medieval Lives of Francis (in Latin); Kajetan Esser, *Die Opuscula des hl. Franz von Assisi: Neue textkritische Edition*. Spicilegium Bonaventurianum 13 (Grottaferrata, 1976), on which the modern translations of the writings of Francis have, until recently, been based (a revised 2nd edition was published in 1989).

16. See the Bibliography for references to their principal works.

17. Raimondo Michetti, "Francesco d'Assisi e l'essenza del cristianesimo," in *Francesco d'Assisi fra storia, letteratura e iconografia*, ed. Franca Ela Consolino (Soveria Manelli, 1996), 42.

18. Frédéric Ozanam, *Les poètes franciscains*, 61–62.

19. Cf. Jean-Marie Mayeur, "Tiers ordre franciscain et catholicisme social en France à la fin du XIXe siècle," in *Mouvements franciscains et société française* (Paris, 1984), 181.

20. Antonio Gramsci, *Quaderni del carcere*, Vol. III (Turin, 1975), 2036.

21. Leonardo Boff, *François d'Assise, force et tendresse: Une lecture à partir des pauvres* (Paris, 1986) (Engl. trans.: *Saint Francis: A Model for Human Liberation*, trans. John W. Diercksmeier [New York, 1982]).

22. Albert Jacquart, *Le Souci des pauvres: L'héritage de François d'Assise* (Paris, 1996).

23. Ernesto Balducci, *L'Uomo planetario* (Milan, 1985); Ernesto Balducci, *Francesco d'Assisi* (San Domenico di Fiesole, 1989). On this individual and his work, see the comments of Grado Giovanni Merlo in his *Tra eremo e città* (Assisi, 2007), 4–15.

24. Cf. J.-M. Tichi, "Assise dans l'imaginaire français des XIXe et XXe siècles," in *Cent ans de présence des Clarisses françaises à Assise (1908–2008)* (Florence, 2008), 315–336; Jean-Dominique Durand, *L'Esprit d'Assise* (Paris, 2005); François Boespflug and Yves Labbé, *Assise dix ans après* (Paris, 1996).

25. Cf. Christian Renoux, *La Prière pour la paix attribuée à saint François: Une énigme à résoudre* (Paris, 2001).

26. John V. Tolan, *Saint Francis and the Sultan: The Curious History of a Christian-Muslim Encounter,* 294–307.

27. Cf. Tolan, *Saint Francis and the Sultan,* 299–314.

28. *Paradiso,* XI, 64–66, trans. Jacqueline Risset, 111.

29. Julien Green, *Frère François* (Paris, 1983) (Engl. trans: *God's Fool: The Life and Times of Francis of Assisi* [San Francisco, 1985]); cf. also Julien Green, *Journal 1943–45,* in *OEuvres complètes,* Vol. IV (Paris, 1975), 741.

30. Renan, *Nouvelles études d'histoire religieuse,* 334; the Galilee program which Renan mentions here is that of the preaching of Jesus in Galilee, at the start of his public life, as it is described in the Gospel of Mark.

31. Gramsci, *Quaderni dal carcere,* Vol. III, 2086.

32. Giovanni Miccoli, "La storia religiosa," in *Storia d'Italia,* Vol. II, 1 (Turin, 1974), 787.

33. Miccoli, *Francesco d'Assisi: Realtà e memoria di una esperienza cristiana* (Turin, 1991).

34. Cf. See the previously cited articles of Raimondo Michetti, "Francesco d'Assisi e l'essenza del cristianesimo," and André Vauchez, "François d'Assise rendu à l'histoire: L'oeuvre de Giovanni Miccoli."

PART IV. THE ORIGINALITY OF FRANCIS AND HIS CHARISM: THE WRITINGS OF FRANCIS

1. Until quite recently (2010), the touchstone has been the critical edition of Kajetan Esser, *Die Opuscula des hl. Franz von Assisi.* Spicilegium Bonaventurianum 13 (Grottaferrata, 1976), upon which the French and English translations were established. Cf., respectively, Théophile Desbonnets, Jean François Godet et al., eds., *François d'Assise. Écrits.* Sources chrétiennes 285 (Paris, 1981), and Regis A. Armstrong, J. A. Wayne Hellmann and William Short, eds., *Francis of Assisi: Early Documents,* Vol. I (New York, 1999).

7. THE EXPERIENCE OF GOD

1. *A Blessing for Brother Leo,* in FA:ED I, 112.

2. "*Tu es tota dulcedo nostra,*" quoted from *The Praises of God,* in FA:ED I, 109.

3. Sigmund Freud, *Malaise de la civilisation* (1929), ed. and trans. Ch. and J. Odier (Paris, 1971), 52–53 (Engl. trans. as *Civilization and Its Discontents*, trans. James Strachey [New York, 1962]), 49.

4. *The Praises of God*, 1–2, in *FA:ED* I, 109.

5. *ER* 23:1–11, in *FA:ED* I, 81–86.

6. *Admonition 1*, 5, in *FA:ED* I, 128.

7. *CTC* 2, in *FA:ED* I, 113.

8. Cf. Christian Bobin, *Le Très Bas*.

9. *EpFid* (Long), 4–5, in *FA:ED* I, 46.

10. 1Cel 86, in *FA:ED* I, 256.

11. 2Cel 199–200, in *FA:ED* II, 374–375; the actual citation is from 2Cel 200, 375.

12. *First Letter to the Custodes*, in *FA:ED* I, 55–56.

13. 2Cel 196, in *FA:ED* II, 373.

14. *Test* 20, in *FA:ED* I, 125.

15. *EpFid* (Long), 49–53, in *FA:ED* I, 48–49.

8. A NEW RELATIONSHIP TO SCRIPTURE

1. Walter Map, *De Nugis curialium*, 1, 31, ed. M. R. James (Oxford, 1914), 60–61 (partial Engl. trans. in Rosalind B. Brooke, *The Coming of the Friars*, Historical Problems: Studies and Documents 24 (London, 1976), 151–152.

2. *EpFid* (Long), 34, in *FA:ED* I, 47–48.

3. *The Office of the Passion*, in *FA:ED* I, 139–157.

4. 3Soc 28, in *FA:ED* II, 85.

5. *Test* 14, in *FA:ED* I, 125.

6. 2Cel 91, in *FA:ED* II, 306, and AC 93, 196.

7. *LR* 10:7–8, in *FA:ED* I, 105.

8. 2Cel 189, in *FA:ED* II, 367–368.

9. Jordan of Giano, *Chronicle*, chap. 8, 24.

10. Théophile Desbonnets, "La lecture franciscaine de l'Écriture," in *François d'Assise un exemple?* (Paris, 1981), 61–72 (Engl. trans.: "The Franciscan Reading of the Scriptures," in *Francis of Assisi Today*, 37–45).

11. *Office of the Passion*, XV:7, in *FA:ED* I, 156.

12. *Homilia* VIII, in *PL*, 76, 1004. The pope himself had borrowed this from an apocryphal gospel, the proto-gospel of James. Cf. Felice Accrocca, "'Natus est pro nobis in via' (*Officium Passionis* XV, 7). Gregorio Magno fonte di Francesco d'Assisi," *Collectanea franciscana* 70 (2000), 337–343.

13. *ER* 9:5, in *FA:ED* I, 70.

14. See the excellent index of scriptural citations that appears at the end of the edition and French translation of the writings of Francis: *Écrits*, ed. Théophile Desbonnets et al., Sources chrétiennes 285 (Paris, 1981), 349–356.

15. Jacques de Vitry, *Letter I*, in *FA:ED* I, 579.

16. Jacques de Vitry, *Historia occidentalis* (c. 1221/25), in *FA:ED* I, 582.

17. *ER* 1 and *LR* 1:1, in *FA:ED* I, 63 and 100, respectively.
18. Cf. Isabella Gagliardi, *Pazzi per Cristo: Santa folia e mistica della Croce in Italia centrale nel XIII e XIV secolo* (Florence, 1997), 69–133.
19. *AC* 18, in *FA:ED* II, 132–133. On the exact meaning of this expression, cf. Maria Pia Alberzoni, "'*Unus novellus pazzus in mundo*': Individualità e affermazione del carisma," in *Das Eigene und das Ganze: Zum Individuellen im mittelalterlichen Religiösentum*, ed. Gert Melville and Markus Schürer (Berlin, 2002), 269–301.
20. *Admonition 7*, in *FA:ED* I, 132.
21. Cf. Alfonso Marini, "'*Vestigia Christi sequi*' o '*Imitatio Christi*'? Due differenti modi di intendere la vita evangelica di Fr. d'Assisi," *Collectanea franciscana* 64 (1994), 89–119.
22. *ER* 22:2, in *FA:ED* I, 79.
23. *CTC* 13, in *FA:ED* I, 114.
24. *Admonitions 20–21*, in *FA:ED* I, 135.
25. *ER* 3:13 and *LR* 3:14, in *FA:ED* I, 66, 102.
26. *A Letter to Brother Leo*, in *FA:ED*, I, 122–123.
27. 2Cel 214, in *FA:ED* II, 386.

9. FRANCIS, NATURE, AND THE WORLD

1. 2Cel 168–171, in *FA:ED* II, 355–357.
2. Ms. Little, 197, in Rosalind B. Brooke, ed. and trans., *Scripta Leonis, Rufini et Angeli sociorum S. Francisci* (Oxford, 1970), 301; cf. Edith Pasztor, "Fonti francescane e storia del francescanesimo nel Duecento," in Edith Pasztor, *Francesco d'Assisi e la "Questione francescana"* (Assisi, 2000), 273–289.
3. 2Cel 111, in *FA:ED* II, 321.
4. E. M. Michalcyk, "Une compilation franciscaine du XIVe siècle," *Archivum Franciscanum Historicum* 76 (1983), 77.
5. Matthew Paris, *Chronica maiora*, Vol. III, 132–133.
6. Cf. F. D. Klingender, "St. Francis and the Birds of the Apocalypse," *Journal of the Warburg and Courtauld Institute* 16 (1953), 13–23.
7. 2Cel 47, in *FA:ED* II, 279.
8. *Admonition 5*, 2, in *FA:ED* I, 131.
9. Renan, *Nouvelles études d'histoire religieuse*, 332.
10. *Salutation of the Virtues*, 5 and 14, in *FA:ED* I, 164–165; *SP* 118, in *FA:ED* III, 366.
11. *Deeds*, 23, in *FA:ED* III, 482–485; *Fioretti*, 21, in *FA:ED* III, 601–604. The Parisian preacher begins his account with the word *legimus* ("we read" or "we have read"), which implies that he was referring to an existing text. He stresses, moreover, the wolf's doing of penance. Cf. Nicole Bériou, "La reportation des sermons parisiens à la fin du XIIIe siècle," in *Dal pulpito alla navata: La predicazione medievale nella sua recezione da parte degli ascoltatori* (Florence, 1989), 91–92.
12. *LMaj* 8:11, in *FA:ED* II, 594.
13. Henri d'Avranches, *The Versified Life of Saint Francis* (Appendix II), in *Fontes Franciscani*, 1242 (Latin text).

14. *"Passio sancti Verecundi,"* in *Saint François d'Assise: Documents, écrits et premières biographies,* 1436.

15. *CTC* in *FA:ED* I, 113–114.

16. *Admonition* 5, 2, in *FA:ED* I, 131.

17. Cf. Bernard Le Bras, *Le "Cantique des créatures" de François d'Assise. Étude littéraire, analyse sémiotique. Vers de nouvelles perspectives,* thesis (Paris-Sorbonne, 1982).

18. Honorius Augustodunensis, in *PL,* 172, 258.

19. Cf. Bernard Forthomme, *Le Chant de la création selon François d'Assise* (Paris, 2006).

20. Teilhard de Chardin, *L'Énergie humaine,* in *OEuvres,* Vol. VI (Paris, 1962), 53.

21. Henri Rey-Flaud, "Les fondements métapsychologiques de 'Malaise dans la culture,'" in *Autour de "Malaise dans la culture" de Freud,* ed. Jacques Le Rider and Michel Plon (Paris, 1998), 24–25.

10. FRANCIS AND THE CHURCH

1. *AC* 60, in *FA:ED* II, 163.

2. Stephen of Bourbon, *Tractatus de diversis materiis predicabilibus* (c. 1250–1260), 4th part: "Le Don de force," in *Anecdotes historiques,* ed. A. Lecoy de La Marche (Paris, 1877), 264–265; and in *Saint François d'Assise. Documents, écrits et premières biographies,* 1440.

3. Stephen of Bourbon, *Tractatus de diversis materiis predicabilibus,* 264–265.

4. *Letter to the Entire Order,* 44, in *FA:ED* I, 120.

5. *First Letter to the Custodes,* 1, in *FA:ED* I, 56.

6. *Test* 1 and 14, in *FA:ED* I, 124, 125.

7. Jacques Dalarun, *Francis of Assisi and Power* (Saint Bonaventure, NY, 2007), 41–51.

8. Gal 1:11–12.

9. Eudes de Cheriton, *Sermones super evangelia dominicalia* (Paris, BNF, lat. 16506, ff. 203vb–204ra), trans. in *Saint François d'Assise. Documents, écrits et premières biographies,* rev. 2nd ed., 361. As this sermon is dated from 1219 and the early Franciscans arrived in Paris in 1217, one must assume that this English secular cleric, who was then living in Paris, received this account from them. Cf. Fernando Uribe, "La Parabola della donna del deserto nelle primitive fonti agiografiche francescane. Sviluppi redazionali e interpretativi," *Antonianum* 82 (2007), 247–281.

10. *Letter to a Minister,* 2, in *FA:ED* I, 97.

11. Yves Congar, "Neuf cents ans après," in *L'Église et les églises, 1054–1954. Neuf siècles de douleureuse séparation entre l'Orient et l'Occident. Études et travaux sur l'unité chrétienne offerts à Dom Lambert Beauduin,* Vol. I (Chevetogne, 1954), 85–86.

12. Jacques de Vitry, *Letter I,* in *FA:ED* I, 579.

13. 3Soc 66–67, in *FA:ED* II, 106–107.

14. *Vita Gregorii papae IX,* ed. L. Muratori. Rerum italicarum scriptores III, 1 (Milan, 1723), 575a, rpt. in *Testimonia minora,* 12 (Engl. trans. in *FA:ED* I, 603).

15. *LR* 12:3, in *FA:ED* I, 106 and *Test* 31–33, in *FA:ED* I, 126–127.

16. *Test* 25, in *FA:ED* I, 126.
17. 3Soc 63, in *FA:ED* II, 105.
18. Cf. Michael F. Cusato, "*'Gubernator, protector et corrector istius fraternitatis.'* The Role of Cardinal Hugolino, Lord of Ostia, as Protector of the Order of Friars Minor, 1217–1226," in *Institution und Charisma. Festschrift für Gert Melville zum 65. Geburtstag,* ed. Franz J. Felten, Annette Kehnel, and Stefan Weinfürter (Cologne, 2009), 491–502.
19. Maria Pia Alberzoni, "*'Unus novellus pazzus in mundo.'* Individualità e affermazione del carisma," in *Das Eigene und das Ganze. Zum Individuellen in mittelalterlichen Religiösentum* (Berlin 2002), 269–301.
20. *Test* 27–28, in *FA:ED* I, 126.
21. Georges Bernanos, "*Martin Luther*" [1943], in *Bernanos par lui-même,* ed. Albert Béguin (Paris, 1954), 182.
22. Georges Bernanos, "*Journal d'un curé de campagne,*" in *OEuvres romanesques,* Bibliothèque de la Pléiade 155 (Paris, 1961), 1082–1083.

11. THE GOSPEL IN THE WORLD

1. Jacques de Vitry, *Historia occidentalis,* chap. 32, 1, in *FA:ED* I, 582.
2. Burchard of Ursperg, *Chronicon,* in *FA:ED* I, 593.
3. See the two sermons of Eudes de Châteauroux ("*Homo quidam descendebat de Jerusalem*" and "*Si quis inter vos*"), trans. Jacques Guy Bougerol, in "Saint François dans les sermons universitaires," in *Francesco d'Assisi nella storia,* Vol. I (Rome, 1983), 175–176, 179.
4. Cf. *Les Sermons et la visite pastorale de Federico Visconti, archevêque de Pise,* ed. Nicole Bériou (Rome, 2001), 778–779.
5. Cf. Patrick Henriet, "*'Verbum Dei disseminando.'* La parole des ermites prédicateurs d'après les sources hagiographiques (Xe–XIIe siècle)," in *La Parole du prédicateur, Ve–XVe siècle,* ed. Rosa Maria Dessì and Michel Lauwers (Nice, 1997), 153–185.
6. 2Cel 108, in *FA:ED* II, 318–319, and especially AC 108, ibid., 215–216; cf. Jean Pierre Delumeau, *Arezzo, espace et société (715–1230)* (Rome, 1996), 1401.
7. Jacques de Vitry, *Historia occidentalis,* in *FA:ED* I, 585; *Sacrum Commercium* 63, in *FA:ED* I, 552.
8. *Test* 24, in *FA:ED* I, 126.
9. AC 101, in *FA:ED* II, 204.
10. ER 23:7, in *FA:ED* I, 83–84.
11. *Letter to the Rulers of the Peoples,* 2–5, in *FA:ED* I, 58.
12. Cf. Jacques Le Goff and Jean-Claude Schmitt, "Au XIIIe siècle: Une parole nouvelle," in *Histoire vécue du peuple chrétien,* Vol. I, ed. Jean Delumeau (Paris, 1979), 257–279.
13. Philippe Buc, "*'Vox clamantis in deserto.'* Pierre le Chantre et la prédication laïque," *Revue Mabillon,* ns, 4 (1993), 9.
14. Lateran IV, canon 10, in *Decrees of the Ecumenical Councils,* Vol. I, ed. and trans. Norman P. Tanner (London, 1990), 239–240.

15. 3Soc 33 and 54, in *FA:ED* II, 88, 99.
16. Lateran IV, canon 3, in *Decrees of the Ecumenical Councils*, Vol. I, 233–235, esp. 233.
17. 1Cel 37, in *FA:ED* I, 216.
18. AC 69, in *FA:ED* II, 172–173.
19. Ibid., 74, p. 177.
20. Cf. G. G. Meersseman, *Dossier de l'ordre de la Pénitence au XIIIe siècle* (Fribourg, 1982); and André Vauchez, *The Laity in the Middle Ages: Religious Beliefs and Devotional Practices*, ed. Daniel E. Bornstein (Notre Dame, IN, 1993), 107–127.
21. *EpFid* (Long), 30–32, in *FA:ED* I, 47.
22. 1Cel 37, in *FA:ED* I, 215–217.
23. Jacques Dalarun, *Francis and the Feminine* (Saint Bonaventure, NY, 2006).
24. *ER* 12–13, in *FA:ED* I, 72–73.
25. Jacques Dalarun, "François et les femmes," in *Dieu changea de sexe, pour ainsi dire* (Paris, 2008), esp. 127–154.
26. Cf. *Processo di canonizzazione di Chiara da Montefalco*, ed. Enrico Menestò (Florence, 1984), 78, 236.
27. Ovidio Capitani, Introduzione to Michel Mollat, *I poveri nel Medioevo*, trans. André Vauchez (Bari, 1982), xxiii ff.

12. A CULTURAL MEDIATOR OF A NEW RELIGIOUS SENSIBILITY

1. Cf. Rosa Maria Dessì, "Prière, chant et prédication dans la '*lauda*,' de François d'Assise à Machiavel," in *La Prière en latin de l'Antiquité au XVIe siècle*, ed. Jean-François Cottier (Turnhout, 2006), 245–272.
2. Innocent III's opening sermon at the Fourth Lateran Council (1215) (Engl. trans. in *Pope Innocent III, Between God and Man: Six Sermons on the Priestly Office*, trans. Corrine J. Vause and Frank C. Gardiner, Medieval Texts in Translation [Washington, DC, 2004], 55–63).
3. 3Cel 159, in *FA:ED* II, 458–459.
4. 2Cel 106, in *FA:ED* II, 316–317.
5. 1Cel 84–87, in *FA:ED* I, 254–257. Cf. Chiara Frugoni, "Sui vari significati del Natale di Greccio nei testi e nelle immagini," *Frate Francesco* 70 (2004), 35–147.
6. Sur le *sermo humilis*, cf. Nino Scivoletto, "Problemi di lingua e di stile degli scritti latini di San Francesco," in *Francesco d'Assisi e francescanesimo dal 1216 al 1226* (Assisi, 1997), 112.
7. Frédéric Ozanam, *Les Poètes franciscains en Italie au treizième siècle* (Paris, 1852).
8. "Colui che e sire della cortesia," in *Vita Nuova*, XLII, 3 (Engl. trans: *La Vita Nuova* [London, 1969], XLII, 9). See also *The Divine Comedy*, Vol. III, *Paradiso*, VII, 91, ed. and trans. Robert Hollander and Jean Hollander (Verona, 2007), 165.
9. Raoul de Houdenc, *Li romans des ailes de prouesse*, quoted by Erich Köhler, *L'Aventure chevaleresque. Idéal et réalité dans le roman courtois* (Paris, 1974), 135 (Engl. trans. Guy F. Imhoff and Michael F. Cusato). Cf. Lise Battais, "La courtoisie de François d'Assise. Influence de la littérature épique et courtoise sur la première

génération franciscaine," *Mélanges de l'École française de Rome, Moyen Âge* 109 (1997), 131–160.

10. Peter of Blois, "Liber de confessione sacramentali," in *PL*, 207, col. 1088, cited by Martin Aurell, *La Légende du roi Arthur* (Paris, 2007), 236.

11. Jacques Le Goff and Jean-Claude Schmitt, "Une parole nouvelle," in *Histoire vécue du peuple chrétien*, Vol. I, ed. Jean Delumeau (Toulouse, 1979), 257–280.

CONCLUSION: FRANCIS, PROPHET FOR HIS TIME . . . OR FOR OURS?

1. 1Cel 82, in *FA:ED* I, 251: "*Novus certe homo et alterius saeculi videbatur.*"

2. 2Cel 54, in *FA:ED* II, 283. Cf. Pietro Messa, "San Francesco d'Assisi tra agiografia e profezia," *Convivium Assisiense* 7 (2005), 103–143.

3. John of La Rochelle, sermon "*Creavit Deus,*" in Jacques-Guy Bougerol, *Saint François dans les premiers sermons universitaires*, 189–190; and Bonaventure, *LMaj* Prologue, 1, in *FA:ED* II, 526.

4. Cf. the series of texts brought together and commented on by Nicole Bériou in her article "Saint François d'Assise premier prophète de son ordre dans les sermons du XIIIe siècle," in *Les Textes prophétiques et la prophétie en Occident*, ed. André Vauchez (Rome, 1990), 535–556.

5. "*Verba fratris Conradi,*" in *Opuscules de critique historique*, ed. Paul Sabatier (Paris, 1903), 370–392.

6. *Test* 14, in *FA:ED* I, 125.

7. Régis Debray, *Un Candide en Terre sainte* (Paris, 2008), 304.

8. Marie-Dominique Chenu, "L'expérience des Spirituels du XIIIe siècle," *Lumière et vie* 2 (1952), 88.

9. *Anonymous Chronicle of Siena*, in *Rerum italicarum scriptores* 2, XV, 6 (Bologna, 1933), 48.

10. Michel Mollat, *Les Pauvres au Moyen Âge* (Paris, 1978), 148 (Engl. trans: *The Poor in the Middle Ages*, trans. Arthur Goldhammer [New Haven, 1986], 120).

11. Jacques Le Goff, "Francis of Assisi between the Renewals and Restraints of Feudal Society," in *Francis of Assisi Today*, 9 (republished in Jacques Le Goff, *Héros du Moyen Âge: Le saint et le roi* [Paris, 2004], 33–42).

12. On all of these questions, see Giacomo Todeschini, *Franciscan Wealth: From Voluntary Poverty to Market Society*, trans. Donatella Melucci (Saint Bonaventure, NY, 2010).

13. *Test* 35–39, in *FA:ED* I, 127.

14. Charles Perrot, *Jésus* (Paris, 2000), 4.

15. *Test* 31–33, in *FA:ED* I, 126–127.

16. To employ the title of the book by Roberto Lambertini and Andrea Tabaronni, *Dopo Francesco: L'eredità difficile* (Turin, 1989).

17. Cf. Roberto Lambertini, *Apologia e crescità dell'identità francescana (1255–1279)* (Rome, 1990).

18. According to the apt phrase of Grado Giovanni Merlo; see his *Tra eremo e città. Studi su Francesco d'Assisi e sul francescanesimo medievale* (Assisi, 2007), 506.

BIBLIOGRAPHY

GENERAL WORKS

(*N.B.* This bibliography is not intended to be exhaustive; it lists only the works that were consulted in the process of writing this volume.)

Brooke, R. *The Image of Saint Francis: Responses to Sainthood in the Thirteenth Century.* Cambridge, 2006.

Capitani, O. *Figure e motivi del francescanesimo medievale.* Bologna, 2000.

Desbonnets, T. *From Intuition to Institution: The Franciscans.* Trans. Paul Duggan and Jerry Du Charme from *De l'intuition à l'institution: Les Franciscaines.* (Paris, 1983.) Chicago, 1988.

Francesco d'Assisi e il primo secolo di storia francescana. Turin, 1997.

Frugoni, C. *Francis of Assisi: A Life.* Trans. John Bowden from *Vita di un uomo: Francesco d'Assisi* (Turin, 1995). London, 1998.

Gratien de Paris, *Histoire de la fondation et de l'évolution de l'ordre des Frères mineurs au XIIIe siècle.* (Rpt. Rome, 1982.) Paris, 1928.

Le Goff, J. "Francis of Assisi between the Renewals and Restraints of Feudal Society." In *Francis of Assisi Today,* ed. C. Duquoc and C. Floristán, 3–10. Concilium 149/9. New York: 1981.

———. *Saint Francis of Assisi.* Trans. Christine Rhone from *Saint François d'Assise* (Paris, 1999). London, 2004.

Leonardi, C., ed. *La letteratura francescana.* Vol. I, *Francesco e Chiara d'Assisi* xiii–clxxvii, Milan, 2004; Vol. II, *Le Vite antiche di San Francesco* xiii–xliv, Milan, 2005.

Manselli, R. *St. Francis of Assisi.* Trans. Paul Duggan from *San Francesco d'Assisi,* 2nd ed. (Rome, 1981). Chicago, 1988.

Merlo, G. G. *In the Name of Saint Francis: A History of the Friars Minor and Franciscanism until the Early Sixteenth Century.* Trans. Raphael Bonnano and Robert J. Karris from *Nel nome di San Francesco: Storia dei Frati minori e del francescanesimo sino agli inizi del XVI secolo* (Padua, 2003). Saint Bonaventure, NY, 2009.

———. *Tra eremo e città. Studi su Francesco d'Assisi e sul francescanesimo medievale.* Assisi, 2007.

Miccoli, G. *Francesco d'Assisi. Realtà e memoria di un'esperienza cristiana.* Turin, 1991.

Rusconi, R., ed. *Francesco d'Assisi. Storia e arte.* Milan, 1982.

———. *Francis of Assisi in the Sources and Writings.* Trans. Nancy Celaschi from *Francesco d'Assisi nelle fonti e negli scritti* (Milan, 2002). Saint Bonaventure, NY, 2008.

Vauchez, A. *Francesco d'Assisi e gli ordini mendicanti.* Assisi, 2005.

BIBLIOGRAPHY BY CHAPTERS

1. Francesco di Bernardone

Caby, C. "L'érémitisme au XIIIe siècle entre solitude du coeur et contraintes du droit." In *L'Ordre des Chartreux au XIIIe siècle*, ed. J. Hogg, A. Girard, and D. Le Blévec, 13–26. Salzburg, 2006.

Da Campagnola, Stanislao. *Francesco e francescanesimo dei secoli XIII–XIV.* Assisi, 1999.

De Beer, F. *La Conversion de saint François selon Thomas de Celano.* Paris, 1963.

Fortini, A. *Assisi nel Medioevo.* Assisi, 1940.

———. *Nuova Vita di San Francesco.* 5 vols. Assisi, 1959.

Maire-Vigueur, J.-C. *Cavaliers et citoyens: Guerre, conflits et société dans l'Italie communale, XIIe–XIIIe siècles.* Paris, 2003.

Maranesi, P. *Facere misericordiam. La conversione di Francesco d'Assisi: Confronto critico tra il Testamento e le biografie.* Assisi, 2007.

Vauchez, A., ed. *Ermites de France et d'Italie (XIe–XVe siècle).* Collection de l'École française de Rome 313. Rome, 2003.

2. Brother Francis

Cusato, M. "La Renonciation au pouvoir chez les Frères mineurs au XIIIe siècle." 4 vols. Diss., Sorbonne, 1991.

Dalarun, J. *Francis of Assisi and Power.* Trans. Anne Bartol from *François d'Assise ou le pouvoir en question. Principes et modalités du gouvernement de l'ordre des Frères mineurs* (Paris, 1999). Saint Bonaventure, NY, 2007.

———. "*Sicut mater.* Une relecture du billet de François d'Assise à frère Léon." *Le Moyen Âge* 113 (2007), 639–668.

Dal Pino, F. *Il laicato italiano tra eresia e proposta pauperistica nei secoli XII–XIII.* Padua, 1984.

Dolso, M. T. "*Et sint minores.*" *Modelli di vocazione e reclutamento dei Frati minori nel primo secolo francescano.* Milan, 2001.

Esser, K. *Origins of the Franciscan Order.* Trans. Aedan Daly and Irina Lynch from *Origini e valori autentici dell'Ordine dei Frati minori* (Milan, 1972; 1st ed. in German, *Anfänge und ursprüngliche Zielsetzungen des Ordens der Minderbrüder*, Leiden, 1966). 1970.

Flood, D. *François d'Assise et le mouvement franciscain.* Paris, 1983.

Flood, D., and T. Matura. *The Birth of a Movement.* Trans. Paul Schwartz and Paul La-
chance from *La Naissance d'un charisme: Une lecture de la première règle de saint
François d'Assise* (Paris, 1973). Chicago, 1975.

Lambert, M. *Franciscan Poverty: The Doctrine of the Absolute Poverty of Christ and the
Apostles in the Franciscan Order.* 2nd ed., Saint Bonaventure, NY, 1998.

Lobrichon, G. "L'évangélisme des laïcs dans le Midi (XIIe–XIIIe siècles)." In *Évangile et
évangélisme (XIIe–XIIIe siècles),* 291–310. Cahiers de Fanjeaux 34. Toulouse, 1999.

Maier, C. *The Preaching of the Crusade.* Cambridge, 1994.

Meersseman, G. G. *Dossier de l'ordre de la Pénitence au XIIIe siècle.* 2nd ed. Fribourg, 1978.

Merlo, G. G. "La conversione alla povertà nell'Italia dei secoli XII–XIV." In *La conversione alla povertà nell'Italia dei secoli XII–XIV,* 3–32. Spoleto, 1991.

———. "Le stimmate e la 'grande tentazione.'" In *Intorno a Frate Francesco,* 131–156. Milan, 1993.

Miccoli, G. "Francesco e La Verna." *Studi francescani* 97 (2000), 225–259.

Militia Christi e crociate nei secoli XI–XII. Milan, 1992.

Paul, J. "L'érémitisme et la survivance de la spiritualité du désert chez les Franciscains." In
Les Mystiques du désert dans l'islam, le judaïsme et le christianisme, 133–145. Gap, 1975.

———. "La signification sociale du franciscanisme." In *Mouvements franciscains et société
française, XIIIe–XXe siècle,* ed. A. Vauchez, 9–25. Paris, 1984.

Pellegrini, L. "L'esperienza eremitica di Francesco e dei primi francescani." In *Francesco
e francescanesimo dal 1216 al 1226,* 281–313. Assisi 1977.

Tolan, J. *St. Francis and the Sultan: The Curious History of a Christian-Muslim Encounter.* Trans. by the author from *Le Saint chez le sultan. La rencontre de François d'Assise
et de l'islam. Huit siècles d'interprétation* (Paris, 2007). Oxford, 2009.

Vauchez, A. *The Laity in the Middle Ages.* Ed. Daniel E. Bornstein. Trans. Margery J.
Schneider from *Les Laïcs au Moyen Âge. Pratiques et expériences religieuses* (Paris,
1987). Notre Dame, IN, 1993.

———. *The Spirituality of the Medieval West.* Trans. Colette Friedlander from *La Spiritualité du Moyen Âge occidental, VIIIe–XIIIe siècle,* 2nd ed. (Paris, 1994). Kalamazoo,
MI, 1993.

3. Becoming Saint Francis

Barone, G. *Da Frate Elia ai Spirituali.* Milan, 1999.

Frugoni, C. "L'ombra della Porziuncola nella Basilica superiore di Assisi." *Mitteilungen
des Kunsthistorischen Institutes im Florenz* 45 (2001), 245–293.

Lobrichon, G. *Les Fresques de la basilique inférieure d'Assise.* Paris, 1985.

Michetti, R. *Francesco d'Assisi e il paradosso della 'minoritas.' La 'Vita beati Francisci' di
Tommaso da Celano.* Rome, 2004.

Romano, S. *La Basilica di San Francesco in Assisi. Pittori, botteghe e strategie narrative.*
Rome, 2001.

Schenkluhn, W. *San Francesco in Assisi: Ecclesia specialis.* Milan. 1994 (1st ed. in German, Darmstadt, 1991).

Trexler, R. "The Stigmatized Body of Francis of Assisi Conceived, Processed, Disappeared." In *Frömmigkeit im Mittelalter*, ed. Klaus Schreiner, 463–498. Munich,
2002.

Vauchez, A. *Religion et société dans l'Occident médiéval.* Turin, 1980.

———. *La Sainteté en Occident aux derniers siècles du Moyen Âge.* 2nd ed. Rome, 1988.

4. The "Second Death" of Francis

Alberzoni, M. P. *Chiara e il papato.* Milan, 1995.

Bartoli, M. *Clare of Assisi.* Trans. Sister Frances Teresa, OSC, from *Chiara d'Assisi*
(Rome, 1989). Quincy, IL, 1993.

Bougerol, J. G. "Saint François dans les premiers sermons universitaires." In *Francesco
nella storia*, ed. Servus Gieben, 173–199. Rome, 1983.

Cocci, A. "Chiara e l'ordine francescano." In *Chiara d'Assisi e la memoria di Francesco*,
67–86. Fara Sabina, 1994.

Cusato, M. "Elias and Clare: An Enigmatic Relationship." In *Clare of Assisi, Investiga-
tions*, vol. 7. ed. M. F. Hone, 95–115. Saint Bonaventure, NY, 1993.

Maranesi, P. "Nescientes litteras." *L'ammonizione della regola francescana e la questione
degli studi nell'Ordine (sec. XIII–XVI).* Rome, 2000.

Potestà, G. L. *Il tempo dell'Apocalisse. Vita di Gioacchino da Fiore.* Rome, 2004.

Reeves, M. *The Influence of Prophecy in the Later Middle Ages: A Study on Joachimism.*
2nd ed. Notre Dame, IN, 1993.

5. Medieval Interpretations of Francis

Accrocca, F. *Franciesco e le sue immagini. Momenti dell'evoluzione della coscienza storica
dei Frati minori.* Padua, 1997.

Cook, W. R. *Images of Saint Francis from the Earliest Images to 1320.* Florence, 1999.

Dalarun, J. *The Misadventure of Francis of Assisi.* Trans. Edward Hagman from *La Mala-
venture de François d'Assise* (Paris, 2002; 1st ed. in Italian, *La Malavventura di Francesco
d'Assisi: Per un uso storico delle leggende francescane*, Milan, 1996). Saint Bonaventure,
NY, 2006.

———. *Vers une résolution de la question franciscaine: La Légende ombrienne de Thomas
de Celano.* Paris, 2007.

Dalarun, J., M. Cusato, and C. Salvati. *The Stigmata of Francis of Assisi: New Studies,
New Perspectives.* Saint Bonaventure, NY, 2006.

Fleming, J. V. *From Bonaventure to Bellini: An Essay on Franciscan Exegesis.* Princeton,
1982.

Frugoni, C. *Francesco e l'invenzione delle stimatte. Una storia per parole e immagini fino
a Bonaventura e Giotto.* Turin, 1993.

Gardner, J. "Stone Saints: Commemoration and Likeness in Thirteenth-Century Italy,
France, and Spain." *Gesta* 46 (2007), 121–134.

Gieben, S., ed. *Francesco d'Assisi nella storia, secoli XIII–XIV.*, 2 vols. Rome, 1983.

Motte, I. E. "François d'Assise, un autre Christ?" *Lumière et vie* 143 (1981), 39–58.

Pellegrini, L. *Frate Francesco e i suoi agiografi*. Assisi, 2004.

Scarpellini, P. "Iconografia francescana nei secoli XIII–XIV." In *Francesco d'Assisi. Storia e arte*, ed. R. Rusconi, 91–126. Milan, 1982.

6. Francis between History and Myth

Brejon de Lavergnée, M. "Ozanam et Assise. Genèse du regard romantique sur le Moyen Âge." *Études franciscaines* n.s. 1 (2008), 89–111.

Michetti, R. "Francesco d'Assisi e l'essenza del cristianesimo." In *Francesco d'Assisi fra storia, letteratura e iconografia*, ed. F. E. Consolino, 37–67. Soveria Manelli, 1996.

Migliore, S. "Francesco d'Assisi e le origini dell'arte del Rinascimento." *Rivista di storia e letteratura religiosa* 31 (1995), 15–44.

Paul Sabatier e gli studi francescani. Spoleto, 2003.

Renan, E. *Nouvelles études d'histoire religieuse*. Paris, 1884.

Sabatier, P. *Vie de saint François*. Paris, 1893–1894.

Tichi, J. M. "Assise dans l'imaginaire français des XIXe et XXe siècles." In *Cent ans de présence des Clarisses françaises à Assise (1908–2008)*, 315–336. Florence, 2008.

Vorreux, D. *François d'Assise dans les lettres françaises*. Paris, 1988.

7. The Experience of God

Cacciotti, A., ed. "Verba Domini mei." *Gli opuscula di Francesco d'Assisi a 25 anni della edizione di Kajetan Esser, OFM*. Rome, 2003.

De La Roncière, C. "La Nativité dans la dévotion de saint François d'Assise." In *La Nativité et le temps de Noël. Antiquité et Moyen Âge*, ed. G. Dorival and J.-P. Boyer, 231–244. Aix-en-Provence, 2003.

Rotzetter, A., W. Van Dijk, and T. Matura. *Gospel Living: Francis of Assisi, Yesterday and Today*. Trans. E. Saggau from *Un chemin d'évangile. L'esprit franciscain hier et aujourd'hui* (Paris, 1982). Saint Bonaventure, NY, 1994.

Russo, D. "Saint François, les Franciscains, et les représentations du Christ sur la croix en Ombrie au XIIIe siècle." *Mélanges de l'École française de Rome. Moyen Âge* 96 (1984), 647–717.

8. A New Relationship to Scripture

Izzo, I. *La semplicità evangelica nella spiritualità di S. Francesco d'Assisi*. Rome, 1971.

Messa, P. *Le fonti patristiche negli scritti di Francesco d'Assisi*. Assisi, 1999.

Vauchez, A. "Les écrits de saint François: Une réponse à la contestation hérétique?" In *Francesco d'Assisi e gli ordini mendicanti*, 15–26. Assisi, 2005.

9. Francis, Nature, and the World

Cardini, F. "Francesco d'Assisi e gli animali." *Studi Francescani* 78 (1981), 7–46.

Forthomme, B. *Le Chant de la création selon François d'Assise*. Paris, 2006.

Klingender, F. D. "St. Francis and the Birds of the Apocalypse." *Journal of the Warburg and Courtauld Institute* 16 (1953), 13–23.

Le Bras, B. "Le Cantique des créatures de François d'Assise. Étude littéraire, analyse sémiotique. Vers de nouvelles perspectives." Thesis, Sorbonne, 1982.

Marini, A. Sorores Alaudae. *Francesco d'Assisi, il creato, gli animali.* Assisi, 1989.

Pasztor, E. "Fonti francescane e storia del francescanesimo nel Duecento: San Francesco, l'agnellino e la scrofa." In *Francesco d'Assisi e la questione francescana,* 273–289. Assisi, 2000.

10. Francis and the Church

Alberzoni, M. P. "*'Unus novellus pazzus in mundo.'* Individualità e affermazione del carisma." In *Das Eigene und das Ganze. Zum individuellen in mittelalterlichen Religiösentum,* ed. G. Melville and M. Schürer, 269–301. Vita regularis 16. Münster, 2000.

Cusato, M. "*'Gubernator, protector et corrector istius fraternitatis.'* The Role of Cardinal Hugolino, Lord of Ostia, as Protector of the Friars Minor (1217–1226)." In *Institution und charisma. Festschrift für Gert Melville zum 65, Geburtstag,* ed. F. J. Felten, Annette Kehnel, and S. Weinfurter, 491–502. Cologne, 2009.

Messa, P. "Il carisma d'interpretare il carisma di San Francesco d'Assisi." In *Charisma und religiöse Gemeinschaften im Mittelalter,* ed. G. Andenna, M. Breitenstein, and G. Melville, 65–90. Münster, 2005.

Rusconi, R. "*Moneo atque exhortor . . . Firmiter praecipio.* Carisma individuale e potere normative in Francesco d'Assisi." In *Charisma und religiöse Gemeinschaften im Mittelalter,* 261–279.

11. The Gospel in the World

Cannon, J. and A. Vauchez. *Margherita of Cortona and the Lorenzetti.* Philadelphia, 1999.

Dalarun, J. "*Dieu changea de sexe, pour ainsi dire.*" *La religion faite femme (XIe–XVe siècle).* Paris, 2008.

———. *Francis of Assisi and the Feminine.* Trans. Paula Pierce and Mary Sutphin from *François, un passage. Femme et féminité dans les écrits et les légendes franciscaines* (Arles, 1997). Saint Bonaventure, NY, 2006.

Henriet, P. "*Verbum Dei disseminando.* La parole des ermites prédicateurs d'après les sources hagiographiques (Xe–XIIIe siècle)." In *La Parole du prédicateur, Ve–XVe siècle,* ed. R. Dessi and M. Lauwers, 155–185. Nice, 1997.

Le Goff, J., and J.-C. Schmitt. "Au XIIIe siècle: Une parole nouvelle." In *Histoire vécue du peuple chrétien,* ed, J. Delumeau, 257–279. Toulouse, 1979.

Rusconi, R. "*'Forma Apostolorum':* L'immagine del predicatore nei movimenti religiosi francesi ed italiani nei secoli XIIe–XIIIe." *Cristianesimo nella storia* 6 (1985), 513–542.

Zerfass, R. *Der streit um die Laienpredigt.* Freiburg, 1974.

12. A Cultural Mediator of a New Religious Sensibility

Bartoli Langeli, A. *Gli autografi di Frate Francesco e di Frate Leone.* Turnhout, 2000.

Bologna, C. "Il modello culturale francescano e la letteratura volgare delle origini." *Storia della città* 26–27 (1985), 65–90.

———. "L'ordine francescano e la letteratura nell'Italia pretridentina." In *Letteratura italiana*, vol. I, *Il Letterato e le istituzioni*, 727–797. Turin, 1982.

Cardini, F. "L'avventura di un cavaliere di Cristo. Appunti per uno studio sulla cavalleria di San Francesco d'Assisi." *Studi Francescani* 73 (1976), 127–198.

Dessi, R. M. "Prière, chant et prédication: À propos de la *lauda*, de François d'Assise à Machiavel." In *La Prière en latin de l'Antiquité au XIIIe siècle*, ed. J.-F. Cottier, 245–272. Turnhout, 2006.

Conclusion

Bériou, N. "Saint François d'Assise, premier prophète de son ordre dans les sermons du XIIIe siècle." In *Les Textes prophétiques et la prophétie en Occident*, ed. A. Vauchez, 535–556. Rome, 1990.

Covi, E., ed. *Francescanesimo e profezia.* Rome, 1985.

Lambertini, R., and A. Tabarroni. *Dopo Francesco: L'eredità difficile.* Turin, 1989.

Messa, P. "San Francesco d'Assisi tra agiografia e profezia." *Convivium Assisiense* 7 (2005), 105–143.

Prinzivalli, E. "Francesco e il francescanesimo: Consapevolezza storiografica e prospettive." In *Francesco d'Assisi fra storia, letteratura e iconografia*, ed. F. E. Consolino, 69–81. Soveria Manelli, 1996.

Todeschini, G. *Franciscan Wealth: From Voluntary Poverty to Market Society.* Trans. Donatella Melucci from *Ricchezza francescana: Dalla povertà volontaria alla società di mercato* (Bologna, 2004). Saint Bonaventure, NY, 2009.

Van Dijk, W. "Signification sociale du franciscanisme naissant." *Études Franciscaines* 35 (1965), 2–12.

Venanzi, M. *"Come le stelle del mattino." Le profezie di Francesco d'Assisi.* Florence, 2007.

INDEX